Salaula

Salaula

The World of Secondhand
Clothing and Zambia

Karen Tranberg Hansen

The University of Chicago Press
Chicago and London

KAREN TRANBERG HANSEN is professor of anthropology at Northwestern University. She is the author of *Distant Companions: Servants and Employers in Zambia, 1900–1985* and *Keeping House in Lusaka* and the editor of *African Encounters with Domesticity.*

The University of Chicago Press, Chicago 60637
The University of Chicago Press, Ltd., London
© 2000 by The University of Chicago
All rights reserved. Published 2000
Printed in the United States of America
09 08 07 06 05 04 03 02 01 00   1 2 3 4 5

ISBN: 0-226-31580-0 (cloth)
ISBN: 0-226-31581-9 (paper)

Library of Congress Cataloging-in-Publication Data

Hansen, Karen Tranberg.
    Salaula : the world of secondhand clothing and Zambia / Karen Tranberg Hansen.
        p.   cm.
    Includes bibliographical references and index.
    ISBN 0-226-31580-0 (cloth : alk. paper)—ISBN 0-226-31581-9 (paper : alk. paper)
    1. Costume—Zambia.   2. Fashion—Zambia.   3. Used clothing industry—Zambia.
    4. Clothing trade—Economic aspects—Zambia.   5. Material culture—Zambia.
    6. Zambia—Social conditions.   7. Zambia—Economic conditions.   I. Title.

GT1589.Z33 H36 2000
381'.45687—dc21
                                                                            99-462387

⊛ The paper used in this publication meets the minimum requirements of the American National Standard for Information Sciences—Permanence of Paper for Printed Library Materials, ANSI Z39.48-1992.

For Ilse Mwanza and Mette Shayne

Contents

Illustrations, Maps, and Tables

Illustrations

Acknowledgments

When I noticed the trade in imported secondhand clothing growing rapidly in Zambia in the late 1980s and decided that I wanted to figure out what this was all about, I never imagined how far and wide this project would take me, either physically or intellectually. My understanding of secondhand clothing consumption as a Zambian cultural economy of taste and style came about through the intertwining of two unusual strands of inquiry. One is tracing the West's surplus of used clothing donated to charitable organizations and their links with commercial textile recyclers and graders who profit from the export trade of that clothing. The second is examining the secondhand clothing trade in Zambia and its many actors, from small-scale traders and state regulatory agencies, to the millions of consumers who satisfy their clothing needs and desires from secondhand markets. The book that has resulted from these two inquiries casts special light on clothing consumption. It is intended for people who are interested in Third World development issues; charity, relief aid, and business; recycling; clothing, style, and fashion; and African regional history and popular culture. While the book is a result of my own research agenda and interpretive approach, there are many additional points of relevant detail to consider from a variety of angles. I hope that it will invite further investigation.

My inspiration to tease out a cultural economy of taste and style from secondhand clothing consumption in Zambia is easy to pinpoint. It goes back to a series of lively exposures to African textile and costume arts that I received between 1979 and 1982 at the University of Minnesota, where Joanne Eicher and Fred Smith brought together prominent scholars from the field of African decorative arts. The exquisite arts of West African textiles and dress design prompted me to rethink the West's influence on long-held dress practices in Zambia. In the intervening years, I have explored many tracks with a view to disentangling the economic and cultural dimensions of secondhand clothing encounters in Zambia.

During my research for this book I received far more encouragement, support, and help from people and institutions than I can acknowledge individually. Family, friends, and colleagues from near and far have kept my clipping files expanding, and there is no end to the stories, suggestions, and leads I have received from across three continents. Still, some very specific acknowledgments are in order.

My fondest gratitude is to Norah Rice of Mtendere township in Lusaka, who has worked with me during all my years of research in Zambia, beginning in 1971. She inspired my interests in the cultural politics of consumption. As my friend and special confidante, I am deeply indebted to her. I thank the members of her spatially extended household and the residents of Mtendere township who have personalized the ambiguous meanings and experiences of development for me.

During all my stays in Zambia I have enjoyed affiliation with the Institute for Economic and Social Research (formerly the Institute for African Studies). Oliver Saasa, director during the years of this research, and his staff made me feel welcome throughout the years. At the University of Zambia, Mubanga Kashoki, Hugh Macmillan (now in South Africa), and Mwelwa Musambachime (now in Namibia) played central roles in working out the historical dimension of this project. Other regional scholars provided leads and advice, including George Bond, Virginia Bond, Brian Callahan, Sam Chipungu, Jeremy Gould, Bogumil Jewsiewicki, Phyllis Martin, Jacob Mwanza, Achim von Oppen, Andrew Roberts, Roger Sanjek, Lyn Schumaker, Owen Sichone, and Luise White. Between 1992 and 1999 in Zambia, Damiano Chonganya, Oscar Hamangaba, Monica Macmillan, Phillemon Ndubani, Chris Simuyemba, and Bradford Strickland assisted me with a variety of very specific research tasks.

Several individuals involved in charity and the commercial secondhand clothing trade took time from their work to discuss industry matters with me in the United States, Canada, several countries in Europe, and Zambia, where I visited sorting plants and thrift and upscale resale stores. The freshman students in my course on clothing and culture explored the Chicago-area resale-store scene on several occasions. Because charitable organizations, recyclers, resale-store owners or managers, and wholesalers in Zambia operate publicly, I have used real names and actual firm designations throughout.

The research on which the book draws was possible thanks to faculty grants from Northwestern University (1992, 1997, and 1999), the Social Science Research Council (1995–96), and the Wenner-Gren Foundation for Anthropological Research (1995–96). In 1993 I was a member of a research team contracted by the Danish Foreign Ministry for a brief assessment of the effects of the secondhand clothing trade in Zambia and Zimbabwe (Denconsult 1993). Part of this book was drafted while I was a fellow at the National Humanities Center with support from the National Endowment for the Humanities from 1997 to 1998. In 1998 I also enjoyed a four-week residency at the Rockefeller Foundation's study center at Bellagio, Italy. Among the many inspiring colleagues I met during that year, Gladys Marie Fry, Narendra Panjwani, Brigitte and John Reader, and Claude Reichler will remain special to me.

Because this project took on a life of its own, my discussion in the introduction and in chapters 7–9 draws some observations from published papers. They include "Dealing with Used Clothing: *Salaula* and the Construction of Identity in Zambia's Third Republic" (1994), "Transnational Biographies and Local Meanings: Used Clothing Practices in Lusaka" (1995), "Second-Hand Clothing Encounters in Zambia: Global Discourses, Western Commodities, and Local Histories" (1999), and "Gender and Difference: Youth, Bodies, and Clothing in Zambia" (n.d.). Beyond these very identifiable influences, the concerns of this book arise from my previously published works, extending those interests in new directions.

On the personal front, friends and colleagues have been patient and supportive in seeing this project through. They include Paul Berliner, Jean and John Comaroff, Dwight Conquergood, Kathy and Paul Freund, Maria Grosz-Ngaté, Bonnie Keller, Robert Launay, Candace Rudmose, and Peg Strobel. And Elizabeth Colson, Jane Guyer, Beverly Lemire, Hugh Macmillan, and Carter Roeber read parts of or the entire manuscript, offering invaluable advice. If I have not listened well enough, they know whom to blame. I thank them all, as I do David Brent and the editorial staff at the University of Chicago Press for their constructive roles in seeing this project through its final stage.

I took most of the photographs in this book. The major exceptions are several photographs from the colonial period, taken by Peter Fraenkel in the 1950s and reproduced here with his kind permission. Special credits are given when relevant, including for two cartoons reproduced from the Zambian print media. The maps were prepared in the Geography Program of Northwestern University.

Two special persons deserve recognition because of their dedicated work, much beyond any bounds of duty, keeping me up to date on news, filling in gaps in the relevant literature and scholarship, and more. They both have retired now. Recognizing their professional skills and critical scholarly role in this project, I am delighted to dedicate this book to Ilse Mwanza, research affiliate officer at the Institute for Economic and Social Research of the University of Zambia in Lusaka, and Mette Shayne, reference librarian and Francophone Africana bibliographer in the University Library at Northwestern University. Without them, this book's story would not have been told.

Introduction: The World of Salaula

> Outside the factory were stacks of rags piled up in heaps, gathered in from far and wide. Each rag had his history, each could tell his own tale; but we can't listen to them all. Some were domestic rags, others came from foreign countries. (Andersen [1835] 1976:453).

There is a magic of clothes in Hans Christian Andersen's fairy tale "The Rags." The story transforms antagonistic Danish and Norwegian rags into sheets of paper carrying written expressions that erase long-standing national hostilities. It is the proximity of rags from many different countries that generates both the magic of distinction and its dissolution in the reworking of rags into paper.[1] When Andersen wrote this tale, many rags were turned into paper, unlike today when only a small proportion of our used clothes travel that route. In fact, much more money can be made from the international export trade in secondhand clothes. This book suggests that a magic of clothes is still at work in the processes through which secondhand clothing from many countries in the West comes to assume new lives in Zambia.

The World of Salaula is the name of a secondhand clothing store in the city of Ndola on the Copperbelt of Zambia, where I saw garments displayed on hangers, much like in the West's thrift stores, in 1993 and 1995. The term *salaula* means, in the Bemba language, "to select from a pile in the manner of rummaging," or for short, "to pick." Commonly used since the mid-1980s, the term describes, graphically, the selection process that takes place once a bale of imported secondhand clothing has been opened in the market and consumers select garments to satisfy both their clothing needs and their clothing wants. They all want to cut a good figure, and purchasing their clothes from salaula markets is a means to that end. Adult Zambian men like to dress in formal suits with smooth lines that present a tidy body silhouette, and adult Zambian women prefer dresses with a variety of decorative accents that present their mature bodies without exposing them. And many young adults of both sexes like to experiment with style. What matters in their clothing selections is not the Western origin of suits and dresses but that these garments have been incorporated into local dress repertoires so long ago that today they are Zambian icons of acceptable wear.

Encompassing the global canvas of the secondhand clothing trade, this book's world of salaula is about much more than local market scenes and dress practices. Intertwining two unusual strands of inquiry, this exploration begins where most other work on clothing has stopped. Few scholars and observers, in Africa or the West, have gone beyond superficial reactions, condemning secondhand clothing imports and deprecating their local effects. Even fewer have inquired into the meanings such clothes evoke for their wearers or have addressed the sometimes ambiguous roles of such garments in everyday lives. To be sure, the export of used clothing from North America and northwestern Europe to developing countries such as Zambia may at first sight appear to be a textbook example of the West's continued exploitation of the rest of the world. And there is no doubt that the recent rapid increase of secondhand clothing imports into Zambia is a sad testimony to the powerless position of the country's textile and garment industry in a highly competitive and crowded global apparel market. Yet such observations have little resonance with popular sentiments about salaula. The passivity these observations attribute to the end of the commodity chain must be tempered by acknowledging the worlds of opportunity that clothing opens up for its consumers.

Local preoccupations with dress make clothing needs and desires converge in the consumption of salaula, shaping this market by cultural specificities of judgment, preference, and style. These cultural referents place a premium on the discerning skills of consumers, involving them actively in driving the demand side of this market. Turning the issue of the secondhand clothing trade from a colorful market scene, or a side issue of commerce, into a complicated industry, this book's focus on clothing consumption sheds unusual light on the development predicament in a country like Zambia.

Although Zambia has participated in the international secondhand clothing trade since the early decades of the twentieth century, if not earlier, markets selling commercially imported used clothing in this part of Africa began growing noticeably in the mid-1980s. They saw enormous expansion and proliferation in the early 1990s, becoming more important retailing sites than ever before in a vast worldwide commodity circuit that involves many countries in Africa, other parts of the Third World, the former soviet republics, and eastern European countries. This trade does not exclusively target Third World countries,[2] yet sub-Saharan African countries are among the world's largest importers of secondhand clothing.

The secondhand clothing trade is a gray area both empirically and conceptually. In empirical terms the extent and scope of this global commodity chain are hazy and so are the economics of the relationship between the charitable organizations and commercial textile recyclers who are the single largest source of this expanding and profitable trade. In conceptual terms the term *salaula* reconstructs the West's cast-off clothing into a desirable commodity without making reference to its origin or provenance, in effect submerging its history of production, in the form of "sourcing," and prior ownership, once retailers place secondhand clothing bales for sale at the end of the chain in Zambia. Indeed, consumers here explain the presence of salaula as a result of "donations" from the West, as is the case with so much else in Zambia.

From the supply side at the point of sourcing in the West through all intervening stages to the point of consumption in poor countries like Zambia, the secondhand clothing trade is surrounded by a charitable guise. The mapping of some phases of its changing history in this book remains preliminary. There are several reasons for that, which I discuss shortly, but perhaps the most striking difficulty is the lack of contemporary scholarly interest in considering secondhand clothing consumption as anything other than the flip side of Western fashion and mere satisfaction of basic clothing needs. But clothing consumption has complex effects on how people organize their livelihoods, and the manner in which they conduct their everyday lives touches on the production and distribution relations that are available to them. In effect, because economic and cultural issues intersect in people's dealings with clothing, the salaula phenomenon in Zambia raises conceptual problems for anthropologists and other social scientists who are trying to make sense of "economic" relationships in our late-twentieth-century world.

The popularity of salaula in Zambia can be explained in part by drawing on anthropological work that views consumption as the means by which people define themselves and their world (Friedman 1994b). But because consumption is about much more than identity, its study becomes the context for broader explanations (Miller 1995a:30–34). If we frame the secondhand clothing phenomenon in Zambia society as a politics of identity in terms of the intellectual shift from production to consumption, we lose sight of something that is very important: people do not respond to things only because they are good to think with but above all because they make a difference to their livelihood. "The ways in which people respond to and use meanings," suggest James Carrier and Josiah Heyman (1997:361), "have material, social and cultural consequences for themselves and those meanings." For consumers in Zambia, secondhand clothing not only mediates desires but also dresses bodies. Wearing clothes rather than rags gives dignity to people with few means, and this is an important reason why clothing constitutes a major dimension of well-being in Zambia. Explaining why this is so invites attention to past and present shifts in the regional and global political economy and their effects on preoccupations with clothing in Zambia.

In this introduction I first discuss why imported secondhand clothing is not just any commodity, but a rather special one because of its ability to mediate both individual and collective identities and desires. I briefly sketch some changing contours of the international secondhand clothing trade. Next, I discuss the relevance of the paradigmatic shift toward consumption in explanations of the salaula phenomenon in Zambia, suggesting that the relevance of this shift depends on what type of commodity we examine in relationship to which consumers, when, and where. Turning to salaula in Zambia, to questions about clothing needs and desires, I suggest that the work of production does not end in consumption, but that in fact it begins there. In effect, in Zambian dealings with salaula, the work of "consumption" has complicated implications in the realm of "production." Ben Fine and Ellen Leopold's notion (1993) of commodity-specific systems of provision provides a constructive approach to capturing such interactions.

Clothing: A Special Commodity

Clothing is not just any commodity but one that mediates between self and society in ways that have radically changed over the *longue durée* in the West, according to Richard Sennett (1992), and that are changing at an accelerated pace in much of the Third World. Prior to the French Revolution, suggests Sennett, when people operated in a hierarchically structured public world, clothes treated the body as a mannequin, a vehicle for marking well-established distinctions. When you presented yourself in public through dress, everyone knew how to relate to you, depending on your status as a noble, commoner, or journeyman. With the transformation of the old order, public and private were redefined, long-held rules of distinction became confused, new socioeconomic differentiations pulled in many directions, and the terms of how society understood human expressivity and self-fashioning shifted from presentation to representation (39–42). No longer a neutral frame, the dressed body became part of new identity strategems.

Mediating between self and society in a very special way, this unique power of clothing was recognized long ago by Erasmus of Rotterdam when, anticipating the coming of the modern individual, he likened dress to "the body of the body" (Elias 1978:78), in this way capturing how bodies are "worn" through attributes of the person. Anthropologists often call on Terence Turner's characterization (1993) of the body as a "social skin" that invites us to explore both the individual and collective identities that the dressed body creates. The point is not that clothing possesses this power inherently, but that it mediates it in an interactive process through which the self is expressed/presented in possession. Daniel Miller's notion (1987) of objectification is relevant here as the process by which people actively realize themselves in the objects they acquire and consume. There is an experiential dimension to the power of clothing, both in its wearing and viewing. Juliet

Ash (1996:219–20) has suggested that clothes relate to our feelings perhaps more than any other designed artifacts and thus "require 'subjective' as well as 'objective' analysis ... The interconnections," she notes, "between clothes as objectively worn and the subjective sensation of wearing them and seeing them being worn indicate a possible variety of identities."

The reasons that scholarship on markets and dress in Africa has overlooked using clothing are not hard to identify. They include, among others, a concern with center-periphery relations and the exploitative and oppressive effects of Western institutions and forms on subaltern lives, Marx's preoccupation with commodity fetishism as a mode of "false" representation, and a hostile, if not elitist and paternalistic, stance on the global spread of mass consumption and its assumed adverse effects on local cultures. Specialist scholarship on textiles and dresses in Africa used to be long on describing and cataloguing details of form and fabric (Eicher 1969; Picton and Mack 1989) and so intent on aesthetic appreciation and symbolic analysis (H. Hendrickson 1996; Picton et al. 1995) that it has been almost oblivious to the social and cultural significance of local dealings with the West's discarded clothing. In the West in recent years, secondhand clothing consumption has attracted the attention of fashion-conscious consumers, the news media, and scholars of cultural studies and popular culture (Cosgrove 1989; McRobbie 1989). Their focus has been largely on the upscale side or on the creation of alternative lifestyles and not on the needy and thrifty dimensions of practices involving used clothing, that is to say, its charitable guise. Recent scholarship also notes the incorporation of fragments of "ethnic" clothing into garments produced for Western tastes (Ehlers 1993; C. Hendrickson 1996). But there is little substantive work on either the incorporation of the West's discarded garments into clothing practices in the Third World or the commercial involvement of charities with the exporters of such clothing.

The popularity of imported secondhand clothing in a country like Zambia provides evidence of much more than dressing bodies in a faded and worn imitation of the West. There is no denying that the growing secondhand clothing market gives evidence of a trickle-down effect of Western fashion, yet such explanations can be qualified by acknowledging the influence on dress style from the bottom up. To be sure, such influences travel in both directions, across class lines, between urban and rural areas, and worldwide. Even then, as Ann Bermingham (1995:12–13) has noted, the trickle-up corrective to the direction of the flow of influence retains the model of emulation and continues "to map the flow of cultural forms strictly along class lines," understanding consumption, she adds, "within the terms established in the seventeenth and eighteenth centuries."[3] Such a model cannot explain popular Zambian dealings with salaula. While clothes certainly can be worn to emulate and convey status or rank in affirmation or disguise, they may also have other ends. Their selection is, as Beverly Lemire (1997:3) reminds us, "replete with personal, economic, and cultural considerations." Bermingham's conclusion is relevant to clothing. The study of consumption "may include," she suggests (1995:13), "but must finally move beyond the idea of emulation to embrace structures of appropriation, circulation, and bricolage, and the complex workings of aesthetics, fantasy, discipline, and sexuality."

If clothing is a special commodity because of the way the dressed body mediates both individual and collective desires, secondhand clothing is perhaps an even more interesting commodity to study in its transfer to Africa. In effect, its incorporation into local dress repertoires offers a special exposure on the interaction between the local and the West. The cultural and political struggles that are played out on the body surface imply a continuing tension in the meeting between local practices and ideas and Western forms. I suggest that this tension contributes importantly to the vitality and dynamism of the "new" cultural forms whose combination of elements is always in process.

Secondhand clothing consumption in Zambia is about much more than imitating Western fashion. It is a story about individual and at times idiosyncratic dress practices that are informed by local cultural norms about etiquette and sexual decorum. The emerging clothing system is always in process, its meaning generated in particular contexts. It is the very process of appropriating imported dress conventions, putting one's own mark of judgment and taste on them, that makes them local. For clothes are not worn passively but require people's active collaboration. The presentational form (Miller 1987:87), the "look" that results from this process in Zambia, does, as Hollander (1978) suggests for Western clothes, have references to pictures, to a spectrum of desirable ways of looking at any given time, that have obvious Western traces. Yet such images are also tied up with local Zambian notions of the body and sexuality, distinctions drawn by gender, generation, and class, and fueled by the economic imperatives of everyday living, and the relative power of the state. Aside from fulfilling basic clothing needs, secondhand clothing consumption is also about liking, wanting, and desiring, thus constituting practices through which social identities are both constructed and contested. This is why dressing and dressing up is both an end in itself and a means that may entail a certain liberatory potential (Miller 1987; Wilk 1990; Wilson 1985).

The Secondhand Clothing Trade: Mapping Histories

In much of the contemporary West, secondhand clothing makes up fringe, or niche, markets. Today income distribution, purchasing power, affordable mass-produced garments and apparel, and concerns with fashion have reduced the need for large segments of the population to purchase used clothing. But well into the nineteenth century, used clothing constituted the effective market for much of the population except the very rich. As this book demonstrates, in a country like Zambia where the cost factor is enormously important, secondhand clothing is both desired and needed.

The secondhand clothing trade may have a long history but not one of unbroken continuity between the early modern era and the present. The sketch I provide below suggests at least a three-phase process marked by changes during the mid- to late nineteenth century, followed by shifts in the 1940s and again in the 1980s. While the last two phases relate directly to this book's observations, an overview of past involvements in the used clothing trade helps to demonstrate the changing importance of this particular commodity against the backdrop of distinct politico-economic and cultural conjunctures both in domestic and export markets.

Past and present, the export trade in used clothing has been closely linked to the costs of domestic garment manufacture in a process on which historians have begun to throw new light (Lemire 1997; Perrot 1994; Roche 1996). As long as domestic consumption of secondhand clothing constituted an effective demand, the export of this commodity was limited. The specificities of this trade in home and export markets are difficult to capture because of a widespread tendency in both historical and contemporary records on trade and commerce to refer to clothing without identifying its status as new or used. A historical sketch of this trade can at best be preliminary because of the very nature of secondhand clothing consumption, which exhausts the material evidence of its own history through extensive wear. Until well after the beginning of ready-made garment production, clothes went through many lives, passed down, resold or exchanged for other goods, altered or mended, and resewn before they reached the final phase of their journey and were recycled as rags into paper. "The success of the second-hand clothes trade can only be commemorated," suggests costume historian Madeleine Ginsburg (1980:121), "by their absence from museum collections of material survivals. [But it] would be an injustice to pay a similar complement to its history, of interest in its own right and as an aspect of the garment history."

Some of the shifting contours of the early secondhand clothing trade in domestic markets can be mapped through recent work, largely by historians who have offered suggestive evidence, drawing for example on probate and court records, of the importance of dealings with secondhand clothing at least from the sixteenth century onward. By 1600, if not earlier, the secondhand clothing trade flourished in major European cities, including Paris, London, Amsterdam, Nuremberg, Parma, and Genoa (Braudel 1973a:435,

1973b:810; du Mortier 1991; Gallo 1991; Lemire 1997; Musiari 1991; Perrot 1994; Roche 1996; Seidel 1991). The trade and its associated markets, stores, and pawnshops often concentrated in specific areas, in London the high end of the trade in Monmouth Street and lower down the scale along Rosemary Lane and Petticoat Lane (Ginsburg 1980: 124; Ribeiro 1991:87), and in Paris along the Rue de la Grande Friperie near Les Halles and the old Temple neighborhood (Perrot 1994:42–52; Roche 1996:349–52). Until after the French Revolution, guild regulations organized this trade, and sartorial rules of dress influenced who could wear what. In many European countries, rules and regulations prohibited tailors from manufacturing ready-to-wear clothes. England abandoned clothing regulation early in the seventeenth century, and the colonies followed soon thereafter (Lemire 1997:20–22; Shammas 1990:298). The revolution broke the statutory dress hierarchy in France and helped set into motion "a system of differentiation and management of signs determined not by law but by social norms" (Perrot 1994:20). More prosperity, greater market opportunities, and more openness in social structure increased the demand among all classes for fashionable clothing, much of which was satisfied from the secondhand clothing market (Lemire 1991a).

So valuable were secondhand clothes in terms of both needs and desires that thefts of clothes were frequent and the reputation of used clothes traders sometimes was dubious (Lemire 1990). Itinerant "old clothes men," many of Jewish background, traded clothes across the countryside, so that garments continued to change hands (Lemire 1997:75–93; Spufford 1984). They bought rags as well, linen rags to be made into paper, and wool and cotton rags, which from the early 1800s were shredded and spun into yarn for "shoddy" cloth for the incipient ready-to-wear clothing industry (Ginsburg 1980:128; Jubb 1860). Given the lower cost and ready availability, it is not surprising that secondhand clothing was popular. From North America Egal Feldman (1960:5) quotes one observer who stated that "prior to the Civil War, the trade in second hand clothing was perhaps more important than that in ready made."

Historical work has begun to push back the date of the origin of ready-made clothing production into the late seventeenth century, long before the development of advanced factory technology in spinning, weaving, and sewing. While the industry did not serve a modern mass market prior to the nineteenth century, hundreds of thousands of ready-made garments were prepared for specialized markets (Chapman 1993; Lemire 1997:20–22; Sharpe 1995). So-called slop shops sold ready-made clothes, first for seamen on long voyages. Governments contracted for military clothing, prison uniforms, and garments for the convicts in the penal colony established in Australia in 1788 (Ribeiro 1991:88). In the late eighteenth century, slop merchants were exporting ready-made clothes for the slave market, "mainly in the US and West Indies" (Ribeiro 1991:89). Tailors were reorganizing their production methods to manufacture ready-made civilian clothing, first work clothing and then everyday wear (Perrot 1994:52–56). Ready-made outerwear did not assume the same level of importance until later in the nineteenth century. Most of the early mass production was geared toward men's clothes. While both workshop organization and technology for mass production were available in the mid-nineteenth century, the production of women's readywear did not reach the levels of men's until the beginning of the twentieth century (Green 1997:39).

From the mid-eighteenth century on, the availability of more affordable cottons and wools began gradually reducing home markets in secondhand clothing at the same time as early mass-producing tailoring firms made new clothing more affordable (Lemire 1991b). Still, even though it was not considered a very attractive occupation, in New York's growing immigrant community people of Jewish background played a prominent role in the secondhand clothing trade between the 1840s and 1860s. Operating on the strategic fringes of the clothing market, Jewish clothing traders were among the pioneers who went on to promote clothing markets in the South and West (Feldman 1960). By the 1850s in Europe, the used clothing trade had decayed (Lemire 1988:22). Specialist retailers and early department stores in London and Paris now sold new clothing at the same price as good secondhand (Perrot 1994:51–56). "New came to mean brand new to the buying public, not the newest item added to one's wardrobe," according to Beverly Lemire (1988:23). In the process, attitudes to wearing secondhand clothing changed from being commonly accepted across most segments of society to being associated with the poor.

What were the export connections of this trade?[4] Beverly Lemire (1997:32–39) has provided insights into how clothing featured as a staple commodity in the Atlantic trading network. In the seventeenth and eighteenth centuries, London was one of the chief sources of ready-made clothing (Lemire 1997:33–34), both new and used. Naval, merchant, and slave ships carried stocks of clothes for their own use and for trade on their voyages. The British Navy carried clothes for its crews to far-flung naval ports, for example, in Portugal, Newfoundland, and the West Indies (Lemire 1997:155, n. 82) as it must have done to ports on major trade routes along the West African coast and South Africa, when rounding the Cape of Good Hope. Ready-made garments, among them undoubtedly used clothes, were part of the cargo of slave ships (Levitt 1991:37–39); they are mentioned in the cargo of ships of the Royal Africa Company, for example (Davies 1975:178, 234). Describing "what Africans got for their slaves," Stanley

Alpern (1995:10–11) lists both new and used clothing, including shirts, jackets, cloaks, gowns, hats, caps, scarves, ties, belts, gloves, stockings, slippers, and shoes. He also describes a line of notions for African weavers and tailors. To be sure, both garments from the early slop production and used clothes ended up on African bodies.

Like any other commodity in demand, secondhand clothing was sourced and traded across vast distances. In the first half of the eighteenth century in the Netherlands, the market for secondhand clothing had expanded so much and the trade had become so profitable that it "proved worthwhile to ship old clothes from England to the continent and still sell them with a handsome profit" (du Mortier 1991:123). London was then a center for the wholesale traffic in used clothes (Naggar 1990:181). By the middle of the nineteenth century, Britain exported a good volume of this commodity to Ireland (Ginsburg 1980:124). Bales of used clothes were also exported to Belgium, France, the Netherlands, and South America, purchased by wealthy merchants from different parts of Britain and Europe. Old-clothes hawkers still performed the first stage of the sourcing. The export trade from Britain continued toward the end of the century "as is confirmed by the case of Solomon Joseph, who was a dealer in new and second-hand clothing and was said to have bought his merchandise for colonial export" (Naggar 1990:181). By the late nineteenth century in Paris, reasonably priced ready-to-wear competed so effectively with secondhand clothes that the used clothing trade had declined significantly. From then on, notes Philippe Perrot, the trade in secondhand clothes became limited to exports, especially to colonial Africa. According to one source with a somewhat overwrought description: "Even the most shopworn garments take on new life when they cross the ocean. In other climes they become fancy goods: the soldier's red trousers and epaulettes are at a premium; the black kinglets grab the uniforms of generals and prefects, and even the gowns of academics and the livery of lackeys" (Perrot 1994:71).

The profitable potential of the secondhand clothes market in colonial Africa was seized after the two world wars when surplus army clothing was exported by used-clothing dealers in the United States and Britain and on the Continent. According to Phyllis Martin (1995:164), by 1920 there was a large trade in secondhand clothes "dispatched to Africa through European and American suppliers who specialized in the business. The availability of army clothing and men's work clothing from the early production of ready-to-wear are among the reasons that the histories of secondhand clothing consumption in Africa are distinctly gendered. Men's greatcoats and jackets came first, and only much later did women's wear begin to enter used-clothing consignments for export. This took place in the interwar period. But the substantive growth of the African secondhand clothing export market is a post–World War II phenomenon, a product of both supply and demand: a vast surplus of still wearable used clothing in the West, and growing desires and needs for clothes in Africa where socioeconomic transformations catapulted more and more Africans into new markets as consumers.

Developments in the post–World War II export trade of secondhand clothing have depended overwhelmingly on the clothing-collection activities of major charitable organizations who supply both domestic and foreign secondhand clothing markets. The charities have a long, and changing, involvement with secondhand clothing. In both Europe and the United States at the end of the nineteenth century, philanthropic groups collected and donated clothes to the poor (Ginsburg 1980:128), changing early in the present century to an approach that stressed self-help rather than outright donation. In the post–World War II period, shifts in income distribution and growing purchasing power enabled more consumers than ever before to buy not only new, but more, clothes, including fashions and styles oriented toward specific niches, for example, teenage clothing, corporate and career dressing, and sports and leisure wear. Such dress practices produced an enormous yield of used but still wearable clothes, some of which ended up as donations to charity.

Many charitable organizations began emphasizing store sales in the late 1950s, among them the Salvation Army, for which the sale of used clothing was the largest single source of income in the United States by the 1960s (McKinley 1986). Consumers in the West today donate a vast proportion of the clothes they no longer wear to charitable organizations who sell some of the donations in their thrift shops while disposing of their massive overstock at bulk prices to commercial secondhand clothing dealers. As I describe in detail in part 2, the charitable organizations are the largest single source of the garments that fuel today's multibillion-dollar-a-year international trade in secondhand clothing.

The charitable organizations dominated the secondhand clothing retail scene in the 1960s and 1970s. During the 1980s they were joined by a variety of special secondhand clothing stores operating on a for-profit basis that began appearing with names, in the Chicago area, like Crowded Closet, Flashy Trash, Hollywood Mirror, Hubba Hubba, Bewitched, and Strange Cargo. Although most of the specialty resale stores cater to women, some stock garments for both sexes, and there are stores for children's clothing as well. Men's stores are beginning to appear, for example, Gentlemen's Agreement on the Upper East Side of Manhattan (*New York Times,* 14 December 1997) and Second Time Around, in the middle of Boston's Newbery Street (*Wall Street Journal,* 20 January 1997). Some stores operate on a consignment basis, selling "gently worn" designer clothes both for women and men; others source in bulk from commercial secondhand clothing vendors; and some use both sources.

Rarely featuring words like *used, secondhand,* or *thrift* in their names, most of these recent stores target specific consumers, for example, young professionals who want high-quality clothes at modest prices or young people keen on retro and vintage fashion, punk, and rave styles (McRobbie 1989). There is a vigorous resale market for designer clothes in specialty stores whose customers buy designer labels to wear as "investment dressing" much like collectors buy art (*New York Times,* 4 June 1996). And "thrift shopping" appears to have developed a new cachet, providing a pastime for vintage junkies/connoisseurs who are on the lookout for rare finds (*New York Times,* 28 September 1997). The garments that do not sell easily in these new stores are bulked and donated "to charity," according to information my students and I obtained from store owners and managers in the wider Chicago area in the last half of the 1990s. We also have evidence that some of these businesses dispose of their surplus at bulk prices to commercial secondhand clothing dealers.

This preliminary sketch of some of the shifting contours of the secondhand clothing trade appears to explain its dynamics with reference to the history of clothing manufacture, first tailor-made and then factory-produced garments. But it is also, in the longer haul, a cultural story about consumption and about the importance of clothing, both new and old, to modern sensibilities, embodying new social and cultural abilities to discriminate. This is the magic of clothing. No longer guided by sartorial rules or fulfilling merely functional needs, clothing became an agent of social change (Martin 1994). To bring this observation to bear more explicitly on the secondhand clothing phenomenon invites a closer look at consumption.

The Turn toward Consumption

What helps account for the recent engagement with consumption in anthropology and other disciplines? There are many potential contending genealogies, and this account is merely one. At its most obvious, historical and analytical issues intersect. Ongoing transformations of the late-twentieth-century global economy are recasting the roles of production and consumption as engines of growth, challenging conventional accounts of development trajectories. Our knowledge of the world as one has improved vastly compared to the days when, for instance, in Africa we discussed whether or not to call rural cultivators peasants (Fallers 1961), when local populations were considered contemporary ancestors and were studied as if they were outside time and space (Wilmsen 1989). The historical turn in anthropology, combined with growing concerns with globalization and transnationalism, makes us grapple with a variety of not-so-local processes that are affecting the livelihoods of the people we study and their experiences of being in the world on changing terms.

Part of the impetus in the new scholarship on consumption has come to us from history (Campbell 1987; de Grazia, Quilligan, and Stallybrass 1996; Goldthwaite 1992; Thirsk 1978; Weatherill 1988). The questioning of accounts of the birth of consumer society as a product of supply-side capitalist market-driven economies is revealing that consumption has a longer and more complex history that does not stretch back unchanged to the sixteenth century but lends itself to a different periodization than the conventional one. Arjun Appadurai (1997:28–33) suggests that, rather than searching for a preestablished sequence of institutional change, we might explore particular conjunctures that help set into motion different consumer "revolutions." For research on developing countries, such insights not only invite a rethinking of local and external production/consumption dynamics; they also raise the possibility that we may in fact be exploring consumption sensibilities that differ from those we have long taken for granted.

The early history of consumption is "culturally suppressed" (Bermingham 1995:3). That is to say, a variety of reigning explanatory frameworks are in part to blame for impeding our grasp of the broader significance of consumption. When consumption is seen as the end point of the economic circuit, what is consumed is no longer a commodity but a use value, and when it is realized in the final act of consumption, there is nothing left to explore (Narotzky 1997:103). Economistic accounts of consumption that allot it a secondary role after production or that focus on commodities rather than on consumers leave little scope to explore the workings of consumption and the diverse and changing social relations that individuals and collectivities are constructing through their consumption of objects.

Popular Zambian preoccupations with salaula richly support Appadurai's argument (1986) that commodities are socially constructed and that things have social lives. Because a commodity does not always remain where it was produced, it can be said to have a "social life" whose value and meanings change as it moves through time and space. In the process a commodity acquires a cultural biography (Kopytoff 1986). Friedman (1991) has added an important caveat by suggesting that it is not the things themselves that are the point of departure but rather the strategies within which they are embedded. In effect, he argues that "things do not have social lives. Rather, social life has things" (161).

Recent work on consumption brings questions about culture and agency to bear on explanations of how people shape and create conceptions about themselves and their world through their involvement with objects. Daniel

Miller (1995b) has suggested that this shift could occur only when the foundational status of culture in anthropology changed into an emergent status. With the "expunging of latent primitivism," he suggests, " . . . culture itself will no longer be regarded as an attribute to be lost or gained, but rather as a process or struggle by which all peoples of the world attempt to make sense of the world and make claims to social and material forms and institutions" (269). Because consumption concerns what people do with things and how things fit into their lives, the issue of agency, rather than the relentless hand of the market, comes to the fore. In this view, consumption is about how people use things and how cultural beliefs and practices shape their appropriation of such things, with consequences for the wider contexts of their lives.

As with all turns of the explanatory pendulum, this one has begun to shift. Even Daniel Miller (1997), probably the most vocal and central proponent of consumption as the vanguard of history, reminds us not to lose sight of production. The same point has been made emphatically and from a variety of perspectives in a number of other works (Carrier and Heyman 1997; Fine and Leopold 1993; Narotzky 1997; Roseberry 1996). Pointing to the lack of political economy in much of the new anthropological work on consumption, James Carrier and Josiah Heyman (1997) have remarked on the "ironic" timing of the boom in work on this subject. "It has occurred," they note, "while the practice of consumption has been threatened . . . [when] real incomes have decayed in many countries peripheral to Western capitalism" (356). In their view, concerns with class and inequality might be brought to bear on the study of consumption through analysis of household reproduction. Susana Narotzky (1997:209–211) has suggested much the same with her means-of-livelihood approach. But while Carrier and Heyman are turning the timing of the boom in consumption studies into an extraordinary fact, they do not follow this up. They stop short of spelling out the implications of their own observations for our understanding of the relationship between consumption and development, and they fail to acknowledge the role specific commodities may play in people's efforts to make a living in "peripheral countries."

Needs and Desires

Clothing goes to the heart of widespread understandings of well-being in Zambia.[5] Because they mediate identity in different ways, few other imported secondhand commodities, for example, cars, spare parts and tires, electrical appliances, and computer equipment, cast as revealing a light on the work of consumption as does secondhand clothing. Its consumption traverses a wide field of social practice across class and between rural and urban areas that both gives effect to cultural normative values and helps to transform them. That is to say, we need to reckon with people's preoccupations with clothing if we are to understand the process of becoming modern in this part of Africa, and thus local experiences of development. More than thirty years of independence from British colonial rule have not brought the developmental attributes of modernity within general reach in Zambia. In terms of too many indicators, among them education, health, longevity, child mortality and nutrition, formal employment, and wages, Zambians in the first half of the 1990s were worse off than they were in the mid-1970s (GRZ and UN 1996). In their narratives about development, they construe the modern through its objective attributes: education, occupation, and wealth. At the very least they want satisfaction of basic needs such as food, schooling, work, housing, health services, and transportation.

People in Zambia also want well-dressed bodies. While the crossover appeal of imported secondhand clothing no doubt is due in part to its affordability to poor consumers, the popularity of salaula cannot be accounted for only because it satisfies basic clothing needs. Clothing desires are equally important. Unlike the scholarly literature, which is having a hard time with the normative aspect of the relationship between consumption and development (James 1992:vii), many Zambians keenly express their subjective interpretations and desires. And clothing is at the dead center of widespread understandings of well-being. That much of this clothing in recent years has been imported secondhand garments does not reduce the power of this commodity to mediate modern sensibilities but has rather accentuated the role it plays in externalizing identity in everyday life. For not only does salaula give people what they need, namely clothing they can afford; it also gives them what they want, namely the ability to dress rather than wear rags. As a metaphor, "wearing rags" stands for lack of access. The widespread replacement of rags with salaula, which is replete with meanings of choice and selecting, invites a move of the explanatory focus from needs to desires and in particular to questions about how people deal with clothing.

Because secondhand clothing connects with bodies both literally and figuratively, salaula consumption mobilizes public opinion at many levels of society. Several popular songs written since the late 1980s praise the "goodness" of salaula. At least one music video has been produced about salaula. Consumers themselves are providing ample evidence of the attraction of salaula by flocking to secondhand clothing markets. And salaula retailing and its many ancillary services provide work for people who do not find wage-labor jobs. Turning to critique, the growth of the salaula trade has spurred a public debate about production versus consumption in which manufacturers associations have taken a lead, arguing that the growth of salaula imports is destroying the domestic textile and clothing industry. Because it ignores the social and cultural issues that make this commodity important in people's lives, such criticism does not even begin to consider the ways in which the subjective, normative dimensions of consumption interact with welfare and development.

At issue in the anticonsumption criticism is an implicit distinction between primary or basic needs versus secondary or social desires that are considered frivolous. The result is a need/want distinction that construes as "natural," rather than historical and social, the conditions of production, distribution, and consumption that have brought about the salaula phenomenon and help to reproduce its significance. Because rigidly drawn need/want distinctions do not acknowledge the interaction of social and cultural factors, they fail to reckon with how consumption affects socioeconomic developments. Such distinctions run into trouble when called upon to explain the popularity of salaula, the consumer practices that are arising around it, and ultimately people's desires for clothes. When purchasing salaula, consumers also make want-based judgments. In effect, when confronted with actual consumption practices, the explanatory rhetorics of need and want distinctions may clash (Campbell 1998). While salaula consumption undoubtedly satisfies basic needs, it also mediates social and cultural desires that have important material and economic implications, affecting household activities and welfare. These implications are perhaps more adequately accounted for when we reckon with the entire chain of activities that embed the consumption of this particular commodity. What is more, such an approach must reckon with gender, which for the study of a commodity like clothing constitutes a critical category of analysis (de Grazia 1996).

A Salaula System of Provision

How do we account for the preoccupations with clothing in Zambia and, in particular, the surge in the consumption of imported secondhand clothing in recent years? The salaula phenomenon in Zambia may be examined within a framework that recognizes both economic and social factors, including the cultural meanings different people attribute to clothing. Ben Fine and Ellen Leopold (1993) have suggested that a "vertical approach," recognizing differences arising around the consumption of distinct commodities, may provide richer insights than analyses that have tended to approach consumption horizontally, that is to say, by appealing to general factors that apply across society and across consumption as a whole. Their idea of a "system of provision" sets the role of consumption "within a much different perspective, one that views it as determined both historically—and therefore varying over time in strength and influence—and jointly with other variables within separate systems of provision which are themselves subject to significant long-term change, achieved at different rates and with different consequences" (23).

A system of provision invites us to explore a "comprehensive chain of activities between the two extremes of production and consumption, each link of which plays a potentially significant role in the social construction of the commodity both in its material and cultural aspects" (Fine and Leopold 1993:33). Depending on the questions of concern, alternative approaches might be called on to trace the changing dynamics of commodity chains, complexes, or regimes, although few take in all the sites along the way (Alessandro et al. 1994; Gereffi and Korzeniewicz 1994; Marsden and Little 1990; Mintz 1985; Steiner 1994).[6] The system of provision offers a constructive approach to examining the international secondhand clothing trade; it provides building blocks from across the economic circuit and takes consumption seriously as a cultural economy that shapes production rather than the other way around.[7]

The secondhand clothing phenomenon can be viewed as a subsystem of provision in its own right, distinct from the system of provision of new garments with which it articulates in complex ways. This system has a history, and a changing one comprising distinct phases that have been shaped by economic, political, and cultural forces. Although parts of this system have been in place for a long time, I suggest that we may speak of the emergence of a secondhand clothing system of provision in its own right in the post–World War II era. The dynamics of this system have changed in many ways from the mid- to late 1980s on as a result not only of global restructuring of production and consumption practices but also of shifts in international arrangements for foreign loans, aid, and relief to Third World countries.

Because it enables me to follow the flow of secondhand clothing from its source in the West to its final point of consumption in Zambia, the idea of considering the secondhand clothing export trade and the local consumption practices that have arisen around it as a system of provision provides a rich organizational frame for this book. To place the salaula phenomenon in Zambia within that frame requires an outline that sketches the economic and cultural practices that make up the production, distribution/exchange, and consumption circuit through which this commodity travels. In effect, each chapter adds new parts to this unfolding story across time and space, with some surprising twists along the way.

The Research and the Book

The secondhand clothing trade is an unusual industry with peculiar problems that arise from the uneasy relationship between "charity" and commercial interests, and the ways these are organized. While its spectacular increase in Africa since the mid-1980s has taken place alongside the growth of the international humanitarian-aid industry, secondhand clothing export is less about charity than it is about profits. Indeed, used clothing as outright donations in crisis and relief situations plays a very minor role in an export process that is overwhelmingly commercial.[8]

In the West today the secondhand clothing trade both in domestic and foreign markets is dominated by nonprofit charitable organizations and private textile recycling/grading firms, often family owned. Its financial side has largely eluded public scrutiny. Thriving by an ethic of giving in the West, the major charitable organizations look like patrons in a worldwide clothing-donation project. Their extensive interactions with textile recyclers/graders add a commercial angle to their dealings about which there is little substantive knowledge. The textile recyclers/graders truck used clothing they purchase in bulk from the charitable organizations across the United States and northwestern Europe to warehouses/sorting plants near major port cities. The clothes are often sorted under poor work conditions by poorly paid workers, some of whom are recent immigrants from countries where the clothes will be sold. At the receiving end, for example in Zambia, the local operations of the secondhand clothing trade are contested by representatives of the state, manufacturers, importers, and retailers who do not always see eye to eye with consumers about the significance of this commodity.

The secondhand clothing trade poses several research problems due to uneven records and, in particular, to the widespread tendency not to distinguish between used and new clothing. These problems are not unique to historical research but persist in contemporary records. Difficulties in accounting for the more recent scope of this worldwide trade are aggravated by the special nature of this industry. For example in the United States, the world's largest exporting nation of secondhand clothing, it is hard to come by basic figures for total sales, number of companies, and volume and value of clothing collected, sold in nonprofit thrift stores, disposed of commercially, and exported.

Representatives of the industry, both in the West and in Zambia, are not particularly anxious to discuss their activities, although I have indeed met people who provided much detail. My research into this process since the early 1990s has taken me into secondhand sorting operations in North America, northern Europe, and Africa. I have had both good and bad times attempting to conduct extensive interviews, in person as well as by phone, using lists of exporters available from chambers of commerce, for example in the Netherlands, and the yellow pages in Belgium.

There is little conventional scholarly work on the process with which this book is concerned. Because both archival and contemporary evidence on the secondhand clothing trade in Zambia is spotty, this book attempts to piece together a larger story by way of suggestive interpretation. For the contemporary circumstances surrounding the sourcing of secondhand clothing in the West and its retailing in Zambia, I have drawn extensively on news media reporting, largely in print but also on radio and television. This introduces obvious problems of representation as well as media bias. In Zambia, for example, the *Zambia Daily Mail* and *Times of Zambia* are state-owned and government-controlled, whereas the *Post,* the main independent newspaper, is very outspoken against the government; the contents and coverage reflect these relationships. What is more, investigative reporting in Zambia as elsewhere is occasionally faulty. And it is above all sensationalist. While getting some elements of a story right, media interpretation is often slanted. This applies particularly to reports on the commercial connection to the secondhand clothing activities of major charitable organizations both in the United States and Europe. Still, without access to news media sources, I would not have been able to delineate the contours of this trade and its shifts over recent years. Acknowledging the many qualifications we must apply when using such accounts, I have kept this evidence in full view, listing all details in the references.

My account of the Zambian side of the secondhand clothing story draws on several periods of field research undertaken between 1992 and 1999 with wholesalers, retailers, consumers, and a variety of special-interest groups both in the capital, Lusaka, and across the country. I also spent time in many archives inside and outside of Zambia. The specific methodological approaches are discussed in the body of the book when they become relevant to particular arguments. But above all, my appreciation of the significance of clothing to and in people's lives in Zambia is a product of my scholarly engagement with that country for close to three decades. This book is about the personal side of the country's development predicament as understood concretely by a large proportion of the population through their preoccupations with clothing.

People in Zambia and in "the West" exist in each other's space, as is evident in the global circuits of the secondhand clothing trade. There are few models for a book that tries to incorporate both ends of this relationship in a unified account. This book deals with a macroscale process: the expansion of the international secondhand clothing trade into a region that some still consider "peripheral." Zambia and the local concerns of its citizens are inextricably bound to the macrolevel, and so this book is equally about what local clothing practices tell us about what it means to be a Zambian, a woman or a man, of a certain age and position, in our late-twentieth-century world.

The flow of secondhand clothing across its worldwide circuit from source to final destination is central to the overall structure of this book at the same time as specific moments and places along the way provide the contexts for detailed examination. The book's two parts situate clothing engagements, both new and used, in time. The two parts are divided by the shift in import regime and value of the mid- to late 1980s when salaula had become part of everyday parlance and clothing practice.

Part 1, "Dealing with Clothing," concerns broad questions about clothing encounters in this region of Africa. Its two first chapters, roughly divided by the end of World War II, explore the acquisition of clothing-consumption competence, clothing access, and the localization of European-style dress. These observations form the local context in which the operation of a secondhand clothing system of provision is evident by the World War II period. Chapter 3 examines the organization of this trade and its historical niche in interactions between the Belgian Congo and Northern Rhodesia from the interwar period until independence in 1964. Chapter 4 broadens out these discussions by exploring postcolonial developments related to clothing and dress practices, among them questions of dress, nationalism, and politics in the immediate preindependence period and after, including most of the time of the second republic (1972–91).

Part 2, "A Secondhand Clothing System of Provision," focuses on Zambian dealings with clothing during the third republic. Recent shifts in the secondhand clothing system of provision have made the local trade and consumption of salaula grow in a big way, which I have examined on the ground from many angles since 1992. The six chapters that constitute this part take us inside the secondhand clothing system of provision from the point of "donations" to charities in the West, through the interventions of commercial middlemen in textile recycling, exporting, and shipping, on to Zambian markets and beyond, into Zambian lives and gendered social relations. It deals as well with the politics the growing import of secondhand clothing has given rise to. In short, trying to capture the special magic of clothing by examining how used clothes "from the West" acquire "new" lives in Zambia, this book provides tangible evidence of local attempts to reckon with a changing world both in cultural and instrumental terms and against the backdrop of a changing economic and political landscape.

PART

1

Dealing with Clothing

1 Clothing Encounters

If the power of the dressed body derives in part from the special nature of clothing as a commodity, as I suggested in the introduction, its significance in particular cases has to do with the circumstances that have made it appear special. Since the early days of the colonial encounter in what came to be known as Northern Rhodesia and now Zambia, Western-style clothing became and has remained a centerpiece of consumption, a focal point of everyday life, in effect, constituting the key token of modernity. But we cannot explain the social and cultural significance of clothing consumption unless we examine how this commodity has been delivered and how it has entered people's lives. The chapters in part 1 are a brief attempt to do so.

Cloth and clothing were key commodities in the political economy of the West's encounter with Africa. African bodies and dress were among the first encounter topics in the writings of European explorers, missionaries, and early ethnographers throughout the nineteenth century and the first decades of the twentieth, and they often continue to be topics of interest. Colonial descriptions of dress practice provide glimpses of an ongoing battle over clothing and specifically the question of who has the power to define what is correct dress. They are heavy with bias and caricature that have shifted over time. Africans make such comments themselves, equally skewed and stereotyped, and influenced by distinctions of class, locality, gender, and religion.

In the first part of this chapter, I introduce some of the many actors and processes involved in making Africans into commodity consumers of clothing. For a glimpse of some of the tensions arising over African appropriations of clothing, I turn to a widely used schoolbook in the Bemba language, *Ifya Bukaya*. One of its chapters features the stock character of migration stories: the smartly dressed returned male migrant (Comaroff and Comaroff 1987). The influences of migration and school are strikingly at odds in this text's treatment of African dress practice. The tensions between these influences persisted into the post–World War II years and remain with us today in the distinction between need and desire, which I return to at several points in this book. For my discussion of African reactions to dress and its growing appeal during the first half of the twentieth century, I draw on a variety of contemporary studies, an oral history project that was carried out in Luapula by students from the University of Zambia in the early 1970s (Musambachime

n.d.),[1] and my own interviews about clothing consumption with elderly people in Luapula Province in 1995.

Cloth, Clothing, and Migration

Cloth and clothing were central commodities in the long-term transformations that brought "the market" to this part of Africa and gradually made local
people dependent on it as consumers. While the economic transformation
project never developed a fully fledged capitalist system of production, it did
introduce the kind of personal identity space we usually associate with
modernity. This new outlook made claims at village, urban, and state levels
for new sensibilities of space, time, and the self, detaching individuals, to
varying degrees to be sure, from larger kin groupings and polities in an ongoing engagement with the developmental aspects of the modern: education,
occupation, and wealth. In local experiences a commodity like clothing went
to the heart of widespread notions of well-being, playing active roles in constructing visions of the future.

Textiles and clothing played pivotal roles in the political economy of the
West's expansion and in the triangular North Atlantic slave trade that helped
fuel Europe's industrial revolution, constituting both a supply and a demand
side across this broader region (DuPont 1995:180). In the West's engagement
with Africa from the fifteenth century on, "cloth became the principal
medium, assisted by beads, bullets, gunpowder, and conus shells; as their use
increased not only was economic specialization greatly stimulated but also
the whole pattern of exchange began to be expanded beyond recognition . . .
[assuming] the force of a creative mobility" (Gray and Birmingham 1970:7).
Historical scholarship has richly documented the role of cloth as a major European export commodity to West Africa in connection with the slave trade
and throughout the colonial period (Johnson 1974; Nielsen 1979; Reikat
1997; Steiner 1985). In addition to cloth and manufactured goods, major
trading companies and individual merchants shipped a miscellany of ready-
made clothing, both new and old, as a trade commodity to West African destinations from the 1600s on (Alpern 1995:10–11; Davies 1975:178, 234).
Indian prints were traded up and down the West African coast. By 1750,
Manchester-produced cloth had been modified to suit African tastes with
prints and patterns that appealed to consumers in different parts of West
Africa (Nielsen 1979:469).[2]

Although no comparable work exists on the scale and nature of cloth imports into East and south-central Africa, there is ample, but scattered, evidence
that cloth and clothing first entered local societies through the activities of
Swahili and Arab slavers and Portuguese traders both from the east (Mozam-

Map 1 The Republic of Zambia, 1997

bique) and the west (Angola), long before trading companies such as the
African Lakes Corporation became active in the region during the early colo-
nial period (e.g., Matthews 1981; Miller 1988; Roberts 1970; St. John 1970;
Sutherland-Harris 1970).[3] When Manuel Gaetano Pereira, the son of a Portuguese trader at Tete, a Portuguese entrepôt on the Zambezi River, reported to
Jose Maria de Lacerda e Almeida, governor of the Sena Rivers Province in
Mozambique, about his visit to Kazembe III, king or paramount chief of the
Lunda in the Luapula region in 1798, he noted that the king was in touch with
both coasts. Kazembe already had at his court goods "from the west coast, like
looking glasses, tea-sets . . . plates, cups, velorio beads, missanga, cowries
and woolen goods." In return for slaves delivered to Angola, he received

"stuffs like flannel, durante, sarafina." The king's dress displayed these influences: "his usual clothing consists of a large silk cloth with a belt like a bandolier . . . his legs are covered with cowries, velorio beads, pipe-shaped beads and others of different colours" (Cunnison 1961:65).

Calico and cotton cloth had already penetrated the interior by the mid–nineteenth century. When the Monteiro and Gamitta expedition passed through the territory of King Kazembe IV in 1831, it was pressed by demands for fine cloth, not the standard cotton cloth used in exchange for food and labor. At that point in time the king had little need for contact with Tete, for he was already well supplied. In fact, he showed the expedition boxes containing "two large bundles of silk and woolen clothes of all colours; ten boxes of beads and stones, and forty shot guns and six limiting carbines wrapped in lace-trimmed cloth" (Cunnison 1961:73–74).

Encounter descriptions such as these indicate that the new commodities that functioned as media of exchange and measures of wealth were initially the monopoly of kings and chiefs who extended their use through tribute channels and distributed them through the kinship system. As trade slipped away from local power and kinship connections, becoming increasingly oriented toward market exchange, the role of kings and chiefs as clearing agents weakened. Throughout the region imported cloth largely of British and East Indian manufacture came to be widely used as a currency for the headload work of carriers and porters, and it served as a medium of exchange in the food and grain trade during the days of caravan travel in the nineteenth century until the advent of motor transportation in the 1920s (Hansen 1989:31–51). From a luxury good once controlled by kings and chiefs, clothing had become a commodity that was exchanged for labor, services, or other goods, and it was increasingly purchased with money. A rare thing had become a necessity that people craved.

People in Zambia have been clothing-conscious for a long time. Throughout most of the nineteenth century, ordinary people's dress in this part of Africa exposed the body; it consisted of bark cloth, skin, and hides, and a variety of body adornment. Only in the extreme northeast border region (Gouldsbury and Sheane 1911:288–89) and in the Zambezi valley had cotton weaving been practiced on a very limited scale (Davison and Harries 1980; Wright 1993). Drawing on London Missionary Society records from 1891, Robert Rotberg (1962:583–84) notes how missionaries preached against "heathen" undress and "encouraged both men and women to obtain shirts, dresses and other foreign objects." "For the first half of the [twentieth] century," observes Luig (1997:61) from interviews with Valley Tonga elders, "clothes became the most prestigious commodity . . . [they were] the main prerequisite by which an African could acceptably enter European controlled areas." By this time Western-style clothing had come to matter to Africans not only in their interaction with Europeans but also in the changing contexts of their everyday lives. Godfrey Wilson (1941–42, 2:18) acknowledged this when he noted that clothing among African mine workers in the late 1930s was "the chief medium in which obligations to country relatives [were] fulfilled." Africans in Broken Hill (now Kabwe), he said, "are not a cattle people, nor a goat people, nor a fishing people, nor a tree cultivating people, they are a dressed people." This preoccupation with clothing was not only an urban phenomenon. The rural Bemba, judging from Audrey Richards's observations (1968, 216–18) in the early 1930s, constantly spoke about clothes and took an intense interest in them.

First traders and prospectors, then missionaries, white settlers, and government officials were among the many actors introducing both cloth and clothing, and along with them new notions of the body and propriety, including dress conventions. Missionaries who have received prominent attention in scholarship on early clothing encounters on the southern African frontier (Comaroff and Comaroff 1997) were not the first or only actors to introduce new dress conventions in Northern Rhodesia, where at the turn of the nineteenth century there was so much trading cloth in circulation that its wage value had become severely depressed (Morrow 1985:34). In the late 1800s and early 1900s mission societies operating within this region, such as the Christian Missions to Many Lands, in their dealings with the Lunda king (Kazembe), were more interested in converting local authority figures than they were in African bodies and dress (Rotberg 1965a:67–71). Other missions focused more on teaching Africans craft and industry than they did on clothing their bodies (Morrow 1985:33). At this point in time, many African men had already begun labor migration to the Belgian Congo, Southern Rhodesia, and South Africa. The clothing practices that arose in these many encounters drew on influences from the missions, migration, and school as well as on African normative notions about the body and sexuality. What is at issue in these encounters, as I argue throughout this book, was not so much antecedents and origins as Africans making these dress practices their own.

The imposition of taxes in the early 1900s provided additional incentive for men to leave their home villages in search of jobs to earn cash. By the mid-1930s more than 50 percent of the able-bodied male population was working for wages away from home, as many outside the territory as in it (Roberts 1976:171). J. Merle Davis ([1933] 1968:54) was struck by how the "desire for trinkets and the White man's castoff finery gave place to a conscious desire for blankets, showy clothes, the European knife and axe, the mirror, mouth-organ, gramophone, sewing-machine and bicycle." In this changing regional socioeconomic context, new ideas of wealth, civilization, and maturity came together in clothing, the acquisition of which for a long time hinged on labor migration (Vail and White 1991:256–61).

During the first decade of this century, clothing access depended on location in relationship to the shifting centers of economic activity, and on the building of roads and railways. Major roads were not cut through the Gwembe Valley, for example, until the early 1950s, when it became connected more closely with activities emanating from Lusaka, the rapidly growing capital. Prior to this, Valley Tonga labor migration had taken men to Southern Rhodesia, especially Bulawayo. In comparison, the Plateau Tonga who lived near the railway that was built in the early 1900s took advantage of their good soil and their proximity to roads and rails, raising cash crops to supply grain and other foodstuffs to the growing mines. They developed local entrepreneurship and experienced social mobility through education (Colson 1962:610–11; Dixon-Fyle 1983). With the Gwembe Valley's relative isolation from developments elsewhere in Northern Rhodesia, local and gendered dress etiquette persisted longer there than in many other parts of the country. In 1949 Elizabeth Colson (personal communication) was told that returning labor migrants disposed of long trousers long before going home because women would not look at them, fearing they must have some skin disease or other problem if they were so intent on covering their bodies; the women for their part could be seen wearing skimpy hide and skin dress until well after World War II.

Cities and towns were crucial settings where migrants acquired not only knowledge about consumption practices but also insights into how to pursue them. Many migrants were engaged in domestic service, which was the chief labor relationship in which African men were socialized into working for whites from early on, and it remained the second-largest African employment sector, after mining, for most of the colonial period. Servants saw European dress conventions and new fashions at first hand, and they learned how to look after clothes. Because of their knowledge of the European way of life, including dress etiquette, style, and care, domestic servants were often consulted by workers in other jobs. But their privileged access to their employers' hand-me-downs must not be interpreted merely as emulation. Servants had little choice in this matter. Their substandard wages, partly paid in kind, limited their ability to purchase clothes. Their knowledge of the dress domain remained far from a monopoly, especially after some job mobility came within reach for African men during the late colonial period (Hansen 1989:164–65).

Migrant experiences in urban contexts constituted crucial contexts for the acquisition of clothing-consumption skills. So did schools. With the spread of education and the value system that went along with it, European-style dress became a sign of progress and success. In the view of some, education earned you the right to dress European-style. But the dressed body also had the power to create an appearance independent of school. This applies to men's dress practice much more than to women's. In general, because colonial authorities attempted to keep them back in the rural areas, women were less exposed than men both to migrant labor and education, thus catching on more slowly as clothing consumers. In effect, the story of clothing practices in Zambia is a deeply gendered one.

Chishimba's Suit

Most schooling during the colonial period took place in mission schools. At least two generations of Bemba-speaking people from Northern Rhodesia who went to Catholic primary school between 1929 and 1950 know *Ifya Bukaya* (White Fathers 1931), their first and second Bemba readers. The literal translation of the Bemba reader's title is "things that are familiar" or "things from around here."[4] One of the chapters, "Chizimba abwela ku Kongo" (Chishimba comes back from the Congo), encapsulates divergent but widespread views on African dress practice.[5] A literal interpretation conveys to the youthful readers of this chapter a cautionary if not moralistic tale about the importance of school and the excesses of migration. A less straightforward reading suggests several contending issues that arise in this text's discussion of the significance of dress and its graphic depiction of clothing.

Figure 1 reproduces the line drawing that accompanies the chapter about Chishimba's return from the Congo. The drawing depicts three students, Philip, Jacob, and Mulenga, sitting along the roadside; they are wearing school uniforms of shorts and simple tops; they are barefoot; and each has a book in his hands. One of them is pointing at a strikingly dressed young man, who is walking down the road. The gaze of the two other students is fixed on the attire of the person whom the narrative describes as "dressed in a pair of striped khaki shorts, looking very smart, with shoes and gray socks, a shirt and a stiff collar, and a jacket, with a walking stick in his right hand, while in his left hand he has a cigarette, which he is smoking while holding it between his middle two fingers and walking proudly. He has also made a shade line [parting] in his hair, which he has smoothed to make it look like a white man's shade" (65).

Wondering who the smartly dressed person is, the three friends realize that he is Chishimba, "the one who refused to start school the year we all started" (65). Chishimba tells them that the Congo "is very nice, it is not like this country of ours, can't you see how I have come back, now I am well off and can't be compared to some people who are just monkeys" (66). In this part of

Figure 1 "Chizimba abwela ku Kongo."
Illustration from White Fathers 1931:66.

Africa, some whites condescendingly used the term *monkey* for Africans to imply that they belonged to a "lower" species. It is not surprising that the three friends take offense at Chishimba's use of this word. Jacob intervenes, "Really, are you calling us monkeys?" He exclaims Bemba proverbs, which Chishimba does not understand. Then Mulenga explains what Jacob meant: "He is saying that, although you are dressed in expensive and smart-looking clothes . . . , don't show off. You are not alone and we shall one day be able to acquire what you have." With disbelief Chishimba answers: "Never! Where will you get such things from? Look at the way you are. Look. Can you say you are really dressed?" Taking his turn, Philip answers: "Yes. We shall continue dressing the way we are. We are not bothered. We are concerned more with our education and performance in school."

Taunting Chishimba, the three friends go on to ask him whether he went to school in the Congo and whether he can read, write, and understand mathematics. When he answers no to all these questions, Jacob exclaims: "You are placing yourself where you do not deserve to be . . . Do not show off just because of the clothes you have, as they are nothing. It is better to acquire knowledge and dignity, as these are the real riches [signs of wealth]. Let us tell you. We are not concerned with dressing properly and smartly at the moment. We are still young and more concerned with education because this is the time to acquire knowledge, and when we grow up it may be too late" (67).

The first specific issue in this mission-authored narrative is migration, specifically to the Belgian Congo, and the role of migration in making Africans consumers of clothing. The second issue concerns schooling and postponement of gratification. These two issues come together in the evaluation of African dress practice, which in Chishimba's story are exaggerated in the voice of the three African schoolboys. The significance of this issue arises, I suggest, from the drawing, specifically in Chishimba's performance gestures and the way he is put together with clothing. While I shall have more to say about migration to the Congo in chapter 3, the three issues invite commentary.

Migration created its own folklore that found expression in songs, anecdotes, and stories, as well as in chapters in schoolbooks such as this Bemba reader. The main character was the returned migrant, smartly dressed, who provoked a variety of reactions on his return. And apparel—a suit, hat, and a walking stick—was among the items associated with returned migrants and as such metonymically with the city and/or new ways he had left behind. Readers and listeners would interpret such stories differently, depending on their location in the race- and class-divided society.

In the mission-inflected voice of the three African schoolboys, Chishimba is taken to task for migrating to the Congo before getting any education; he was, they remembered, "the one who refused to start school the year we all started." It seems that, from the mission point of view, clothing should be a reward for completing the educational process, and indeed, unlike Chishimba, the schoolboys are prepared to postpone the acquisition of clothes until they finish school. Last but not least, an evaluation of dress practice arises from the drawing of Chishimba's performance gestures and the specific garments he is wearing. There is little doubt that his attire is constructed in a manner that is meant to cast doubt on his "taste," in effect on his competence in putting together the elements of "proper" dress style. The issue is not so much that his clothes are wrong but that he wears them differently. Standing cross-legged, with one hand resting on his walking stick, he is gesticulating proudly while smoking. Clearly, his dress is ill-matched: cuffed striped shorts under a checked jacket with a tight waist. An oversize handkerchief sticks out of his pocket. He is wearing spats as well.

The modern man that arises from this story is educated and knows his station. To him, clothes and fashion are a wasteful and frivolous preoccupation pursued by uneducated people who are concerned only with the present and lack knowledge and the wisdom to think ahead and plan for the future.

Chishimba's overdone dress is a result of misdirected labor. Turning the odious appellation "monkey" back at him with his uncouth, exaggerated manners and buffoonlike attire, who doesn't even know Bemba proverbs, the schoolboys in their nondescript clothing appear to have the upper hand: knowledge and future orientation. Although it is at some distance, they foresee an inevitable future toward which they are forging; extending the taken-for-granted tropes of the story, we imagine that, once they have arrived, they will dress properly and respectfully according to their station—in khaki suits, to be sure, thus keeping "in their place."

In the Eyes of the Beholder

The growing importance of matters of dress and clothing style in everyday African life was not immediately apparent to European observers who often described the emerging styles of dress in strongly evaluative terms. W. H. Anderson (1919), the first Seventh-Day Adventist missionary among the Plateau Tonga, was amused when commenting on the arrival at church of five men who just had returned from Bulawayo in 1905.

> The first one to enter was a boy of about sixteen years of age. He had on a woman's chemise, reaching down to just below his knees, and trimmed at bottom, neck and sleeves with torchon lace. Another one had purchased a man's shirt, but decided to wear it in a style a little different from the customary way. He had turned it upside down, thrust his legs through the arms, tied the tail of it up around his waist, and was wearing it for a pair of trousers. Another one had purchased a large, heavy pair of hobnailed shoes, and some stockings of the kind that men wear when playing golf, reaching above his knees. Around his loins he had the usual jackal skin and above that a woman's corset, upside down. (309–10)

"We had a climax in the sermon at that point," he added.

This missionary's astonished rendition of the very real way in which Africans were involving themselves creatively with dressing was more often outweighed by condescending depictions. When British travel writer Eileen Bigland (1939:96) described the "native store" at Shiwa Ngandu, the estate of prominent politician Stewart Gore-Browne in the Northern Province in the mid-1930s, her choice of words showed utter disdain: "Suspended from ropes were gaudy silk handkerchiefs, frightful striped shirts, several pairs of suspiciously second-hand trousers, a jinga [bicycle] horribly rusted, and two mackintoshes." Almost two decades later Barrie Reynolds (1968:207), who in 1956 and 1957 examined the material culture of the Gwembe Tonga prior to their relocation before the building of the Kariba Dam on the Zambezi River, provided a commentary much in the same vein: "the simple costume of the nineteenth century is in striking contrast to the garb of the twentieth-century . . . [A] youth . . . was observed wearing, besides a brightly coloured shirt and brief shorts, a garish check cap, white-rimmed sun-glasses, football socks and Wellington boots; this was in the height of the dry season. This mode of dress is admittedly extreme, but nowadays most men wear at least some items of cast-off or cheap European clothing, of which shirts and trousers are the most common."

The construction of a character like Chishimba in the White Fathers' Bemba reader dismisses African preoccupations with clothing as lack of competence and most certainly of taste, and dressing up as a vain and wasteful activity, but worst of all as a pursuit inappropriate to their station in the race- and class-divided order of colonial society. It is not surprising that such reactions are contained in the story of Chishimba's return, for they abounded in colonial society at large. The smartly dressed returning migrant unsettled the role of clothing consumption in marking social difference. I will not here go into the contemptuous discussions about whether or how Africans should dress and wear shoes that still found echoes in the 1930s and 1940s except for the following example (Hansen 1989:42–43). This discussion lingered in the question that the Reverend H. E. Wareham of the London Missionary Society's Mbereshi Mission in Kawambwa in 1931 asked Secretary for Native Affairs J. Moffat Thomson: "Is it the policy of the government to discourage the use of European clothing?" Noting that "natives have been made to feel that the wearing of European clothing was held up against them and prejudiced their chances," the minister went on to explain that he had discouraged this usage himself, "but not recently for it has become universal. I do not refer to shirts and shorts," he added, recognizing that they had become general dress items for African men (NAZ/ZA 7/4/26).

Judging from Wareham's letter, growing African preoccupations with dress and style upset widespread European concerns with keeping Africans "in their place." While accepting that African men wore shirts and shorts, many Europeans were highly ambivalent about African desires for clothing once the most basic clothing needs were covered. J. Merle Davis ([1933] 1968:42) expressed this unease in his comments on changing rural life when he traveled through Northern Rhodesia in the early 1930s: "his clothing shows some changes; the former nakedness or bark cloth garments have given place to a medley of gaudy trade cotton garments covering the body indifferently from shoulder to knee, and the blankets when the nights are cold. This has been slightly supplemented in recent years by nondescript cast-off apparel and cheap factory-made clothing brought in by returning mine and domestic workers."

Davis's suggestion ([1933] 1968:43) that "ambition to succeed in the European system of wage-earning slumbers, and the fires of emulation burn low" might perhaps have applied to rural Africans in the depression years of the early 1930s, but did not hold up well with subsequent developments, most certainly not on the urban scene. Those developments struck Eileen Bigland on a visit to the mine township in Mufulira in the mid-1930s. Astonished by their clothing, she described African women as "dressed with a sophistication unknown farther north [in the rural Northern Province]—hats with feathers adorned their woolly heads, cheap silk frocks in gay colourings or jumpers and skirts their bodies, European shoes with pointed toes encased their feet" (Bigland 1939:187). Not all Europeans, of course, were equally amazed by African dress practice. Inspired by his observations from work for the London Missionary Society on the Copperbelt from 1933 until his death in 1943, R. J. B. Moore had a good eye for detail when characterizing this period's African dress practice. "The African urban dweller to-day, whatever his work," Moore explained (1948:72–73), "can no more exist without a smart rig-out of clothes than he could have managed yesterday without bow and arrow . . . Crowds at beer halls and football matches where everyone is dressed in European fashion show how universal is the new standard of clothing."

African Clothing Sensibilities

Clothing remained a high priority in African consumption decisions throughout this period as the migratory process moved people, goods, and ideas across the wider region. The mine workers Wilson (1941–1942, 2:80) studied in Broken Hill in the late 1930s spent more than half of their cash wages on clothes.[6] Clothing was the primary good migrants transferred to rural areas. "The new ambitions of the country dwellers," Wilson noted, "have reduced the proportional significance of food to them; they still want food, but wanting clothes, saucepans and bicycles too, they would rather go hungry than do without them . . . the wealth which young men send or give them is hardly ever turned into food" (52).

The amount and variety of clothing in recorded travel kits of returning migrants illustrate the high value attached to clothes both by migrants and people in their home villages. David Mwanza, who went with his father from the Eastern Province to Southern Rhodesia when he was twelve years old in 1936, worked on a European farm for one year. When beginning their return journey home, he related that "we went to the store. I bought shorts, a shirt, a belt, a sweater, a hat and tennis shoes" (Marwick 1974:149). When he was around sixteen years old in 1949, Sindikani Phiri left home in the same region to seek work in Southern Rhodesia. He first worked on a dairy farm near Gwelo, then in a shoe factory. "When I was in Southern Rhodesia," he explained, "I was earning good money and on returning [in 1951] I had thirteen pounds, a bicycle and other things, such as shorts, [long] trousers, six shirts and a jacket" (Marwick 1974:145).

Observations like this are available from many regions, for example, in a detailed recording of the contents of travel kits of migrants returning home from the Copperbelt in the early 1930s, which lists a profusion of clothes (Davis [1933] 1968:401–2). Transfers of clothes from towns to the rural areas continued well into the 1950s in Luapula as Aron Chinanda remembered: "Those who had relatives working on the Copperbelt used to have clothes sent to them. Sometimes relatives on the Copperbelt used to send money, and a person would take the money to one of the shops in Mansa and buy clothes . . . he could buy clothes for himself and his wife" (Musambachime n.d. #26). While statements such as these do not distinguish between new and used clothing, a good proportion of what returning migrants from the north brought home from the Congo consisted of *kombo,* as secondhand clothing was called in Luapula. By late in World War II, "the once familiar blue print dress ha[d] almost entirely been replaced by these Congo dresses" (NAZ/SEC 2/875). At this time, clothing no longer served as a store of wealth in the manner described for the 1930s. Wilson (1941–42, 2:35) had noted that the "possession of unused clothes enables the Africans to visit their rural homes . . . , and provides security against the sudden loss of a job . . . These clothes are kept, sometimes in boxes in their own houses, sometimes in the stores where they are purchased." A legal ordinance from 1915 had regulated the "box system" that enabled migrant workers to accumulate clothing in stores, either for safekeeping or as a security against payment. Developments in society at large during the war years made this arrangement obsolete, and in 1948 a repeal of the ordinance went into effect (NAZ/SEC 2/294).

The first call on wages by migrants in towns was clothing, according to an official publication on trade, noting that "the Native coming in or back from the reserves usually arrives or returns in rags." The priority items were "khaki shirts and shorts and the wardrobe will then gradually be built up with fancy shirts, hat, shoes, socks, belt and possibly a suit" (Board of Trade 1954:11). It would not be wrong to say that secondhand clothing represented the first type of ready-made clothing that Africans could afford to buy, especially when considering their limited income and the poor quality of imported Indian and Japanese garments available in the local shops. Persons of the senior generation with whom I discussed clothing consumption spoke of kombo as garments with better fit, superior quality, longer duration, and last but not least, as more fashionable style. "These clothes were not seen in the shops," recalled Geoffrey Mee from his youth in Luapula during the war (16 May 1995, Lusaka). Still, the tailor played an insufficiently recognized role in responding to clothing demands and desires, not only by fabricating very basic garments such as shorts and school uniforms but also by fashioning clothes requiring more skill such as suits and elaborately styled dresses. Aside from mining and domestic labor, which employed a great number of migrants, the tailor's craft was an important activity that enabled men to find employment almost everywhere. Translating clothing needs and desires into garments, tailors contributed importantly to the process of making Africans knowledgeable and discriminating consumers of clothing.

"Those who came back from the Congo," remembered Longboy Chakomaulwa, ". . . were considered to be rich. This is because they wore nice clothes" (Musambachime n.d. #38). A touring officer who in 1949 commented on the ready availability of secondhand clothes from the Congo in village stores in Luapula barely understood their appeal when he noted, "With the eventual stage that Africans wear their clothes to, even this market must reach saturation sooner or later, unless Africans start possessing two or three sets of clothes" (NAZ/SEC 2/894). Nor did the panel that in the early 1940s discussed a commissioned report on African urban costs of living understand how clothing mattered, as I discuss in more detail in the next chapter. In A. L. Saffrey's report (NAZ/SEC 1/1363) on a minimum standard of living, one specific issue provoked criticism. His suggestion that African women should have several dresses did not sit well at all.

Saffrey explained: "The house to house investigation showed that most women have at least five or six dresses. These dresses are constantly worn, usually in rotation, and cannot be regarded as capital goods accumulated for presents when visiting the villages. An old dress is occasionally given away to a relative, but nowhere did one find stocks of new clothes such as were found by Godfrey Wilson at Broken Hill" in the late 1930s (NAZ/SEC 1/1363, appendix 2 of extracts of first report).

The Saffrey report remarked on the gendered dimension of clothing consumption. When trading kombo in Luapula villages in the 1940s, Ellie Mukonko and his young coworkers were often pressed with specific orders from women who had more limited access to and choice of clothing than men who had been migrant workers. "What I want is a dress" was a common order with specification of size and style (25 May 1995, Mansa). When women came to towns in larger numbers during and after World War II, they went for the new fashions with abandon (Parpart 1994:250–54). A report on the commercial prospects of the colony in the early 1950s when purchasing power had improved somewhat noted that a man's "first expenditure is on clothing for himself and his womenfolk and the latter usually see to it that they are not overlooked . . . [T]he native woman . . . attaches considerable importance to matters of design, style and fashion in her dress goods and she generally knows just what she wants in the way of cloth[ing] when she goes shopping. Just as fashions change in our Western world, so, often for unaccountable reasons, certain designs or colours in cotton piece-goods, for instance, suddenly lose popularity and become quite unsaleable" (Overseas Economic Surveys 1950:28).

Women in towns usually had several dresses, as Saffrey had noted, and style was an issue as well. R. J. B. Moore (1948:57) was particularly impressed by African women's sense of style: "There are many dazzling frocks . . ., evening dresses bought from ladies in the European town, coloured handkerchiefs on heads, crocheted caps or stylish hats worn on one side." All of this resonated with popular culture, such as a song in town English and Nyanja by Alick Nkatha, the most famous vocal artist of the 1950s, in which a domestic servant sought to entice a woman by promising her a "New Look" dress (ama new look ni plenti).[7]

> Come live with me in the yards
> You're gonna get bread an' butter
> I have everything
> New Look in Plenty.
> You will have so many dresses
> you'll be changing clothes all day.
> . . . .
> If we two appear in public,
> young men will be shaking
> because of your beautiful clothes
> (quoted in Hansen 1989:163–64)

Agnes Mwalimu, a sixty-five-year-old storekeeper at Mushinka market in Mansa, and some of the men I interviewed commented on women's display of changing fashions (24 May 1995, Mansa). The flared skirts and dresses with gathered sleeves that were common in the 1950s gave way to sleeveless dresses in the 1960s. High heels were worn for special occasions. Women who were less outgoing would wear hand scarves rather than hats. During our conversation, Mrs. Mwalimu took pains to point out that a *chitenge* (printed cloth) dress in the 1950s merely was a wrap around. That is in fact the dress of the female bearer in the offical coat of arms introduced at independence in 1964.

African men were also fashion conscious. A report on the colony's commercial prospects took note of this: "the men, especially those who work in towns and earn higher wages, are keen observers and imitators of European fashions and can be found animatedly discussing shop window displays of European garments. Khaki drill is still one of the staple classes of cloth on sale for native wear throughout the area, as nearly all working natives possess one or more of such suits (open-necked shirt either with 'shorts' or 'slacks') but their taste, especially in the towns, is definitely for the flamboyant, and the more recent North American styles in shirts, ties, slacks, jackets and hats accordingly have a large popularity" (Overseas Economic Surveys 1950:28). The elderly men I interviewed in Luapula keenly described the shifting fashions and the changing preferences in clothes. The tight trousers that were the rage in the 1940s, for example, gave way to very wide trousers in the 1950s. Ordinary khaki drill was not the issue as Reverend Wareham had noted. African men had worn shorts, Mr. Chisakula and other men explained to me, for a long time; the army and police were wearing khaki shorts as well. In fact, in the 1950s African men considered one type of khaki drill to be special. It was known as "ruler's style" and described by Mr. Chisakula as the dress style of the district commissioner (D.C.), consisting of shorts, short-sleeved shirt, and knee-high stockings; "we all went for that," he said (26 May 1995, Mansa). In fact, this dress style is precisely that of the male bearer on the official coat of arms that was designed at independence.

Shoes also have a story of their own. They were expensive and not readily available either new or secondhand; many people grew up wearing sandals made from tires, canvas shoes, or no footwear at all. Mrs. Mwalimu remembered that she wore her first pair of good shoes in 1964, at the celebration for independence (24 May 1995, Mansa). Mr. Chisakula recalled the attraction of new shoes that migrants from Wankie or Bulawayo in Southern Rhodesia brought along when returning to Northern Rhodesia. Those shoes made a special creaking sound that attracted women, he told me. Mr. Kamuti also remembered the creaking shoes from Southern Rhodesia (29 May 1995, Mansa).

Hats were an important part of good dress according to Mr. Kamuti, who smiled when he described how in the early 1960s fashions from across the region could be seen around the Mushinka welfare hall in Mansa on weekends. From his remarks it is clear that people took extreme pride in clothing and displayed it boldly, with an air of style about them. Here you would really see people dressed up, he told me, including a man in blazer and waistcoat, his shirt sleeves rolled up with an armband, wearing a busby hat and a walking stick, and smoking a pipe; this was a person who had been to South Africa. Those who had been to the Congo had their own way of showing clothing off; men would wear collarless shirts, and some put on striped trousers. This "craze for foreign,"[8] which continues to resonate in postcolonial Zambia, was captured then, according to Mr. Kamuti, in a song by Alick Nkatha about how people went abroad to seek wealth and brought back goods from the Congo and South Africa.

In short, dressing and dressing up had become part and parcel of everyday

African life in both rural and urban areas in ways not immediately appreciated by the ruling European minority. This ambiguity helps explain the problematic role of clothing in the story of Chishimba's return from the Congo.
Ifya Bukaya was produced and read within a race- and class-divided society
that limited the horizon of African mobility. Regardless of station, stylish or
extravagant dress on African bodies was subject to negative if not outright
hostile remarks from within both church and secular white society. While
wage labor in colonial society did require bodies to be dressed, there were informal, though clear, rules for how far to go. With immediate clothing gratification rather than delayed, the Chishimba of this story seems to lack the
knowledge to play by those rules. The notion of modernity that emerges from
this story is a linear projection of colonial wisdom, discounted by race, that
leaves little room for diversity of experiences and for the possibility that
clothing consumption in everyday African life might mediate quite different
sensibilities than those Europeans took for granted (Miller 1994:68).

2 Clothing Needs and Desires

African preoccupations with dress and showy attire made clothing a powerful medium for debate. From his research in Broken Hill in the late 1930s, Godfrey Wilson (1941–42, 2:18) noted how Africans discussed clothes "unceasingly, in much the same way villagers discuss their cattle; they are tended lovingly and carefully housed in boxes at night." "Every African man of whatever social grouping," he commented, "tries to dress smartly for strolling around the town, or for visiting in his spare time, and loves to astonish the world with a new jacket, or a new pair of trousers of distinguished appearance. Women," he went on, "behave the same way; and they judge husbands and lovers largely according to the amounts of money which they are given to spend on clothes" (18).

When J. Clyde Mitchell and Arnold Epstein described the importance of Western-style clothing in African status aspirations on the Copperbelt fifteen years later (Mitchell 1956:12–14; Mitchell and Epstein 1959:32), the colony's economic and political circumstances had changed so much that we may consider the post–World War II period as a turning point for our analysis of African dealings with clothing. What differed was that the ability to fulfill clothing desires had come within reach of a much larger proportion of the African population than before the war. What is more, the ruling European minority no longer was the final arbiter of dress, for reasons that I explain later in this chapter. Distinct African clothing practices had existed along with the European-approved khaki suit for quite a while. But by the postwar era Africans had definitely made Western-style clothing and dress practices their own. At this time rural women were no longer content with ordering one dress from hawkers of secondhand clothing. During the war years they migrated to towns in growing numbers in spite of official attempts to keep them in the villages. As Saffrey noted in his report (NAZ/SEC 1/1363), urban African women commonly had more than one dress. And the khaki suit no longer satisfied wage-employed men. The European difficulty in acknowledging this change in dress practice finds expression in household-budget studies, particularly in tensions arising in efforts to draw distinctions between clothing needs and clothing desires.

Such observations convey growing impatience with the efforts of the colonial government to keep Africans in their place. Household-budget surveys

Figure 2 Two workers ("ironing boys") at Fraenkel senior's dry-cleaning establishment in Lusaka in the 1950s, dressed in their "Sunday best" of suit, hat, and tie. Photo by Peter Fraenkel, reproduced with permission.

Figure 3 Child receiving milk from mother dressed in 1950s sleeveless dress. Archive photo from Zambia Information Services, reproduced with permission.

assessing clothing consumption, among other matters, are one body of evidence for the study of the battle over needs and desires, which I explore in the next section. Clothing had come within reach, but within limits, and in the second section, I discuss how African clothing consumption was curtailed by government policy on the colony's development during the last two decades before independence. In the last section I describe the pride of place that dress had come to assume in everyday and leisure-time interaction.

How Much Is Enough/Too Much?

When between 1945 and 1948 Phyllis Deane (1953:33), a noted British economist, made firsthand inquiries into the living conditions in different parts of Northern Rhodesia, she was so struck by the poor standard of consumption among the African population that she characterized it as "demonstrably low, even by colonial standards. It is an inescapable conclusion," she added, "that development has somehow passed these people by." Describing village living as "bleak and monotonous," she presented a slightly better picture of the towns: "standards of dress are higher in the urban areas, and while one ragged set of clothes might be good enough in the villages it is not sufficient for the more sophisticated social standards of the towns, where a man has also to clothe his wife and children with more care" (32).

Questions about what was "good enough" and "sufficient" for Africans especially in the urban areas continued to be raised by the colonial government during World War II and the postwar years, when the economy experienced a boom and labor power was scarce. One way of harnessing Africans to work in order to increase productivity was to improve their living circumstances in towns, especially by providing family housing, rather than single quarters for migrant workers, and wage increases. But just how much was enough?

The colonial government undertook a variety of not very systematic inquiries into urban African expenditures, beginning in 1941 with an attempt to establish a cost-of-living index for African miners on the Copperbelt (*Final Report of the Commission of Inquiry* 1950:182) and some budget data collections throughout the war. In 1947 public concern over the rising cost of living during and after World War II prompted the appointment of a Cost of Living Commission (Customs Department 1950:3). While at least two government-sponsored cost-of-living surveys were carried out during the years preceding independence in 1964,[1] they covered only urban African households, and there was no reliable collection of income disposition data for the population as a whole. Some investigators included rural budget surveys when conducting research of much broader scope (Allan et al. 1948; Brelsford 1946; Colson 1958; Kay 1964), yet these studies drew on very small samples from which it would be hard to generalize. What is more, the cost of clothing varied from area to area, and prices and wages changed so much during the war and postwar years that household expenditure patterns must have been affected by them.

Despite the precautions we must take when interpreting these household-budget studies, and regardless of what specific analysis or sample base they draw on, most of them show that the two largest items in urban African budgets were, first, food and, second, clothing. This order tended to be reversed in some rural areas.[2] The available, very provisional, observations about expenditures on clothing as compared to food in urban households suggest that the relative proportion of income spent on clothing might have decreased as wages improved somewhat during the period in question.[3] While none of these studies distinguish between new and used garments, secondhand clothing constituted an important supply of ready-made clothing in the war and postwar period. From the Belgian Congo across the Copperbelt and Luapula flowed a large volume of kombo into other parts of Northern Rhodesia, and considerable quantities of secondhand clothing kept entering and circulating in the colony during the 1950s (Overseas Economic Surveys 1950:20). Given wartime restrictions on imports, there is no doubt that secondhand clothing was an important source of affordable garments.

The massing of Africans with growing consumer needs and desires in the colony's growing towns posed obvious problems to the powers that be. Just what, and where, was the proper place of the growing urban African population in this rapidly changing society? What improvements should be made so as to curtail the development of an established urban African working class that might not agree with the principles and practices of colonial governance? The discussion that surrounded official attempts at arriving at a standard budget or establishing a poverty datum line for urban Africans demonstrates the contentious nature of these questions, which at their core were political.[4] When discussing African clothing consumption, colonial authorities were in effect talking about another subject, embedded in the political future, but not immediately apparent in the contemporary clothing terms of discourse.

When A. L. Saffrey's preliminary findings on African urban living were presented to the Advisory Board on African Labour in 1943, all hell broke loose. Saffrey had been appointed labor officer in 1942 and charged with the task of ascertaining the extent to which Africans had become urbanized, or in the language of the day, stabilized, which is to say, committed to living in towns rather than returning to the rural areas as the colonial government had expected labor migrants to do during the previous decades. Saffrey found a high degree of stabilization and suggested that the process was likely to continue. His estimates for minimum requirements (apart from food) for a family of four provoked irate commentary, especially his suggestion that African urban women needed several dresses. His "house to house investigations" showed that "most women have at least five or six dresses." In the preliminary report he explained that "one of the most difficult items to assess when estimating a reasonable minimum standard is the quantity of clothes to be allocated. European type clothes are to the African a sign of prosperity and advancement, and one of the first things the wage earner buys with his first month's pay is, not pots and pans, but a shirt or a pair of trousers for himself and a dress for his wife" (NAZ/SEC 1/1363).

Compound managers and other labor officers expressed doubts about the accuracy of Saffrey's observations, which representatives from the Chamber of Mines went to great pains to discredit. "The fact that most women have at least five or six dresses," one of them argued, "is surely an indication that their incomes are not inadequate" (NAZ/SEC 1/1363). In the end the report was considered to be confidential, it was not published as a government document, and it was circulated only informally in labor management circles. It is not surprising that Saffrey's report provoked debate. Much before its time in recognizing that African urban life was becoming a permanent phenomenon, the report invited official acknowledgment that Africans who lived in towns were there to stay and that this entailed recognition of their changing living requirements. As Saffrey argued: [I]n ascertaining a reasonable minimum standard for clothes and covering it is obvious that one must be guided by the desires of the people but not bound by them. At the same time, one must give due consideration to the changing standards that have come about and are continuing at increased tempo in the urban areas" (NAZ/SEC 1/1363).

Saffrey's report was shelved. The subject of clothing came in for some discussion in a report by David Bettison (1959), an anthropologist, about African living conditions in Lusaka. This study had been commissioned by the Housing Board to provide information on whether low-income Africans who lived in employer-provided or employer-paid housing could afford to pay economic rents. In the context of this investigation, Bettison sought to calculate a poverty datum line that covered minimum needs in the "scale of preferences and in the biological and social requirements of persons—food, clothing, fuel and light, transport to work, and tax" (93). Bettison defined "a minimum of clothing at a standard to ensure decency" (xxii), specifying it in terms of cost rather than contents, thus avoiding the question of just how many dresses to include in a minimum standard for urban African women.

In their discussion about standards of dress, colonial authorities drew a sharp distinction between basic clothing needs and clothing desires, which they considered unnecessary. The importance of upholding such a distinction resonated with European sentiments in some segments of colonial society at

large. For instance, in a 1949 newspaper article advocating racial segrega-
tion, the writer noted that, although the African could live comfortably on
much less than whites, "he wants to wear boots and hats and European clothing—which are unhealthy and unsuitable—, and his wife wants to wear
dresses, silk stockings and high-heeled shoes and hats—also unsuitable and
unbecoming." "Even when they step out of place and into whites' clothing,"
this writer concluded, "they will never be anything but poor imitations of the
higher race" (*Central African Post,* 27 October 1949).

Dividing needs into those that were basic minimum standard and those that
were not is arbitrary. Beyond the bare requirements of physical survival, all
needs are socially and culturally constructed. Saffrey recognized that much
when he encouraged officials concerned with labor management to acknowledge the changing standards of urban life, letting African desires guide, but
not bind, them. Phyllis Deane clearly observed in the mid-1940s that one set
of clothes was not sufficient in towns. In the African view clothing needs and
desires increasingly went together. But the ways in which Africans pursued
needs and desires were hemmed in, rather than given scope for expansion, by
the system of colonial governance within which they dealt with clothes.

Consumption Space, Trading Place, and African Opportunity

Questions about African clothing needs and desires cannot be explained
without reference to the social, economic, and political conditions that structured their livelihoods during the last decades of colonial rule. Between 1939
and 1947 the cost of living for Africans had increased by about 100 percent
(*Colonial Annual Report* 1947:7). Most retail prices of textiles and clothing
more than doubled between 1939 and 1943 (*Final Report of the Commission
of Inquiry* 1950:245). Because of wartime import restrictions, clothing demand far outstripped supply, and Africans, as noted above, eagerly purchased
kombo, which traders brought across from the Belgian Congo.

Although the colonial government never envisioned Africans as permanent residents of towns, urban stabilization for at least part of the growing
African population became accepted colonial policy in the 1950s. The economy had gained new momentum during World War II and the Korean War,
when the copper industry boomed, secondary industries developed in muni-
tions and auto parts, and the construction sector grew. In short, continued labor shortages throughout the economy after the war invited new thinking on
both housing and work. More family housing was built for Africans in towns,
and women who had migrated to town alone were no longer repatriated to the
villages. Compulsory schooling for the lower grades was introduced in many
of the towns in the early 1950s. Better-educated Africans experienced some

upward mobility, and African miners began to perform some of the tasks previously reserved for whites (Burawoy 1972). African pay scales finally increased, and real wages that had eroded significantly during the war began to
improve (Baldwin 1966:87). The change in the mid-1950s to a cash-only
wage instead of cash and food rations also affected purchasing power by giving people more money to handle. But although more Africans had more
money in their hands than ever before, there remained considerable disparities in purchasing power. In Northern Rhodesia in 1952, African wages and
salaries constituted only one-fifth of total national income (Overseas Economic Survey 1955:67).[5]

These developments took place against the backdrop of a rapidly changing
political scene. The 1950s were highly charged both racially and politically,
a tension that was prompted by widespread African opposition to the Federation of Rhodesia and Nyasaland, which the Colonial Office nevertheless imposed from 1953 to 1963 (Epstein 1992a). This opposition contained the
seeds of rapid political mobilization and a nationalist struggle resulting in political independence in 1964. In this atmosphere the colonial government was
slow or reluctant to recognize the potential of the growing African market for
consumer goods. In effect, more Africans now had the ability to buy, but their
possibilities were still limited. Colonial economic developments simultane-
ously pushed Africans toward and held them back from full engagement with
the market. Throughout most of the federal period, urban spatial policy
continued to segregate social and economic opportunity by race, restricting
African trade to a limited array of goods in designated places, and providing
practically no credit arrangements to stimulate the development of entrepreneurship. Africans were expected to purchase goods for their households in
the townships and in so-called second-class trading areas where largely In-
dian-owned stores sold a larger and more varied stock than traders in the
townships. When going into the European parts of town to shop, Africans
were dealt with through hatches on the side or back of stores. Many small-
scale traders, including women, made a living not because of, but in spite of,
colonial rules and regulations. In short, colonial rule did not do much to encourage the growing ability of Africans to consume. Rather, the government
was reluctant to promote new production and marketing practices.

When the colonial government considered questions about expanding the
manufacturing sector of Northern Rhodesia, reactions were cautious, if not
negative. A committee established to advise the government on the findings
of an official report about the development of secondary industries (Busschau 1945) concluded in 1948 that the European population was too small to
justify domestic production and the African population too poor to constitute
much of a market (Advisory Committee 1949:54). The only industry consid-

ered to be "deserving" of government support was the cement industry, which was indeed established. In the mid-1950s the country had an African population of close to two and a half million and a European population that had doubled since the war years to some sixty-five thousand (Kay 1967:29). At that time, a small number of blanket and garment industries had been established in Livingstone and Lusaka by private initiative. In all of Northern Rhodesia in 1954 there were just three factories "primarily devoted to clothing manufacture and a number of concerns operating machines as a subsidiary business" (Overseas Economic Survey 1955:84). In fact, Northern Rhodesia never developed a domestic manufacturing industry to speak of save in activities supplying the copper mines. The country suffered "both from the narrowness of its industrial market and its nearness to areas where the market is much larger" (Baldwin 1966:181). These nearby areas were South Africa and Southern Rhodesia, where many of Northern Rhodesia's manufactured goods originated, enjoying "empire preference" on payment of customs and tariffs. Textiles and clothing as well as other commodities were also imported from Great Britain, India, Hong Kong, and in the early 1950s from Japan (Overseas Economic Survey 1955:37–42). Last but not least, there was imported secondhand clothing as well, coming through as kombo from the Congo.

Given the limited scale of local secondary industry in Northern Rhodesia, it is not surprising that manufacturers gave little consideration to innovations in marketing techniques such as advertising to capture the growing ability of Africans to consume. Most strikingly, for the purpose at hand, there was hardly any advertising of clothing and textiles. The principal method was print advertising, mainly in the papers Europeans produced for African readers. The chief privately owned European papers, among them the *Livingstone Mail* (1906), the *Northern News* (1943), the *Central African Post* (1948), and the *Central African Mail* (1960), did reach and were read by some Africans, yet they catered largely to European readers. The government-owned African press, *Mutende* (1936–52) and its successor the *African Eagle* (1953–62) in four local languages (Bemba, Lozi, Nyanja, and Tonga) in addition to English, and the monthly radio magazine *The African Listener,* which aimed to educate, inform, and entertain, focused largely on news items of local interest, social affairs, and sports (Kasoma 1986). These papers did feature advertisements directed toward Africans for a limited range of goods and with little imaginative appeal. Advertisements were mostly line drawings, strip cartoons, and occasional photographs. Bicycles and bicycle accessories were among the main goods advertised, followed by patent medicines, toiletries, and cosmetics (Board of Trade 1954:28); household cleaning products, such as floor polish and detergent, and foodstuffs and beer were featured as well (Kallmann 1998). But clothing and textiles rarely were the focus in these advertisements. Some of the African papers intermittently featured women's pages that offered European advice on dress and style (e.g., *African Listener,* March 1957, April 1957).

Clothing Competence, Performance, and Distinction

To be sure, Africans continued to be preoccupied with clothing through the last two decades of colonial rule, buying it eagerly and displaying it with panache. In fact, there was little else they could do with their hard-earned cash, which, although wages increased gradually over these years, came nowhere near European earnings. The general European affluence of the mining towns, according to a study from the late 1950s, was "unequalled in any other white community in Africa" (Holleman and Biesheuvel 1973:12, 35–36). The leisure-time lifestyle that developed there revolved around entertainment, clubs, cars, holidays, and shopping. Because of the desire for luxury goods among this segment of the population, consumer goods were a big portion of the colony's imports (Quinn 1965:678).

By law African urban workers could own neither land nor homes; except for a few, they could not afford cars or expensive furniture. Because of their limited purchasing power, the effective consumer demands of Africans continued to concentrate on food and clothing (Barber 1961:172). In the late 1930s, when Africans were "striving for new purposes and new kinds of wealth," Wilson (1941–42, 2:15) had described how they concentrated "their attention on the one readily available item of European wealth which gives them an immediate appearance of civilized status, namely clothes." In this situation, he explained, the "intense desire for European clothes which characterizes the Africans in Broken Hill today is inevitable, for it is, generally speaking, the only form in which their underlying desire for a civilized status, comparable to that of the Europeans, can find satisfaction" (15). What Wilson observed in the late 1930s held true for most of the colonial period. This struck Hortense Powdermaker on the Copperbelt in 1953–54 when she recalled how, in the United States, the latest model of a prestige car, a professionally decorated apartment, the "right address," and expensive clothes all were significant. "Because of the low standards of living in Central Africa," she explained, "clothes were generally the most important means of display" (Powdermaker 1962:96).

The potential African market for clothing remained largely untapped by local industry and barely explored by advertisers. As my discussion of household-budget surveys indicates, the size of that market is difficult to quantify because of inadequate studies. But there are other ways of exploring that market, for example, in qualitative terms through consumption practices, tastes, and styles. I take up these issues below, beginning with consumption access, questions about emulation of "Europeanness," and the rise of distinction in a clothing-consumption universe that was far less homogeneous than the market segmentation into "European" and "African" implies.

Because of the limited scope of the colony's domestic garment manufacture, Africans turned to many other sources to fulfill their clothing desires. Tailors experienced brisk business, judging from the steep rise in the importation of sewing machines: from 935 in 1940, declining to only 217 in 1943, and increasing to 3,458 in 1952, when it was estimated that at least 80 percent of the machines were sold to Africans (Customs Department 1950:90; Board of Trade 1954:14, 34). Used clothing from many sources found a popular market. In the early 1940s, according to R. B. J. Moore (1948:58), "a European only has to tell the houseboy that there are some old clothes for sale, for a large and interested crowd to throng at the back door. At police sales of deceased's estates [Africans] run each other up to absurd prices for socks, shirts and old suits. A European church wanting to raise money only has to organize a jumble sale of clothes in a compound to be sure of successful results." And then there was kombo, secondhand clothing brought across from the Congo. It is important here to recall Geoffrey Mee's comments about secondhand clothing from his youth in Luapula in the 1940s, namely that "these clothes were not seen in the shops."

Last but not least were the mail-order firms in the United Kingdom and South Africa. From my discussions in Luapula about clothing access prior to independence, it appears that mail-order firms were an important source for new and stylish clothing. Mr. Chisakula (26 May 1995, Kashikishi) and Mr. Kamuti (29 May 1995, Mansa) recalled that quality shoes and good-looking jackets were purchased from mail-order firms, among them Edwards and Oxendale in England. Drawing on his detailed memory about clothing style, Mr. Kamuti described a particularly well liked blazer from the early 1960s in brightly colored narrow stripes of yellow, green, and red and with gold metal buttons.

Already in 1932 J. Merle Davis ([1933] 1968) had commented on the growth of a flourishing mail-order business by J. D. Williams and Oxendale companies in England among African miners on the Copperbelt. He described how a number of workers would pool their orders to avoid processing charges. He explained mail-order purchases as a defensive strategy "as throughout Northern Rhodesia the prices charged Natives by White and Indian storekeepers are ethically unjustifiable . . . It is short-sighted mercantile policy and will act as a boomerang on the Rhodesian trader" (73–74). Even during World War II, when import quotas and currency restrictions reduced the volume and variety of clothing available for purchase, Africans eagerly turned to mail-order firms abroad. R. B. J. Moore (1948:57–58) reported from around 1943 that a "man in town becomes a catalogue fiend. Overseas mails are loaded with catalogues from Oxendales and other mail order firms. Almost any evening a group of men may be seen in a compound or location sitting on dirty boxes poring over a catalogue for clothes, while one who can write makes out the order."

Hortense Powdermaker's paraphrase (1962:94) of a conversation between two African miners provides an example of the types of garments Africans purchased from mail-order catalogues as well as of local reaction to their acquisition. At the center of attention was an overcoat from Oxendale in Great Britain. One of the men described three other kinds of overcoats featured in the catalogue but added, "[T]hey are not good. The one which this man ordered is wonderful. In June [the winter in this part of Africa] he will be wearing it to the beer hall, since he is a strong drinker, and people will all be looking at him. The coat is brown in color and has very long hair. If he wears it in town, policemen can be asking from where he got it. The other day when he put it on, three Europeans asked him where he got it." The two friends both wanted to obtain such a coat, one of them wanting to order it before visiting in his village: "People at home will just fall off the chair when they see that coat."

Were Africans imitating Europeans, and what is the meaning of the "civilized status" to which Africans, according to some contemporary observers, aspired through dress? An official report characterized "the African [as] a great imitator and this applies to his purchasing habits. He likes to buy what the European buys although where clothes are concerned he is less inhibited as to colour" (Board of Trade 1954:11). Another commentator also described Africans imitating Europeans "though on a lower scale, in making imports form a notable part of their consumption. A postal catalogue from either Britain or the Republic of South Africa," he went on with reference to the early 1960s, "seems to be indispensable for every African in steady employment: clothing, bicycles, radios and gadgets seem to be preferred" (Quinn 1965:678).

But imitation is a quite different matter from wanting to become "like" Europeans. Class-bound models of consumption run into trouble when they are called upon to explain socioeconomic mobility in the colonial situation. Recognizing this helps to qualify the criticism that has been leveled at prominent anthropological interpretations of African preoccupations with clothing during the late colonial period in this region. This is the work of J. Clyde Mitchell and Arnold Epstein.

To be sure, clothing mattered in Mitchell's work on *kalela*, a popular dance

Figure 4 Amon Chapusha, former household servant, in double-breasted jacket, with fellow workers outside Fraenkel senior's dry-cleaning establishment in Lusaka in the 1950s. Photo by Peter Fraenkel, reproduced with permission.

Figure 5 Messenger wearing suit, tie, and hat, with delivery bicycle in the 1950s. Photo by Peter Fraenkel, reproduced with permission.

on the Copperbelt, as it did in his and Epstein's analysis of urban African prestige and status rankings (Mitchell 1956; Mitchell and Epstein 1959). Kalela dancers were teams of young migrant workers, dressed in "well-pressed grey slacks, neat singlets, and well-polished shoes." Their dancing, and the accompanying drumming, was overseen by a "king," who in the team Mitchell observed always dressed in sharp contrast to the dancers, wearing a "dark suit, collar and tie, hat, and a pair of white-rimmed sunglasses." A "doctor" and a "nurse" encouraged the dancers, making sure that they were neat and tidy. None of the young dancers had white-collar or lower professional jobs, yet they were "dressed smartly in the European style" (Mitchell 1956:2–3).

When Bernard Magubane (1971:425) criticized this work for interpreting African dress practices as emulating Europeans, he not only misread the intents of these works but also dismissed the significance of their findings.[6] By interpreting such dress practices as imitation, only the familiar is brought within view, that is, the "Europeanness," while the local drops out of sight. Mitchell (1956:16) clearly recognized this when he remarked that the "European way-of-life has now become so much a part and parcel of life in the urban areas that the Europeans themselves have faded into the background." What Mitchell and Epstein captured in their analyses of status ranking was how the incorporation of European-style clothing articulated African perceptions of class, status, and ethnicity during the rapidly changing colonial situation. As Mitchell later explained (1987:145), African appreciation of European lifestyle "was not simply a reflection of the value system of the metropolitan country [but of] some of the contradictions inherent in colonial society."

At the core of these dress practices is a disjuncture, embedded in the late colonial political economy, between African aspirations and possibilities. In this context clothes were much more than a means of emulating white lifestyle. The crossover appeal of European-style clothing was enormous because clothing consumption constituted the most readily available practice for popular expression of African aspirations. In effect, the strikingly dressed dancers in kalela enacted their ambiguous roles in a colonial occupational structure still underpinned by race. And clothing played a major part in this process in which already in the late 1930s, as Wilson (1941–42, 2:15) had noted, "Africans were striving for new purposes and new kinds of wealth" (my emphasis). These aspirations grew more marked as the colonial era drew to its close. Just before independence in rural Serenje District, for example, Norman Long (1968:164–65, 192) took note of the importance of consumption, including clothing, in emerging notions of wealth, power, and status. The new men of importance wore suits, owned consumer durables like furniture and household equipment, drank tea, and ate European-type foods.

By the time of Long's work, it no longer made sense to speak of Africans wearing European clothes. They had clearly made European-style dress conventions their own in their active engagement with a changing world. Judging from contemporary descriptions from which I have drawn throughout these chapters, Africans eagerly put themselves together with clothing they appropriated from a wide variety of domestic and foreign sources: shops, stores, and hawkers; tailors; mail-order firms; locally obtained secondhands; and imported kombo. The dress practices that arose from this medley of sources were not much influenced by local print advertising, which rarely featured clothing and textiles. Knowledge about clothing consumption was above all practical knowledge, acquired from participation in group activities and individual networks in urban life both at work and at home, in recreation and entertainment, and at markets and in the streets. In such interactions the visual impact of being noticed was in focus, involving a sharp eye for detail, active recall of bodies in dress, and constant and detailed talk about clothing matters.

Preoccupations with dress styles were important social and cultural processes. The effects of dress were produced in performance, by people presenting themselves for display and knowing that they looked good, for example, when strolling round the town, in markets and beer halls, at dances, and during country visits. In Nkatha's song about New Look dresses, young onlookers shook with delight, and Powdermaker's miner had villagers fall off their chairs when looking at a well-dressed person who, in Wilson's words (1941–42, 2:18), astonished the world with "clothing of distinguished appearance." In short, clothing mediated new aspirations with a lot of verve through display and eye-catching styling that made its "European" origin merely one of many inspirations.

Uniforms and Robes

In the colonial order of things, hierarchy was everywhere, and everyone was supposed to keep to their place, especially Africans who worked for Europeans in situations where clothing marked difference. Domestic servants, messengers, court clerks, police, and many others wore uniforms. But when dressed in his "Sunday best" from kombo, an office orderly was barely distinguishable from a clerk. The few urban budget surveys that were undertaken drew largely on samples of households headed by wage-employed men whose desire for distinction in dress might have been more attainable than that of many others. In fact, the potential African clothing market was more segmented than the previous discussion implies. Certainly the rural people whom a visiting miner might impress by a new mail-order overcoat had less

Figure 6 Chief's messenger in uniform with office bicycle in village setting in the 1950s. His wife is wearing a knitted cap, a puffed-sleeved top with a yoke around the neck, and a wrap-around skirt. Photo by Peter Fraenkel, reproduced with permission

access. And villagers knew that, because of the long history of labor migration and the resulting widespread circulation of people, goods, and ideas. Many of these new inspirations had been locally appropriated. John Barnes offers telling evidence of this from his work among the Ngoni in the eastern part of the country. A photo depicting young men in collared shirts and T-shirts is accompanied by a caption that reads "A Jimi Roja dance at an installation ceremony. This dance, named after an American band leader, is allowed only on important occasions" (1959: Plate 15).[7] Indeed as George Kay (1964:89) reported from Chief Kalaba's village in Luapula in 1959–60, where 76 percent of the able-bodied men were away in search of work: "[U]rban behavior and cultural practices are known and to some extent desired . . . the villager will himself compare his lot with that of the urban dweller, and with the life he personally experienced in urban areas."

In the rural areas people also desired distinction. Villagers dressed in garments they bought at provincial stores and farm shops, from tailors and itinerant traders in kombo. Clothes made up the bulk of goods returning migrants brought home with them. Most villagers possessed at least one set of clothes, even if ragged, as Phyllis Deane had noted (1953:32). During World War II, people of rank in the rural political structure of indirect rule cried out for new distinctions to be made, judging from a protracted discussion during the war years among provincial commissioners and the secretary for native affairs about the desire of Africans at different levels of the native administration for special dress. Men who worked in the rural native courts wanted uniforms and badges of rank, while chiefs wanted robes, headdresses, and decorations (NAZ/SEC 2/1234).

This was not the first or only time that chiefs had called for clothing to signal their rank. Around the time that the Colonial Office took over the administration of Northern Rhodesia from the British South Africa Company in 1924, Ngoni, Chewa, and Kunda chiefs at an *indaba* (Zulu for meeting) in Fort Jameson (Chipata) requested Governor Stanley to ask King George to provide them with uniforms, gun licenses, and salary increases (Ranger 1980:353; Tapson 1957:62–65). The 1940s discussion about upgrading the official dress of rural native authorities took twists and turns because the chiefs did not agree about what constituted "dignified dress in keeping with their status." Only the paramount chiefs of the Lozi, Bemba, and Ngoni had some type of special dress (NAZ/SEC 2/1234, Provincial Commissioner, Northern Province [Kasama] to Chief Secretary, 23 June 1941). The Litunga (paramount chief, or king), Lewanika of the Lozi, referred to then as Barotseland, had been provided with a uniform of British admiral of the fleet when attending the coronation of Edward VII in London in 1902. When he returned, he promptly incorporated it into Lozi ritual. Since then, every Litunga has worn such a uniform on important occasions, for instance, during the annual *kuomboka* ceremony in which the king leads the people from their dry-season homes on the Zambezi floodplains to higher ground (Prins 1990:101).

In response to the chiefs' call for official dress in the 1940s, the secretary for native affairs asked all provincial commissioners to supply him with suggestions and requisitioned copies of photographs of chiefs in official dress from across the region. Robes had in fact been issued previously to all chiefs holding court, except in Barotseland, where the king wore the uniform given to his father; the lower chiefs in Barotseland also wore robes. In 1938 the first issue of robes with gold or silver braid, depending on rank, had been purchased from an Arab merchant in Zanzibar. Aside from the color of the braid, these robes did not clearly distinguish between senior and subordinate chiefs. In 1944, when this discussion took place, many of these robes had fallen into disuse because of wear and tear. Most chiefs had no headdresses, and many wore "shabby European clothes." Some now wanted uniforms, badges, and hats for themselves while passing the old robes on to their subordinate councillors (NAZ/SEC 2/1234, Chief Secretary to Provincial Commissioners, 22 November 1944). In the words of Chief Nsokolo of the Mambwe Native Authority, "We now want uniforms: coats, trousers, shirts and ties; we know how to wear them now" (NAZ/SEC 2/1234, minutes of Northern Province Regional Council meeting, 22 May 1944).

Many chiefs applied themselves with gusto when conveying their views on the matter of official dress. They all wanted clothing that could command respect, something that only chiefs had the right to wear. From Eastern Province in 1945, the chiefs in the Petauke Native Authority wanted "a tailored uniform of a distinctive colour not to be used by commoners, with braid on lapels and cuffs, and a chain of office; the uniform to consist of trousers and tunics and peaked caps, badges and braid of tribal chiefs to be different from those of lesser chiefs." In the Lundazi Native Authority, the chiefs suggested "white trousers with white jacket of military cut with brass buttons, shoulder straps—epaulettes—with gold braid, and perhaps brass buttons or more gold braid on the cuffs, together with a white helmet." And in the Fort Jameson Native Authority the younger chiefs went for "a dark suit, shoes, and a 'chief's hat'" (NAZ/SEC 2/1234, Provincial Commissioner, Eastern Province, to Chief Secretary, 23 April 1945). But some provincial commissioners suggested that the whole exercise contradicted the official attempt to build up a "modern edifice of administration on the ancient foundations of tribal organization . . . A European type of dress must come sooner or later," one of them argued (NAZ/SEC 2/1234, Provincial Commissioner, Kasempa, to Chief Secretary, 5 March 1945). The provincial commissioner for Eastern Province suggested much the same (NAZ/SEC 2/1234).

This long-winded discussion seems not to have mattered very much in the larger scheme of things, "as its application would mean using labour and material which might be directed to war purposes" (NAZ/SEC 2/1234, Chief Secretary's handwritten note on correspondence from Provincial Commissioner, Northern Province (Kasama), 23 June 1941). Only after the war, in 1946, were black robes approved for native authority councillors and arrangements made for their production by import of cloth through the Crown agent in 1947. That year, a badge/medallion depicting the Northern Rhodesian fish eagle and the name of the native authority area was approved for the use of native authority councillors. And lower-level native authority employees were to be issued with symbols denoting their rank (NAZ/SEC

2/1234, Chief Secretary, circular minute, Recommendations, 20 January 1947).

It is not clear from the information at hand how native authorities reacted to this lackluster outcome of the long discussion aimed at upgrading their status through dress. What is clear is that the administrative system of indirect rule had stripped them of much of their previous power and authority. At the bottom in the chain of colonial command, they served in rural courts and at ceremonial functions. Migrants no longer heeded their authority, and even women and children left the villages without their permission. Yet even if this particular discussion was inconclusive, it demonstrates the very real significance of clothing and the power of this special commodity in mediating desires, in this case the chiefs' wish to assert their rank and status.

We Want Dresses

Where were African women in discussions of their clothing during the late colonial period? Did they only speak by their action, leaving the villages in ever growing numbers as men had done previously? At least three issues are involved in pushing women onto the sidelines of this era's clothing discussion. One is the deeply gendered history of clothing consumption, which through labor migration drew in African men much earlier than African women. Another concerns normative assumptions about gender and authority that constructed men as heads of households, as the authority in charge of clothing transfers to wives and dependents. A third issue arises from the available sources, which, although they were not all written by men, overwhelmingly report the opinions of men, both African and European, about African women's clothing needs and desires. Taken together, these issues help to hide the story of African women's active engagement with clothing.

There is one platform where women stepped into fuller view with a discourse that casts some light on the significance of clothing in their everyday lives. That is the native courts in both rural and urban areas, to which some people brought their domestic troubles and in the language of clothes spoke about conjugal relations and problems on the domestic front.

In court women's dress, or lack thereof, was a barometer of the quality of conjugality and gender relations that was immediately understandable to the African court councillors and the people attending court. Martha and her husband David, for example, had been quarreling because Martha had a lover. In the suit David brought against her for desertion in a Plateau Tonga native court in the late 1940s, he explained to the court councillor that Martha had returned her clothes to him when she refused to have intercourse with him. When David discovered that she had a lover, he explained that then he knew "that was what gave her power to refuse the clothes I bought for her." But Martha, who never had become pregnant during their four years of marriage, argued that it was David who had taken her clothes. "Why do you take my clothes when we fight?" she had asked him (Colson 1958:194). In the court's assessment, not only did David's behavior demonstrate that he lacked power over Martha, but he had not even completed the bridewealth payments for her. In this case the court granted a divorce (Colson 1958:193–205). In one of many urban cases from the late 1950s in which a husband's lack of support is demonstrated, Brenda asked for divorce in the Ndola Urban Court on the grounds that her husband frequently beat her, did not provide her with "traditional" medicine to facilitate conception, and above all that he "did not clothe her" (Epstein 1981:82). Mangaleti went to the same court, also seeking divorce, and her case reveals some of the entangled meanings of clothing in the context of urban everyday life. She explained how her husband had supported her when she first came to live with him: "My husband would give me 200s. out of his earnings. But after I had taken only a shilling to buy relish [vegetables/meat] he would come and take the rest of it off me and spend it on beer. One day my mother took the 200s. which he had given me, and I used some of it to buy two dresses. I put the dresses away in the hut and then when I came back later, I found that he had burned them" (Epstein 1992b:26).

It seems from the court record that the husband, Cewe, was playing around. Giving evidence, Mangaleti's father alleged that his son-in-law "was fornicating with every girl he saw." Cewe had brought Mangaleti back to her parents at a stage when she insisted that she still wanted to remain with him. The father-in-law's version of the clothing purchase referred to a quarrel. Cewe had become furious when Mangaleti returned from the store with two dresses: "No, you only had £1. There's no-one who can buy two dresses for £1." Mangaleti's father went on to explain how Cewe then "took the dresses, tore them up and burned them because of his jealousy" (Epstein 1992b:27).

Two dresses rather than one, purchased for an amount that would not cover their cost, meant to Cewe that someone else, a man, had given them to Mangaleti. But the court showed little sympathy for his jealousy. Wasting his money on beer, Cewe had not kept his wife properly; he had not given her sufficient money for herself, and he had been rude toward her parents. Judging that he had not fulfilled his obligation to care for her, the court ordered Cewe to compensate Mangaleti because he destroyed the dresses and admonished him to honor and respect his in-laws (Epstein 1992b:31–32).

Indeed, as Wilson noted (1941–42, 2:18), some women did "judge husbands and lovers according to the amounts of money they are given to spend on clothes." There was the cultural expectation, as Martha's and Brenda's cases illustrate, that husbands provide wives with clothes. The nature of the male-female relationship was both expressed and reconfigured through clothing. The normative expectation that men dress women has a reverse side that provoked David to take back the clothes he had bought for Martha when he realized that she had a lover. It also gave rise to the kind of suspicion Cewe expressed over the question of who pays for women's dresses and particularly so if their clothes look expensive or extravagant. The flashily dressed woman and her paramours is a well-worked theme in popular songs of this era (Epstein 1981:259–60; Powdermaker 1962:233–34, 240–41).

But in the urban setting some women did earn money in their own right, largely through small-scale trade and a variety of services, as few of them at this point found wage-labor jobs. Indeed, the domestic servants and tailors I introduced in chapter 1 were mostly men. The tensions that urban women's new spending capacity introduced into normative assumptions about men's household control sometimes produced domestic trouble that led to court. Such situations have been described in rich detail in the Copperbelt studies conducted during the latter half of the 1950s by Hortense Powdermaker and Arnold Epstein. Their work captures some of the charged tensions in gender relations on the domestic front and beyond that were fueled by rapid socioeconomic change, including women's growing consumption abilities and new dress options (Epstein 1981; Powdermaker 1962).

To be sure, African preoccupations with dress made clothing a powerful medium for debate involving African men, women, and the powers that be, for the various reasons described in this chapter. Clothing was of course much more than a medium of debate. Because of its enormous appeal to popular sensibilities, it was an important trade good that accounted for a good part of consumer expenditure. The ramifications of popular African preoccupations with clothing were not immediately apparent to government and local manufacturers who did little to promote local clothing production. As a result of African entrepreneurship, clothing in its most affordable form, secondhand, provided ready-made garments to poorly supplied rural areas, enabling men to wear "respectable" clothes rather than rags and meeting some of rural women's growing desires for dress. During World War II and the postwar years, secondhand clothing became increasingly available in towns, satisfying both basic clothing needs and desires for "a smart rig-out of clothes . . . For the ill-paid there are secondhand goods in plenty," noted R. J. B. Moore from the Copperbelt (1948:72–73), "from Europeans' back doors, from hawkers importing from the Congo and from more well-to-do friends." The Congo connection to which I have frequently referred is my special concern in the next chapter.

3 Secondhand Clothing and the Congo Connection

Secondhand clothing, known on both sides of the border between Northern Rhodesia and the Belgian Congo as kombo (plural *bakombo*),[1] was an important clothing source for Africans. From the early part of the twentieth century, the bulk of these garments reached Northern Rhodesia from Katanga in the Belgian Congo through Luapula[2] and across into the Copperbelt. The trade grew particularly rapidly during World War II and the immediate postwar years, when import restrictions caused scarcities of all kinds of commodities, including clothing. This chapter turns to the Congo connection in the secondhand clothing system of provision. My exploration of the reasons that Luapula occupied a prominent niche in this trade draws on several factors that help to set the local context for the subsequent discussions.

Why Luapula? With its rivers and lakes this region had been a crossroads in both historical and cultural terms (Legros 1996; Miracle 1969; Moore 1937; Roberts 1970). Luapula has a long history of involvement in short- and long-distance precolonial trade, including slaves, and it has seen the coming and going of a variety of peoples between what in the late 1800s was known as the Belgian Congo and Northern Rhodesia. During the opening decades of the twentieth century, many people from Luapula migrated to Katanga in the Congo, where they acquired not only skills as workers but also experience as consumers. From the 1930s on they worked on the Copperbelt of Northern Rhodesia. And clothing, new and used, was the chief commodity they brought back home with them.

Migrant labor, kinship relations, and trade that made people move across this wider region were much facilitated by the building of railways and roads. In the post–World War II years all these factors came together to make the population of Luapula valley more prosperous than that of many other regions. Anthropologist Ian Cunnison (1959) commented on the cosmopolitan atmosphere of the valley, which local people in the late 1940s spoke of as *ku mikoti,* "like the copperbelt" (*koti* is Bemba for "hole," here an underground mine). Describing paramount chief Kazembe's village as "a Paris of pleasure," Cunnison was impressed by its variety of activities and sophistication (25–26). Like many contemporary observers he was especially struck by the local clothing scene: "The businesslike rags they wear on their fishing expeditions are replaced on Sundays by white shirts, creased trousers, polished shoes and felt hats; while the women vie for brightness of dress and head-cloth" (2).

This impression of sleek prosperity and great energy was the result of trade in two commodities that embraced Luapula and Katanga, linking them with the Copperbelt, the Northern Province, other parts of the territory, and ultimately Europe and North America. This was the two-way trade in fish from Luapula to the Katanga mines in the Congo and secondhand clothes, imported from North America and Europe into the Congo and taken across the border into Northern Rhodesia. In effect, fish and secondhand clothing stimulated the early growth of entrepreneurship in Luapula. "Development of Northern Rhodesia started here from Luapula," explained Kapaso Chisakula, a sixty-seven-year-old businessman whom I interviewed in 1995 about his involvement in the kombo trade in one of his stores in Kashikishi, a fishing and trade town on the Zambian side of Lake Mweru. He noted matter-of-factly: "We master this business" (25 May 1995, Kashikishi).

"A journey down the Luapula Valley is like paying a visit to a camp of American Armed Forces," noted a district commissioner in 1950 with reference to secondhand clothing imported from the Belgian Congo (NAZ/SEC 2/877). African recollections and colonial documents from this period pertaining to Luapula contain plenty of references to the trade in imported used clothing. Most of the existing scholarship on the colonial economic landscape of this region has concerned its shifting fortunes in fishing and as a labor reserve (Bates 1976; Cunnison 1959; Gould 1989; Musambachime 1981, 1995; Poewe 1981). While mentioning the secondhand clothing trade in passing, this work has left its significance largely unexplored. Because used clothing rarely is distinguished from other garments in the colonial records, I draw a sketch of the contours of this trade and its attractions from a wide variety of sources, including my own interviews. I consider, in sequence, questions pertaining to sourcing, the role of the Belgian Congo as entrepôt in this trade, its extensions into the Copperbelt and Luapula, and the rise in African entrepreneurship around the trade in fish and kombo.

Sourcing and Import Regimes

Imported secondhand garments played an active part in the growing African preoccupation with clothing from the early decades of this century. Such clothes appear to have been readily available in the 1920s in the Belgian Congo (Dobkins n.d.), which extended its growing trade to Northern Rhodesia in the 1930s, if not earlier, and onward (Davis [1933] 1968:42). Traveling by foot from Likasi (Jadotville) in the Congo in 1922 toward the Angolan diamond fields in their search for work, Moss Dobkins and his partner George

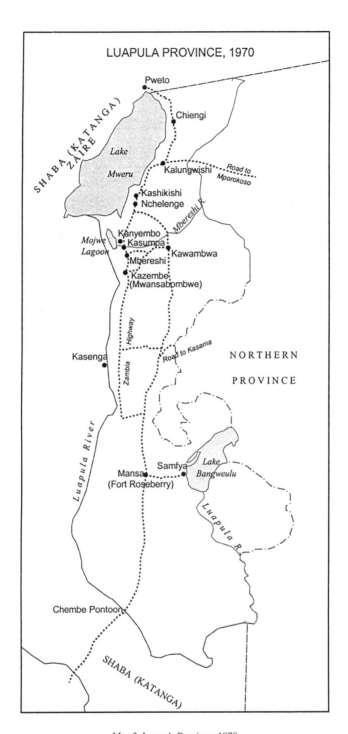

Map 2 Luapula Province, 1970

Sterling brought trade goods to pay for food and carriers. Among the goods were fifty yards of cloth, including white calico, black drill, and khaki. In his notes Dobkins (n.d.) described their difficulty in selling cloth by the yard. Speculating that perhaps the local Africans had no more money or that they were "looking for second-hand goods which were plentiful at that time in the Congo," he concluded that secondhand clothing was not a good commodity for this kind of trade because it was "too bulky to carry . . . if the transfer was by carriers" (70).[3]

So commonly available had secondhand clothing become in Northern Rhodesia by 1925 that the government passed a public health regulation requiring disinfection (Government Notice 78 of 1925). Although this regulation was repealed in 1943, its possible reintroduction became an issue in the early 1960s when the risk of secondhand clothing as a medium in spreading major epidemic diseases was discussed (especially with reference to smallpox). On that occasion it was pointed out that "a considerable proportion of secondhand clothing which has been brought into this territory from Katanga Province . . . is completely uncontrolled owing to the enormous length of the frontier involved" (NAZ/MH 1/5/2).

These efforts at official regulation of some aspects of the secondhand clothing trade between 1925 and 1962 form a convenient frame for my discussion of the Congo connection. The time frame is relevant because it encloses some important peaks in the international trade in secondhand clothing. The export potential of this commodity increased considerably at points of sourcing in Europe and North America along with the massing of army-surplus clothing after the two world wars. Easy border arrangements with the Belgian Congo made Katanga a convenient point of transshipment for secondhand clothing into Northern Rhodesia.

Last but not least, the heyday of the secondhand clothing trade into Luapula and the Copperbelt was during World War II and immediately thereafter, especially from the 1940s through the early 1950s, when war-related import quotas made new clothing and textiles both scarce and expensive. A wide range of import regulations and price controls were observed in Northern Rhodesia during and following the war (Kanduza 1986:221). These restrictions prevented retailers from buying goods in cheaper markets, and importation from dollar sources was allowed only if the goods were essential and not available from sterling sources. Piece goods and clothing fell into this category (Customs Department 1950:217).

Exceptions from the import restrictions were occasionally permitted for specific commodities. In 1945, for example, colonial officials asked their superiors in London whether the wartime quotas for imports from sterling and dollar areas might be stretched to include more secondhand clothes from the

United States (NCCM/KMA 131). Brief dispensations from the quota rulings seem to have been made between 1947 and 1948, when total clothing imports into Northern Rhodesia from the United States doubled in value, much of it in the words of a commercial observer "probably related to the very considerable quantities of second-hand civilian clothing for natives in which the U.S.A. has done a large volume of business in the territory." He also expressed concerns about alternative sources of supply "as second-hand civilian clothing suitable for this large African demand appears to be unobtainable in sufficient quantity from sterling sources" (Overseas Economic Surveys 1950:20). Indeed, another official commenting on the large demand argued that there was "no question of dollars being made available for direct importation by the government of secondhand clothing ex U.S.A." (NAZ/SEC 2/896). Many of these regulations remained in effect until 1953. The supply problems were accentuated by the difficult dollar position throughout the British Empire, which with devaluation of sterling in 1949 caused price increases. Only in the late 1940s did the government suspend duties on many foodstuffs, textiles, and clothing in an effort to keep down the cost of living (Customs Department 1950:6).

The Belgian Congo as Entrepôt

The bulk of secondhand clothing entered Northern Rhodesia through Katanga in the Belgian Congo. This routing was influenced by several factors. They include developments of the transportation system, the Belgian role in the secondhand clothing trade, the Congo franc as legal tender, customs arrangements, and the attractions of Elisabethville and Katanga as centers of migration and consumption. A few remarks highlight the major issues.

Roads and railroads were central in the development of Katanga and its interaction with Luapula and the Copperbelt (Katzenellenbogen 1973; Yelengi 1997). The north-south railroad from South Africa to Bulawayo in Southern Rhodesia across the Copperbelt arrived at Elisabethville in 1910. The Benguelo railway from Lobito Bay in Angola reached Katanga in the early 1930s. It took only twenty-seven days to ship goods from London to Ndola on the Northern Rhodesian side of the border via Lobito in Angola, as compared to two months for goods moved from southern and eastern African ports (Kanduza 1986:125). In the first half of the 1920s several roads were constructed, among them the Fort Rosebery (now Mansa)–Kapalala–Ndola road, the Fort Rosebery–Bangweulu road, and the Fort Rosebery–Elisabethville road (Mwansa 1992:16). The road across the Congo pedicle was not completed until around 1946. These improvements in the transportation system gradually displaced the kind of human porterage Moss Dobkins had de-

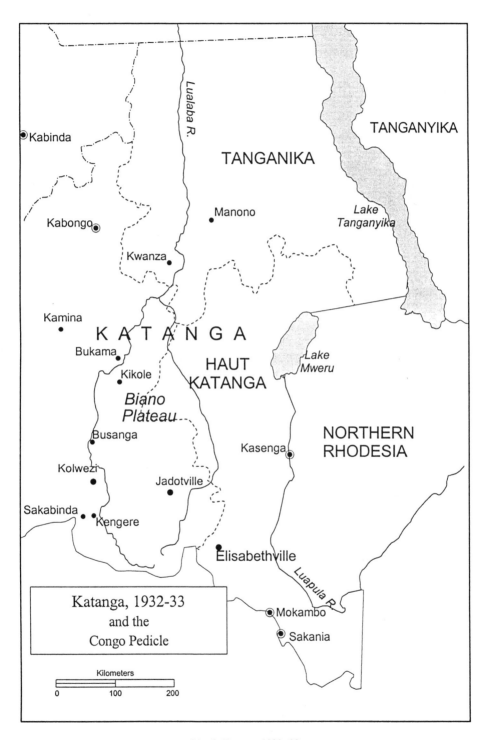

Map 3 Katanga, 1932–33

scribed. In addition to the dugout canoes that Africans had operated on Luapula's rivers and lakes for decades, bicycles found extensive use in transportation, as did, in the 1950s, buses and trucks.

The long involvement of Belgium in the secondhand clothing trade is an
important factor in making the Congo a convenient destination for secondhand clothing shipments from abroad. Indeed, metropolitan developments
helped to propel the Congo into a prominent role in the regional secondhand
clothing trade during and after World War II. Agreements between the United
Kingdom, the United States, and the exiled government of occupied Belgium
prompted the expansion of war-related production, especially of strategic
minerals such as uranium, in the Congo, where Africans were pressed to work
both in production and military campaigns. The foreign trade of the colony
was increasingly oriented toward the United States (Helmreich 1983;
Williame 1983). After the war Belgium was in a better economic situation
than many other countries in Europe because of revenues generated by the
huge war effort in the colony. There African wages had increased gradually
during the last years of the war and after. But the strong local demand for
clothing was met neither locally nor by suppliers in Europe, where both textiles and garments were rationed well into the 1950s.

Imported secondhand clothing met this demand. In the years after World
War II, the annual yearbooks listing European firms that supplied the colony
contain references to dealers in *friperie,* the French term for secondhand
clothes, from Belgium (e.g., Annuaire du Congo 1948). Clothing recyclers in
Belgium had access to a large network of foreign suppliers with extensive
knowledge of the trade, many international contacts, and easy access to the
world's major ports. Secondhand clothes were sourced across northwestern
Europe, including Paris, London, Amsterdam, and Brussels, as well as in the
United States (SAA/SAB/DEA 204 A10/16/IX). Because of clothes ra-
tioning in much of northwestern Europe, little clothing was cast-off, and
North America was a frequently used source. Some of the "American"
clothes that so impressed touring officials in Northern Rhodesia might well
have been transshipped via Europe where Belgium and the Netherlands, as I
discuss in part 2, long have been both importers and exporters in the international secondhand clothing trade.

Not all the secondhand garments that entered Northern Rhodesia from
across the Congo had been sourced commercially. Churches and mission societies also brought in secondhand clothing. How much of this particular
flow of garments in fact was sold for profit is hard to ascertain. A case in point
was a dispute in Sakania on the Congolese side of the border not far from
Ndola in 1944–45, between the Belgian administrator René Marchal and
Father Marcel Antoine, the superior of the Salesian Mission. The case, which

was never proven, involved allegations that the mission sold a variety of goods, especially bales of secondhand clothing, for profit in Northern Rhodesia (Verbeek 1987:283).

Trade was facilitated by the Congo franc, which had served as legal tender on both sides of the border since 1909, one year after the Congo Free State became the Belgian Congo (Musambachime 1995:62).[4] While British sterling circulated freely in Katanga especially during World War I, the franc became more common after 1920 and remained in use in Luapula until the Congo crisis in 1960 (Bates 1976:88–89). Migrant Africans from Luapula who worked in the Katanga mines used their francs to purchase goods in the Congo, especially clothes, which were both cheaper and more stylish than in their home districts (NAZ/KDF 6/1/11, 1923–24). The franc was so much preferred to the sterling in Luapula "that the natives have got so used to being paid in Belgian money that they are extremely averse to change, and insist, at any rate at present, on a much higher price if paid in our money" (NAZ/KDF 6/1/11, 1926). Commenting on the circulation of the franc in the Kawambwa area in 1950, one official noted that "habit dies hard, and the people still think in terms of francs. The prices of goods are quoted in francs as much as in sterling; tax-payers offer francs with which to pay their taxes; and some labourers still ask to be paid their wages in francs because of the not unfounded fear that if they go shopping in the Congo with sterling, the Greek traders will swindle them over the exchange" (NAZ/SEC 2/877).

Customs arrangements helped make Katanga a strategic entry point for secondhand clothing to Northern Rhodesia. For customs purposes Northern Rhodesia was divided into two zones known as the Congo Basin and the Zambezi Basin.[5] About a third of the territory, largely the northeastern part, fell under the Congo Basin treaties, which maintained low tariffs and prevented discrimination against any country's imports. This is in contrast to the Zambezi Basin, which was subject to reciprocal customs agreements with Southern Rhodesia, the Union of South Africa, and the protectorates, giving "empire preference" to several classes of goods. Goods passing between the two zones within Northern Rhodesia paid a duty (Kanduza 1986:60).

The shorter hauling distance by ship and rail to central African markets than to South African ports encouraged the import of Japanese merchandise, especially textiles and clothing, in the Congo Basin free-trade-convention area (Kanduza 1986:125) after the Great Depression as well as during the early years of the Second World War. During the last half of the 1930s, for example, Japan supplied about "one-third by value of all outer and underclothes, hats, hosiery, enamelled ware and cheap cutlery" that was imported into Northern Rhodesia (Department of Overseas Trade 1939:35–36). Direct import into this region also included secondhand clothing from Europe and North America that flowed without customs tariffs from the Congo into Northern Rhodesia until the first half of the 1950s.[6]

Stricter regulations of the flow of secondhand clothes from the Congolese side were put into place in the early 1950s, when the Belgian authorities limited the amount of clothing that could be taken into Northern Rhodesia to "the normal requirements of a man and his family" (NAZ/SEC 2/896). Additional customs posts began to be built along the Northern Rhodesian side of the border to prevent smuggling, for example, at Lukwesa at the Luapula River just across from Katabulwe in the Congo. When African traders who had been used to buying secondhand clothing at Mokambo complained of harassment by border officials, they were instructed about "the Congo law. Any Northern Rhodesian African is permitted to bring out with him, once in three months, two new jackets. If he does not bring out two jackets in that period, he can bring out four shirts, or if not four shirts, instead of that he can bring out four dresses or if he does not like dresses for his wife, he can bring out two pairs of trousers. If he has no need of trousers, he can bring out two overcoats" (Record of the Second Meeting of the Western Province African Provincial Council 1951:39).

Northern Rhodesian officials doubted that their Belgian colleagues would be able to reduce the flow of kombo across the border. "This prohibition is only loosely enforced," commented an official tersely with reference to the new border arrangements (NAZ/SEC 2/878, comment on tour report 6/ 1951). Another official was even more outspoken: "Their efforts are unlikely to be successful so long as Belgian customs wards are offered substantial awards by the local shopkeepers" (NAZ/SEC 2/896). A district assistant, probably a young man fairly fresh in the field who had an eye for style, commented that "such a ban would result in a rather less colorful community, as the cotton prints retailed in the piece by Messrs African Lakes Corporation, and Booth (mostly made in India) are dowdy in the extreme" (NAZ/SEC 2/ 878, no. 6 of 1951).

Last but not least, Katanga's role as entrepôt in the regional secondhand clothing trade also had to do with the attractions of its chief city, Elisabethville, as an important center for exchange and consumption that had turned into the most cosmopolitan place north of the Limpopo. As hub of the Congolese mining industry, Katanga Province hosted a large European population, engaged in mining and commerce, and it attracted African migrant laborers from a very wide region (Fetter 1976; Higginson 1989; Perrings 1979). This growth prompted increased demand among all classes for clothing, and with it, a desire to own and display clothing.

In the late 1920s and early 1930s Elisabethville had several stores operated by Jewish and Greek traders. Several of them dealt in clothing with the city's growing African population (Fabian 1990:99–101, 150). Large volumes of textiles and clothing were imported to satisfy the demands of both the European and African populations. Textiles and ready-made clothing from Britain made up a major part of imports during the 1920s while *pagnes* (printed-cloth wraps) for the African market overwhelmingly came from Belgium. Great Britain was then a major source for secondhand clothing to the African market, including jackets, trousers, vests, and hats (Sendwe 1994:9, 27). These developments were overshadowed during the years following the Great Depression and before World War II, when Japanese exports of textiles and garments grew to such an extent that they gave rise to allegations about dumping (OC 393/201.385.01). By 1937 so many Japanese goods were available that they almost eliminated European and American secondhand clothes from the local clothing market (Sendwe 1994:28). But it did not take long for kombo to be back in popular demand, prompted by increased costs of living and by general scarcities of the Second World War period.

When men from Luapula described their migration experiences to Katanga, it was the availability of attractive clothing that made a difference to what through the 1920s were rough and dangerous years of mine work when health hazards and casualty rates were alarming (Fetter 1976:110–11; Higginson 1989:19–57). The African workforce on the Katanga mines in the post–World War I period was primarily from the northeastern parts of Northern Rhodesia and the more remote northern parts of Katanga (Higginson 1989:43). Several recruitment agencies were active in the region, and while many young men from Luapula performed contract labor, *icibalo,* on the mines, some went on the long journey to Katanga on their own. Some of them worked as domestic servants and some, like Patrick Nshenda, worked as a tailor during two stints in the Congo, beginning in 1934 (Musambachime n.d. #24). Chungu Kanswe explained: "There was also . . . icibalo . . . I myself went to Kakontwe [near Jadotville] in the Congo for eight months . . . before going on contract labor we would be given a blanket and also 3 yards of cloth" (Musambachime n.d. #6). The vast majority of men like Chungu Kanswe went to work on the Katanga mines, so many in fact that the Northern Rhodesian government appointed an inspector and three vice consuls in Elisabethville to observe working conditions in Katanga (Fetter 1976:41; Higginson 1989:26).

Part of the wage of recruited workers was deferred and paid when they returned. Many workers spent the cash part of the wage while they were in the Congo on material goods, especially on clothing. Practically 90 percent of this, according to one source, was "spent on trade goods, with cloth[es] being the most favoured item" (Musambachime n.d. #31). J. B. Mwansabombwe explained: "[W]hile in the Congo the contract labourers used to buy clothes which were packed up in huge iron-boxes before they came home. When they arrived at Mansa, they reported to the Boma [administrative headquarters] authorities and they were paid [deferred wages]. The money that they had been paid in the Congo was just used for buying clothes and other commodities there" (Musambachime n.d. #2).

Marko Mwelwa pointed to a widespread problem for the returned migrants: "When a person returned after working in the Congo, he would not have enough money to start a business. The little money that a person received while on contract would be spent on immediate necessities" (Musambachime n.d. #27). And Lasaila Nkandu remembered: "Those contract labourers also came back fairly well off, especially as regards clothes because they spent all the francs that they were paid in the Congo on clothes" (Musambachime n.d. #10). To be sure, the limited stock available to African consumers on the Luapula side of the border helps to explain this purchasing pattern. "In those days," explained Batolomeo Katwai, "one couldn't find a wide range of items in an African store [in Luapula] . . . a store owner only had clothes, soap and matches on his shelves . . . The bulk of commodities were clothes and they were usually bakombo" (Musambachime n.d. #15).

Across the Copperbelt: Mokambo

During the Second World War and immediately thereafter, Africans from many parts of Northern Rhodesia and beyond converged on the north, purchasing secondhand clothing at border-crossing points to the Belgian Congo both on the Copperbelt and in Luapula. While some ventured all the way to Elisabethville to purchase secondhand clothing, others obtained it at Mokambo, which is likely to have been the destination for a group of Africans from Lusaka who in 1943 had made a "practice of going to the Congo in order to purchase secondhand clothes . . . owing to the diminished supplies" (NAZ/SEC/1/1970). That same year, a compound manager in Mufulira commented on "a band of natives . . . [who] had walked [all the way] from the Fort Jameson district [now Eastern Province] to purchase at Mokambo" (NCCM/KMA 20). Indeed, in the late 1940s Africans traveled from as far away as Bulawayo in Southern Rhodesia across Northern Rhodesia to Mokambo in the Congo and brought back secondhand clothes for resale (Gussman 1952:88–89).

Mokambo's role in the kombo trade grew in response to demands from Northern Rhodesia. Recalling their involvements in this trade at Mokambo from the early 1940s through the mid-1950s, two Congolese men born in 1918 and 1920, Jean Mukuta Ngosa and Maurice Kabemba, remembered the many Africans and Europeans from Northern Rhodesia who came to Mokambo to purchase furniture, foodstuffs, and above all kombo when mining centers like Mufulira began growing from the early 1930s on (4 and 5 March 1998, Mokambo).[7] During the war years and until the early 1950s, they explained, Africans in Northern Rhodesia who experienced scarcities of all kinds of goods flocked to Mokambo to purchase kombo in order to resell it back home. What ready-made clothing was available there was sold by Indian storekeepers; it was expensive and of poor quality. There was barely any choice of clothing. As regards fabric, the only colors Africans could buy at the Northern Rhodesian side were khaki, black, and white. These two Congolese traders and others like them purchased bales of secondhand clothing in Elisabethville, traveling back and forth by train. They retailed at Mokambo, and some walked across the border under the cover of night to sell their goods in Mufulira, typically to persons they had come to know through this trade; they and their helpers bartered kombo in the rural areas around Mokambo as well.

Like many others on the Copperbelt side, Harry Nkumbula, who rose to political fame in the struggle for independence and after, also dealt in secondhand clothes. When teaching at Mufulira Central School in the late 1940s, his "weekend pastime was to cycle to the Congo (Zaire) border town of Mokambo to buy secondhand clothes to sell and thus supplement his income" (Mwangilwa 1982:19). The most famous of the many people who did some trade in secondhand clothing from the Copperbelt is undoubtedly Kenneth Kaunda, Zambia's first president. Describing his trials and tribulations during the years prior to his full-time political involvement, Kaunda (1962:30) explained how he and his wife "determined to work together to improve our standard of living" when they both were employed at a boarding school in Mufulira in 1948.

> In order to increase our combined income . . . we decided to buy second-hand clothes from Mokambo, just over the Congo border, and send them up to my home [Chinsali in the Northern Province] to be sold for a small profit. People were permitted by law to cross into the Congo and to buy second-hand American clothes, but each person was only allowed to bring back one jacket and one dress or shirt. At the end of the month when I had received my salary, I would organize a group of schoolboys and on a Saturday afternoon we would cross the border at Mokambo and come back wearing the strangest assortment of clothes.

In 1949 the Kaundas moved back to Chinsali, where Kaunda became active in political mass mobilization. Through savings he obtained the three things that he needed most urgently in this transition: "We saved up to secure bicycles to enable us to move about and attend meetings freely. We decided to purchase watches in order to be on time for such meetings. My wife and I decided we should also get a sewing machine to help us to repair whatever second-hand goods I could bring back from Katabulwe that needed mending before selling . . . The small savings from our meagre monthly pay packets, plus what we managed to raise from the sale of second-hand goods helped us to purchase our three main requirements" (36).

The rest of Kaunda's reminiscences about kombo moves the focus from Mokambo to Luapula. Chinsali was far from the "sources" of secondhand clothes on the Congolese border. Kaunda describes how he "would cycle for over three hundred miles up to Katabulwe across the Luapula River in the then Belgian Congo with some of our neighbours and we would cross the Luapula back to Northern Rhodesia and then would come the scramble to load them on the . . . lorries. All this was terribly strenuous. And then came the long race cycling home to try and arrive back before our goods. During my absence from the farm, my sister took charge of the farm labour and my wife dealt with the second-hand clothes shop" (39). The trip took about three days, Kaunda recalled, and some of the clothes were sold in Kasama, the provincial headquarters of Northern Province (18 July 1997, Lusaka).

Men like Nkumbula and Kaunda went into professional politics, while others took up the secondhand clothing trade on an intermittent or full-time basis. Although people from other parts of the territory and beyond it certainly also were involved in this activity, it was people from Luapula who developed mastery of the kombo trade, extending it into other provinces.

Luapula Entrepreneurship

Luapula's rise to prominence in the kombo trade was the result of close interaction between the trade in fish and secondhand clothes by Congo-based Greek and African entrepreneurs in Luapula. The entrepreneurial success of this region was facilitated by legislation that expanded African participation in trade from the 1930s on but particularly during World War II and after (Mwansa 1992). African stores appeared throughout the region because it was easier to get hawking and trading licenses. These developments were the subject of extensive commentary by touring colonial officers. One of them suggested that access to goods for resale was one of the main problems of the village shop owners around Fort Rosebery, who basically could buy their stock from four sources: the Copperbelt, the Congo, European and African stores in Fort Rosebery, and an African cooperative society in Fort Rosebery. At that time "purchases in the Congo were almost entirely confined to second-hand clothing." This writer stressed both the expense and time involved in travels aimed at obtaining stock as a way of explaining why many village stores remained small and poorly capitalized (NAZ/SEC 2/902).

The growth of the Katanga mines helped create the demand for foodstuffs, including fish. Both mine workers and foodstuffs had to be brought in from the larger region. And because workers received food rations as part of their remuneration, the demand for foodstuffs at the mines increased. The Luapula region had no European farmers to speak of. From the early days of the operation of the mines, Africans from Luapula brought fish and produce across to the Congo, using the small town of Kasenga on the Congolese side of the border as a collection and transit point. Participating in this growing trade between the lower Luapula valley and Elisabethville, traders walked or biked; they covered the 220-kilometer distance in seven to ten days by foot, or in three to four days on bicycle (Musambachime 1995:55).

By the early 1920s Greek traders and fishermen had established a commercial center at Kasenga, built ice plants there and at Kilwa, an island in Lake Mweru, and constructed packing facilities. A steamer made weekly runs along the Luapula River and into Lake Mweru, stopping at regular intervals to purchase fish from villagers. The Greeks also started using local timber to build Greek-style fishing vessels with wood-burning or charcoal-powered engines, which in the late 1940s were replaced by diesel engines (Musambachime 1995:58). Plying the Luapula River to and from Lake Mweru, some boats took up ice and brought down fish, while others took up goods to supply the small trading centers that sprang up along the river.

One of those developing trade centers was Katabulwe, mentioned by Kaunda, some thirty miles north of Kasenga where a dozen Greek stores on the river's edge were well supplied with consumer goods, including "plenty of secondhand American dresses, men's clothes, blankets, etc." (NAZ/SEC 2/876). While there, "the fishermen spend most of their money buying second-hand American clothes" (NAZ/SEC 2/877). The African crews transported not only fish and foodstuffs, but also passengers and sometimes merchandise such as the popular Congolese Simba beer as well as secondhand clothing to be exchanged for fish or sold for money. When the boats were full, the crews returned to Kasenga, where a fleet of trucks transported the fish to the mining centers of Katanga (Bates 1976:25).

Some of the Greek traders established considerable goodwill with African fishermen from Luapula "due to the regularity of their custom and incentives which include loan of expensive nets, financial assistance with boat construction and trade-good barter"; among the latter kombo was a major commodity (NAZ/SEC 2/879). The fish and kombo trade brought cash to the more successful African participants. "They have either built, or are building," according to one report, "brick houses and stores. The stock in trade doesn't vary very much . . . consisting chiefly of frocks, shorts, trousers and shirts, cycle spares, etc. . . . The biggest sales are for secondhand cotton frocks from the Belgian Congo" (NAZ/SEC 2/878, no. 6 of 1951). Not all were equally successful. In 1943, when he was in his early twenties, Sefeli

Chibwe traveled often from Fort Rosebery (now Mansa) to Samfya (on Lake Bangweulu), where he bought fish for resale. He set up a small store near Fort Rosebery, which he operated for around eleven years. There he sold "clothes from the Congo, the types of clothes which were known in those days as bakombo." He used to go by bus from Fort Rosebery to Kawambwa and from there to Kasenga in the Congo. But he went bankrupt and closed the store in the mid-1950s (Musambachime n.d. #3).

In investing their earnings this generation of early entrepreneurs pursued a number of strategies, either singly or in combination. Some invested their earnings in the fish trade, acquiring their own motor boats and buying fish to resell. Others turned to transport, purchasing buses and trucks. And still others used their earnings to establish small stores up and down the valley, where they retailed fish and kombo to marketeers from the Copperbelt. Ready cash and the availability of European trade goods encouraged settlement near sources of stock. Cunnison (1959:27) noted that in the late 1940s the "two most concentrated areas are near Kashiba and near Lukwesa, the former within easy reach of Kasenga, the latter immediately opposite the Congo trading post of Katabulwe and on the river route to Kasenga." This regional concentration shifted in the 1950s when the colonial government encouraged the sale of fish from Luapula on the Copperbelt rather than in Katanga (Poewe 1976:134). Already by the 1940s African entrepreneurs had extended their trading reach to Lake Bangweulu, which became an important site in the fish/secondhand clothing nexus.

Trading Kombo

Kombo was an important trade commodity in the rise of the first generation of Luapula-based African entrepreneurs. *Generation* is a fitting term here, as the men who acquired skills and resources from kombo trading in the 1940s and 1950s often passed them on to their sons or nephews or, in exceptional cases, to their daughters. "Our father used to be a trader in kombo," recalled Mr. Kapapula; "we were all brought up and educated by the same trade" (29 May 1995, Mansa). Reminiscences like these sketch a story of African involvement in the kombo trade with the assistance of or stimulation from the Greek traders and fishermen with whom they dealt in fish and foodstuffs.[8]

The most well known of the men who participated in the kombo trade extended it in the 1940s from the valley and lakes onto the plateau and beyond. For example, the Mwenso brothers extended their activity from Mansa to Johnson Falls and Mulundu, and into the Northern Province to Kasama, Mporokoso, and as far as Mbala, and they ran a bus service to Mufulira on the Copperbelt (NAZ/SEC 2/878, no. 10 of 1951). Luka Mumba had taken kombo across from the Belgian Congo, including Elisabethville and Mokambo, from the early 1940s (Gann 1969:377).[9] He linked his activities in Mansa and Samfya on Lake Bangweulu, building a hotel in Mansa and acquiring a boat that traveled between Mamfuli and the islands (Annual Reports on African (Native) Affairs 1958), and he transported fish from Lake Bangweulu to the Copperbelt. Kapapula senior built several stores along the lake, one of them at Lukwesa, as did Luka Mumba, and one of the Kapapula daughters set up shop in Kabwe. The chief stock in these new stores was secondhand clothing. "Next to clothing, which probably forms from 60–70% of most stores, the largest stocks were held in paraffin and soap, with smaller stocks in hardware" (NAZ/SEC 2/876).

The trade in kombo grew from small beginnings. Mukonko senior, born 1901, who in the late 1930s traded in grain, roots, and legumes with villagers, had kombo in his inventory. He sent his young son Ellie with an uncle on bicycles to purchase bales of kombo at Kasenga in the Congo; on their return, they sold the goods from home shops or exchanged them for beans and groundnuts. Later they went all the way to Elisabethville through Matanda; at this point Mukonko senior employed people with bicycles to help in the trade. After dividing up the bales, he sometimes returned directly home, leaving Ellie in charge of the workers to go into the villages with dry goods like soap, salt, and calico in addition to kombo. They also took orders, noting name, size, and type of garment to deliver on their next trip (25 May 1995, Mansa).

In the late 1940s Kapapula senior sent his sons with kombo on bicycles into the fishing camps along the river. They took a limited supply of dry goods, some dresses, trousers, and shoes, which they sold for cash or exchanged for fish. They would go in a group of four to six young people with as many "helpers," biking five to ten miles a day and camping overnight. Usually villagers would feed them. "This is how we learned management," said Mr. Kapapula, born 1935, a prominent businessman in Mansa who owned stores, buses, and trucks and had been a road-construction contractor, among many other things (29 May 1995, Mansa).

Mr. Chisakula told me how he and his brother after school were sent into the villages by their father to sell kombo. Initially they walked. Later, using bicycles, they would put a basket with kombo on the back of the bicycle and display dresses in front. Having learned the tailor's trade at a very young age in a Greek store, Mr. Chisakula received most of his education at Mufulira, where he later worked as a clerk for the mines. He returned to Luapula in 1952, setting himself up in the fish and kombo trade. He opened a store in Kashikishi on Lake Mweru in 1956, trading fish and kombo until 1958. During subsequent years he built several other shops and a rest house and bar, and purchased trucks, among other things (25 May 1995, Kashikishi).

During the late 1950s traders in Luapula found it increasingly difficult to bring in secondhand clothing from the Congo (Annual Report on African (Native) Affairs 1959). Aside from the intensification of border control, many factors converged in making the Congo a less desirable location than before. In the postwar period people from Luapula tended to look for work on the Copperbelt rather than in Katanga. The color bar was beginning to crack, as evidenced in the involvement of Luapula Africans in a diverse field of trade and business. On both sides of the border, this was a period of national-ist mobilization that resulted in a state of emergency in Northern Rhodesia in 1957 and prompted the violent exodus of Europeans from the Congo in 1960. There had been "riots" on the island of Kasenga in 1955 when Africans demonstrated against the Greeks and struck against people employed by them (NAZ/SEC 2/882).

The orientation of trade away from the Congo did not escape official notice in Luapula: "International uncertainty at the effect of Congo independence has been detrimental to the development of trade and industry which had im-proved annually over the last few years . . . The refusal of banks and other bodies to accept the Congo franc resulted in a marked reduction in trade in the Luapula valley and on the lakeshore of Lake Mweru. Much of the trade in past years has been conducted in francs and traders have found themselves left with large amounts of useless currency which they are unable to convert into goods and with which they cannot pay off their trading debts" (Annual Re-port on African (Native) Affairs 1960).

All my interviews with second-generation men of the kombo trade point to the late 1950s and early 1960s as the period during which they invested their profits in other commercial activities. The kombo trade was always under lo-cal control, its success depending on local insights into business opportuni-ties, personal skills in pursuing them, willingness to take risks, and above all practical knowledge. Accumulating start-up capital from the kombo/fish trade, some traders diversified their businesses in the late 1950s, acquiring boats, trucks, buses, restaurants, rest houses, and shops. When Mr. Chisakula said that "development in Northern Rhodesia started here in Luapula," he had in mind the improved livelihood that resulted from better transportation and services, which not only helped to cover basic needs but also mediated personal desires. The kombo trade thrived because it was fed by widely shared sensibilities that revolved around the importance of dress and style. Because clothing has remained central to widespread understandings of well-being, dealings with clothing continue the story about changing socio-economic experiences that were part of Northern Rhodesia's transition from colony to independent nation.

4 Dressing the New Nation

Others cry out for smart berets,
we cry out for our country.
Others cry out for suits.
We cry for the iron in our soil.
Our wealth has been taken from us.
Alas, our iron.
Mothers, cease your weeping.
Fathers, do not cry.
I ask, "what are you going to do about it?"
(Fraenkel 1959:132)

Kenneth Kaunda, who traded in kombo from the Congo before involving himself in full-time politics, wrote this song about self-respect and autonomy during the last half of the 1950s before the banning of the Zambia African National Congress and the formation of its successor, the United National Independence Party (UNIP). At independence in 1964, Kaunda became president of the Republic of Zambia. Questions about clothing and its production were important to the new nation, since independence meant, among many other things, producing what previously had been imported.

The Congo connection in the secondhand clothing trade forms the point of departure for this chapter's discussion of dress and the new nation. Political developments on both sides of the border but particularly in the Congo created a commercial climate in which the secondhand clothing trade in Luapula, the Copperbelt, and across the country declined during the late 1950s. In Lusaka imported secondhand clothing was not readily available during the first decade after independence. To be sure, there were always a few secondhand clothing traders in city and township markets, as I noted during my first period of research in the capital in the early 1970s. They sold used garments they had sourced at the door of expatriate households or purchased at house sales or from traders who maintained contacts across the border to Zaire. In fact, commercial import of secondhand clothing was prohibited at this time.

Questions about clothing consumption and textile and garment production assumed both cultural and political importance as the new nation's leadership sought to achieve economic self-sufficiency in efforts to erase the legacies of external dependency that the colonial regime and the federal period in particular had left on the economy. This chapter briefly explores the politics of dress from two angles. One has to do with the emergence of dress styles and their shifting contextual evaluations. The other concerns the rise and decline of a textile and garment manufacturing industry. Processes pertaining to both of these angles of inquiry converged in the mid- to late 1980s in the reappearance of the secondhand clothing trade, providing the preconditions for its exceptionally rapid growth and popularity and thus the backdrop for part 2 of this book.

The Question of National Dress

Zambia presented itself symbolically to the world of nations with a newly designed coat of arms (Fig. 7). The new republic's heraldic imagery features black and white wavy lines representing the Victoria Falls, with a fish eagle on top and a crossed hoe and pick underneath it. The eagle stands for freedom and the ability to rise above problems, the hoe and the pick for farming and mining (Hobson 1996:5). To the left and right of the shield stand a man and a woman, the man dressed in bush jacket and shorts, and the woman in a cloth tied at the waist, a square-necked shirt with puffed sleeves, and beads. They both wear sandals. At their feet are symbols of the country's natural resources: a maize cob, a mine headframe, and a zebra. At the bottom of the depiction is a narrow, horizontal banner with the postcolonial political motto: One Zambia, One Nation. The country's many ethnic groups, a total of seventy-three according to an official handbook, were to be melded into one unitary polity, Zambia (Brelsford 1965).

When the ministerial consultative committee for the independence celebration asked Zambian artist Gabriel Ellison to design the new coat of arms, it insisted on human figures as bearers. Considering quite a variety of suggestions for how to dress the bearers, the consultative committee members settled on the dress style that was widespread during the two decades before independence, and that is the style Mr. Kamuti and Mrs. Mwalimu described in chapter 1. The all-male members of the committee agreed more easily on the male bearer's dress than that of the female bearer. The designer had proposed a variety of birds as bearers, arguing that human bearers were unlikely to withstand the effects of time (Gabriel Ellison, 12 September 1997, Lusaka). Subsequent developments in dress styles indicate that she indeed was right in her argument.

The coat of arms does not feature any regional or "tribal" dress styles of the kind worn by paramount chiefs on ceremonial occasions. In fact, in the new

Figure 7 Coat of arms of the Republic of Zambia.

republic with the political motto "One Zambia, one nation," regional dress did not constitute a public issue. Special dress was certainly worn, such as at the Lozi *kuomboka*, where Lewanika wore his admiral's uniform, and other regional celebrations where chiefs donned a bricolage of Western clothing and local paraphernalia. A photo captured the occasion of the *mutomboko* ceremony at Mwanzabombwe (Kazembe) in the late 1960s (Fig. 8). All the chiefs have fly whisks in their hands and wear striking headgear, signaling their status. They include the Lunda paramount chief Mwatakazempe from Luapula in a jacket and a flowing multicolored tiered skirt; Lunda chief Ndunga from North-Western Province with a jacket in animal-print material and a double wrapper skirt; from Eastern Province, visiting Ngoni chief Mpezeni with jacket, chief's medallions, and a leopard skin worn on top of a

Figure 8 Visiting chiefs at a *mutomboko* ceremony at Mwanzabombwe in Luapula Province, late 1960s. From right to left, Lunda paramount chief Mwatakazempe from Luapula Province; Lunda chief Ndunga from North-Western Province; Ngoni chief Mpezeni and a Chewa chief, probably Chief Undi, both from Eastern Province.
Archive photo from Zambia Information Services, reproduced with permission.

skirt; and a Chewa chief, probably Chief Undi, in a long loose gown, complete with solar topi and sunglasses.

In effect, the new nation made little effort at defining itself through dress. When Kenneth Kaunda in the mid-1950s was the second in command to Harry Nkumbula, the president general of the African National Congress, he once wore a loincloth at a demonstration (Fraenkel 1959:181). He did not continue to do so, unlike Gandhi, who during the years of Indian cultural nationalism always wore a *khadi* (homespun) loincloth (Bean 1989; Tarlo 1996:76). Nkumbula, by contrast, at public events often wore his London School of Economics blazer (Fraenkel 1959:173), a garment that resonated much better with African men's ideas about good dress practice than did loincloths. The suit that features in Kaunda's song at the outset of this chapter might in fact have been a veiled reference to Nkumbula, who was widely known as a very sharp dresser. Kaunda and his followers had split from Nkumbula's African National Congress party in 1958 over disagreements of policy, forming the Zambia African National Congress.

What to wear did become an issue as independence approached. "Because we did not have a national dress as such in Zambia," recalled Vernon Mwaanga (1982:95), a long-term politician, on the occasion of his appointment as deputy high commissioner in the United Kingdom prior to independence in 1964, "the High Commissioner's wife improvised togas of African print . . . It turned out to be a very ordinary piece of red and white stripe[d] cloth material . . . available from the shops [in London]." During Zambia's independence celebration, Kenneth Kaunda and some of his colleagues wore similar attire. The style was modeled on Ghanaian wraps. Sources in the National Assembly in the Parliament of Zambia hold that President Kaunda at the annual opening of the assembly always wore a Ghanaian cloth that had been presented to him by President Nkrumah. Parliamentarians refer to this cloth as *kanga,* an East African Swahili term for printed cloth.[1]

But the dress practice of men wearing cloth draped around the body never took hold as "national dress." That role was played for a while by the bush suit of colonial vintage, with the important addition of long trousers rather than shorts. In this way a slightly revised version of the dress of the human bearers on the coat of arms becomes an example of a created tradition that Zambians sometimes call "national" or "traditional" dress. President Kaunda helped popularize this dress practice that became known locally as the "safari suit" and sometimes was called a "Kaunda" in neighboring countries. Vice president Simon Kapwepwe, who had been a member of the committee discussing the design of the new coat of arms, was the only politician in the First Republic to staunchly advocate a cultural nationalism in the arts that also referred to dress. While his colleagues donned safari suits, which became almost de rigueur in government and parastatal offices, Kapwepwe often wore a loose short-sleeved print shirt made of colorful fabric.

Unlike men's dress, which never turned into a public issue during the first and second republics, women's dress and their dressing "properly" provoked intermittent public reactions, as they continue to do. Recurring debates, first in the early 1970s and recently in the 1990s, revolved largely around miniskirts and tight clothing, with trousers/jeans playing subordinate roles. The 1970s debates were expressed by the House of Chiefs, supposedly the guardians of tradition and authority, and by the Women's Brigade, an auxiliary body of the ruling party, UNIP, and ostensibly the advocate of women's affairs as wives and mothers. The House of Chiefs in fact in 1971 proposed a motion to ban miniskirts, yet it was not instituted into law (Republic of Zambia 1971).

Railing at miniskirts and advocating "traditional dress" for women, the House of Chiefs and UNIP's Women's Brigade constructed women's dress as "respectable" when it reached below the knees and did not reveal "private parts," which in this part of Africa includes thighs. Chibesa Kankasa, the chair of the Women's Brigade in the early 1970s, added fuel to the miniskirt debate by conflating dress practice with women's "proper roles" as wives and mothers (Schuster 1979:160–65). Kankasa played a prominent role in the development of the "traditional" chitenge (printed-cloth) suit: a skirt or a wrap and a top of printed cloth, increasingly more elaborately tailored. Her personal hallmark was an elaborately folded headscarf in the West African manner. About a decade later, when the miniskirt long had passed out of fashion, the president's wife, Betty Kaunda, who often wore chitenge suits, advised women to dress decently, look natural, and "discard all foreign modes of dressing which [are] not compatible with local taste." Urging Zambian women to "guard their independence for the benefit of [the] future," Mrs. Kaunda said that "we should not copy everything that comes from foreign countries, but only good and decent attire" (*Times of Zambia,* 4 February 1985).

A step along the way in the development of the safari suit and chitenge dress styles is illustrated in a photo of a formal occasion in the late 1960s (Fig. 9). The two central figures exchanging greetings are Kenneth and Betty

Figure 9 President Kaunda greeting his wife, Betty, on a formal occasion in the late 1960s. The person between them, with a walking stick, is Mr. Reuben Kamanga, and behind him are Mr. Changufu (in a white shirt) and Mr. Chitambala.
Archive photo from Zambia Information Services, reproduced with permission.

Kaunda. The president's bush jacket has not yet achieved the slim silhouette it later obtained. Mrs. Kaunda's two-piece chitenge suit, though simple in style, is well tailored. She and the other female companion wear simple headgear, while the president is sporting a distinctive hat.

Clothing and Textile Independence

The Zambian society in which safari suits and chitenge dresses were worn on formal occasions experienced what was, by African standards, a booming economy, until the early 1970s. World-market prices for the main source of revenue, copper, were very favorable. The government and the majority party, UNIP, of the first republic (1964–72) set about developing the new nation through heavy public expenditures, expanding the educational system, establishing import substitution industries, building utilities and transport infrastructure, and acquiring majority shares in mining and export-import enterprises.

I noted at the outset that achieving independence meant, among other things, producing what previously had been imported. While this applied to textile and garment manufacturing in particular, the goal pertained across industrial sectors. The effects of colonial and federal policies that had restrained Northern Rhodesia's industrial development were conspicuous. An economic survey mission established by the United Nations and the Economic Commission for Africa just prior to independence in 1962 to provide advice on industrial development noted that only eight out of twenty-nine industrial categories supplied the local economy by 50 percent or more (UN/ECA 1964:76). Only 10 percent of the country's consumption of textiles was met by local production in 1962; the rest was imported. The survey mission estimated consumer demand to consist of blankets (12 percent), knitwear (14 percent), clothing (44 percent), and cloth sold retail as piece goods (30 percent). "At 26 yds *per caput* (in 1962)," this report observed, "textile consumption is high compared with elsewhere in Africa, and equal to that of Southern Rhodesia" (UN/ECA 1964:77).

In 1962 there were about nineteen garment manufacturers in Zambia, with only two factories employing more than 100 workers (UN/ECA 1964:77). During the immediate postindependence years, notable growth was experienced in food processing, tobacco, and chemicals as well as in textiles and clothing (McGrath and Whiteside 1989:172). The general growth in the market for locally produced goods was the result partly of the rapidly growing urban population with improved purchasing power and partly of import restrictions imposed on goods from the south after Southern Rhodesia's Unilateral Declaration of Independence from Great Britain in 1965.

The textile industry was an outcome of these new developments. In 1967 the Zambian government, the Commonwealth Development Corporation, and private enterprise established Kafue Textiles of Zambia, Ltd., in Kafue, a small town some forty kilometers south of Lusaka. The factory began production in 1969. Until 1995 the Swiss firm Maurer Textiles held 22 percent of the shares and operated Kafue Textiles in tandem with its sister company SOTEXKI in Zaire. In the early 1970s Mulungushi Textiles, Ltd., was set up in Kabwe, 140 kilometers north of Lusaka, as a parastatal company. The Chinese government provided loans and technical support, and production started in 1982 (Guille 1995). Privately owned weaving and spinning plants opened up as well, and small-scale garment manufacturing grew. An indication of this comes from a directory of manufacturing firms compiled by the Industrial Development Corporation (INDECO), which in 1970 listed eighty-five manufacturers of wearing apparel, ranging from safari suits, men's conventional suits, women's dresses, skirts, and blouses, to industrial clothing, uniforms and school uniforms, and underwear (INDECO 1970). And an industry directory from 1976 contained at least 115 manufacturers of wearing apparel of much the same range as the 1970 list, plus seven textile manufacturers and three manufacturers of knitwear (ZIMCO 1976).[2]

During those years, rural to urban migration became more massive than during the late colonial period as more people moved to towns expecting jobs, housing, and better lives. Between 1969 and 1980 the urban share of the total population jumped from 29 to 43 percent (Karmiloff 1990:302). Some benefits were experienced, particularly by women, who had not been well represented among the wage-employed during the colonial period. In the new nation de jure job discrimination hardly existed except in underground mining. The first cohort of well-educated women easily found salaried work in the government's many new departments, and more women were seen in previously male-dominated employment fields (Schuster 1979).

These developments began to slow down during the Second Republic (1972–91), when the government of the one-party state introduced a socialist-inspired command economy (Gertzel, Baylies, and Szeftel 1984). The Middle East oil crisis followed by a steady economic decline due to plummeting world-market copper prices and poor political planning squashed expectations about leading better lives for the great majority of the Zambian population (Woldring 1984). The second republic turned increasingly phobic, blaming the poor economic performance on foreign influences that were alleged to buttress the white minority regimes in the region, both in Rhodesia (now Zimbabwe) and South Africa.

From 1974 on, the contribution of the manufacturing sector to GDP declined until a partial recovery in 1984, per capita real incomes dropped, and

She's wearing his clothes

The greatest pride of the Kafue Textiles weaver is seeing his product worn in style — that's why the entire work force of Kafue Textiles goes to great lengths to see that you get the very best.

Using the choice of the Zambian cotton crop, the best of Zambian designs and the highly developed marketing team of Kafue Textiles, we ensure that you get the finest quality fabrics. Our shops in Lusaka and Ndola offer you the widest range of materials in Zambia. You can find KTZ materials in nearly all wholesale outlets in Zambia — a sure sign that our materials are respected by both wholesalers and consumers alike. Kafue Textiles combines the latest techno-

logy, the produce of Zambian farmers, the highly trained technical staff, exciting traditional designs and knowledge of the Zambian market, to give you just what you need. For industrial or domestic use, the best materials money can buy is KTZ fabrics.

BE PROUD — ITS MADE IN ZAMBIA

KAFUE TEXTILES
OF ZAMBIA LTD.
Head Office: P.O. Box 131, KAFUE.
Telephone: 311501, Telex: ZA 70020

Figure 10 Advertisement from Kafue Textiles of Zambia, Ltd., appearing in the *Times of Zambia*, 25 February 1984, p. 2.

the rural/urban terms of trade deteriorated (Karmiloff 1990:299–301). Foreign loans and aid programs from the International Monetary Fund (IMF)/World Bank and international donors helped to tide the economy over from the mid-1970s on, setting the government on a course of increasingly tighter fiscal and economic reforms. As one of many efforts to reduce the outflow of foreign exchange, "the Party and its Government," the second republic's most commonly used political term, banned the importation of clothes from mail-order firms (*Zambia Daily Mail,* 7 January 1982).

Clothing remained central to people's experiences of well-being during those years when, according to one observer, "buoyant private and public consumption supported the textile and clothing sub-sector in the face of overall decline" (Karmiloff 1990:299). Rural people experiencing development passing them by expressed their disenchantment in the language of clothing, for example, in appeals from the residents of Kasumpa village in Luapula during a visit of a district governor in 1972. In their petition they said: "Look at us, Mr. Governor. Some of us are dressed in rags. But that does not mean we are lazy. It is because we have no employment. Go, Mr. Governor and get us schemes [development projects]; or help our farmers; or mine our minerals. Go and get us jobs" (Bates 1976:213–14).

As the Zambian economy continued its downward slide during the 1980s, it became increasingly difficult to dress in "good attire." Secondhand clothing was classified as a "nonessential" good for the import of which the Party and its Government did not allocate foreign exchange (BBC, 17 June 1980). By the mid-1980s total merchandise imports had dropped to about one-third of their 1970 volume, falling by about half between 1980 and 1985 alone (Makgetla 1986:396). The two state-owned textile factories exported most of the country's high-quality cotton cloth and yarn. At the same time, severe import restrictions and declining availability of foreign exchange increased the costs of raw materials and equipment, limiting local production both of fabric and ready-made garments. Factories closed down intermittently because of lack of imported inputs. During those years it was dress in general rather than women's clothes in particular that drew public attention. How, for instance, could police work effectively when wearing pata pata (flip-flops; *Times of Zambia,* 26 October 1986), teachers draw respect from students when poorly dressed (*Times of Zambia,* 28 April 1987), and newspaper vendors expect to sell the dailies when wearing rags (*Times of Zambia,* 6 June 1987)? So scarce was good clothing during the 1980s that army personnel on the Copperbelt were punished for allowing their wives to wear military attire (*Times of Zambia,* 28 January 1987). The key words of that time were *scarcity* and *unavailability,* and the most common sight in towns was queues of consumers waiting in long lines to purchase essential commodities.

It was also during the long, hard years of the second republic that the promise of gender equality proved illusory in many fields, including politics, education, and employment. As formal-sector employment contracted, so did women's presence among the wage-employed. Few women obtained jobs that men could do. Instead, they turned to informal-sector work in ever growing numbers, often providing the margin that made survival possible in the face of men's shrinking wages. But as heads of households, Zambian men have conventionally had cultural claims on their wives' incomes, time and attention, and sexual services. By the end of the 1980s, the disjuncture between those claims and actual economic strategies made the hierarchical nature of gender relations increasingly problematic both on the home front and in society at large (Hansen 1997).

Economic Liberalization and Salaula

When multiparty elections in 1991 ushered in the third republic and a policy of rapid liberalization, the poor economic performance of the two previous decades had turned Zambia, in United Nations categories, into one of the world's least-developed countries. Continued foreign lending had turned Zambia's per capita debt into one of the highest in the developing world. During the last years of the second republic, after Kaunda had terminated loan arrangements with the IMF/World Bank in 1987 and reinstated them in 1989, initial attempts had been made to open up the economy by improving the investment climate, relaxing the foreign-exchange allocation system to allow imports by more enterprises, and lifting a wide range of price controls.

Like many other countries in Africa where one-party states with centralized economies were giving way to reform in the post–cold war era, Zambia in the 1990s was up for sale. Privatization of major national assets is under way in an international bidding process in which several once important players have reappeared. Tate and Lyle, for example, bought up the national sugar company that it owned before the company was nationalized. Meanwhile, established international mining interests with previous involvement in Zambia, like the Anglo-American Corporation, purchased major parts of the former parastatal mining corporation. A flood of imports are entering the country and being sold from new local branches of major South African chains, making clothing and housewares available to the medium-income and upscale consumer market. While this consumer segment is being targeted from abroad, all manner of imported goods are sold to ordinary consumers by street vendors and itinerant traders, some of whom work on commission for formal firms. Many of these goods enter Zambia illegally in the "suitcase" trade involving men and women who travel by bus, rail, private car, and plane to destinations within the region and beyond to purchase items that are in popular demand in Zambia.

Zambia's world of small-scale trade and manufacture developed as a parallel African economy during the colonial period, largely in urban areas, restrained by occupational and spatial regulations based on race. While the independent government did away with race as a principle in structuring the economy, trade restrictions on licensing requirements and the location of economic activity remained in effect. The state's unsuccessful control and ownership of the retail trade during most of the second republic helped accelerate the growth of an informal economy that has since expanded everywhere.

The gradual opening up of the economy since the late 1980s affected clothing supply by allowing direct commercial importation of secondhand clothing into Zambia. During the previous decade of deteriorating economic developments, the two government-owned textile factories, Kafue Textiles of Zambia, Ltd., and Mulungushi Textiles, operated in a near monopoly situation with very little competition from imports. The number of privately owned clothing manufacturing firms began to decline (*Times of Zambia,* 30 June 1988, 29 June 1989). Many factories operated at reduced capacity, and closures became common (*Times of Zambia,* "High Prices," 21 June 1986). Because of the difficulty of importing raw materials and technology, locally produced textiles and garments were not only expensive but also of poor

Figure 11   Billboard advertising fabrics manufactured by Kafue Textiles of Zambia, Ltd., near factory in Chilanga in 1992.
Author's photograph.

quality and drab style. What is more, inflation was eroding the already limited purchasing power of the vast majority of the population, and formal employment was shrinking. It is not surprising that Zambians flocked to their local markets once secondhand clothing began appearing in greater volume from the mid-1980s on and that its availability in rural areas was interpreted as a sign of progress. From the point of view of the growing number of consumers for whom expectations about leading better lives have been disappointed, the role of clothing as an index of well-being and a mediator of widespread sensibilities was accentuated rather than diminished.

By the mid-1980s imported secondhand clothing was already known by a name of its own in Lusaka, Eastern Province, and Southern Province.[3] This term is *salaula,* a Bemba word that means "to select from a pile in the manner of rummaging." In the border region of Malawi, the Nyanja term *kaunjika,* meaning "to pile up," "to heap," is often used, while *kombo* is the term still used in Luapula for secondhand clothing. The trade in this commodity across the Zaire/Zambia border had continued since the post–World War II years with intermittent twists and turns, depending on political and economic developments in the two countries. By the mid-1980s "northern traders" from the regions adjacent to the border of Zaire and Tanzania were in fact transporting bales from Zaire all the way down to Lusaka. There the contents of the secondhand clothing bales were retailed from a few locations in the light industrial area and from Kamwala, at that time the capital's largest market that had been established for Africans during the colonial period. The longest-standing importers of secondhand clothes with this background whom I met during the course of my research began selling salaula in Lusaka in 1986 and 1987. One of these firms was owned by a Tanzanian African, and the other by two brothers of Namwanga background, an ethnic group on the border of Tanzania. Familiar with the brisk trade of secondhand clothes in Tanzania, the owners of both firms established modest enterprises in Lusaka and went on to build warehouses, importing salaula and other commodities. In Kitwe and Chipata, and probably elsewhere, some regular clothing stores added salaula to their inventory (*Times of Zambia,* "Salaula Defended," 21 June 1986, 13 June 1991).

Between 1989 and 1992 the direction of the flow of secondhand clothing from Zaire to Zambia changed. The reduction of the Zairean trade may be attributed to a combination of factors, including restrictions or outright harassment of Zairean traders operating in Zambia, the change of political regime in Zambia, and above all a series of political upheavals in Zaire. While the clothing-consuming public began to worry about a possible collapse of the salaula supply from Zaire, the Lusaka City Council briefly considered importing secondhand clothing from Europe to sell to the public at "cheap prices. But the project was shelved for unexplained reasons" (*Times of Zambia*, 19 November 1991). By 1992 hardly any traders in Lusaka imported used clothing from Zaire. Traders from Luapula now traveled all the way to Lusaka to purchase salaula.

Throughout the 1980s urban and rural Zambians increasingly relied on salaula because of the deterioration of the local textile industry, rapid inflation, and the overall economic decline that severely eroded their purchasing power during the last decade of Kaunda's second republic. In the popular view, after years of standing in queues and ending up empty handed because people had little money and clothing was not readily available, salaula made it possible for ordinary people to wear clothes rather than rags. It also enabled more consumers than ever before to make choices in a booming clothing market without having to be talked down to by hostile shopkeepers set on selling their limited range of dull clothes.

Salaula was popular in urban and rural areas alike. Rural areas, which in the mid-1980s I heard characterized with statements like "There is nothing there—they don't know sugar, tea, bread, clothes, what it is like," were described in 1992 with some optimism: "There is even salaula now." After the long hard years of the Kaunda regime's austerity programs and deteriorating terms of trade between rural and urban areas and between Zambia and the rest of the world, commentaries on the recent rapid increase in salaula availability and consumption expressed not only disenchantment with the previous government and its party but also the attainability of hopes and aspirations.

Not everyone, of course, praises salaula. In Zambia, as in some other countries in Africa, garment and textile manufacturers associations and labor unions have blamed the secondhand clothing import for destroying local industry and have criticized government for not adequately assessing tariffs and duties on imports of this commodity. Calling for "leveling the playing field" through tariffs and custom fees, such groups commonly allege without much foundation that secondhand clothing imports are charitable "donations" that escape taxation or are smuggled, thus reducing government revenue. While I turn to the politics of these arguments for Zambia in chapter 10, I wish to note here the two most important factors that must be reckoned with in evaluations of the effects of salaula consumption. One factor is the steady deterioration of purchasing power in Zambia since the mid-1970s and the impoverishment of a larger proportion of the population, which makes salaula the chief source of clothing for growing numbers of households across Zambia's rural and urban areas. The second factor has to do with the special powers of clothing in mediating notions of self and society, which make this commodity different from any other in terms of indexing welfare and development. That is to say, the economic and normative notions that converge in salaula consumption pertain to matters that go far beyond the supply-side arguments made by representatives of textile and garment manufacturing firms. In effect, people in Zambia want well-dressed bodies.

Crazy for Foreign

The popular Zambian columnist who once a week wrote under the name Kapwelwa Musonda in the *Times of Zambia* for more than thirty years reached the core of local clothing sensibilities in a 1981 piece called "Made in Zambia?" The young female public relations officer of this story had bought a dress "from the U.K." on installments from a Zambian Airways stewardess who visited offices to sell. "She just brought it from London and it is the latest thing in fashion. I hear this particular dress is the rage in Europe," she explained. Giving his story an ironic twist, Musonda has the woman meet several other women wearing the same dress. In the end she gives it to an office orderly, explaining, "I wouldn't want to be found dead in any dress made in Zambia" (*Times of Zambia,* 11 August 1981).

Acknowledging that some Zambians fly to Zimbabwe, Botswana, and even London to shop, Kapwelwa Musonda expressed his amazement "at our desire and preference for imported goods." The active engagement with things foreign connects Zambian preoccupations with clothing in the colonial period and at present. "It is difficult," said Ilsa Schuster (1979:80) in her study of white-collar women workers in Lusaka during the first half of the 1970s, "to exaggerate the hunger for a full wardrobe in the latest fashion trends from Britain or Italy." This hunger, she added, "is matched by a passion for variety and change." The demand for imported clothes is often remarked on negatively—if not explicitly, then by implication. Yet it is fairly easily accounted for in supply terms, as indicated by my discussions of the limited scope of the textile and garment industry during the late colonial period and after independence. There never were many locally manufactured garments available, especially for consumers looking for quality and fashion. But the desire for imported clothing has to do with factors other than supply. It is fueled by widespread Zambian preoccupations with cutting a fine figure. Consumers of both sexes who are able and willing to spend money on clothing have always shunned the products of the local garment industry (*Zambia Daily Mail,* 7 January 1982, 1 September 1995; *Times of Zambia,* 29 June 1989, p. 5). The attraction of salaula across Zambia's socioeconomic spectrum, except at the top, is precisely that it makes available a profusion of styles that allow consumers to put themselves together in garments that are "not very common" and are considered "unique" and "exclusive," as I discuss in chapter 8.

The fact that salaula is imported and not local enhances its attractiveness to local consumers. The "craze for foreign" that informs clothing consumption of both salaula and ready-made garments does not produce emulation in any direct sense. The Zambian clothing scene does not represent a passive copy of imported dress conventions. Fashion here, as elsewhere, always quotes existing styles, making them over in new ways. Clothing engagements pull in many directions, generating a creative tension in the meeting between local practices and ideas about dress and a variety of influences from elsewhere. Today these influences are not all Western inspired; some are products of increasingly active inter-African contacts. It is this tension that contributes creatively to the vitality and dynamism of the Zambian clothing scene, whose "new" combinations of elements continually shift. The emergent clothing system is always in process, its meanings generated in particular contexts, as I illustrate below.

New Culture

When President Chiluba took over after Kaunda's defeat in 1991, he presented himself to the nation in a double-breasted suit with matching tie and handkerchief. This style was rapidly picked up in the salaula markets, where tailors became busy restyling big trousers, closing jacket vents, and turning large single-breasted jackets into double-breasted ones. In fact, the safari suit disappeared almost overnight when President Chiluba chose to wear double-breasted suits. His dress style fitted well with Zambian men's clothing preferences, for they all hold that a man must have a proper suit. Some of the "new" men in power also dress Chiluba-style: in double-breasted suits with floral ties and matching handkerchiefs. The local term for this dress style is "new culture," which the press also uses for the liberalized economic regime and political opening up under President Chiluba and the new set of values supposedly ushered in by political and economic reforms.

The issue of women's dress has been less straightforward than men's during the third republic. Young women's wearing of miniskirts has provoked several ugly events involving public stripping, which I discuss below. The first lady, Vera Chiluba, vacillates between wearing highly tailored Western-style suits and dresses, often with hats, and increasingly elaborate chitenge outfits with headties or headwraps. Truly pan-African in their distribution, chitenge dresses offer Zambian women a garment in or through which their imagination and play work in ways that miniskirts, tight blouses, and jeans do not allow. Yet even in chitenge wear, as I discuss below, there are limits to how women can present their dressed bodies in public.

The details of the dress of President Chiluba and the first lady are observed with excruciating attention to detail and commented on widely. This includes the president's silk ties and handkerchiefs as well as his shoes, some of which have elevated heels or are dress boots with pointed toes and built-up heels (*Post,* 9 April 1997). But above all, the president's suits are in focus. Popular columnist Geoff Zulu described the men's clothing scene in 1995: "Since the advent of the third republic, Zambians have apparently discarded the famous Kaunda suits of the second republic for the more flamboyant Harrods or Saville Row or Serioes suits accompanied by what some people call 'new culture'" (*Sunday Mail,* 12 February 1995). When President Chiluba was seen wearing a high collar, fully buttoned-up, single-breasted pin-striped suit on some public occasions in 1997, his attire was likened to Kaunda's suit by the opposition paper, which lamented that his policies resembled Kaunda's but were even worse (*Post,* 18 July 1997). Judging from my watch of media reporting, the president was not seen wearing such suits in public again. Zambian men with whom I discussed this suit suggested that it was a present from President Mwinyi of Tanzania or President Kabila of the Democratic Republic of the Congo. And they commented that President Chiluba had visited the Congo too many times during the first months after Kabila assumed power in

Figure 12 "Yuss at Large," *The Post,* Wednesday, 14 May 1997.

May 1997. These observers viewed the president's dressed body as "quoting" past sources and making allusions to a political culture that is very different from that embodied in the "new culture" of the double-breasted suit.[4]

Zambian women's dressed bodies are subject to much more critical scrutiny than men's, and first lady Vera Chiluba's dress is no exception. "Much as I understand the new culture which accompanied the third republic, I am against the way of dressing of our first lady," wrote a Lusaka woman in a letter to a newspaper editor. As wife of a president, Vera Chiluba is regarded as an executive, she said. "It is not advisable for an executive to wear outfits with flamboyant colours," she argued, suggesting that "whoever furnishes the first lady's wardrobe supply her with clothes which reflect seriousness" (*Weekly Post,* 20–26 August 1993).

The first lady's mannerisms come in for criticism as well, as in a letter to the editor from a Lusaka man who expressed his "disgust" at seeing her with a nose ring on national television. "Nose rings," he said, "are acceptable in Asia but not in a country like this one, they are associated with low class wayward women of loose morals." He also wondered if the first lady had somebody to advise her on her wardrobe. "She must not embarrass us by wearing flamboyantly coloured tight fitting clothes which she has no body for," he argued. Commenting on the "ungraceful and uncultured" ways in which she pulled her facial muscles and eyelids, he asked, "Has she not gone to school to get groomed?" (*Post,* 29 May 1997). Another Lusaka writer, a woman, continued this theme: "while we appreciate her very humble background and education, she should learn to conform with modernity and avoid embarrassing mannerisms that are out of taste." Even in "African tradition," she went on, "it is absurd and unacceptable for an elderly woman to 'parade' herself in public like Vera" (*Post,* 26 November 1997). Not everyone agreed, of course, and at least one male commentator from Lusaka took the matter of the nose ring to refer to "cultural knowhow." "It is part of the rich Zambian cultural heritage, just as ear piercing, elbow and ankle rings . . . check out with the National Heritage Commission for the roots of some Zambian practices," he advised (*Post,* 4 June 1997).

The women with whom I discussed the first lady's dress style were less aggressive in their reactions than these commentators. Most of them thought that the first lady goes "too far" with her choice of clothing and that, to be sure, she needs a better fashion consultant. They wondered which tailor/s make her extravagant chitenge outfits. Vera Chiluba certainly bears the brunt of adversarial commentary that disparages her ordinary background and casts doubt on her seriousness and thus on her abilities and intentions with the Hope Foundation, a social welfare group she launched soon after her husband took office. As head of the foundation, she frequently tours the country-

Figure 13 "Yuss at Large," *The Post,* Tuesday, 29 July 1996.

side, visiting townships, hospitals, and prisons, delivering speeches about self-help, and leaving behind a trail of gifts, most of which have been donated to the foundation, among them salaula, chitenge, bedding, foodstuffs, drugs, sewing machines, and hammer mills. These activities do not take place without controversy. Doubting her motives, some NGOs have criticized the first lady for her "parading of poor people and distribution of handouts" (*Post,* 20 May 1998). The Hope Foundation's funding sources are uncertain, but clearly, in the view of many, advocating self-help to people who already are busy trying to make a living and presenting them with salaula and hammer mills is a stopgap that does little to relieve the country's extensive poverty.

The term *new culture* may well have conveyed the initial optimism many Zambians expressed about better opportunity and more access in their new multiparty state in the early 1990s. While the expectations of the wearers of new-culture suits and ties from salaula have faded considerably, consumers from most walks of life except the very wealthy continue to rummage the piles of salaula, putting their lives together as best they can. They do not rummage at random but follow normative cultural presuppositions about the dressed body that vary by class, region, and, above all, gender and age. In effect, diverse reactions to the Chiluba suit, the first lady's dress style, and miniskirts illustrate some of the highly ambiguous meanings about both freedom from needs and normative constraints that people in Zambia read into clothing consumption.

A Secondhand Clothing System of Provision

5 The Sourcing of Secondhand Clothing

How do the West's used clothes reach Zambia? Which processes and actors are involved in the rapid growth both of the export trade and the local consumption of secondhand clothing throughout much of Africa since the mid- to late 1980s? Worldwide exports of used clothing from North America and northwestern Europe increased dramatically in the last two decades. To be sure, the little-known role of the established charitable organizations in the commercial secondhand clothing trade casts unexpected light on the uneasy relationship of poverty to wealth that entangles both ends of this global commodity circuit.

The organization and significance of this rapidly growing export trade have changed in many ways since the post–World War II period, as have the circumstances that are shaping local clothing demands. The massive import of secondhand clothing in many African countries is a result of local and external developments that have to do with the opening up of centrally organized political economies. What is more, international humanitarian aid in the 1980s and 1990s became an important industry, affecting local livelihoods (de Waal 1997:65–85; Maren 1997; Sogge 1996). And more than ever before, both the supply and demand of used clothing are driven by concerns with fashion, individual dress styles, and "looks." Consumers in poor countries like Zambia are using their own judgment and taste when dressing in garments from the West's huge surplus of used clothing.

Part 2 of this book examines this system of provision from several angles. A system of provision, as I explained in the introduction, may be approached as a commodity specific chain of activities in the economic circuit between the West and Zambia, connecting questions about production, distribution, and consumption, and the cultural practices that surround them (Fine and Leopold 1993:15). The chapters that follow consider a variety of activities that constitute "the production" of secondhand clothing in the West; import, wholesale, and distribution practices through which salaula is brought into circulation in Zambia; and the local clothing retail scene. I examine the hard work involved in clothing consumption, and cultural practices that give local meaning and significance to salaula consumption. The politics that have arisen around salaula are far from trivial, and I explain why in the book's penultimate chapter.

The "production" of salaula consists of processes involved in the sourcing of secondhand clothing in the West, including activities entailed in realizing value from used garments through domestic and foreign clothing resale and textile fiber recycling. Before the clothes that we no longer want ever reach Africa and other export markets and after they have traveled from our closets as donations to the charitable organizations, they have been dealt with by textile salvagers and rag graders, brokers, national trade groups both of textile and waste recyclers and of thrift store owners and managers, and occasionally labor unions. The relevant parties in the Netherlands, for example, include the Centraal Bureau Fondsenwerving (central bureau of fund-raising) that oversees the collection efforts of the charitable organizations and to which they report; this bureau interacts on their behalf with government and the clothing-donating public vis-à-vis the commercial collectors.

These actors and many others, including container firms and shippers, play diverse roles in an immense, profitable, but barely examined worldwide trading network that exports millions of dollars worth of used clothing in a commodity trade that has grown more than sixfold worldwide over the last fifteen years. In the pages that follow, I briefly describe the overlapping activities of some of the chief players in the production process of secondhand clothing: the charitable organizations and for-profit used clothing resellers who are the chief source of this commodity; the rag traders and textile and waste recyclers who enhance its value; and the textile brokers and exporters, especially those involved in African markets. The chapter closes with a discussion of how the potential profit of used clothing is prompting deception, if not illegality, at many stages of the worldwide secondhand clothing trade.

"Producing" Secondhand Clothing

The secondhand clothing system of provision begins in private households and homes. Its largest single source is the garments consumers in the West give to charitable organizations such as the Salvation Army, Goodwill Industries, and St. Vincent de Paul in the United States, and Oxfam, Terre, Abbé Pierre, and Humana in Europe, to mention just a few. The economic potential of our clothing donations arises because of two circumstances: one is that consumers in the West purchase a large volume of textile products: in France in the early 1990s, for example, about 15 kilograms per person per year (*Chicago Tribune,* 13 October 1992, p. 6), and in the Netherlands and Germany 8–10 kilograms per individual a year (Wicks and Bigsten 1996:9); and the second is that today almost all textile fibers can be recycled. In short, the economic prospect of this trade arises from the huge surplus of used garments, each of which may have many possible future lives. What is more, growing environmental concerns in the West in recent years have enhanced both the profitability and respectability of the rag trade and given its practitioners a new cachet as textile salvagers and waste recyclers. A recent advertisement for used denim garments by a Brooklyn-based exporter, for example, described its products not only as having "a great price point" but also as being "environmentally friendly—100% recycled" (*Journal of Commerce,* 20 April 1999).

According to a United States–based industry spokesperson, today's international secondhand clothing trade might be considered a "win-win-win-win situation": the purchase and sale of used garments from charities relieves consumers of unwanted clothing, charities obtain much-needed funds, textile recyclers find a reliable supply of clean used clothing, and people in developing countries—where much of the clothing goes—have the opportunity to purchase affordable garments (Winchester 1995:105). We might add to this "win list" that the secondhand clothes export also keeps a large volume of used clothing out of landfills.

Long-established charitable organizations are the chief recipients of used clothes, although consumers also donate garments to statewide and local organizations such as school and community groups. Some also pass better garments on to used clothing stores that sell on consignment, reducing their own risks by paying only for the merchandise that sells. Judging from scattered evidence, in the United States in recent years two of the largest national charitable organizations that accept clothing donations and operate thrift stores, the Salvation Army and Goodwill Industries, between them took in about 75 percent of the used clothing donated nationwide (*Los Angeles Times,* 28 July 1997, p. A1).

There is little substantive evidence of how much clothing in fact is donated to charitable organizations in the United States or of how they use it. It is certain, however, that annual giving to nonprofit organizations in general has grown since the mid-1980s (Nonprofit Almanac 1996–97:2–3). The financial information provided by organizations submitting tax-exempt information to the Internal Revenue Service (IRS) does not provide specific data on donations in kind. And surveys of giving rarely list and differentiate between gifts in kind (e.g., AAFRC 1998; Nonprofit Almanac 1996–97). Some nonprofit organizations, for example the Salvation Army, provide blank receipts, which donors fill in with their own value estimate. Some donors itemize such information, which the IRS does not analyze systematically.[1] This is much in contrast, for example, to the Netherlands, where national legislation mandates release of detailed information about both clothing donations and their resale. Some states in the United States require charitable thrift stores to provide evidence of this relationship to the donating and consuming public.

A few studies, my own interviews, and intermittent reporting in the news media permit a sketch of the situation in the United States in the 1990s. Clothing collections by charities produces an enormous yield, by one estimate some 100 million tons annually (*Los Angeles Times,* 29 October 1992). About half or less of these clothes reaches the charity thrift stores, according to this report, while the rest is sold in bulk to more than 300 firms in the clothing-recycling business. A very small portion is given outright to the poor. Indications of what proportion of donated clothes the charitable organizations sell in thrift stores and to commercial graders differ, depending on source, regional variation, and shifting developments of export markets. Environmental concerns may play a role as well.

At Goodwill operations in Kentucky in 1995, for example, about 60 percent of the donated clothes were sold in local thrift stores, while 39 percent of the rest that were deemed to be of "exportable quality" were sold to textile salvagers, and 1 percent simply were thrown away (*Courier-Journal,* 30 December 1996). The Salvation Army's central operation in Chicago sold between 25 and 30 percent of donated clothing in its downtown store in 1997, disposing of most of the rest to graders (Graham Allan, 28 July 1998, Chicago). In 1998 Illinois Salvation Army thrift stores participated in a voucher program, providing three free work outfits to welfare recipients participating in a work program (*Chicago Tribune,* 5 October 1998). The Salvation Army regularly provides clothing donations as disaster relief.

A recent academic survey of Goodwill and St. Vincent de Paul thrift-store operations nationwide suggests that these two organizations receive some 700 million pounds of used clothing as consumer donations annually (Francis, Butler, and Gallett 1995:28). About one-third of the donated clothing was sold in the thrift stores of these organizations while one-half was sold to the textile salvage industry, primarily for export. Only a small proportion of the donated clothing was sold to recyclers of textile waste and an even smaller portion was disposed of in landfills (28–29). Some organizations include additional steps before assigning clothes that do not move easily to the bulk heap for commercial resale. Goodwill branches in Santa Ana and Long Beach, California, for example, hold daily "as is" sales that are attended by swap meet and street vendors who purchase clothes at $1.80 a pound (*Los Angeles Times,* 28 July 1997, p. A13). Goodwill Industries in Toronto had a "buy-the-pound" room at the back of the headquarters where shoppers in 1994 paid one Canadian dollar a pound for all that they could carry. More than half of the clothes donated at Goodwill's Toronto operations in 1994 was compressed into huge 2,000-pound bales and sold at $0.15 a kilogram to the textile salvagers, largely used-clothing dealers, most of whom were targeting the secondhand clothing export market (Chris Thornton, 3 October 1994, Toronto).

The resale of secondhand clothing takes many forms. In addition to the long-established nonprofit organizations like the Salvation Army and Goodwill Industries, local school and community groups raise funds for their activities by reselling donated clothing. The for-profit secondhand clothing business, largely specialty oriented, sources from textile recyclers and scours estate sales and urban and rural flea markets. There are used-clothing chain stores as well, among them Ragstock in the Midwest and Urban Outfitters, that purchase used clothing in bulk. The list includes, according to a news report, a publicly traded company, Grow Biz International Inc. of Minneapolis, with 19 corporate stores and some 1,000 franchises, and planning to open another 250 during 1997 (*Wall Street Journal,* 20 January 1997, p. 1). Other traders specialize, particularly for export, in very specific garments such as jeans and sneakers (*New York Times,* 22 August 1994). Vintage stores like Chicago's Hollywood Mirror recently established outlets in Japan. A trade group, the National Association of Resale and Thrift Shops, estimates that membership during 1996 increased 12 percent, to 1,000 (*Wall Street Journal,* 20 January 1997, p. 1). Between 1990 and 1999 in Britain, the number of secondhand resale stores on high street grew by two-thirds, with turnover more than doubling (*Independent,* 10 February 1999). In short, the growth potential of the clothing resale market appears to be tremendous at both the low end and the upscale end.

The nonprofit thrift shops of some of the large charities like Goodwill Industries and the Salvation Army provide employment and job training. Other charities, including the American Cancer Society, operate their stores for profit with a mixture of volunteers and paid managers. The clothes that do not sell in the specialty secondhand stores are given to local charities, according to some store operators, or sold in bulk to wholesale textile recyclers, as are a large portion of the clothes consumers donate to the charitable organizations.

Most people who donate garments to charitable organizations are not aware of how their donations are disposed of. Put simply, consumers donate so much clothing that the charities cannot handle it. This constitutes a topic to which the news media occasionally return, harping on how much of the clothing donated to charities does not reach the poor and needy but is sold to textile recyclers, who are reported to make tremendous profits from the resale and export of clothes. Even then, the work of the charitable organizations does benefit from the revenues created by such sales. Goodwill Industries and the Salvation Army combined are reported to take in nearly $100 million a year from secondhand clothing sales (*NBC Nightly News,* 7 December 1997). They use this revenue to support a variety of programs such as Goodwill's job training for the disabled and the Salvation Army's shelter and treatment programs for homeless people, alcoholics, and drug abusers (*Los Angeles Times,*

28 July 1997, p. A13). In the United States the Salvation Army is the largest single provider of such services, which are supported entirely by funds generated from resale operations.

Major charities like the Salvation Army and Goodwill Industries are considering strategies to avoid selling the surplus clothes, unsorted in bulk, to the textile salvagers. They want to steer the accumulation of profit away from the middlemen, that is, the textile salvagers and recyclers who resell and export, and to harness more money for their own programs from clothing donations. There are other models. For example, one nongovernmental organization (NGO) headquartered in Scandinavia, Development Aid from People to People (DAPP), operating under the name Humana in many European countries, sends unsorted clothing to Third World countries, especially in southern Africa.[2] Sorting the clothes in Zambia, DAPP in turn sells them wholesale and resale, using the income to finance local development projects. Like the major charitable organizations, it also uses commercial middlemen to dispose of part of its surplus European clothing collections. Suggestions for different strategies considered in the United States and Canada include increased in-house fiber recycling and the pooling of clothing donations from clothes-collecting charitable organizations, expediting its movements, and making it available for humanitarian assistance and development (Raymond Braddock, 4 October 1997, Salvation Army, Toronto; John Mitchell, 7 November 1994, Salvation Army, Ottawa; Chris Thornton, 3 October 1994, Goodwill Industries, Toronto).

Such strategies have ramifications for the costs and personnel needs of the charitable organizations. Some of today's recycling is expensive, as it requires clean rags of natural fiber. Additional labor and management skills are needed for in-house sorting of the vast surplus of donated clothes into different grades and export categories and for organizing local and foreign logistics of an export trade. Some European charities have found the resale dimension to be so troublesome that they are making little use of secondhand clothing donations in emergency situations any longer, as was the case for Red Cross and Oxfam operations in Zambia in 1993; and some no longer collect clothes at all, including Caritas and Brot für die Welt (bread for the world) in Germany (Wicks and Bigsten 1996:35). Meanwhile, in an effort to ensure good returns on their sale of used clothing, Goodwill and the Salvation Army in the United States are reported to be using brokers to stimulate competitive bidding by the textile salvagers (*Los Angeles Times,* 28 July 1997, p. A13; *Sun,* 28 September 1997).

The charitable organizations use several parts of the textile-recycling network. Because they lack skilled personnel, and because used clothing is a potentially profitable commodity, charities in North America and Europe commonly contract out the right to collect in their name to commercial dealers, some of whom also manage charity thrift stores in return for a percentage of earnings. Examples in the mid-1980s included ten thrift stores of Amvets (American Veterans of Foreign Wars) in Illinois, California Council of the Blind, and Disabled American Veterans in many states (*Los Angeles Times*, 27 September 1987). In such transactions, a large share goes to the thrift-store operator. For example, in a Florida arrangement in the mid-1980s, the store operators made $2.55 for each dollar turned over to the charity (*Los Angeles Times*, 27 September 1987). In 1992 Goodwill branches on Long Island offered a textile salvage company a flat rate of $350 a bin plus 5 cents a pound, recognizing also the cost of the bin, maintenance, transportation, and processing costs (*New York Times*, 9 February 1992).

Across the United States and western Europe, competition for used clothes increased during the 1990s. The entry of the former soviet republics and east bloc countries into the secondhand clothing market since the early 1990s increased the price at source, prompting expanded collections to meet the growing demand. Charitable organizations and commercial dealers alike are looking for wider access to the increasingly valuable supply of donated clothing. Depending on local zoning regulation, they try out a variety of solicitation techniques in addition to the conventional store drop-off, among them door-to-door collection, which yields a better-quality product, telephone appeals, curbside pickup, and outdoor collection bins in highly frequented places. In a recent pilot program in southeastern Wisconsin, the county granted Goodwill Industries access, for a fee, to donated clothing at its recycling facility. County recycling trucks collected the clothes on the curbside in residential areas. The demand for used clothing was so high that local branches of Disabled American Veterans, St. Vincent de Paul, and the American Council of the Blind protested this decision as detrimental to their own clothing-collection efforts (*Milwaukee Journal Sentinel*, 11 February 1999). The commercial clothing recyclers in their turn are competing with one another for contracts with the charitable organizations. In countries where commercial solicitation is legal, for example, Belgium, textile salvagers lobby municipal governments for permission to collect locally and, for a fee, make arrangements with supermarkets for the placement of collection bins.

Textile Salvaging/Recycling

Because every piece of clothing has many potential future lives, textile recycling is a lucrative business. The textile recycling industry, today's version of a previous era's rag trade, comprises salvagers and graders, fiber recyclers,

Figure 14 *(top)* Dropping used clothing in UFF (Development Aid from People to People) bin in Copenhagen 1997. The caption on the bin means "clothing collection for the benefit of people in the Third World." Author's photograph.

Figure 15 *(middle)* Humana secondhand clothing store on high street in Brussels, 1996. Author's photograph.

Figure 16 *(bottom)* Customers purchasing clothes "buy-the-pound" at Goodwill Toronto store in 1994. Author's photograph.

and used-clothing dealers, brokers, and exporters. "Used clothing" includes not only garments but also shoes, handbags, hats, belts, draperies, and linens. The textile recyclers sort and grade clothing and apparel into many categories, some for the domestic vintage or upscale market, and others for export; some for industrial use as rags, and others for fiber. Blue jeans, especially Levi Strauss 501, the original button-fly jean created in 1853 for miners and cowboys in the West, are popular in many European countries and find a particularly huge market in Japan. Sneakers get new lives overseas too, for example, Nike's Air Jordan (*News and Observer,* 22 November 1997). The traders who deal in used commodities with special appeal tour college campuses, advertise in local papers, and organize trade-ins with established department stores and firms.[3]

Wool garments are another used commodity with a specific flow, exported from the United States and Europe to Italy, where since the late nineteenth century the world's largest wool-regeneration industry has been located in Prato, near Florence (Piore and Sabel 1984:214). Here wool is unraveled, dyed, and respooled, ready to be used again. For instance, from the operations of his two Sacramento-based textile salvaging firms, Markess Export Company and American Wiping Rag Company, Lorenzo Gomez exported 15 percent of his merchandise to Italy for reprocessing in the late 1980s (*Sacramento Bee,* 26 March 1990). Some of the nonwool garments in consignments destined for Prato subsequently travel to Resina, between Herculaneum and Napoli, where they are retailed in open-air markets much like those in Africa. Italian commercial textile dealers also purchase from this stream for local store sales and export. One such dealer claimed to be the largest Napoli-based secondhand clothing exporter to Africa and that he was controlling the Italian secondhand clothing export to East Africa (A. Formisano, 17 March 1998, Portici/Napoli).

The size and scope of the textile recycling industry is likely to be more diverse than reported in information provided by the Council for Textile Recycling, which was founded in the early 1990s.[4] The 350 members of this group removed annually, according to a fact sheet, some 2.5 billion pounds of postconsumer textile waste. Recycling 93 percent of the collected textiles, these firms export more than half in fairly equal proportions of used clothing and fibers for reprocessing, and sell a quarter to rag graders and fiber recyclers; about 7 percent ends up in landfills (table 1).

Among the more than 300 commercial firms in the textile recycling industry in the United States in the mid-1990s, approximately 50 large textile salvagers (rag graders) did the bulk purchasing by the trailer load or in bales from both charities and for-profit organizations and shops. Grossman Industries, Inc., of Columbus, Ohio, which has been in the textile recycling busi-

Table 1. Destinations of U.S. Recycled Postconsumer Textile
Products (percentages)

	Domestic	Export	Total
Used clothing		35	35
Fiber for reprocessing	7	26	33
Wipers (rags)	25		25
Landfill	7		7
Total	39	61	100

Source: Council for Textile Recycling [1997?].

ness for over fifty years, sourced used clothing from a ten-state region in
1989, stretching from New York City to Chicago (*Business First–Columbus,*
6 November 1989). When in 1990 Lorenzo Gomez's eight-ton truck from
Markess Export Company made the rounds of thrift shops in northern California, it collected about 100,000 pounds of used clothing a week (*Sacramento Bee,* 26 March 1990). At factory setups, the collected garments and
apparel are then sorted. The employees unbind the large bales and do a first
rough sorting into resalable clothes and rags. Vintage clothing is put aside.
Torn and stained items are put away, only to reappear at a later stage of this
process as industrial rags (wipers) or to be ground into fiber for car insulation,
rugs, or blankets (*Los Angeles Times,* 29 October 1992). A second sorting dis-
tinguishes numerous categories by garment and fabric type. Then the clothes
are graded by quality, compressed, and baled. The sorting categories reckon
with changing seasonal demands, different markets, and occasionally with
customer specification.

Some firms operate their own rag companies, thus ensuring not only constant supply but also, and perhaps more profitably, more control of the production process and earnings. This is the case of Continental Textile
Corporation of Milwaukee, which established Wipeco, a wiping-rag company in Chicago, and of American Wiping Rag Company, set up by Sacramento-based Markess Export Company. The largest commercial sorting
operation in western Europe, which in the mid-1990s sorted at least 250 tons
of secondhand clothing a day, is the recently established Boer and Smaal
Holding, comprising four sorting plants in the Netherlands (Gebotex, Marbo
Recycling, Rutimex, and C. Boer and Zoon), one in Belgium (Evadam), plus
one commercial collecting company, Curitas, also in Belgium. The head of
its international sales division in 1996 was eighty-two-year-old Gerard
Mendel, founder of Evadam and Curitas, who began his secondhand clothing–collection career after World War II by purchasing surplus military
clothing in Europe (31 July 1996, Brussels). In those days, he told a reporter,

Figure 17 Opening plastic bags of donated clothing at Humana's sorting plant near Utrecht, 1997. Author's photograph.

Figure 18 Sorting bins at Plevier's sorting plant near Roosendaal, the Netherlands, 1997. Author's photograph.

secondhand clothing was referred to as Congo, perhaps not so surprising in view of Belgium's colonial history (*Knack,* 29 May 1996, p. 20).

After the final sorting the better grades are exported to Central American countries such as Costa Rica, Honduras, and Guatemala, and to Chile in South America. The lowest grade goes to African and Asian countries. Most recyclers compress sorted garments into 50-kilogram bales while some press unsorted bulk clothing into bales weighing 300 or even 500 kilograms. The bales are wrapped in waterproof plastic, bound with metal or plastic straps, placed in containers, and shipped. Depending on legislation in the receiving country, the clothes may or may not be disinfected and fumigated before they are shipped.

In both Europe and North America many of these textile recycling firms are family-owned businesses that have been in the trade for a long time. Others are relative newcomers, sometimes recent immigrants who know the potential of the secondhand clothing trade from their former homes in Third World countries. The identifiable participants are firms of Jewish and Middle Eastern background with long-term involvement with the textile and clothing trade, and more recently established firms with backgrounds in south Asia, particularly India and Pakistan, some of whom are recent immigrants to Europe and North America from Africa. One Toronto dealer with Middle Eastern background grew up in Lubumbashi in Zaire in a family involved in the import of secondhand clothes. Leaving Zaire during the early 1970s, he established his own firm in Toronto. We know this trade and the market, he told me (Griffin Minimpex, 4 October 1994, Toronto). The Italian exporter I spoke to near Napoli had lived in pre–civil war Rwanda, where he became familiar with the popularity of this trade. Still others learned about the secondhand clothing trade from being employed in it and then starting out on their own, such as members of the Ellison family, introduced below.

Information from the Council for Textile Recycling suggests that the textile salvage industry as a whole in the United States in the first half of the 1990s employed some 10,000 semiskilled and marginally employable workers at the first sorting level and some 7,000 workers at the final stage. The sorting is largely manual and very labor intensive. Many operations use a system of barrels or bins for different categories of clothes while others use a conveyor-belt system. Some combine the two, as I found at Humana's sorting plant near Utrecht, one of Europe's largest single operations in terms of volume. The minimum wage and unpleasant environment that often characterize this work have prompted strike action in the United States. From northwestern Europe where minimum wages and social benefits are much higher than in the United States, some clothing recyclers have relocated their sorting operations in eastern Europe, where wages are lower and the demand

Figure 19 Compressing a 500-kilogram bale of used clothing at Humana's sorting plant near Utrecht, 1997. Author's photograph.

Figure 20 Five-hundred-kilogram bales ready for shipment at Humana's sorting plant near Utrecht, 1997. Author's photograph.

for secondhand clothes is growing. At least two of the twenty firms I con-
tacted in the Netherlands in 1997 had relocated their sorting operations in
Hungary.

The long-standing sourcing relationship between charitable organizations
and textile recyclers may be changing. Some reports indicate that the textile
salvaging/grading business has declined in recent years. Baltimore "used to
be the capital of used clothing" in the post–World War II period. The "nation's biggest" salvage operation, according to one source, Schapiro and
Whitehouse, graded a million pounds of used clothing every week in the
1960s, serving as a training ground for people who set up their own operations (*Sun,* 28 September 1997). But in less than a generation, the number of
salvage firms in Baltimore dropped from fifteen to two. Major recyclers in
Dallas, St. Louis, and Philadelphia have closed as well (*Sun,* 28 September
1997). Some recyclers blame the charitable organizations, which are increasingly using brokers to drive up the market price, thus bypassing the salvagers.
The rapid growth in worldwide demand for secondhand clothing during the
first half of the 1990s might have intensified the relationship between charitable organizations and brokers, which is problematic in any circumstance.

Most of the large textile recyclers in the United States involved in buying
and reselling for export are near port cities along either coast and the Great
Lakes. The decline in the number of salvage firms in Baltimore may have to
do, among other things, with the shift of containerized cargo shipping away
from its port in favor of the Port of New York and New Jersey, which has
deeper navigation channels. Because secondhand clothing from the United
States is a desired commodity in Mexico, where its import for resale is prohibited, it is retailed in stores and warehouses along the U.S. side of the border from the Gulf of Mexico to the Pacific Ocean (*New York Times,* 12
November 1997).

In Europe for historical and geographic reasons, the chief commercial
sorting capacity is available in the Netherlands and Belgium within easy access to the world's major ports. Among the world's largest importers and exporters of secondhand clothing, commercial firms in these countries sort and
grade tons of secondhand clothing exported in bulk from Germany and Scandinavia, where the local capacity to handle this stage of the process is very
limited. In 1983 in West Germany, for example, 49 percent of the country's
used clothing was exported to the Netherlands and Belgium-Luxembourg for
sorting and 60 percent of the country's used wool products to Italy for reprocessing (Hopfinger 1985:209). In Denmark there are a few small commercial
textile salvagers and one large firm, Tåstrup Produkthandel (Tåstrup product
trading), with which local charitable organizations such as the Salvation
Army and International Children's Aid have made contractual arrangements.

This firm was established in 1917 by the grandfather of the present owner and expanded particularly during and after World War II. It exports to Africa, the Middle East, and eastern Europe (*Politiken,* 28 August 1996). Given the limited sorting capacity, it is not surprising that close to half of Denmark's total export of secondhand clothing in recent years has gone to Belgium-Luxembourg and the Netherlands (Danmarks Statistik 1988–97). In the southern region of Norway in 1999, the Salvation Army loaded 90 percent of its clothing donations in the bags in which they were received directly onto trucks bound for sorting centers in the Netherlands (Gunhild Hagestad, personal communication, 9 May 1999).

The news media have been quick to point out that, while textile recycling may not make much money for the people who do the labor-intensive work of sorting, the profits of this trade have made some recyclers very wealthy. Among them is Ed Stubin, who in 1987 described himself as "one of the top ten" exporters to Africa (*New York Times,* 16 February 1987). He is president of Trans-American Trading Company in Brooklyn, started by his father in the early 1940s. The Domsey Trading Corporation in Brooklyn was founded by German Jewish immigrants fifty years ago and today is run by the grandchildren. This firm, which has often been in the news because of labor violations, is estimated to have grossed $40 million in 1996 and is described as one of the largest secondhand clothing exporters on the East Coast (*New York Times,* 9 June 1997). One of the big-timers in the trade is California-based Vahan Chamlian of Armenian background, described in 1997 "as the world's largest dealer" in secondhand clothes. Arriving from Lebanon some forty years ago, today he owns three sorting plants and grossed $78.6 million in 1996 from the recycling and export of secondhand clothes. Chamlian recently opened an operation in Germany where secondhand clothing from the United States is sorted to fill orders from across Europe (*Los Angeles Times,* 28 July 1997). Last but not least, the Ellisons today run thrift stores in almost every state and are descendants of five Ellison brothers, two of whom split from the Salvation Army in 1949 and 1951 over disagreements about how to organize used-clothing operations. Nearly 100 Ellisons together with their in-laws, associates, and former employees are said to be involved in this specialized trade (*Los Angeles Times,* 27 September 1987).

Export

Anecdotal accounts from the exporting and importing ends of the international trade in secondhand clothes tell a story of growth over the last decades, with noticeable increases during the first half of the 1990s. The precise details of this trade are elusive for many reasons. The chief source, commodity trade statistics compiled by the UN on used clothing based on reports from individual countries, is incomplete. For example, Zambia has not reported any import data for this commodity to the UN since 1978. References to used-clothing exports to Zambia are available intermittently in the commodity export listings of other countries, for example, the United States. Some statistics list volume while others list U.S. dollar value, which introduces problems not only of consistency and comparability but also of changes in exchange rates.[5]

In general the information provided by the UN commodity statistics must be approached with many qualifications for the reasons discussed above and for the widespread tendency to underestimate used-clothing export consignments in terms of both volume and value. And even if they are available, country-specific statistics on imports of used clothing are not very accurate because of a variety of illegal practices surrounding the import, including smuggling across international borders. Finally, while there are no UN worldwide statistics on used clothing for charitable exports in crisis situations, a proportion of used clothing collected and exported from donors in the West for emergency purposes is sold for profit on arrival, thus ending up in the commercial market.

Drawing on UN commodity trade statistics for exports of used clothing, Steven Haggblade (1990) has provided a profile for 1980. The United States was then, as it is today, the world's largest exporter in terms of both volume and value, followed by Germany, the Netherlands, Belgium-Luxembourg, and Japan. In 1980 these top five exporters supplied more than 90 percent of the world's used clothing, the United States alone contributing some 45 percent (510). As table 2 indicates, while these five countries have remained the world's top exporters, some other countries have become increasingly involved since 1990. But if the United States is a major used-clothing exporter in terms of volume and value, its per capita clothing collection is far below

Table 2. Major Secondhand Exporters, 1980–95 (U.S.$ millions)

	1980	1990	1993	1995
United States	73.1	174.2	292.2	340.5
Germany	22.8	118.4	149.3	187.0
Netherlands	18.3	91.4	87.1	126.9
Belgium-Luxembourg	16.7	84.4	86.3	110.7
Japan	9.0	46.7	39.1	50.2
Italy		41.1	52.7	68.2
United Kingdom		34.2	60.9	88.4
France		35.6	39.1	47.0

Sources: 1980 figures, Haggblade 1990:512; 1990 and 1993 figures, UN 1995:60; 1995 figures, UN 1996:60.

that of several other countries in the West. Belgium-Luxembourg and the Netherlands were among the major exporters in terms of weight of used clothing per capita in 1990 with 6.6 kilograms and 3.5 kilograms, respectively; in comparison, Denmark exported 1.5 kilograms and the United States 0.55 kilograms per capita during that year. The high figures for the first two countries probably reflect their role as major importers of secondhand clothing for sorting and subsequent reexport (Wicks and Bigsten 1996:5).

Between 1980 and 1995 worldwide exports of secondhand clothing grew sixfold: from a value of U.S. $207 million in 1980 to $1,410 million in 1995 (Haggblade 1990:508; UN 1996:60).[6] In 1995 the United States exported some U.S. $340 million worth of used clothing, compared to U.S. $174 million in 1990. According to a U.S. Commerce Department specialist, that amount represents only what is shipped abroad in compressed bales and does not include garments piled loosely in containers as filler or smuggled across the Mexican border. He estimated the total export to be double the official figure (*Plain Dealer,* 25 January 1998).

The already large share of the United States in the worldwide export may increase even further in the near future if recently proposed policy passed in 1998 by the European Union (EU) on waste disposal, including secondhand clothing, from member countries is in fact implemented as intended. Third World countries who have agreed not to accept the import of particular categories of waste from EU member states might in fact not have fully appreciated the inclusion of secondhand clothing on the list of prohibited waste categories. Concerns have been raised about this matter in Ghana and Uganda, both countries that conventionally have imported large volumes of secondhand clothing from Europe, and are likely to be raised by other countries as well (Africa News Service, 31 December 1997; BBC World Broadcasts, 6 January 1998; *Indian Ocean Newsletter,* 10 January 1998).[7]

Table 3 lists the world's top ten Third World importers of used clothing. Among them in 1980 were Tunisia and three countries in sub-Saharan Africa, with Rwanda the first by rank in terms of value of imports, followed by Togo and Zaire. The 1990 top ten importers still contained Tunisia and three countries in sub-Saharan Africa, headed by Nigeria, then Benin and Zaire. Tunisia remained in the top ten in 1995, with Uganda in the lead role as a major sub-Saharan African importer of used clothing, followed by Tanzania and Niger.

Aside from featuring several poor countries in Africa, what is striking about this list of the largest Third World net importers of used clothing is the presence of Asian countries with large export production of textile and garments, such as Pakistan, Singapore, India, and Hong Kong. Unlike the Netherlands and Belgium-Luxembourg with large imports but net exports of used clothing, these countries in Asia appear to be importing used clothing

Table 3. Major Third World Secondhand Clothing Importers, 1980–95

Rank	1980	1990	1993	1995
1	Pakistan	India	Hong Kong	Singapore
2	Bangladesh	Pakistan	Singapore	India
3	Tunisia	Hong Kong	Mexico	Tunisia
4	Rwanda	Nigeria	Tunisia	Malaysia
5	Togo	Singapore	India	Uganda
6	Zaire	Tunisia	Chile	Tanzania
7	Jordan	Benin	Malaysia	Pakistan
8	South African Customs Union	Zaire	Pakistan	Chile
9	Syria	Malaysia	Benin	Niger
10	Singapore	Chile	Ghana	Nigeria

Sources: 1980 figures, Haggblade 1990:512; 1990, 1993, and 1995 figures, UN 1996:60.

for domestic consumption at the same time as local textile and garment production is targeting the export market. I return to this observation in chapter 10 when I assess the criticism that secondhand clothing imports are destroying the local garment industry.

Taken together, the countries in sub-Saharan Africa import a vast proportion of world exports of used clothing, amounting in 1995 to close to one-fourth of total exports worth U.S. $379 million, up from $117 million in 1990 (UN 1995:60, 1996:60). The listing of the top ten Third World importers of used clothing indicates shifts in this import to specific countries. In Zambia the value of secondhand clothing imports from all sources was estimated to increase from $1,181,000 in 1990 to $6,881,000 in 1993, decreasing to $3,651,000 in 1995 (UN 1995:60, 1996:60). In 1994 more than half of these imports were from the United States alone (UN 1994:258).

By and large the countries in sub-Saharan Africa have not attracted much attention for trade and investment by firms in the United States. Good export prospects were noted in 1987 for used clothing, which a trade publication described as "a non-traditional export that has continued to expand its roles in Africa" (*Business America,* 25 April 1988). While the secondhand clothing export might not be highlighted during formal U.S. trade promotion events in Africa, it has been featured at other venues. At a 1992 seminar in Chicago, "How to Succeed in Exporting and Importing to Africa," sponsored by the U.S. Small Business Administration, at least one participant heard what she wanted to hear. Veronica DePart hoped to find markets for her used-clothing business. She was especially interested "in Togo and Senegal because they have a used clothing market. But most of the used clothing sold in those countries comes from Europe" (*Chicago Tribune,* 26 March 1992).

In a 1993 publication entitled *Used Apparel Markets in Subsaharan Africa,* the U.S. Department of Commerce acknowledged the potential of the used-clothing market in Africa. That year, used apparel was the eighth largest export to the region, among the top thirty-five of all exports from the United States to twenty-eight sub-Saharan African countries. Angola headed the list in terms of imports by value, followed by Benin, Tanzania, Ghana, Senegal, Djibouti, Zaire, and Zambia, which imported $3,454,000 worth of used clothing, comprising 5.1 percent of all that country's imports from the United States (U.S. Department of Commerce 1993:2–3). The 1997 updated version of this publication listed used apparel as the sixth largest U.S. export to sub-Saharan Africa. The African trade grew almost 38 percent, from U.S. $67 million in 1993 to over U.S. $92 million in 1996 (U.S. and Foreign Commercial Service and U.S. Department of State 1997:1–2). The publications contain notes about the legal barriers for such imports in some countries, for example, Nigeria and Ethiopia—tariffs; banking, credit, and financial arrangements; and contact addresses.

The emergence and disappearance of specific countries, among them Rwanda and Zaire, from the top ten importers indicate how quickly African used-clothing markets change. African markets are very volatile, not only because of civil strife and war, as in the case of Rwanda and Zaire, but also in terms of legislation guiding the entry or prohibition of secondhand clothing import. For example, Senegal observes a 2,000-ton quota on used-clothing imports, and Mali imposes tariff duties in the range of 61–86 percent, ostensibly to protect the domestic garment and textile industry (U.S. and Foreign Commercial Service and U.S. Department of State 1997:20, 23). Above all, monetary policies affecting exchange rates and the very availability of foreign exchange influence the ability of local wholesalers to import. Many African governments come and go, and military regimes and one-party states often tighten the flow of money out of the country by restricting imports, as was the case in Zambia during most of the second republic (1972–91).

There are ample examples of quick shifts in African secondhand clothing markets brought about by political and economic changes. When Cameroon's oil-based economy was in deep trouble, secondhand clothing imports placed that country in the top ten Third-World importers in 1994. Under an IMF/World Bank-supported structural adjustment program, the government reduced civil-service salaries and retrenched thousands of workers. The CFA franc was devalued by 50 percent, and the secondhand clothing trade boomed (Inter Press Service, 10 October 1994). Imports from the United States alone increased 200 percent between 1993 and 1996 (U.S. and Foreign Commercial Service and U.S. Department of State 1997:8). And less than a year after the fratricidal war in Congo-Brazzaville in 1997, during which many people lost homes and property, the secondhand clothing markets in Brazzaville, the capital, were expanding. In a region known for its highly stylized dress preference for expensive, brand-name, imported clothing "from Paris," epitomized in "la sape" (Gandoulou 1984, 1989), residents now flock to used-clothing markets to buy affordable clothing referred to locally as *sola* (to choose; IPS Service Francophone, 4 July 1998).

Government policies in African countries significantly shape the local secondhand clothing trade. In Tunisia in the 1960s and 1970s, for example, the government determined the volume of secondhand clothing imported as well as the amounts distributed to the provinces. Two firms controlled the import of unsorted 100-kilogram bales, largely from the United States. The imports of poor quality, around 40 percent of the total, were turned into rags and reexported, wool to Italy and the rest to elsewhere in Europe. Some 70 percent of the remaining clothing of good quality was reexported to African and Middle Eastern countries. The clothing sold locally was retailed to urban licensed traders and to regional societies in the provinces (van Groen and Lozer 1976).

Some countries have at one time or other banned this import, among them the Côte d'Ivoire, Kenya, and Malawi. And some countries have restrictive policies, for example, South Africa, which allows the importation of secondhand clothing only for charitable purposes rather than for resale except for one garment, overcoats, the demand for which the local garment industry does not satisfy. Zimbabwe allowed secondhand clothing imports for charitable purposes until 1994. But regardless of import rules, African boundaries are highly permeable, facilitating both legal movement and smuggling of secondhand clothes on a grand scale throughout the continent. In South Africa the regulation that charities may import secondhand clothes on condition that they are given away and not sold is widely disregarded. Although tons of secondhand clothing are confiscated on the docks, many containers come through without being checked by customs. Once the merchandise is unloaded, there is little way to prove that it is imported. Because secondhand clothing is readily available, the clothing workers' union has sought to have the law enforced (MNet, 9 November 1997). In spite of import prohibitions in Zimbabwe, large volumes of secondhand clothes are sold in open markets, far more than small-scale traders can possibly smuggle from Zambia and Mozambique, where the import is legal. And although secondhand clothing imports are now banned in Nigeria, there is a brisk transborder trade with Benin and Togo.

Small countries like Benin, Togo, and Rwanda have appeared on the top ten list of importers due to a great extent to their role in transshipment. In 1983 Rwanda was the world's fifth-largest net importer of used clothing and the largest in all of sub-Saharan Africa. Less than half of this import was consumed within the country itself; the rest was reexported unofficially to Zaire, Uganda, Burundi, and Tanzania (Haggblade 1990:506). In the late 1980s and early 1990s Togo had become the trading hub of West Africa, given its geographic location, political stability, and low tariffs. Eighty percent of its imports, including used clothing, were reexported to neighboring countries (*New York Times,* 10 August 1987, p. A8). The capital, Lomé, was the home to more than 400 regional trading companies. With more than 100 firms active in the secondhand clothing business, Togo was described as the used-clothing capital of West Africa (*Business America,* 22 April 1991).

Prices

The market price of secondhand clothing fluctuates, reflecting shifts in international supply and demand, political developments in local and overseas markets, and the changing value of the U.S. dollar. According to sources with long experience in this trade, the market price of secondhand clothing fell in the early 1980s when the demand for industrial use, that is, the rag, wiper, and reprocessing market, was declining. The chief players then were the large charitable organizations that remained in the trade, generating a large part of their income from direct sales rather than resales to the commercial textile salvagers. But during the 1980s, when niche marketing of secondhand clothing in Western markets grew in popularity and the growing export potential to the developing world became widely acknowledged, the market price began to increase. As noted earlier, many commercial textile salvagers increasingly turned their production toward the secondhand clothing export market while supplying rags for industrial use. On the demand side, import statistics reveal a gradual shift from middle- to low-income countries, as is reflected in the steady growth of used-clothing imports to sub-Saharan Africa since the 1980s (Haggbade 1990:517).

The first half of the 1990s experienced a particularly dramatic growth in this export, influenced by the opening up of new markets in eastern Europe, the ongoing impoverishment of much of the Third World, or both. As I noted earlier, the conventional sourcing methods are placed under pressure, challenging both the charitable organizations and the commercial textile salvagers into devising more effective ways of collecting. The large commercial textile salvagers in the Netherlands and Belgium today receive far less clothing for sorting from German firms, for example, some of whom have relocated their operations to eastern Europe, as have firms from the United States, the Netherlands, and Belgium.

After a low in the late 1980s and early 1990s, market prices of used clothing went up. They increased rapidly by the mid-1990s only to decline again very recently. In the United States, for example, "markets opening up in Africa and the former Soviet Union have created a demand that has raised prices," according to one observer, from $0.02 to $0.03 a pound during the late 1980s to $0.14 a pound and higher in 1992 (*New York Times,* 9 February 1992). During the early 1990s used-clothing prices were about $0.08 or $0.09 a pound, increasing in the mid-1990s to $0.22 a pound in most markets (*Journal of Commerce,* 12 June 1996). In the Netherlands in 1996, the price of "domestic origin" clothing (clothing sourced within the country) had risen approximately 25 percent when compared to the previous year, as a result of increased demand from eastern Europe (Plevier, 19 March 1997, Roosendaal, the Netherlands). Recently market prices seem to be sliding downward again to $0.10–0.15 a pound (*Houston Chronicle,* 2 April 1998). One observer estimated that prices dropped almost 70 percent, from $0.25 to $0.12 a pound, during the first half of 1998. He attributed the decline in part to trouble in Third World markets, including political and economic upheavals and natural disaster from Indonesia to Africa and in part to uncertainty and instability of economic developments in eastern Europe (Graham Allan, Salvation Army, Chicago, 28 July 1998).

Once sorted and graded, the sales prices of secondhand clothing increase. They ranged in the United States in 1997 from $0.50 to $1.50 per kilogram, depending on garment type, with quotes (f.o.b.) of $0.66 per kilogram for used winter clothing and $0.77 per kilogram for shoes from a New Jersey supplier (*Journal of Commerce,* 9 April 1997). That year used summer clothing with "no rips" sold for $0.40 a pound (*Journal of Commerce,* 19 November 1997, p. 10C).

Shipping

The introduction of container ships has facilitated and speeded up the surface delivery of goods to far-flung destinations, including secondhand clothing. About 16 percent of the containers with U.S. exports bound for Africa in 1995 were filled with clothing. That year the number of containers in the overall trade on Africa grew by about 27 percent, almost three times as much as on the import side (*Journal of Commerce,* 1 March 1996). The top item shipped inboard to many parts of Africa was used clothing, which was "ahead of machinery and food" (*Journal of Commerce,* 7 November 1996). From the Port of New York and New Jersey, the largest East Coast port, used clothing "can represent up to 70 percent of all shipments to West Africa," according to a president of a U.S.-Africa shipping company (*Sun,* 28 September 1997). And used clothing is one of the most popular commodities shipped to Africa from the Port of Houston (*Houston Chronicle,* 2 April 1998).

Fluctuating prices of secondhand clothing and shifts in worldwide supply and demand that affect them have ramifications at many levels, including the overseas shipment of used garments for sale. In the beginning of 1996, "other markets took a fancy to the used clothing from the United States" (*Journal of Commerce,* 12 June 1996). When the demand grew, the price increased in most markets. These increases had a direct effect on shippers and shipping lines. Trade dropped in part because of currency devaluations in many African countries. According to a spokesperson from one shipping line, U.S. Africa Navigation, given the cost of ocean freight, exporters to Africa lose money if used clothing costs more than $0.18 a pound. This company served the southern range of the trade with West Africa, including the Congo, Gabon, and Angola, "a hotbed for oil exploration and a prime market for used clothing" (*Journal of Commerce,* 12 June 1996). A general problem for shippers is the mostly government-run ports in Africa, where port base rates are expensive and officials charge fines and duties far "beyond those found in other international ports" (*Journal of Commerce,* 1 March 1996). Ship and cargo seizures are common. Because the African trade is a trade of changing niches, including export commodities like cocoa, cotton, and tobacco, the trade lanes between the United States and Africa are tricky under any circumstances. In effect, not only may shippers encounter economic loss because of diminished outbound cargo, but also they may have to move empty containers back to the United States.

African Used-Clothing Markets

Secondhand clothing exporters need local knowledge not only about the political climate, import rules, tariffs, and currency regulations but also about clothing consumption practices in different African countries. Some exporters have lived in Africa, and those who have not visit to familiarize themselves with local clothing markets. During the first year after Lorenzo Gomez left his uncle's secondhand clothing business to set out on his own in Sacramento in 1965, he traveled to Europe and West Africa to develop contacts. Over the next five years, he went to Ghana three times to find markets for his goods (*Sacramento Bee,* 26 March 1990). From the African end, wholesalers feed information to their contacts in North America and Europe about which garments do and do not sell well. In effect, exporters need to reckon with considerable regional variation in Africa's clothing markets. In Muslim-dominated North Africa, for example, used clothing contributed only 7 percent of total garment imports in 1980 compared to the 33 percent in sub-Saharan Africa (Haggblade 1990:508–9). Tunisia is an exception to this, with large imports probably due to long practices of reexport (van Groen and Lozer 1976).

Local dress conventions differ not only in terms of religious norms but also of gender, age, class, and region, informing cultural norms of dress practice and influencing what types of garments people will wear and when. Briefly, in several countries in West Africa, distinct regional dress styles that are the products of long-standing textile crafts in weaving, dyeing, and printing today coexist with styles of dressing introduced during the colonial period and after. In Nigeria and Senegal, for example, secondhand clothing has entered a specific niche. Although people from different socioeconomic groups, not only the very poor, now purchase imported secondhand clothing and use it widely for everyday wear, Senegalese and Nigerians commonly follow long-standing regional style conventions on important occasions, dressing with pride for purposes of displaying locally produced cloth in "African" styles (Denzer 1997:10–12; Heath 1992:21, 28). This is much in contrast to the situation in Zambia, where such textile crafts hardly existed and where people from across the socioeconomic spectrum except the very top are dressing in the West's used clothing. Last but not least, there are invented dress "traditions." In Mobuto Sese Seko's Zaire, for example, the "authenticity" code forbade men to wear Western coats and ties and women to wear jeans. His successor, President Kabila of the Democratic Republic of the Congo, is conservative in matters of women's dress. One of his first edicts after assuming power in 1997 was to ban women's wearing of jeans and miniskirts (*Post,* 22 July 1997).

Deception and Illegality

The secondhand clothing trade is an unusual industry. Few other industries obtain their raw materials free, as do the charitable organizations, or have suppliers, the clothing-donating public, who do not know the important role they play at the start of a long commodity chain. Indeed, the clothing-donating public is generally not aware of either the grand scale on which the charitable organizations commonly dispose of clothing to commercial middlemen or contract out the right to solicit and sell under their name. Charity representations to the public through fund-raising appeals might do well to recognize such practices more explicitly than they do now, as a way of forestalling sensationalist media accounts.[8] For example, when the Danish press in 1992 and 1993 took DAPP to task for selling donated clothing directly to poor people in southern Africa and thereby supposedly adversely affecting the local garment and textile industries, several municipalities considered withdrawing DAPP's permission to place collection bins in public places.[9] One consequence of the debate was that DAPP altered the descriptions of its appeal on collection bins from "clothing and shoes to people in the Third World" (tøj og sko til folk i den tredje verden) to "clothing collection to the benefit of people in the Third World" (tøj og sko til fordel for folk i den tredje verden) to indicate the indirect effect that domestic and overseas sales of donated clothing might have on Third World people's lives.

The commercial connection in the flow of donated clothing need not be problematic. Recent demonstrations of this come from Britain where the Queen's Award for export in 1997 was given to a textile salvager in London's East End, Lawrence Barry. "Charity shops," he explained, "can only sell a relatively small proportion of what they're given, so we buy from them clothing they can't otherwise sell." He described the enormous demand in the countries to which he exported in East, West, and central Africa, the Far East and Middle East, Russia, and eastern Europe. His staff of one hundred workers "export 15 tons of shoes and between 100 and 120 tons of clothing a week . . . When I started I gave out fly posters to people arriving at Heathrow, which kept me in business. These days I travel a lot, and we know our markets" (*Daily Telegraph,* 21 April 1997). In 1998 two recyclers achieved the export award, Ward Shoes for exporting used footwear, largely to Africa, and W. H. Tracey Recyclers for exporting used clothing. The latter firm had its origin in a rag-and-bone business set up by the founder in 1935. Ten years ago the firm began exporting, "when the demand for shredded garments fell." The chief markets are Kenya, the Baltic states, and Pakistan (*Financial Times,* 21 April 1998).

Still, the connection between the charitable organizations and the commercial textile salvagers appears to be problematic to the clothing-donating public because of the disproportionate amounts sometimes earned by those who handle the trade. In the great charity clothes scandal in Britain in 1976, the group of commercial salvagers collecting from the Children's Research Fund, a Liverpool-based charity, earned £75,000 during 1974–75, with £15,000 going to the society and £60,000 to the collectors (Ginsburg 1980:132). I have already mentioned the two Florida operators who made $2.55 for each dollar they turned over to charity from contracts managing thrift stores in the name of charities. According to a news report they realized an annual return of more than 100 percent on their equity by managing ten Illinois Amvets thrift stores in the 1980s (*Los Angeles Times,* 27 September 1987).

Vying for locations to place bins and defending their collection and resale policies, the charitable organizations and textile salvagers are pitted against one another in competition for access to used clothing. Goodwill Industries has complained for years about the commercial salvage companies using donation bins, sometimes under contract by churches and charitable groups and sometimes under bogus names. The prospect of good returns from secondhand clothing sales has lent itself to a variety of abuses, including two textile salvagers, a father and son, paying kickbacks to Salvation Army officers in Philadelphia over a thirteen-year period to assure a steady supply of clothes (*New York Times,* 25 May 1985). What is more, the hidden profitability of used clothing is prompting widespread theft. Each week in 1992 Goodwill Industries on Long Island found seven to ten bins cleaned out by people who climbed in or had access to keys. Some of these thefts were attributed to job-bers collecting for the salvage companies. Three such jobbers were arrested for stealing clothing from St. Vincent de Paul collection bins on Long Island in 1992. Goodwill Industries was ready to press charges in a similar case; it had seven bins stolen outright in the beginning of 1992 (*New York Times,* 9 February 1992). Some charities whose collections have been declining have hired private detectives to find out what is taking place (*Newsday,* 22 Febru-ary 1998). In fact, collection bins are so routinely broken into that some char-ities have reduced their number or removed them entirely from some locations (*New York Times,* 14 November 1995).

Concerns have been raised about the textile salvaging operation once used clothing reaches the sorting point. When two workers were fired after bring-ing union organizers onto company property at the beginning of 1990, strike action erupted at Domsey Trading Corporation in Brooklyn, one of the largest of nearly two dozen secondhand clothing firms on the East Coast. Some 200 workers, many Haitian immigrants, but also Latino and African-Americans, held a prolonged strike over unfair labor practice, low wages, and lack of benefits. Work conditions were poor, and the conduct of manage-ment left much to be desired, including physical violence and racial and sex-ual insults. The Reverend Jesse Jackson, who spoke at a prounion rally when the strike was in its sixth month, reported that he had met with representatives of the governments of Nigeria and Senegal, two of the countries to which Domsey exported, urging their governments "to refuse to buy Domsey prod-ucts" (*Big Red News,* 21 July 1990).

As the strike continued, the International Ladies' Garment Workers' Union and workers from Domsey demonstrated at Salvation Army and Goodwill Industries, urging them to stop selling clothing in bulk to Domsey and calling on New Yorkers to stop donating clothes to the charitable organi-zations (*Women's Wear Daily,* 8 May 1991). The head of Goodwill Industries said that some local agencies were continuing to do business with Domsey on "a highest-bidder basis" (*New York Daily News,* 23 April 1991). While a Sal-vation Army spokesperson explained that "we can't control what happens to our rags once they leave our docks," he did add that the organization had not sold anything directly to Domsey since the strike began (*Women's Wear Daily,* 8 May 1991). Finally in August 1991, eighteen months after the strike began, the district court ordered Domsey to reinstate the striking workers and to pay their back wages (United Press International, 1 August 1991). But four years after the company lost its final legal appeal, work conditions remained oppressive, and Domsey delayed the compensation for back pay (*New York Times*, 9 June 1997).

Deception that turns into outright illegality accompanies the flow of secondhand clothing from the sorting factory to its export destination. Because of incorrect statements of the weight of cargo provided by the exporter who is shipping, cargo-vessel operators carrying used-clothing containers have been penalized at the point of discharge. One such case in 1978 involved a vessel owned by Atlantic Overseas Corporation, which was assessed a customs fine of $655,200 at the port of Abidjan in the Côte d'Ivoire for undervaluation of weight. The case underscores a problem common to shipowners transporting secondhand clothing to Third World countries, according to a news report. A New York district court ruled that the shipper, the export firm of Pioneer Institutional Trading Company, had to pay the fine (*Journal of Commerce*, 23 May 1978). In 1985 the two textile salvagers who offered kickbacks to Salvation Army officers were charged in federal district court in New York with cheating seven shipping companies out of payment for carrying clothes and with underestimating the value of clothing shipments through their Dumont Export Company in Philadelphia. Between 1981 and 1983 they supplied the shipping companies with at least 310 certificates understating the weight of clothes and rags by nearly five million pounds. They also undervalued twenty-one shipments to Italy, Benin, Pakistan, France, and India. The charges carried a maximum penalty of ten years in prison plus restitution and fines (*New York Times*, 25 May 1985).

Farther down the line, at the point of foreign entry, there is deceit, fraud, and corruption as well, in part facilitated by the complications of African bureaucracies in the transfer of port storage and port clearance fees. One of many examples comes from Tanzania, where in 1988 more than thirty Tanzanian importers and customs officials were charged with depriving the country of about U.S. $2 million in customs duty and taxes. Nearly 1,500 containers sat unclaimed at the Dar es Salaam port because authorities at the end of the previous year decided to check the contents of each container against its manifest. When the containers were opened, it was discovered that "whisky had been declared as pesticide, used clothing as fertilizer, and a new sports car as clothing" (Africa News Service, 25 January 1988).

To be sure, as the international secondhand clothing trade is currently organized, donated garments are providing excellent economic returns to some of the parties who are dealing with them. Are they all winners, as boldly argued by the spokesperson for the textile recycling industry in the United

States whom I quoted early in the chapter? Both charities and the commercial textile salvagers are annoyed with repeated media criticism of their practices. The politics that arise from the production of secondhand clothing in the West through the sourcing arrangements described here are real, and they reappear in a variety of forms once our discarded clothes arrive at the end of the line in a country like Zambia.

6 Import, Wholesale, and Distribution

After several weeks at sea, the container ships carrying secondhand clothing destined for Zambia make port along the Indian Ocean. Shipping lasts approximately six weeks from the United States and three weeks from Antwerp or Rotterdam in Europe. Consignments to Zambia are offloaded in the ports of Dar es Salaam in Tanzania, Beira in Mozambique, and Durban, and occasionally Port Elizabeth, in South Africa. For years Dar es Salaam received a good deal of Zambia's cargo, including secondhand clothing, in part because of the country's political stance against white-dominated South Africa. Following the shifts in South Africa since 1990 and the change of regime in 1994, Durban has been increasingly used (*Times of Zambia,* 25 July 1995). And the nearest port, Beira, reopened in 1992 after decades of bloody war, is seeing more traffic in the wake of Mozambique's political stabilization.

Once cleared at port and loaded onto trucks, the containers with bales of secondhand clothing are hauled to warehouses in Zambia. The transport to Zambia takes three to four days. Following the onward journey of the container loads of secondhand clothing from port until they reach the point of consumption in Zambia, this chapter explores the wholesale and distribution practices that have arisen around the growing import of this commodity and introduces some of the actors involved: customs officials from the Zambia Revenue Authority (ZRA), wholesalers, and some of the many traders. Extending chapter 4's brief description of the secondhand clothing trade in the 1980s into the present, this chapter starts when Zaire, now the Democratic Republic of the Congo, no longer was the main conduit for secondhand clothing imports into Zambia. I draw on secondary materials and observations from both urban and rural areas that I made during several periods of field research between 1992 and 1999. I end with a discussion of the recommodification of the West's used garments that is initiated through these processes. Through them and activities related to retail and consumption that I discuss in subsequent chapters, secondhand clothes are redefined as "new" garments.

Import

For the inbound journey from port, most secondhand clothing wholesalers in Zambia use commercial freight companies and their clearing agents. The exceptions to this are a couple of large importers who are involved in general retail trade or other businesses and use their own fleet of trucks. Customs clearance takes place at either the point of entry or at the inland port, Makeni dry port, on Lusaka's southern outskirts. Charitable groups and social welfare organizations may apply to the Ministry of Finance for exemption from duty. For several years DAPP, the Scandinavian-based NGO that funds its development projects in Zambia through local sale of imported secondhand clothing, paid a reduced customs rate because the garments were unsorted. That dispensation is no longer in place.

For customs purpose the assessment of secondhand clothing has varied over the years. In the early 1990s importers paid a flat rate of U.S. $12 for standard bales of around 50 kilograms. In the fall of 1993 the government suddenly placed a rate of $10 per kilogram on imported secondhand clothing only to withdraw it within days after critical interventions by importers (*Times of Zambia,* 9 and 13 September 1993). The rate remained at $1.30 per kilogram for some years. Since the mid-1990s, assessments have followed a simple formula: U.S. $1.50 per kilogram with 25 percent of that value as duty.[1] This formula was chosen in preference to assessing duty on the declared import value of consignments, which exporters often underestimate.

Since August 1992 all importers of secondhand clothing have been required to produce Société Générale de Surveillance (SGS) preshipment documents and to clear their consignments at the point of entry (*Times of Zambia,* 28 June 1992).[2] This clearance procedure ostensibly forecloses a "special delivery" practice that allowed release of sealed containers before payment of duty. Secondhand clothing importers, in particular, had been using this procedure to evade duty, at times in collusion with individual customs officials (*Times of Zambia,* 9 September 1993, 7 October 1993). Special clearance has been practiced intermittently since then, including a trial in 1995, but was revoked a few months later (*Zambia Daily Mail,* 4 March 1995; *Post,* 11 July 1995, p. 3).

Although most secondhand clothing consignments are cleared at the inland port in Lusaka, some continue to clear at border points, for instance, inbound cargo from the north at Nakonde on the Zambian side of the border with Tanzania and some cargo arriving from the south at Chirundu on the Zambian side of the border with Zimbabwe. The border posts to Malawi have experienced increasing traffic since 1994, when Malawi unbanned the importation of secondhand clothing and the port of Beira in Mozambique assumed a more strategic position in this trade. ZRA officials with whom I discussed these matters in 1995 and 1997 suggested that the worst cases of underreporting were occurring along the Malawian border.

In spite of increased customs scrutiny of secondhand clothing consignments, the import is "massively" underreported, according to ZRA officials (5 August and 6 September 1997). One suggested that wholesalers who import several container loads of secondhand clothing at the same time do not declare them all; only one out of seven containers was declared, he said. Another proposed that at least one-fourth of the secondhand clothes that are sold in Zambia had entered the country without being declared for customs purposes. The ZRA has in recent years made seizures of undeclared consignments of secondhand clothing from several large importers, requiring payment of duty and fines. Yet ZRA personnel is stretched thinly along Zambia's vast borders, where some undeclared importation no doubt continues.

Information on the scope of Zambia's secondhand clothing import is not reported to the UN statistical division on world trade and is not available in any systematic form within the country. The SGS data I obtained locally are incomplete.[3] The UN statistics that I discussed in chapter 5 provide only estimates for Zambia. They suggest that Zambia's total import of secondhand clothing grew from an estimated value of U.S. $1,181,000 to $6,881,000 between 1990 and 1993. Total estimated imports into Zambia declined in value to $3,651,000 in 1995 (UN 1996:60) and have fallen slightly in subsequent years. In terms of volume, this import might have been some 7,000 metric tons for the year 1993, probably a very conservative estimate.[4]

The reported export of secondhand clothing from the United States to Zambia grew from a value of U.S. $266,00 in 1990 to a high of $5,015,000 in 1993. It declined during subsequent years to a value of $2,105,000 in 1997. Canadian exports rank second to those from the United States, reported at a value of U.S. $1,476,000 in 1997. Next is Belgium-Luxembourg with exports to Zambia growing in value to $840,000 in 1993, and declining to $340,000 in 1997. Secondhand clothing exports from the United Kingdom grew from a value of $107,000 in 1990 to a high of $525,000 in 1993, falling to $217,000 in 1997. While the UN data I have had access to do not allow an assessment of the total value of actually reported secondhand clothing exports to Zambia, they suggest an overall pattern: imports peaked in 1993, followed by a gradual decline (UN International Trade Branch 1998).[5]

Locally available data from SGS inspection records of customs clearance at Lusaka's dry port between July 1994 and June 1995 list some 142 commercial consignments of secondhand clothing by a total of forty-five importers, of whom ten cleared several shipments while most of the rest cleared only one. The number in this listing exceeds my own suggestion of twenty to thirty sizable importers and is likely to reflect some firms' use of different names for different parts of their operations. The SGS listing indicates a lull in import during the first half of 1995 when wholesalers probably were clearing stock in anticipation of the introduction of a value-added tax (VAT) of 20 percent at the beginning of July. The VAT replaced a previous sales tax of 23 percent. The VAT has since been reduced to 17.5 percent and has not by itself affected this import.

Close to one-third of the consignments on the SGS list were imported from the United States, followed in rank by Canada and Great Britain. Together these three countries exported three-quarters of the consignments listed in the SGS records. The rest came from across Europe where Belgium-Luxembourg, the Netherlands, and Denmark exported several shipments while Italy, France, Spain, and Sweden exported single shipments. Japan was among the exporting countries of secondhand clothing, as were Hong Kong and Pakistan.[6]

The SGS records listed two religious groups, Life Centre Ministries and Kabwata Baptist Church, under the category of commercial import for which duty is paid. Some twenty-eight additional groups that also imported secondhand clothing were classified under a rebate category exempting them from paying duty, including the YMCA, and several churches, parishes, and dioceses. Among them were also a couple of international development organizations, for example Swedish International Development Cooperation Agency (SIDA) and Japanese International Cooperation Agency (JICA). The volumes imported by these groups were minuscule when compared to the commercial import.

Private organizations and churches that import rebated secondhand clothing use them to relieve specific needs such as the Catholic Secretariat's distribution of clothing to schools for the handicapped in 1993 (Denconsult 1993:21). In 1993 the YMCA donated fifteen bales of secondhand clothing to the Hope Foundation, the relief agency established by first lady Vera Chiluba, for distribution to "the needy in rural areas" (*Times of Zambia,* 5 August 1993). But there is no doubt that some rebated clothing ends up in commercial markets. This is one reason that Oxfam, I was told in 1993, no longer imports secondhand clothing into Zambia from its stock of donated clothing in the United Kingdom. There are other reasons that secondhand clothing that has not been cleared for commercial sale is sold. When the Rotary Club of Kabwe in 1992 received several container loads of used surgical tools as a donation from a sister club in the Netherlands, secondhand clothing was used as filler and packaging material. The Kabwe Rotarians advertised the sale of these clothes and used the money raised to support the Kabwe General Hospital, which was also the recipient of the surgical tools (*Times of Zambia,* 28 August 1992).

Much like the exporting side, the importing of secondhand clothing into Zambia has its share of deceptive and outright illegal practices. Customs officials are quick to point out that a good proportion of Zambia's secondhand clothing imports enters the country without payment of duty. The reorganized ZRA is seeking to eliminate involvement of its officers in dubious clearance dealings, by upgrading skills, work conditions, and remuneration. Aside from suspicious dealings by individual ZRA customs officials, in several reported cases rebated secondhand clothing imported by church and social groups for emergency distribution was sold. Even the Lusaka City Council came under fire in 1989 when, in an effort to enhance its dwindling funds, it decided to sell secondhand clothes donated to flood victims by Lusaka's twin city in the Soviet Union (*Times of Zambia,* 6 November 1989). When Minister of State Michael Sata in 1990 was asked to comment on a plan of the Ndola Urban District Council to raise money for its operation through salaula sales, he said there was nothing wrong with the council "exploring for new business." Two council officers were detailed to travel to Taiwan and Brussels to "scout for sources" of secondhand clothes (*Times of Zambia,* 10 January 1990, p. 2).

While there is nothing illegal about an urban council plan to improve finances, it might well be beyond its jurisdiction to engage in import and retail trade. Another more dubious case involved a consignment of clothing donated to refugees by World Vision International in 1990, which was sold on the streets (*Times of Zambia,* 10 January 1990, p. 1). In 1994 the ZRA revealed a "racket" in which a Lusaka firm used a local church to evade payments of customs duty on imported goods, including secondhand clothing (*Times of Zambia,* 27 May 1994, p. 1). And in 1995 the ZRA investigated church ministers from three denominations for using the name of their church to import rebated secondhand clothing to resell for personal gain (*Sunday Times of Zambia,* 7 May 1995). Such examples constitute the tip of an iceberg, the contours of which are difficult to trace because of its vast extent and irregular shape.

Wholesale

The wholesale hub of secondhand clothing is Lusaka, the capital, from where the salaula trade and its associated activities have radiated across the country since the early 1990s. The number of wholesalers has increased steadily, from twenty to thirty sizable firms over the first half of the 1990s, to around forty in 1995. By 1997 some had dropped from the scene, and some importers suggested to me that the saturation point in trade of this commodity might have been reached. Some eight to ten firms have handled the larger part of the trade, half of them remaining in operation throughout while the rest have declined and been succeeded by others. In addition, there is a varying number of short-term enterprises.

There have been shifts in the location of secondhand clothing wholesaling as well. In the mid-1990s the largest single importer, Khatry Brothers, was in Chipata, the provincial headquarters of Zambia's Eastern Province on the border to Malawi. Benefiting from the unbanning of the secondhand clothing import in Malawi, this firm expanded its reach into that country and established outlets in Lusaka and the Copperbelt as well. Some Lusaka firms also have upcountry branches on the Copperbelt, and one of Lusaka's largest, Lamise Investments, has established several outlets in Malawi, as has Khatry Brothers, to make inroads in that new market. And DAPP moved its operational base from Lusaka to Ndola on the Copperbelt toward the end of 1993. DAPP and Khatry Brothers were in the mid-1990s the only groups in Zambia to import large unsorted bales of secondhand clothing and to establish sorting operations on their premises.

Many of the twenty to thirty sizable firms that wholesale secondhand clothing are general dealers who added this commodity to their inventory when the trade began to grow substantially. Some operate other businesses and consider the wholesale of salaula a sideline. They include several long-established firms with Indian backgrounds, some Lebanese enterprises with trading experience from elsewhere in Africa who entered this region after the political shift in 1991, and a varying number of local African-owned firms. Small enterprises have come and gone in this trade, both African and Indian, some of them subcontracting from larger firms. Then there is the NGO DAPP, a longtime and important player in the secondhand clothing trade in Zambia. There was a sense among the long-established secondhand clothing wholesalers I revisited in 1997 that some firms had stopped importing, that there were fewer bales in the warehouses, and that both import and retail might have slowed down somewhat. In fact, the data on 1990–97 exports to Zambia support that impression.

When ordering secondhand clothing consignments from abroad, wholesalers specify garment type and quality. I have heard that factory seconds occasionally are among the clothing consignments, yet I have never seen them marketed in public places. Wholesalers are familiar with shifts in the local market and know that clothing needs and desires vary seasonally. There are times of slow demand, for example, during the months after Christmas when expenditures on school fees and uniforms curtail household budgets. Wholesalers also reckon with complaints by retailers about garments that do not sell easily, such as polyester knit. They know that the market for miniskirts is limited and that women's jeans do not sell well. Many deal with exporters they know through family and contacts. I have met exporters from Australia and Germany in salaula warehouses, visiting Lusaka-based wholesalers to assess the market. And foreign embassies in Lusaka receive

Figure 21 *(top)* Komboland: Quality Salaula, a warehouse owned by Iqbal, Ltd., a wholesaler in Ndola, 1995.
Author's photograph.

Figure 22 *(middle)* World of Salaula, a secondhand clothing retail store also selling used tires in Ndola, 1993.
Author's photograph.

Figure 23 *(bottom)* Salaula Centre, a wholesale outlet in Petauke, a small town in Eastern Province, 1993.
Photograph by Leslie Ashbaugh, reproduced with permission.

occasional requests for commercial contacts by exporters who are new to the Zambian market.

Some brief examples will serve to illustrate the diverse range of salaula wholesale.[7] I have deliberately selected cases that highlight differences of scope, diversity in operation, and shifts over time. The cases demonstrate that the commercial importation of secondhand clothing rarely gives rise to a profitable activity by itself but works best when combined with the wholesale of other commodities that will tide the firm over at times of difficulty. A long time passes from the placing of an order overseas, its filling, shipping, port clearance, and the arrival of goods for customs clearance in Zambia, which easily ties up the capital of a single-commodity trader. Problems at any stage of this process may delay delivery, and increased scrutiny by ZRA customs agents can hold up consignments, resulting in poorly stocked or empty warehouses. Successful wholesalers receive several consignments a month, and because they deal in other goods, they are not too badly affected by delays of delivery or seasonal slumps in salaula demand. The DAPP model that I describe below is an exception to this. A number of small wholesale enterprises have come and gone in Zambia since the early 1990s precisely because they were undercapitalized.

Simbeye Enterprises is an African-owned wholesaler of secondhand clothing, foodstuffs, and essential commodities. The owner's regional background is in the northern corridor, that is, the Zambia-Tanzania border region where people became involved directly with secondhand clothing much earlier than in Lusaka. Namwanga by ethnic background, the owner has wholesaled secondhand clothing since 1987. In 1995, he owned three outlets in Lusaka, including a warehouse and store strategically located next to Kamwala market, Lusaka's oldest "African" market established in the postwar era, within easy proximity of the intercity bus terminal and the railway station. Importing through Dar es Salaam one or two containers every two months from suppliers in the United States, Canada, and the Netherlands, this operation is considerably smaller than that of Lamise (described below). Like other salaula wholesalers whom I interviewed during the spring of 1995, this enterprise experienced slow sales prior to the introduction of the VAT. According to a warehouse employee the owner had begun to express doubts about the future profitability of salaula, considering whether to drop it entirely from his inventory (19 April 1995, Lusaka). He did not do that but rather took a proactive role as chair of the Salaula Dealers' Association, arguing against a 1998 proposal for increased tariffs.

Lamise Investments set up shop and warehouse in Lusaka in 1991 after the shift in regime and beginning of economic liberalization. It is a family-operated wholesale firm, established by a group of Lebanese who left Tanzania for Zambia to explore the new business environment. The headquarters is near Lusaka's town center and close to a major market, Soweto. One of the managers told me (29 July 1992, Lusaka) that he had dealt in secondhand clothes in Dar es Salaam for several years and that the family had been involved with this business for at least fifteen years. The showroom included two types of fabric, one for garments and one for upholstery. In addition to secondhand clothing bales the warehouse held a variety of plastic products for household use and some dry goods. The firm is involved in many other businesses as well. In 1992 Lamise sourced most of its secondhand garments from the United States as it did in 1994 and 1995, judging from SGS records. In 1992 Lamise imported three or four container loads of forty-foot capacity each month through Dar es Salaam and Durban. During the twelve-month period between 1994 and 1995 for which I have data on SGS clearance at Lusaka's inland port, Lamise Investments was the fourth-largest importer of secondhand clothing; it is most likely larger than that, given the practice of the large wholesalers of using different names for different operations. Lamise extended its operations into Malawi after the shift of regime in that country in the mid-1990s, operating both secondhand clothing resale and general wholesale outlets. Consignments bound for Malawi are likely to arrive at Beira in Mozambique, adding to the volume of the firm's already large Zambian import of secondhand clothing.

Chisco Asaar, Ltd., is a general wholesaler whose owner came to Zambia from India in 1979, marrying a Zambian-born woman of Indian background and involving himself actively in the secondhand clothing trade. When I interviewed him at his warehouse near Lusaka's light industrial area in 1992, he received an average of five forty-foot containers per month, most of them from Canada, and he was planning to import more (29 July 1992, Lusaka). Still going strong, this firm was the top importer on the SGS list of commercial importers in 1994–95. I use this example to contrast it to small-time operators, who dropped out of this trade over the years, for instance *Ware Wholesale* behind Kamwala market, whose young Zambian owner of Mambwe background from the Tanzania border region did not import directly but purchased bales from the larger wholesalers for resale (28 July 1992, Lusaka). He and several other small enterprises did not remain long in this business.

Mukampalili provides a different model than those just described, combining aspects of wholesale and retail. This secondhand clothing outlet was opened by a twenty-eight-year-old Zambian woman who joined her retired father's business of selling farm produce after receiving her BA in business administration in the United Kingdom. Her family is from the northern region and is Mambwe by ethnic group. When visiting a brother who was studying in the United States in 1993, she called on a textile salvager in New York State. On her return to Lusaka, she opened Mukampalili in 1994 on premises her father owned near the light industrial area. She began selling wholesale, but when she realized that many customers wanted smaller volumes, she introduced units of clothing, for example, four pairs of trousers, six T-shirts, and so forth. Obtaining a retail license, she also began selling by the piece. When I interviewed her, it was four months since she had ordered her last consignment (21 April 1995, Lusaka). "There is too much work involved," she said, "and getting it here is too much trouble." She doubted she would order another consignment and spoke of plans to open a restaurant and take-away, using produce from her father's farm. When I called on the premises in August 1997, she had done just that and seemed to be doing a vigorous lunchtime business.

Khatry Brothers was referred to by other wholesalers in 1995 as "the king of salaula." Located in Chipata, the Khatry family of immigrant Indian background were general traders who were among the first to enter the secondhand clothing trade in Zambia in the mid-1980s.[8] Expanding into a major trading enterprise with several outlets under different names, both in Lusaka and on the Copperbelt, Khatry Brothers has followed a rags-to-riches path.

After purchasing bales from DAPP and other early wholesalers for some years, Khatry began importing fifty-kilogram bales in the late 1980s. The trade had grown in popularity, and Khatry extended its regional reach by making favorable credit arrangements with many small-scale traders. The trade boomed after 1994, once imports into Malawi no longer were prohibited. It had so much scope that, by 1995, Khatry began importing five hundred-kilogram unsorted bales, hauling them from port on ten new trucks, setting up a sorting operation with three baling machines, and employing some hundred local Africans in sorting and rebaling an estimated 2,500 to 3,000 tons of secondhand clothing per year. In 1995 two-thirds of the clothing was sourced in the United Kingdom and the rest in the United States. Their U.S. supplier in Houston was of Pakistani background. This person and their U.K. dealers, Indian expatriates who were British subjects, had all resided in Africa at some point or other.

While still conducting general wholesale trade, Khatry Brothers established secondhand clothing outlets in Malawi at Lilongwe, Blantyre, and Limbe. When I called on it in Chipata in 1997, Khatry Brothers was clearing its local inventory of secondhand clothing, planning to move its sorting operation to Malawi, and actively investigating the prospect of setting up an operation in Beira in Mozambique, close to port. Continuing the Chipata-based general wholesale trade, Khatry Brothers' future commercial focus in Zambia's Eastern Province would be, one of the brothers told me, commercial farming (12 August 1997, Chipata). Land had been acquired, a dairy started, and an irrigation scheme for citrus and wheat was under way. An abbatoir was under construction, and plans were ready for poultry and egg production as well as for a refrigerated plant and refrigerated trucks to haul frozen foodstuffs to Lusaka markets.

Between 1995 and 1997 the ZRA scrutinized the import practices of Khatry Brothers. The brother I spoke to explained that increased customs duties and VAT made it "impossible" to profit on salaula and that those who did so probably were passing money under the table to the ZRA. But clearing their consignments on arrival from the north at Nakonde or on the Malawian side for imports from Beira, Khatry Brothers, according to other big wholesalers and ZRA officials, had their share of underdeclaration. Seizures had been made and fines imposed, and rumor had it that Khatry Brothers planned to dispute the decision in court.

DAPP combines commerce and charity in its dealings with used clothing in Zambia, according to an agreement of 1985 with the Zambian government that allows the organization to finance a part of its local development projects through the sale of used clothing. The import of large bales of unsorted clothing into Zambia from associated organizations within the Federation for the Pan-European Benevolent Organizations of UFF and Humana in Europe began in 1986. For some years clothing was sorted in DAPP's Frontline Youth Centers, largely for wholesale, and the earnings allotted to the agricultural activities of the centers. A DAPP sorting center was established in Lusaka in 1991 where clothes were sorted and rebaled in forty-five-kilogram bales, 57 percent sold wholesale and 43 percent sold in DAPP retail stores, of which some fifteen were in operation in the towns along the line of rail and a few provincial centers in 1993 (Denconsult 1993:23–24). The retail stores display clothing on hangers much like thrift stores in the West.

DAPP urban retail stores are in strategic locations at or near major shopping streets or markets. There is fierce competition with the commercial wholesalers, especially in Lusaka. DAPP keeps a careful watch of price developments at both the commercial wholesale end and the retail end. When the government suddenly slashed an import tariff of U.S. $10 per kilogram on secondhand clothing in September 1993, DAPP closed most outlets in Lusaka, moving its entire sorting operation to Ndola on the Copperbelt, where there was less competition. Within two years, its average yearly import was back to where it had been previously, at some 500 tons. DAPP has since reopened outlets in Lusaka.

From profits generated by the resale of secondhand clothing, DAPP has launched a variety of development projects staffed by members of the Federation of UFF and Humana, volunteers, and local people throughout Zambia with focus on education, environment, community development, and health. Showcase projects include the Children's Town in rural Central Province, where former street children, orphans, and disadvantaged rural children participate in a five-year program of primary education and vocational training. One of the most recent projects is Hope Humana People to People in Ndola, which assists HIV/AIDS-infected people.

While DAPP's many activities in Zambia put more than 160 local people to work in its shops and sorting centers, teaching them empowerment through self-help (*Africa News Service,* 4 November 1997), the organization also makes money from secondhand clothing sales. The specific relationship between income from clothing sales, local development projects, and the activities of the Federation of UFF and Humana is obscure. But what is clear in relationship to the wholesaling of secondhand clothing in Zambia is that DAPP is in a structurally different position from the commercial importers who source from textile recyclers: DAPP avoids the commercial middlemen, as its clothing consignments are donations. In effect, DAPP's chief expense is transport costs. This simple fact makes DAPP's profit margin from secondhand clothes sales in Zambia potentially much higher than that of commercial dealers. And because DAPP combines commerce and charity, its status as importer remains ambiguous.

Warehouse Sales

Wholesalers typically resell their consignments from warehouses where bales of secondhand clothing are stacked up. Most warehouses in Lusaka are near the major markets where the retail trade of secondhand clothing is concentrated. Some are in the light industrial area on privately owned or rented premises. Many outlets are surrounded with tall spiked fences with tiny gates in front of which customers line up. Most customers are small-scale traders who buy one or two bales for resale in inside or outdoor sections of the large city markets. There are also rural clients and hawkers, and people from Lusaka's medium- to high-income residential areas who resell secondhand clothing privately from their homes or at workplaces in the capital's office buildings.

Customers evaluate wholesalers in terms of whether they stock "good" or "bad" bales, depending on the source and type of bale, and whether they are more or less friendly, depending on their customer practices. Although more than half of Zambia's total import of secondhand clothing is sourced in the United States, customers maintain that American bales are of poor quality. They say that European-sourced clothes show less wear and tear. When it comes to specifics, jeans imported from the United States upset Zambian retailers because of the advanced degree of wear, not to mention holes and rips. Men's trousers are best from France and Italy, customers argue, and Europe supplies better dresses than the United States; the same applies to shoes. The reputation of individual wholesalers shifts depending on source of stock and what is available at any given time at other wholesalers. This information flows through an active grapevine, prompting customers to form lines at the most popular spots. Some lines start forming early in the morning, and at some places customers receive numbers to indicate their place in the queue.

The variety of clothing bales on sale on a given day and their prices are often listed on a blackboard in the yard on the wholesaler's premises or on an inside wall of the storeroom. The inside walls of most wholesale stores have a sign with variations of the following: no credit, no return, no exchange, no refund. That is to say, customers purchase bales entirely at their own risk. I have seen several unhappy customers complaining to no avail over poor merchandise: too many torn, ripped, and damaged garments in a bale; denim material cut off from hip and bottom, purchased as a bale of jeans; or mildewed garments, perhaps from a container that got wet in transit.

Once customers reach the head of the line, they inform the attendant at the desk or counter which type of bale they want to purchase, for example, one containing women's silk blouses. They pay up front in cash, get a receipt, and are approached by one or several male warehouse workers who haul out a bale of the type the customer has specified. Bales have labels such as women's cotton blouses, children's mixed wear, or men's jeans. Most contain only one type of garment, and mixed bales called rummage sell for less. The variety of apparel has diversified considerably since the early 1990s when, for instance, very few shoes found their way into bales. Since then, bales have been available with specific items of underwear such as bras, lingerie, and nightgowns. There are bales of bomber jackets, track suits, shorts, and sweatshirts in addition to standard garments, household linens, and draperies. The warehouse inventory may include bales of ties, socks, scarves, hats, belts, and handbags. Shoes have become a particularly popular commodity.

Some bales carry the name of the country where the garments were sourced. If they do not, the warehouse staff is rarely able, or willing, to specify the source. The customer usually makes that identification once she opens the bale and scrutinizes the labels of garments, some of which still carry tags from the thrift stores in the West. "Good" wholesalers allow customers to look at a couple of bales, decide on which one they want, and briefly inspect the contents when the workman cuts open the plastic wrap at one end of the bale. This practice permits the customer a quick glance at variety of color and quality of fabric. Once a bale has been purchased, it is headloaded or carried

Figure 24 Price list of bales at salaula wholesale store, Lusaka, 1995.
Author's photograph.

Figure 25 Forty-five-kilogram bales in wholesaler's warehouse, Lusaka, 1995.
Author's photograph.

Figure 26 Shop assistants helping woman customer move salaula bale out of wholesaler's premises, Lusaka, 1995.
Author's photograph.

Figure 27 Young customers with salaula bales purchased at Khatry Brothers, Chipata, 1997.
Author's photograph.

Figure 28 Young men headloading salaula bale from wholesaler's warehouse to minibus stop for transportation to periurban township, Lusaka, 1995.
Author's photograph.

by wheelbarrow, and reloaded onto transport such as private cars, legal and pirate taxis, minibuses, and long-distance buses to reach the point of retail.

Table 4 indicates the steady increase of wholesale prices for some of the best-selling secondhand clothing items during the time that I have monitored developments in this trade. The price increases respond to the interaction of several factors both local and external, including ongoing depreciation of the kwacha, the Zambian currency; inflation; shifts in customs and tariff fees; and price increases of original sourced clothes in North America and Europe.[9]

Table 4. Median Wholesale Prices for Bales of Secondhand Clothing (in kwacha)

Year	Children's Wear	Men's Trousers	Men's Shirts	Women's Dresses	Women's Blouses	Women's Skirts
1992	40,000	36,000	44,000	33,000	35,000	34,000
1993	71,000	95,000	65,000	75,000	52,000	65,000
1995	75,000	92,000	125,000	76,000	83,000	69,000
1997	170,000	220,000	250,000	270,000	250,000	260,000

Two striking shifts in wholesale prices are evident in this table, the first between 1992 and 1993, and the second and more dramatic one between 1995 and 1997. The first of these shifts may reflect some of the ramifications on exchange rate and inflation of President Chiluba's quick embrace of very stringent IMF/World Bank structural adjustment measures after he became president of the third republic in 1991. The currency regime was particularly harsh during the early years of the new republic, when the value of the kwacha was allowed to depreciate sharply (Bates and Collier 1993). While the price rise between 1995 and 1997 no doubt continued to be influenced by the slide of the kwacha, it was probably also provoked by the more than doubling of market prices for secondhand clothing in the West in response to growing demand for this commodity on international markets.

Distribution

At the warehouse, bales of secondhand clothing are purchased by marketeers and private individuals, both women and men, who in turn distribute and sell their goods in urban and rural markets, hawk them in the countryside, and transfer them in rural exchanges in return for produce, goats, chickens, and fish. In Zambia's urban and rural markets in the mid-1990s, the secondhand clothing sections were almost everywhere many times larger than the food sections. By then the secondhand clothing trade had spilled from established markets in cities and towns onto main streets. In urban residential areas salaula is also sold from private homes, and traders bring secondhand clothing to city offices and institutions like banks for sale on credit to employees who receive monthly paychecks. In fact, wherever there is a concentration of people who receive regular wages, for instance, commercial farms and tourist lodges, traders from the nearest towns are sure to turn up on payday to sell secondhand clothing. And around all of Zambia's border-crossing points, there is a lively trade in secondhand clothing as well as a good deal of illicit transborder transfer. Focusing on some of these settings and the processes by which secondhand clothing flows across the country, I describe some scenes along the way.

Provincial Scenes

We begin in Luapula Province, which featured prominently in chapter 3's discussion of the secondhand clothing trade during the colonial period. Some of the elderly men whose involvement in the fish and kombo trade I discussed in that chapter and/or their children were in 1995 still engaged in business in general. Some legacies of past Zairean connections were still evident. Some of the elderly men barely had English language skills but communicated with me in French. And some people, both older and younger, spoke Swahili, the lingua franca of Katanga (Fabian 1986). But during the 1960s and 1970s the kombo trade had become subordinated to other activities. Secondhand clothing was not considered an "essential commodity" in the second republic's controlled economy, and it was legally imported only by people who had an import license. In effect, most of the secondhand clothing that was sold in Luapula and elsewhere during those years arrived illegally across the Zairean border. While some Luapula-based traders pursued this trade during those years, it was considered risky and was a far less common activity than it had been during the colonial period and than it was to become from the late 1980s onward.

Since the early 1990s most traders in Luapula have traveled to Lusaka to purchase bales from wholesalers, bringing them back by bus or, if they are large-scale traders, by private transport, a journey of more than 1,000 kilometers when avoiding the Congo pedicle. During the month I spent in Luapula in 1995, a few traders traveled to Ndola on the Copperbelt to purchase bales from DAPP or Komboland, the outlet of Iqbal, one of the large wholesalers. The journey to and from Ndola has its special risks, especially if done by the most direct route across the pedicle, the part of the Democratic Republic of the Congo that abuts Zambian territory. Traders taking this route complained in 1995 about wasting time and experiencing trouble, because Congolese customs officers commonly hassle them and extort money at whim.

Figure 29 Passenger bus from Lusaka with salaula bales on top, Mwanzabombwe (Kazembe), Luapula Province, 1995.
Author's photograph.

Figure 30 Small-scale traders with salaula in front of health clinic, Mansa, Luapula Province, 1995.
Author's photograph.

In the provincial towns of Mansa and Kawambwa, but less so in Kashik-ishi, a fishing and trade town on Lake Mweru, the clothing retail scene in 1995 was dominated by the secondhand clothing trade. There was also an ac-tive trade in markets and small boutiques of ready-made clothing, brought in by "suitcase traders" who traveled to Nakonde and across to Tanzania, some going as far as Dar es Salaam and Zanzibar to purchase stylish, but afford-able, garments largely manufactured in the Far East. Another category of ready-made clothing consisted of garments made to order by small tailor workshops in Lusaka, including batches of men's trousers, women's dresses, girls' dresses, and boys' shorts—all styled in a way that differs from most salaula and barely costing more. There were tailors as well, repairing and al-tering secondhand clothing and sewing garments to order. Many independent tailors were middle-aged men or older, of whom several had working experi-ence in Zaire. The wage-employed tailors in smaller workshops tended to be younger, and some of them were women. Such workshops manufactured uni-forms and specific garments to order, including chitenge dresses.

Secondhand clothing was everywhere: from the main town markets to markets on the outskirts, along streets, and carried along by itinerant traders. The general trading scene at Kawambwa appeared less active than at Mansa, perhaps because of uncertainty about the future of the Kawambwa Tea Es-tates, a major employer whose workers had not been paid for the last several months. Only in Kashikishi on the lake were there more traders in fish than in secondhand clothing. Aside from a few old-timers, most traders had con-ducted this activity for less than five years; many were newcomers to it in the wake of the shrinking purchasing power of wages, job retrenchments, or both. There were more women among the elderly cohort, often single heads of households, and more men among the younger traders. Young women were more frequent among the workers attending stalls than among the inde-pendent operators, among whom were more young men. As in most markets elsewhere, many traders considered the retailing of secondhand clothing a temporary occupation, and some had started it with the hope of accumulating start-up capital for something else. Most of them described their trading ac-tivities as ensuring the means for day-to-day survival and spoke of the diffi-culty of making much more money than what was needed to buy the next bale. In Luapula in general, some marketeers conducted secondhand cloth-ing trade only intermittently during the fishing off-season.

The attractiveness of the secondhand clothing trade depends on what al-ternative opportunities are available as well as on the resources and capital in-dividuals can muster, given their age, sex, and educational, familial, and regional background. The traders I interviewed in 1993 in Kabwe, a provin-cial town on the line of rail some 140 kilometers north of Lusaka, did not see

Figure 31 Salaula for sale in periurban market, Mansa, Luapula Province, 1995.
Author's photograph.

Figure 32 Salaula for sale in market, Kawambwa, Luapula Province, 1995.
Author's photograph.

Figure 33 Hawkers selling salaula, Mansa, 1995.
Author's photograph.

Figure 34 Salaula roadside stand near Landless Corner, south of Kabwe, 1993.
Author's photograph.

much growth potential for their activity. Kabwe's economy was suffering because of the temporary closure of Mulungushi Textiles, Ltd., and retrenchment at Zambia Railways, which is headquartered there. Some of the young male traders I spoke with were laid off by Mulungushi Textiles; while waiting for the factory to reopen, they were considering plans for how to get ahead. One of the most common suggestions made by this cohort of young men in all the markets where I have worked is the idea of taking "courses," among which computer programming and accounting were the most popular. Because Kabwe lies in the shadow of Lusaka, young men frequently think of going to the capital to develop some business or other. Young female traders and workers seemed to be less impatient than their young male cohort with developments in the secondhand clothing trade.

Urban-Rural Connections

Some secondhand clothes move from Lusaka and the provincial towns into the countryside. Tailors and stores that sell ready-made clothing are few and far between in Zambia's rural areas today, probably fewer than during the two decades before independence in 1964. The very low, and deteriorating, levels of rural income are the cause of very modest clothing expenditures among farm households. On a Tonga farm near Monze in Southern Province that raised cattle and grew maize, cotton, groundnuts, beans, and sorghum, no one among the male farm head, his two wives, and their twelve children had received clothing of any kind for the last two years when I visited in 1993. The clothing last obtained in 1991 from an itinerant trader who arrived at the nearby maize grinding mill was secondhand clothing, some of which was bought for cash and some exchanged for maize and chickens. The last brand new clothing bought in this household was a child's school uniform.

   School uniforms were also among the acquisitions in farm households I visited in Kawambwa District in rural Luapula Province in 1995. On this trip I met an itinerant trader whose pile of secondhand clothing was displayed on the ground in front of a rural homestead. He was a Kawambwa Tea Estate's worker trying to make money while waiting to receive his outstanding pay, by selling clothing he brought into the villages on a bicycle. In Kanenga, a village much deeper into the district, farm households acquired clothing largely through barter with traders from Kawambwa who visited them around harvest time. The village settlement that holds the chief's palace had a single trader in secondhand clothes, plus one trader in chitenge and one in canvas shoes, all merchandise that individual traders brought up from Lusaka, traveling by bus. One male farm head in his late twenties had last supplied his wife and three children with clothing one year prior to my visit. On that occa-

Figure 35 Rural shop with tailor-made dresses from Lusaka for sale at Chiawa, Lusaka Rural, 1992.
Author's photograph.

Figure 36 Peasant farmer and his two wives dressed for visitors near Monze, Southern Province, 1993.
Author's photograph.

sion he obtained a pair of secondhand trousers in exchange for eight gallons of maize, a shirt for six gallons, a dress for three gallons, and children's clothing for four gallons. This man owned a bicycle, which he used often for the three-hour ride to Kawambwa, where he had obtained a loan for fertilizer. One of his neighbors, around the same age and with a wife and three children, had not been to Kawambwa even once during the previous year. When the itinerant secondhand clothing trader came through around harvest time, the children and wife were supplied with secondhand clothing in exchange for maize, and one child got a school uniform in exchange for ten gallons of maize. The farmer did not purchase any garments for himself during that visit.

Secondhand clothing finds wide use in rural areas as remuneration for piece work instead of cash. Female casual workers in the early 1990s sometimes preferred to be paid in kind, including secondhand clothing, rather than cash, to prevent husbands from diverting their earnings (Geisler and Hansen 1994:102). Yet the barter value of salaula diminished as more of it became available. At an agricultural training scheme operated by the Seventh-Day Adventists at Chimpempe in Luapula Province, casual workers were remunerated in secondhand clothing from a container load donated to the local Seventh-Day Adventists from Australia. While they first were keen on getting clothes in return for their labor, the workers in 1995 insisted that they would rather have cash. Rural people are realizing that the terms of such exchanges frequently are unequal. A comment in the financial section of one of the papers put this squarely: "Maize is also bartered with salaula or other goods which, when compared to cash payments works out beneficial to the trader rather than to the farmer" (*Post,* 11 July 1995, p. 12). When peasant farmers in North-Western Province complained of lacking a market for their maize and being forced to exchange it for salaula, they described the situation as a "rip-off . . . because the merchandise with which they exchanged the maize was of little value" (*Times of Zambia,* 13 October 1996).

When I first began examining the retailing of secondhand clothing in Lusaka in 1992, the rural areas were the main destination for many of the garments in fabrics, colors, and styles that did not appeal to urban consumers. Urban retailers spoke of the easily recognizable attire of country people who came to town to shop: gaudy colors like orange or poison green, unmatched trousers and jacket, and outmoded ties and hats. Rural women dressed in crimplene dresses (polyester knit), which was just about the last fabric urban women then would be seen wearing; and shoes gave the peasant away, in particular when none were worn. Such disdain does not quite apply any longer. The greater availability of secondhand clothing has made rural residents more concerned both with quality and style. What is more, dynamic urban-rural interchanges of people, goods, and ideas have always made rural residents conscious of lifestyle issues and different ways of making a living. While peasant farmers in North-Western Province perhaps are among the most "remote" from the center of activity in Lusaka, they in fact vocally objected to the advantage urban traders were taking of their circumstances.

Off-Farm Rural Activities

Throughout the 1990s urban retailers of secondhand clothing extended their sales across Zambia's rural areas, particularly to localities where regular wage-earning opportunities exist. A sizable proportion of people who earn monthly wages live on commercial farms and near tourist lodges, often working away from home on a seasonal basis. For instance, some 135 kilometers south of Lusaka near Chirundu, the border crossing to Zimbabwe on the Zambezi River, is Masstock, a multinational commercial farm on which migrant workers grow export crops bound for European markets. Also in the area are a growing number of privately owned tourist lodges, creating work opportunities both for migrants and local people from nearby villages in chieftainess Chiawa's area.

When I first visited Chiawa in 1992, there were a handful of traders of secondhand clothing in the villages, largely returned male migrants. Most of them worked from home, displaying their goods in front of their homesteads; on payday at Masstock, some of them went to the workshop gate with clothing to sell.[10] They sourced by taking the pontoon across the Zambezi River, hitching a ride to Chirundu, and traveling from there by bus to Lusaka. In addition to salaula, some brought back a few tailor-made garments of the types described above and a few lengths of chitenge. The only general store in the area had very little clothing of any kind on display.

This had all changed by 1995. Production at Masstock had shifted from cotton to marigold and paprika. The labor force had expanded from around 700 to 2,000 at peak season, around 60 percent men and 40 percent women. Secondhand clothing traders were flocking to Masstock on payday, so many that the company instituted a sliding payday over the last three Saturdays of the month. Traders came from Chirundu, Kafue, and Lusaka for those dates, sleeping overnight, often in the open, in an area next to the general store and the two bars that had opened since 1992. Unlike in 1992 when I did not see any tailors in the villages, in 1995 there were at least eight, most of them doing repair and alterations. And hardly any village residents traded secondhand clothing any longer.

In addition to selling to Masstock workers, often on credit with specific repayment schedules, some of these traders plied the secondhand clothing sales trail in the small provincial towns from Chirundu on the border up to Lusaka. Similar movements occur in other places with identifiable concentrations of people and money, for example, around Mfuwe some fifteen kilometers from the national park in the Luangwa valley, where there are several tourist lodges and an airport used by local and small international flights. Also in the area is a large rural development project, the Luangwa Integrated Resource Development Program, and a command station for national park rangers and scouts, among others. Like elsewhere in rural Zambia, in the early 1990s the people who lived in this area had very little clothing they could buy, other than trousers, shorts, and chitenge.

One of the first people to establish secondhand clothing trade near Mfuwe came down from Lundazi in 1993 and set up a big shop by local standards, employing six or seven associates and workers to supervise the trade while he remained at Lundazi.[11] He purchased bales there, probably offloaded from consignments bound for Chipata; Lundazi lies two-thirds of the way from Nakonde, the border crossing to Tanzania, to Chipata. Because the trade was popular, he brought bales in every second week, and soon several small-scale operators began to sell salaula along the roadside between nearby villages and the entrance to the game park. But by 1994 the Lundazi-based trader's shop was no longer in operation; a brother had died, and the owner was distressed and gave up the Mfuwe operation. The trading opportunities were taken up by several new entrants to the business. Of the ten or so persons interviewed in this area in August 1995, some were local traders who occasionally sold secondhand clothing, and some were itinerant traders from elsewhere, arriving near payday much like at Masstock. The majority sold secondhand clothing as their full-time occupation, purchasing bales in Chipata some 120 kilometers down the Mfuwe road and occasionally in Lusaka, some 570 kilometers away.

Transborder Trade

Secondhand clothing is exchanged widely across Zambia's borders to neighboring countries that ban this import. There was an active illegal trade through Chipata into Malawi until 1994 when imports no longer were prohibited. Zimbabwe is a popular market with secondhand clothing traders in Zambia. In 1994 the Zimbabwean government restricted the import, which previously had been permitted by charitable organizations (*Herald,* 10 February 1994). A vast amount of secondhand clothing, including bales, continues to be available for sale in public markets throughout Zimbabwe, some of this offloaded en route by truckers hauling consignments from Durban to Zambia. A significant quantity of secondhand clothing is smuggled through Forbes, Victoria Falls, Kanyembo, and Chirundu border posts in northern Zimbabwe by small-scale and not so small-scale traders from Zambia and Mozambique. Some Lusaka-based traders who pursued this trade traveled to Luangwa (previ-

Figure 37 Canoes loaded with salaula at Feira ready for transport across the Zambezi River into Mozambique, 1993.
Photograph by Leslie Ashbaugh, reproduced with permission.

ously Feira) in the southeastern corner of Zambia on the Zambezi River where the borders of Mozambique and Zimbabwe meet. From here the bales were transported by canoe to Zumbo in Mozambique to be exchanged for fish, and then on to Kanyembo on the Zimbabwe side where a bus service connects with Bulawayo, the second-largest city in Zimbabwe.[12]

The most trafficked border crossing between Zambia and Zimbabwe is Chirundu, where the Zimbabwean customs authorities in vain are attempting to curtail the influx of secondhand clothing from Zambia. Their efforts have been directed toward small-scale traders, mostly Zambian and Zimbabwean women who travel in both directions, Zambian women to sell in the south and Zimbabwean women to source in the north. Customs interventions on the Zimbabwean side have consisted of limitations on the number of garments a person was permitted to bring across for "personal use." There are many ways of evading these rules: wearing several layers of clothing with a chitenge wrapped on top, catching rides with truck drivers willing to conceal the goods, and including "children" in the passport to increase the number of items a traveler and her companions may carry. Last but not least, there are corruptable customs officials.

These and other border-crossing practices are risky. Women have been accused of peddling sex (*Zambia Daily Mail,* 16 October 1994). When crossing from Livingstone to Victoria Falls town on the Zimbabwean side of the border in early 1995, several Zambian women were stripped and frisked in public. An officer in charge who claimed "we cannot allow this" said, "These women are unscrupulous and strap themselves in chitenge materials and second hand clothes which they smuggle in to sell and purchase groceries to re-sell in Zambia" (*Zambia Daily Mail,* 26 April 1995). Arrests are made, merchandise confiscated, and fines imposed. Also in 1995 some 700 Zambians, "mostly women cross-border traders," were locked up in Hwange prison in Zimbabwe, some with small children, and charged with illegally bringing in secondhand clothes. The length of time they spent in prison varied, depending on how much clothing they had been found with. In spite of such harassment, one of the arrested women said that she would continue the trade; many of the women had no choice but to go on, she explained, "because their husbands have been retrenched" (*Zambia Daily Mail,* 17 August 1995).

Secondhand clothing by the piece and in bales is among the commodities, including precious and semiprecious stones, ivory, rhino horns, and drugs, that are smuggled widely across borders in this region. The specific exchange value of secondhand clothing depends on socioeconomic and political factors prevalent in particular locations. Many of the countries that share borders with Zambia, among them Angola and the Democratic Republic of Congo, continue to experience political unrest, and violence is still rife in parts of independent South Africa. Small arms, including AK-47 guns, kalashnikovs, submachine guns, cartridges, and grenades, have achieved sad importance. The background is the massive inflow of weapons during the liberation and civil wars, and small arms continue to proliferate in spite of embargoes, often transshipped (Batchelor [1997]; Potgieter [1997]). Small arms have been reported in exchanges by secondhand clothing traders who travel from South Africa through Namibia or Botswana to the borders of Angola, and they most likely feature in exchanges with Zambian traders on that country's long border to Angola as well (TASS, 9 November 1993). [13] Zambian traders no doubt exchange salaula for guns and ammunition at trading centers inside Angola, for instance, Cazombo, that are nodes in a centuries-old trading network. Zimbabwean traders traveling across the border to Mozambique have reportedly brought back not only secondhand clothes but also weapons that feature in the border trade between Zambia and Mozambique (*Southern Africa Chronicle,* 7 October 1996).

Transforming Value

The recommodification of imported secondhand clothing into salaula in Zambia involves several phases (Kopytoff 1986:73). Transactions between overseas suppliers and local importers initiate the process through which the value of the West's unwanted but still wearable clothing is reactivated on local terms. Through subsequent transformations the meanings shift in ways that help to redefine used clothes into "new" garments. These transformations begin in communications between exporters and importers and in on-site visits, continue at the wholesale outlet and in public markets, and are made public in how consumers put themselves together with salaula.

Some of the transformations and the redefinitions that take place through them can be revealed if we look closely at a variety of informal practices that have evolved around the buying and selling of salaula. I close this chapter with brief comments on transformations of meanings that are initiated at points of import and wholesale.

The sorting and grading of secondhand clothing prior to export is guided not only by the West's categories of garment distinctions but also by specifications from the importer's end. The big wholesalers try to reckon with the changing cultural and seasonal demand that place a local mark on what at first sight appears to be a clothing universe determined by the West. These local terms are the seasonally varying terms for what sells, when, and where, and the culturally shifting terms for what is proper dress. Style terms enter as well, both regarding fabric and what is considered to be "the latest."

Once imported bales of secondhand clothing have been stacked in the warehouse and customers specify the type of bale they want to purchase, the transformation process continues. Customers assess their nonreturnable bales with exacting care before completing a purchase. They scrutinize the plastic wrap and inspect the straps to determine that the bale has not been tampered with. Wholesalers who import bales larger than the standard forty-five to fifty kilograms sometimes open, sort, and rebale items. Some importers are said to remove choice items, and clothing presorted in this way is said to end up in shops. The purpose of the customer's scrutiny in the warehouse is to ascertain that the bale has arrived "fresh" from its Western source, untouched by dealer interference, and thus offering a range of "new" items.

A variety of practices pertaining to the retail of salaula continue the transformation of the West's used clothing into new objects in Zambia, as I discuss in the next chapter. Once the bale of bulk garments has been opened, its content is individualized into distinct objects of exchange. At this point, specific items of salaula sell for so much per piece or so much per pile. From then on, once items of salaula have been purchased, they begin their new lives through the ongoing cycle of consumption.

7 Clothing Retail Practices

Some marketeers, traders, and vendors speak of the retailing of salaula as a Pick-A-Lot, the state lottery in Zambia. Selling salaula is a gamble, they say, a "do or die" business. Still others characterize salaula retailing as a business in which you "win some and lose some." In fact, salaula retailing comprises all of those aspects. As this chapter demonstrates, the experience of individual traders depends on many factors, some of which are related to Zambia's changing political economy and others are related to personal skills and resources. While the secondhand clothing retail trade in the post–World War II years did indeed produce some rags-to-riches stories in Luapula Province, it rarely does so now. Today's salaula trade is increasingly an occupational refuge for people who never have had formal sector jobs and retrenched employees both from the public and private sector. It also constitutes a temporary pursuit aimed at accumulating money for other activities. And it serves as a sideline for people who are seeking to extend their earnings from jobs elsewhere.

The explosion of Zambia's salaula market has not only provided an income source for traders and created ancillary enconomic activities for many others. It has also made a profusion of clothing available from which dress-conscious consumers can purchase just the garments they want. "Watch Lusaka," suggested one writer. "All who are gorgeously attired mostly get their clothes abroad." Lusaka's so-called boutiques, he went on, "have become rather like museums . . . neither Lusaka's Cairo Road nor the Kamwala shopping area is the place to look. You have a better chance at the secondhand clothes dealer, the flea market or even the city centre market dealer who jaunts between Lusaka and Johannesburg" (*Times of Zambia,* 26 August 1995).

Focusing on salaula, this chapter turns to the clothing retail scene in Lusaka, the rapidly growing capital whose population was estimated at 1,327,000 in 1995 (UNDP 1995). On first sight the dramatic growth of salaula markets meets the observer's eye as a chaotic mass of secondhand clothing hung up on flimsy wood contraptions or displayed on tables or in piles on the ground. Yet the economic geography of salaula retailing contains several distinct segments that are most noticeable in large cities like Lusaka and that I describe at the beginning of this chapter. Then I examine the participants in the trade, their sales practices, and some of the ancillary activities that have arisen around the retailing of this commodity, including the work of small-scale tailors. In the process I also take note of distinctions consumers draw between different types of used clothes that they do not construe as equally desirable. I briefly outline the contours of the ready-made clothing retail scene and the informal sourcing of garments from "outside." And I close with observations about recommodification, extending the discussion from previous chapters about the transformation of meanings that redefine the West's used clothing into new garments in Zambia.

The discussion in this chapter draws on my research into the organization of the salaula retail trade in several urban markets between 1992 and 1999 and is informed as well by my long-term observations of Lusaka's informal sector. In addition to carrying out interviews, I spent considerable time in these markets, observing the flow of business and the interaction between traders and customers. I have also explored the scope of small-scale tailoring both in markets and in front of shops and have done research with a view to comparing prices and type/quality of garments across the retail clothing sector.[1]

Marketplaces and Trading Spaces

The salaula retail scene that met the visitor's eye in Lusaka in the 1990s con-sisted of sprawling outdoor spaces adjacent to established marketplaces where traders erected ingenious contraptions to display their merchandise. Plastic roofs that sheltered traders and customers against sun and rain took on a sorry look during the dry season as they accumulated sand and dust. Radio music and cries by hawkers increased the noise level. The visitor would have been struck by the volume of trade, especially salaula, and the crowding of people in the streets just off the main city center. But these were recent devel-opments. Lusaka's secondhand clothing retailing scene shifted geographi-cally since this trade began to grow in the late 1980s. Before that, township markets used to have a few secondhand clothing traders who sourced gar-ments at the door of expatriate households or had connections to people who brought used clothing to the capital from Zaire. During the mid to late 1980s Zairean traders began to bring bales of secondhand clothing into Kamwala market, and the first direct importers appeared on the scene. The import grew rapidly in the early 1990s when all townships and city markets included ex-panding salaula sections.

City and township markets have both inside and outside sections, the in-side section consisting of stalls with roofs, while the outside sections merely have demarcations. Open-air traders initially displayed their merchandise right on the ground, gradually building up their stands. In 1992 Lusaka's Soweto market had the largest section of open-air trade. The market itself began developing on privately owned land as a center of produce trade for periurban farmers in the late 1970s. It soon featured Lusaka's largest auto-part section plus the standard trades in small-scale manufacture, repair, and services. It was called Soweto after the largest African township in Johannesburg, where the population was relegated to the periphery of town, with few services provided. Traders called the large salaula section that arose on the bare ground around Soweto market Kambilombilo. The name stems from a rural resettlement center established on the Copperbelt during the second republic with the aim of turning unemployed urban youth into good farmers. The special meaning of the term derives from the fact that the youth who were brought there were left without any provision of services. The term Kambilombilo is used for outside sections of markets elsewhere, where traders are left to their own devises. At Kambilombilo, there is no infrastructure to speak of and no amenities.

Toward the end of 1994, traders in Soweto's outside salaula section and part of the built-up interior market were relocated to yield space for the construction of a new city market. Several months of trouble preceded the move, before traders gave in to the city council's request that they vacate their stands for demolition. In return they were promised stands in the new market (*Post,* 30 September 1994, p. 4, 7 October 1994; 28 October 1994). Some went farther out on the open field, establishing stands underneath tall pylons carrying power cables. Others moved to Kamwala market, where space had become at a premium; many set themselves up on the open field outside the built-up market, next to the railway tracks. They called this section Gabon, a designation that is used in other open-air markets. The connotation is to perish in a disaster, like the Zambia National Football team who died in a plane crash after a match in Gabon in 1993.

Kamwala market had in 1995 some 500 salaula traders, while Soweto had more than 2,000, according to a staff member in charge of fee collection. These are very conservative figures that do not reckon with the masses of salaula traders who spilled onto sidewalks and into main streets near Lusaka's center. The 1997 formal opening of the new Soweto market, now called City Market, did little to halt these developments (Financial Mail, 3–9 November 1998). Many standholders who had fought to be allotted space in the new market structure soon gave up their stands, complaining of lack of customers and high fees charged by the private company managing the market (*Post,* 11 August 1997; *Sunday Mail,* 17 August 1997). Within days of the opening, the city council burned down stands on the outskirt of the new market, yet standholders continued to leave it for the streets in ongoing conflicts

Figure 38 *(top)* Traders and customer at salaula stand
with men's trousers and shirts in the outside section
of Kamwala market, Lusaka, 1992.
Author's photograph.

Figure 39 *(middle)* Trader checking his account-
book at salaula stand with men's trousers and short-
sleeved shirts in the outside section of Kamwala
market, Lusaka, 1992.
Author's photograph.

Figure 40 *(bottom)* Salaula displayed in piles on the
ground in the outside section of Kamwala market,
Lusaka, 1992. A downtown office building is in the
background.
Author's photograph.

between inside and outside traders, police, and management (*Sunday Times of Zambia,* 10 August 1997; *Zambia Daily Mail,* 2 September 1997; *Sunday Mail,* 15 February 1998; *Times of Zambia,* 13 June 1998). In an effort to make street vendors move into established markets, city councils supported by paramilitary and police in April and May 1999 demolished their temporary stands in cities and towns across the country (*Zambia Daily Mail,* 29 April 1999; *Sunday Times of Zambia,* 2 May 1999). While a temporary truce may prevail between vendors and authorities in the wake of this massive intervention, the vendors are likely to return to the streets as they have successfully done on previous occasions.

Within established city and township markets, standholders pay an urban-council levy and a variety of fees, for instance, for security guards, in support of the football team, and almost everywhere to a funeral association. Those who trade from outside sections do not pay the council levy but are usually asked to contribute some of the other fees. The big markets are subdivided into sections, each of which has a chair to mediate problems and to bring concerns to the attention of the market administration. Some standholders sublease their stalls, a practice that adds to the overhead of marketeers who rent. Most city marketeers incur overnight storage costs, as their merchandise is too bulky to be carried between home and work by public transportation. A common practice is to store goods in an inside stand and pay the standholder a monthly fee. There are transportation costs as well, as marketeers commonly pay for both their own and their workers' transport.

Traders and Workers

Salaula traders are young and old, women and men with different educational and employment histories and from many ethnic groups. Some operate in husband-and-wife teams or with relatives. Absentee operators employ assistants or workers while some owner-operators use hired or unpaid help intermittently. A few traders have several stands, but the vast majority are small-scale independent operators. When I began to observe this trade in 1992, women slightly outnumbered men among the independent traders; they tended to be middle-aged, between thirty and forty-five years old. By 1995, women still had a slight edge over men in terms of numbers, although more young adult men than women were entering the trade as independent traders. There were proportionately more young men than young women among the workers/attendants in Lusaka's salaula markets. In 1995 more than two-thirds of these workers were not remunerated for their work other than with food, transport, and occasional items of clothing. They were mostly "kept" relatives of the person operating the stand. "Keeping" relatives in

Zambia means providing them with food, clothing, and shelter; such arrangements are very common in households where relatives provide unpaid domestic work, and they have, it seems, expanded onto the market scene.

More women than men were single heads of households among the 30–45 age category of salaula traders. Yet in all these markets there were more than twice as many unmarried male traders as unmarried females. Many of these young adult male traders lived with their parents or guardians in Lusaka, not having established households of their own. Some of them pursued the salaula trade in the hope of earning enough money to leave this work for something better, whereas many of the middle-aged women retailed salaula to contribute to sagging household budgets.

How do people get their start in the salaula trade? To set up business requires capital to purchase bales and cover the overhead of the trade as well as knowledge about the organization of the trade. Some female traders receive start-up capital from husbands, while others save it from their household allowances. Both these practices are becoming inadequate to generate sufficient money to purchase bales because of the combined effects of inflation and rising bale prices. The most common start is provided by relatives who pitch in money. Loans are very occasionally arranged between kin. Some of the young male independent salaula traders started out on their own after working for someone else, learning the tricks of the trade and acquiring some start-up capital. Young women might have worked for a relative who helped them buy their first bale. Young workers are exceedingly poorly paid, and because the trade is difficult to supervise, it is common knowledge that some workers make money on their own behalf. In the 1990s severance pay or retrenchment packages were often used to launch trading in salaula. Once bales have been purchased, the level of success depends to a great degree on the trader's practical skills and business acumen. It also depends on the quality and style of garments contained in the bales, which is why traders themselves speak of this business as a gamble, a Pick-A-Lot, in which the outcome hinges on chance.

Salaula retailers may be grouped into three categories according to their length of involvement with this business. The most established traders I met had been in this business since the early 1980s, if not before. The second category entered this business during the last half of the 1980s. The vast majority of traders fall in the third category, having begun within the last couple of years. By 1995 there were very few of the old-time traders left, and more than half of all the traders in the markets I investigated had begun this activity after 1991. In short, the salaula retail scene is very much a phenomenon of the third republic.

The old-timers entered the secondhand clothing trade in two ways. Some purchased used clothing from expatriate households, calling directly at the door or identifying sellers, mostly departing expatriates, from newspaper advertisements. For example, a woman born in 1935 in Northern Province, the first in Lusaka's Mtendere township to deal in secondhand clothing in the early 1980s, still obtained most of her supplies in that way as late as 1988. She told me that she started buying bales at Kamwala market when "the Europeans began charging too much; just like Zambians." In 1992 her stand in the inside section of the market displayed the contents of three bales (jerseys, jackets, dresses), and she was planning to buy another bale soon. One of her daughters, whom I remember as a teenager assisting her mother, also had a stand at the Mtendere market. Her husband was studying in the United States, and she sold salaula in order to finance "suitcase trade" to the south. During subsequent years she did travel up and down, but her health declined, and she was dead when I returned in 1997. Her mother, by 1995 still working in the inside section of the market, withdrew from trade, complaining about the competition from the open-air traders.

The second avenue through which well-established traders entered the secondhand clothing trade is a "northern connection," much like the way the early wholesalers got started. Several long-term traders had regional backgrounds in Zambia's northern corridor, adjacent to Zaire and Tanzania, and some were from Luapula. A typical career is that of a trader from North-Western Province, born in the 1930s, who came to Lusaka in 1972. When I met him in 1992, he had a stall inside Kamwala market where he sold clothes from four bales. When he first entered this trade, he traveled all the way to Lubumbashi in Zaire to purchase bales, which he brought back to Lusaka. He had not been to Zaire in recent years, he explained, because bales had become readily available from importers in Lusaka. His wife sold vegetables in the market in one of the townships, where they had their own house and lived with their eight children. Like many well-established traders, this man employed three young workers to assist him in the market. While I found him still active at his stand in 1995, I was unable to trace his whereabouts in 1997.

Many traders who have remained in the salaula business since the late 1980s have weathered difficult times by diversifying. Among them are people for whom the secondhand clothing trade is a sideline activity they follow while holding a regular job, including doctors, nurses, and university lecturers. They commonly had assistants or young relatives supervise the retail activity. This category also includes people who have given up wage labor for salaula, such as a woman born in 1958 who held a social worker's job for thirteen years. When explaining to me in 1992 how she had begun to take unpaid leaves from her job in order to go to Tanzania to buy used clothing and other goods for resale in Zambia, she said that holding a formal job was "a waste of time; there is no money in it." She had quit her position in 1986. On her return from trips to Tanzania, she washed and ironed the clothes and took them around office buildings for sale. Some people in those days "looked down" on used clothes, and she would tell them that "her sister in the U.K. had sent her things to resell." She had worked from an outside stand at Soweto market selling women's clothes for the past year and a half when I met her. Her husband was a self-employed electrician, and they lived in the southern part of Lusaka in a house of their own with their four children.

I noted earlier that more young adult male traders than female are unmarried. Among them was a man in his early twenties, educated through the twelfth grade, who began selling salaula in the late 1980s. When he was declared redundant in 1987 after three years of work as a bricklayer for one of Lusaka's large contractors, Minestone, he used his severance pay to purchase secondhand clothes from Zairean suppliers in Kamwala market. Living with his mother and his retired father, he contributed to household expenses with earnings from his salaula sales and occasional building jobs, which he did on the side.

The third and largest category, those who launched their trade since the early 1990s, consists of people from many walks of life who are in tight economic circumstances. They include recent widows and widowers, divorcees, and young people, especially young men with basic education but no formal job. In this category are also married women and men who sell salaula to ease strained household budgets. Some young men hoped that their earnings would finance a training course, and some young women were selling salaula while waiting for admission into nursing school or teacher's training college. Among them were two brothers from Luapula in their midtwenties whom I met at the Gabon section of Kamwala market in 1995. They had both completed grade twelve and had been trained at trade school, one as a mechanic and the other as an automotive electrician. After working for the now defunct United Bus Company in Kitwe for a while, the younger brother quit his job. He began selling groceries in Kitwe market and used his savings to purchase salaula. He went to Lusaka in 1993 and had been operating from Gabon at Kamwala for one year when his older brother joined him. They both were familiar with this business from their parents, who in the 1980s brought salaula from Zaire into Luapula to their shop at Mansa. The two young traders allotted their profits to the older brother's "suitcase trade" in Zimbabwe and South Africa; he had a passport. Like many other travelers, he purchased products abroad according to specifications from Indian traders. "Salaula," this young man argued, "anyone can do. But traveling is a bit more advanced." Both these young traders expressed hopes of earning good money to create better living circumstances for themselves, including building a house and buying a car. "But what can one do in Zambia today?" they asked. Still unmarried, they shared a rented room in one of the low-income townships.

The third category includes a sizable proportion of persons who lost jobs in the ongoing retrenchment in Zambia's civil service and private sector. While this process started at the bottom ranks, I met several midlevel civil servants with salaula stands in 1995. Many of them were caught in a bind when receiving their severance packages, especially those who had not acquired homes of their own while residing in government housing. Now living in rented accommodation in periurban townships, some of them had turned to salaula trading as a means to ensure household income. "They all come running," commented one of the older traders who worried about the expansion, "wanting to sell salaula."

The ranks of salaula traders are constantly replenished as some people drop out and others enter. Not all recent entrants remain in business. They all complain about the rapidly increasing prices of bales, slow sales, and competition. Yet a twenty-four-year-old man with Eastern Province background and grade-seven schooling considered the salaula trade preferable to his former activity, selling "rocco" (rock) buns and bread from a bicycle near workplaces in Lusaka's light industrial area. When I spoke with him, he was trading from a stand in Kamwala's outside section, specializing in men's coats and jackets. He kept on in this business through 1995, and he seemed, when I met him again in 1997, to be doing reasonably well. But a thirty-five-year-old widower from the north who started selling salaula in 1991 told me in 1992 that he soon would return to his former job as a tailor for a shopkeeper in Soweto market. He complained about losses from a bale of men's trousers, but still wanted to try a bale of men's shirts, hoping that they might sell better and faster. A twenty-two-year-old recently divorced woman educated through grade ten had turned to salaula in 1992 as a way of supporting herself and her child. In her first three months of trading, she purchased four bales and was in the process of clearing the garments from the last two when we met. The slow turnover made her reluctant to consider salaula trading a viable long-term strategy for making a living.

In the past astute traders were able to make good money from the secondhand clothing trade in Luapula, investing it in other businesses and diversifying. Some of the old-time traders who were among Lusaka's pioneers in this business also did well, making enough money to provide their children with an education, build their own homes and at times houses for rent, open small shops in townships, and purchase private cars. But for many others who were involved with the early secondhand clothing trade in Lusaka, this was just one among many enterprises at which they tried their hands. The prospects for accumulation decreased as more traders entered. Several traders who entered this business in the late 1980s were still able to build houses of their own, one of the high priorities at the urban low-income level where affordable housing is scarce. They did so piecemeal, beginning with one core room and adding rooms as and when their means allowed. Indeed, when considering their experiences and changes in the business, some of them pointed to their houses as their only achievement for many years of work. Of course, there are exceptions, as the following case demonstrates. It is noteworthy because of its twist on the relationship between the tailor's trade and salaula.

When I spoke with William Tembo in 1992, he had a fairly well stocked salaula stand inside Kamwala market where he had been trading since the late 1980s. In 1995 I found him in the market's tailor section, operating his own workshop. A brother continued to sell salaula. Mr. Tembo had invested his earnings from salaula in this enterprise, which he started in 1994, purchasing three sewing machines and renting two. He employed up to seven young men with basic sewing skills whom he paid by the piece. One of the two workers I found busy at the machines had been trained at trade school while the other had learned to sew from a friend. Mr. Tembo's workshop produced only one type of garment: men's trousers for the low-income ready-made clothing market. One-quarter of his production was sewn to individual order while the remaining three-quarters were tailored in response to larger orders, for example, of fifty to one-hundred pairs of trousers, placed by people coming to Lusaka all the way from Mbala in the north to Livingstone in the south. While Mr. Tembo admitted his workers only "knew trousers," he also spoke of beginning production of overalls and dustcoats, garments for which there is a specific demand and which are not easily found in salaula.

Sales Practices

That anyone can do salaula is a bit of an overstatement. Successful trading requires insight into marketing strategies, detailed consumer knowledge, and a good deal of business acumen. Chance plays a role as well, since traders never can be certain of the quality and style of garments when they purchase bales at the wholesaler. Traders pursue a variety of sales strategies that are reflected in when they purchase bales, where and how they display their merchandise, and how they price their goods. These strategies have developed with increasing ingenuity since the early 1990s, when salaula marketing commonly took place from a pile of clothes on the ground or, if inside a market, on a table, with a few items hung up. Today most traders except those who operate on city streets display their best clothes on hangers. Special stands and contraptions have been created for this purpose. Poorer-quality garments and damaged items are relegated to piles on the ground.

Figure 41 Fur jackets and bras for sale in Main Masala market, Ndola, 1993. Author's photograph.

Figure 42 Men's shirts for sale at Main Masala market, Ndola, 1993. Author's photograph.

The volume of business in salaula markets at any given time is influenced by customers' ability to purchase and by the availability of bales. Traders adjust their volume of salaula, and thus their purchasing practices, to variations in demand across the work week, to the monthly pay cycles that are observed in different work sectors, and to major shifts in seasonal demand. The first days of the week are slow in many markets, with trade picking up toward the weekend. Most salaula markets stay open over the weekend. The last two weeks of every month is the best time for business. The army receives its pay by midmonth. Demand in general increases from the twenty-first of the month until the twenty-fifth, which is payday in many firms and offices, and traders make sure to have fresh stock at those times. Consumer demand slows down considerably during the beginning of the month when the majority of the wage-employed population has used most of its money on essential purchases and credit installments. The great seasonal low in this trade is between January and April, when most people have spent large amounts on school fees and school uniforms. Demand picks up again in April and May. June and July are the winter months in this region, when both traders and importers make sure to stock winter clothing. Leather jackets, windbreakers, bomber jackets, and even men's full-length wool coats are popular garments then, as are cardigans, jerseys, and wool skirts.

The most common sales method is "one-one." It involves the sale of individual garments that are priced separately. Negotiation over price usually takes place in individual sales, as it does in a practice known as "on order," which involves customers' buying several items at a reduced price with a view to reselling. These are often items that do not sell well in town or that have been damaged. Many rural customers buy "on order" and resell their goods in the villages. During the winter Zimbabweans travel to Lusaka by bus and train to purchase cold-weather clothing such as coats, jackets, wool skirts, and jerseys. They bring along Zimbabwean products to sell or barter in order to finance their trips. Many who do not have personal contacts in Lusaka sleep in the open on the grounds of the intercity bus terminal.

Not all garments sell well, and there are times when business is slow. In an effort to move their merchandise, traders pursue a variety of tactics alone or in combination. Some change trading space, moving from an inside section of a market to the outside, or shifting to another market entirely, for example, from a township to a market in the city center. City-center traders may shift temporarily from a market stand to the sidewalk or street, hoping to clear merchandise. They may hire an adolescent, typically a young boy, to hawk specific items through the alleys in the market. And some traders make regular or occasional rural trips to sell or exchange salaula, bringing back chickens, fish, or produce. Some go to commercial farms around Lusaka near

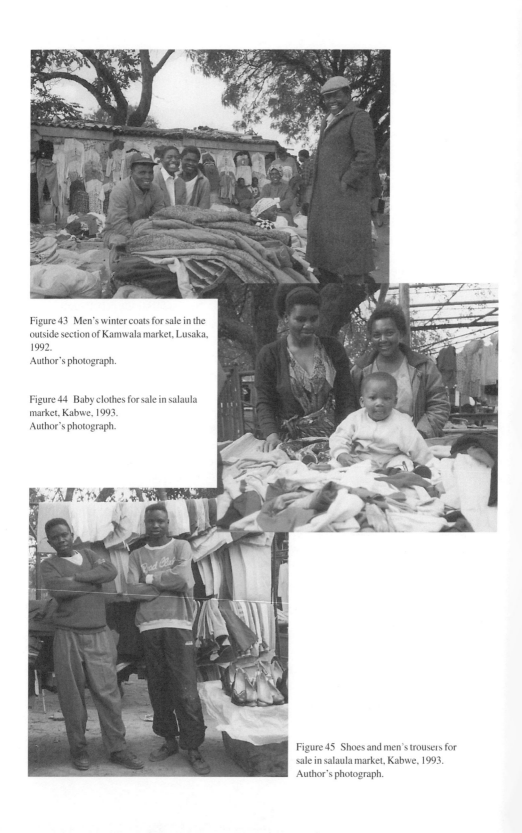

Figure 43   Men's winter coats for sale in the outside section of Kamwala market, Lusaka, 1992.
Author's photograph.

Figure 44   Baby clothes for sale in salaula market, Kabwe, 1993.
Author's photograph.

Figure 45   Shoes and men's trousers for sale in salaula market, Kabwe, 1993.
Author's photograph.

payday, like the traders who travel to Masstock. One young Soweto trader who regularly traveled into the countryside sold the chickens he obtained on such trips to a colleague in the market's poultry section.

Salaula moves best when traders have lots of it, that is, when they keep replenishing stock rather than waiting for merchandise to clear. A certain scale of operation is necessary for a trader to afford regular restocking of several bales every week. A trader has to be able to "win some and lose some." But the vast majority of traders who can afford only a couple of bales at any given time operate so tightly that they can restock only when they have recouped their money through day-to-day sales. Quick sales from taking their merchandise onto the street might generate sufficient money to enable them to purchase again. Chance affects these traders particularly, in that a bale containing many damaged items may push them over the limit, as in "do or die."

Some prospective traders with limited start-up capital and traders who are poorly capitalized pursue a strategy aimed at reducing the uncertainty due to the variable quality of clothes. They "pick," as it is called in the market language. Once other traders open bales, the pickers descend on them, selecting choice garments that they buy on the spot. Then they piece together women's

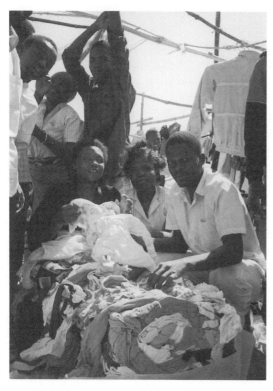

Figure 46 Forty-five-kilogram bale being opened in the outside section of Soweto market, Lusaka, 1993. Author's photograph.

two-piece outfits of individual items that match well and are stylish. The same applies to men's suits and leisure wear. The stands that sell such preselected items are known in these markets as boutiques. They tend to cluster in particular parts of markets near the stands of men's suits, the most expensive garments in the salaula repertoire. Unlike ordinary salaula stands the boutiques often have names such as the "Caroussel Botique" I came across at Soweto market in 1992. It featured cleaned, pressed, and restyled clothing at prices slightly higher than elsewhere in the market. Operated by two young men from the northwestern part of Zambia, this shop advertised its "Imported Cloths" in "London Wise" styles. These young men had traded in second-hand clothing they imported from Zaire for several years, but stopped traveling to Lubumbashi in 1991 because of "the confusion" in Zaire. In 1992 they began to pick their stock at the Soweto market when other traders opened bales.

The "Carrousel Shopping Centre" after which the young men named their stand was the newest development on Lusaka's upscale shopping scene in 1992 when it still was under construction. It was never completed and has in the meantime been sold for redevelopment. Although the Caroussel Botique disappeared during the process of relocation at Soweto market, stalls like it continue to cater to the upscale end of the salaula trade. While the boutique trade reduces the risks of bale purchasing, it does not eliminate other uncertainties. Because salaula from boutiques is more expensive than other secondhand garments, boutique operators are perhaps more vulnerable than other salaula traders at times of low demand. Most of the boutique operators I met were young men who were skilled at choosing their stock with a fine eye for what will sell, a great sense of style, and a flair for making stunning combinations. There were also female boutique traders, including some with tailoring skills who did some sewing to order from their homes.

Most traders keep books, usually exercise books, in which they record when they bought bales, the price, the number of good and damaged items, and the amount of daily sales. They record credit practices as well, such as who purchased what type of garment and the repayment arrangement. Traders in city markets and on streets rarely offer credit except to trusted customers and to people they know. Township market traders who know more about their individual customers commonly extend credit and spend much time at the end of the month trying to collect money owed them. But although many traders do some form of bookkeeping, they have trouble specifying their profit level. Many explained that there is "no use in keeping books because we don't see the money," which is to say that, for the great majority of traders who handle one or two bales at the same time, earnings from salaula readily disappear into daily consumption budgets.

The usual business practice is to recoup the purchase price of the bale as quickly as possible, setting it aside for the next purchase. Earnings beyond that point help to cover household expenses. This balancing act easily gets unsettled by a poor-quality bale, by extraneous circumstances in the market such as a sudden decline in business, by poor skills, and by factors pertaining to the personal life of the trader. Supplying and tending a salaula stall is a time- and labor-intensive occupation. Claims on the trader's time and resources from the household and larger family, the church, or other forces easily divert attention away from trade, reducing earnings. And leaving a stand supervised by an assistant or worker is risky. Although the worker is instructed to count the number of garments sold, there is little guarantee that he has not overcharged or helped himself to stock.

With skillful management, access to capital, and good-quality stock, a salaula trader can indeed make money. When opening a bale, the trader counts the number of garments, taking note of the number of poor or damaged items. She then selects the number of good-quality garments to sell at a specific price on "opening day" and sets the price of the remaining garments. Expecting to recoup her capital, if not more, on opening day, she then reduces the price daily. Consider Mrs. Zulu, who bought a bale of cotton blouses for K30,000 in 1992. The bale contained around 300 items of acceptable quality and 50 damaged items. Calculating that she would sell 200 blouses at a price of K300, she might make K60,000. She might even charge higher prices for the best blouses. After the best blouses are sold, she reduces the price. Business is best when she buys bales regularly, adding new stock rather than selling the contents of each bale before buying again. In this way the trader's profits from a good bale and quick sales may balance losses. Sales do indeed achieve that for many traders even if they cannot specify their profit level, and this is the reason that, in spite of complaints, they keep on with this business.

Genuine Salaula

Not all used clothing is equally desirable. Some previously worn clothes rarely enter the commercial circuit. And certain types of garments offered for sale do not appeal to consumers at all. In short, there is a local cultural politics about sourcing that defines what is "genuine" salaula. A jacket a man might have received upon the death of his uncle, for example, might remind him of the deceased person.[2] A gift of clothing may prompt memories of past events that salaula, an imported commodity that is construed as having no history, is unable to set into motion. This sense of inalienability of the clothing of a deceased person (Weiner 1992) has been challenged in recurring robberies of clothes from newly buried bodies in cemetaries.[3] Telling a chilling story about dire income needs, such events also provide a dramatic twist on practices involved in redefining used clothes into new.

People in Zambia have continued buying salaula in spite of intermittent, disquieting news of thieves exhuming bodies from graves, stripping them of clothes, which they resell (*Times of Zambia,* 22 October 1993, 3 November 1993, 7–9 August 1996). One confessing grave robber who had ransacked eleven graves in Lusaka in 1997 told police that he used to "attend body viewing and burials" during the daytime, only to return to the cemetery at night a few days later. He had earned his living as a hawker by selling graveyard clothes (*Times of Zambia,* 25 April 1997, 30 April 1997). When two unemployed men, one of them a previously convicted grave robber, were caught in a cemetery in Ndola, they carried a plastic bag containing "a gent's suit, white shirt, blanket, neck tie and socks." They explained that they stole the items from the corpse of the late Royson Mwema, a city-council public relations officer. The case of the graveyard thief who previously had been sentenced for "tresspassing at a burial site with the intention of wounding the feelings of the public" but "without reforming" was transferred from the magistrate court onto the high court for sentencing (*Times of Zambia,* "Grave Thieves," 5 February 1998).

Events like these certainly frighten consumers, prompting extreme caution in salaula shopping. How traders and consumers responded to this most vexing issue is evident in changes of clothing display in the boutique sections of the salaula markets. While most of the boutiques I saw in Lusaka in 1992 and 1993 exhibited carefully washed and ironed garments, by 1995 they displayed their goods without such interventions. In fact, wrinkles are preferred. This practice, in the words of vendors and customers, reduces the fear that such garments are "third-hand," which refers to previously used clothing, specifically by Zambians. Secondhand clothing displayed with folds and wrinkles straight from the bale is considered to be fresh from the source, thus genuine.[4] Garments that have been tampered with give rise to suspicion. The real thing, genuine salaula, is described as "new" and "alive" in contrast to clothing that is considered "tired" and "dead." This conceptual construction of second- and thirdhand clothing provides a startling twist on local notions of "used" clothes that I did not encounter in rural salaula markets.

After one of these incidents, a salaula trader advised customers to be "cautious about those people who sell [only] a few items [of clothing]. Our goods are genuinely obtained," he explained. Another trader agreed, adding that it is easy to "distinguish salaula clothes from the secondhand clothes that don't come from bales." He explained "most salaula clothes have distinct paper tags on them and they have that unique smell probably caused by being tied up in bales, so you can tell genuine salaula from suspicous clothes" (*Zambia Daily Mail,* 24 August 1996). As a result, by distinguishing between previously worn clothing and genuine salaula, consumers in Zambia are offering their own interpretation of a process that from a Western perspective appears to be about nothing but asymmetric global/local interactions.

Ancillary Activities

The growing salaula trade has given rise to a variety of ancillary activities, among them services that provide the traders with basic necessities. In the activities that give new lives to undesirable garments, small-scale tailors are playing important roles.

An army of young men pushing wheelbarrows, referred to as "zam-cabs," transport bales into the markets, and headloaders provide this service as well. Many zam-cabs are rented. At Soweto market, for example, one man owns around 100 wheelbarrows that he rents out for a daily fee (*Zambia Daily Mail,* 15 July 1998). The special needs of secondhand clothes traders are catered to by small-scale entrepreneurs who provide them with clothes hang-

Figure 47 Recycling salaula: woman trader weaving mat from clothes scraps in the outside section of Soweto market, Lusaka, 1997.
Author's photograph.

ers, plastic sheeting, and wooden boards for their stands. And numerous young food vendors circulate between the stands, selling water, cold drinks, fruit, ready-made foods, and snacks. Some marketeers and private individuals prepare food at home, bringing it into the market to resell to make a bit of money. When business is slow, some women traders knit or crochet, using yarn they have unraveled from torn or unpopular salaula sweaters to make baby blankets, jerseys, and boots. Others cut damaged garments into small strips, which they weave into doormats. One innovative trader in 1997 made baby boots from remains of quilted fabrics. Few male traders possess such skills. Some men read to pass time, and I have seen anything from Graham Greene to airline magazines and *Time* to Bibles on their stands. The outside section of Soweto market had a Bible study group in 1995, whose members were keenly discussing religious dogma.

Many activities revolve around recycling. Because both traders and consumers are concerned with quality and style, items made of fabrics that do not sell easily are turned into a variety of new garments. Crimplene (polyester knit) trousers and dresses, for example, are cut into pieces and sewn together in contrastive patterns or colors as girls' dresses and boys' shorts. A whole section of Kamwala market is dedicated to these activities carried out by women whom tailors supply with the precut pieces. Curtain material with colorful prints is made into women's dresses and two-piece outfits, and draperies with metallic sheen become men's trousers. One workshop with

Figure 48 Blankets made from salaula sheets for sale near road in Soweto market, Lusaka, 1995. Author's photograph.

Figure 49 Men's trousers tailored from drapery material, Soweto market, Lusaka, 1995.
Author's photograph.

Figure 50 Tailor making sweatshirts from strips of unmatched salaula sweat pants, Soweto market, Lusaka, 1997.
Author's photograph.

Figure 51 Tie-dyed secondhand jeans and T-shirts, Soweto market, Lusaka, 1995.
Author's photograph.

young male tailors outside Soweto market in 1995 specialized in the manufacture of such trousers, adding a special decorative effect of cut-off labels
from other garments. Every time I have returned to these markets, I have observed new forms of recycling. In 1995 I first saw tie-dye in dark and light
contrastive colors applied to used jeans and T-shirts, the T-shirts further
adorned with eye-catching iron-on decorations. And in 1997 I saw tailors
making colorful tops from contrastive colored pieces they had cut up from ill-
matched salaula sweat suits.

Tailors play important roles in these activities. In addition to producing
new garments from discarded clothing, they repair and alter salaula, taking in
or extending garments of the wrong size to fit Zambian bodies, and restyling
trousers and jackets, adding trim and buttons to conform with "the latest" in
the ever-changing style repertoire. Examples including closing vents and
changing large-sized single-breasted jackets into double-breasted ones, and
the addition of one, not two, back pockets to trousers. Trousers with two
pockets, "twin cabs," were not popular but were considered old-fashioned.

But tailors do much more than alteration. While I have monitored these trades, salaula had not "killed" the small-scale tailoring craft, as some feared when I began exploring these issues in 1992. One tailor who had set himself up in Kamwala market after closing shop in one of the townships said then that salaula had destroyed the tailors' work. When I spoke to him in 1995, he sang a different tune. "I sat down for two hours to think of how to beat salaula," he told me. His solution, like that of the many other tailors who keep on working, was specialty production, in his case church uniforms, a regular part of many women's wardrobes in Zambia. Many of the "corridor tailors," as the people who operate sewing machines outside of shops are called in Zambia, that I revisited in 1995 had followed a similar strategy, targeting niche production of garments rarely found in salaula. Some of these tailors produced job lots for established boutiques, while others made chitenge dresses "on order" for suitcase traders who sell them in Zimbabwe and South Africa. There the production of "African-style" dresses is not very wide-spread, and in fact such dresses were known as "Zambia" in the mid-1990s.

If the small-scale tailoring sector in "corridors," on verandas, and in markets is dominated by men, there is another setting in which many women are involved with the tailor's craft. This is home-based production, often by hired tailors, both women and men, organized as a sideline activity by women who work away from home but also by some who pursue it full-time. Such operations may taken place in the home or in servants' quarters in homes in medium- to high-income residential areas. I have seen tailors at work in the

Figure 52 Tailor making women's two-piece office wear, Kamwala shopping center, Lusaka, 1993. Author's photograph.

Figure 53 Senior tailor, his son on the right, and two relatives, all producing office wear and chitenge dresses, Kamwala shopping center, Lusaka, 1997. Author's photograph.

Figure 54 Tailor making office wear and chitenge dresses, Kamwala shopping center, Lusaka, 1995. Author's photograph.

Figure 55 Tailor making girl's dresses and chitenge dresses, Kamwala shopping center, Lusaka, 1995.
Author's photograph.

middle of the living room of two-bedroom flats of bank employees, for example, as well as in the flats of some university lecturers whose wives did not hold wage jobs. Some of these women entrepreneurs go to office buildings soliciting orders. In the mid to late 1990s most of their output consisted of women's two-piece suits "for the office" and chitenge wear. Skirts and blouses are rarely produced in such workshops, as they are available in great variety and attractive styles from salaula.

These tailoring activities, including Mr. Tembo's workshop, have been greatly facilitated by the improved availability in recent years of imported dress fabric in the local shops, compared to the early 1990s. In short, small-scale tailors and the salaula traders need not confront each other in an antagonistic relationship, but can coexist.

Ready-Made Clothing Retail

What are the alternatives to salaula and tailor-made garments? The domestic garment industry had all but disappeared by the mid-1990s, and I discuss the contentious debate about the relationship of the growing secondhand clothing import to Zambia's garment and textile industries in chapter 10. Some brief remarks about the changing supply of ready-made imported clothing will contextualize this chapter's discussion of the changing salaula retail scene.

Consumers in Zambia purchase salaula for three reasons: it is affordable, it offers choice, and it gives better value for money. As I discuss in detail in chapter 8, people at all income levels except the very top purchase salaula for these reasons. Ready-made clothing in most formal shops claims prices that low-income workers cannot afford. How could a domestic servant who in 1992 earned an average monthly wage of around K8,000 fulfill the cultural expectation of presenting his wife with a new dress at Christmas when the least expensive dress in the state-run department store cost between K5,000 and K8,000? A cotton salaula dress at that time cost between K500 and K800, an effective competitor to the ready-made dress. While this example might be extreme, it is far from unusual. The growing proportion of the Zambian population that is earning very little money is making similar calculations, as are medium-income people, whose spending money has become increasingly tight.

The state-owned department stores with their limited stock of drab and dismal-looking clothing had not quite disappeared from the urban retail scene when I began observing the clothing sector in 1992. An eye-catching newspaper announcement featuring a smartly dressed young couple, placed by the Zambian Posts and Telecommunications Corporation (PTC) in 1993 to introduce a mail-order service by Sonny Boys, a Cape Town firm, might have done something to satisfy Zambian dress desires, but before the firm ever got off the ground, the PTC denied it permission to operate (*Times of Zambia,* 19 June 1993; *Weekly Post,* 11–19 August 1993). The state-owned department stores have since been privatized, and by 1995 branches of South African chain stores had appeared in some of their locations. While the clothing that is offered for sale in these stores was produced for the low end of the market, it is not readily affordable by low-income Zambian consumers.

The general supply of ready-made imported clothing has increased considerably since the early 1990s because of relaxations of import restrictions and currency controls. In addition to the chain stores I just mentioned, more upscale boutiques have appeared, many of them in connection with ongoing shopping-center development. By 1997 one of these centers featured a bridal store owned by a Middle Eastern woman who was selling and renting gowns imported from the United Kingdom and Thailand. The sad appearance of the previous era's ready-made clothing scene has been replaced by a vibrant look that changes quickly from season to season. The clothing scene includes increasingly elaborate "African-style" dresses, the latest of which in 1997 were referred to as "Nigerian." While a few of these garments were brought from West Africa, most of them are produced locally by Zambian tailors, in job-lot arrangements with the more exclusive boutiques. Some tailors also produce job lots for shops of women's two-piece outfits of a particular style, the mid-1990s preferred type of "office wear" in this region.

The diversification of the capital's ready-made clothing supply is to some degree the result of the personal initiatives of suitcase traders who cater to both the high and the low end of the clothing market. Before Zambia Airways, the national airline, was liquidated at the end of 1994, airline stewardesses were actively involved in bringing in clothes from "outside," as this source is commonly called in Zambia. A study of *makwebo* women (Bemba for "buying and selling"), or dealers as they are sometimes called, during the closing years of the second republic details the journeys by road, rail, and air of largely middle-class, well-educated women traveling abroad in groups of two or three, bringing in clothes, shoes, and dress and suit fabric as well as vehicle and machinery spare parts, electrical goods, and groceries. Mauritius was a particularly popular destination for the purchase of fabrics in the late 1980s (Siyolwe 1994:100–110, 121–22). A study from the mid-1990s describes successful production units with boutique-style outlets in downtown Lusaka, operated by well-educated women married to wealthy men, who are able to travel abroad and take design and fashion courses. They concentrate on producing "high quality fashion garments for high income clients who prefer imported clothing from London, Paris, and New York" over what they perceive as "cheap" local wear (Kasengele 1998:96–97).

Although "dealers" and suitcase traders might have brought in dress and suit fabrics in the past when such goods were less readily available, today most of the women with the profile described above bring in fashion goods rather than fabrics. No longer facing import and currency restrictions, these apparel entrepreneurs flew in 1997 as far as New York and Bangkok to purchase clothing, shoes, and accessories for sale in Lusaka's growing number of exclusive shops as well as by private arrangement.[5] London and Dubai remained regular sourcing destinations on their itineraries. Just like the secondhand clothing import, these sourcing trips were often facilitated by personal contacts. The garments brought in by this trade are expensive, with dresses easily costing in the range of a civil-service monthly salary, which in 1997 was between K90,000 and K154,000.

Suitcase traders catering to a less upscale group of consumers continue to travel to South Africa, Zimbabwe, Tanzania, Mauritius, and India to purchase more affordable apparel. On their return these traders sell some of their merchandise on commission to established traders and the rest to traders on the perimeter of city markets, for example in a section of Kamwala known since the mid-1990s as Zambia-Zaire. Some traders sell goods like these from home, often to individuals who have commissioned them to bring back a very particular type of garment, or they might call on office buildings to sell to the people who work there.

The chief attraction of garments from "outside" is style, not price. A low-paid secretary might commit herself to buying on a personalized installment plan to avoid a one-time expenditure of considerable size. This active concern with style and the preoccupation with cutting a fine figure can readily be satisfied from salaula markets, which is one reason for their attractiveness to people across most of Zambia's class spectrum. These style concerns had not yet, during my last visit in 1999, brought with them a noticeable search for brand-name clothing in the salaula market. Yet neither style issues nor clothing markets are ever static but develop in complex ways, one of which might be a preoccupation with brand names in the secondhand clothing markets in the future. The beginnings of brand-name recognition might already have occurred. By 1997 an upscale men's clothing store had appeared in downtown Lusaka, the first to feature Dior, Armani, and Versache garments. Given the flair of tailors for capturing what is in vogue, such names might soon appear on tailor-made garments. And given the keen ability of Zambians to create astute terms and special meanings, I would not be surprised to see brand names on the signs of salaula boutiques.

Recommodification

The transformation of the West's cast-off clothing into new garments in Zambia, initiated in interactions at the point of wholesale, continues through the retail process. Unhinged from its origin, the decommissioned value of the West's discarded clothing is charged anew in the retail process. The process of redefinition hinges on the meaning of the term *salaula*—selecting from a pile in the manner of rummaging. Practices that express this are evident, for example on "opening day," when a bale is cut open for resale, its contents are counted, and individual items are assessed for quality and price. At this moment, when the clothes are ready to enter into another cycle of consumption, it is important that they have not been meddled with. Both traders and customers prefer to open bales publicly, so that customers can select on the spot. A bale that is opened in the market in full view is considered to contain "new" garments. If it were opened privately at home, the trader might put aside choice items, causing customers to suspect that they are being presented with a second cut and not "new" clothing.

The desire for "newness" is particularly evident in the boutique section of the salaula market, where traders piece together outfits from garments they carefully select when bales are opened. Unlike at the "Caroussel Botique" at the old Soweto market, where garments in 1992 were pressed and ironed, in recent years the clothes displayed in the boutique section of Lusaka's salaula markets are hung up "fresh" from the bale, that is, with wrinkles and folds. Prewashed and ironed clothing in the opinion of traders and customers alike leaves the suspicion that the clothes are "thirdhand," meaning previously owned and worn by Zambians.

The most obvious changes to the West's used clothing involve recycling and alteration. These and many other transformations that take place through dress practice, in how, where, and when the body is put together with clothes, offer rich evidence of both traders and customers working actively at giving new lives to the West's used garments, and in the process making salaula into their own creation. Focusing on the hard work of consumption in the next chapter, I continue to trace shifts in the register of meaning of clothes.

8   The Work of Consumption

What are the actual processes through which consumers in Zambia acquire salaula? There is much more at stake in buying salaula than a mere exchange of cash, or barter, for clothes. If the wholesale of salaula is selective in the clothing consignments it purchases from the West to retail in local markets, so are consumers in the garments that they purchase. A vital dimension of the demand side is cultural taste and style. These matters make conventional distinctions between need and desire converge in consumers' valuation of garments not only for their use but also for the meanings they attribute to them. In short, consumption is hard work, a kind of invisible production, according to Michel de Certeau (1988:30–31), that is not revealed in numerical tabulations of household expenditures. Instead consumption may be understood through the practices and meanings consumers bring to bear on how they use things.

When shopping "from salaula," consumers' preoccupation with creating particular appearances is inspired by fashion trends and popular dress cultures from across the world. They draw on these influences in ways that are informed by local norms about bodies and dress. Such observations are by no means unique to secondhand clothing consumption but parallel what takes place in appropriations of external dress influences elsewhere in Africa and beyond, the specificities depending significantly on the shifting cultural politics of their local settings (Durham 1995; James 1996; Tarlo 1996). This is to say that the work of consumption is situated in histories "whose conjuncture has to be examined, alas, case by case" (Appadurai 1997:42–43).

Turning to questions about clothing demand and desire in Zambia, this chapter follows the flow of salaula from the retail scene into households, examining clothing consumption from the point of view of residents in some of Lusaka's different neighborhoods. The areas include Kamanga and Kaunda Square as well as parts of Rhodes Park, Woodlands, and Kabulonga. The first two consist of self-built housing, one a squatter settlement and the other a site-and-service scheme,[1] and are inhabited by a low- to medium-income population. The last three are medium- to high-income areas of mainly rental houses accommodating a large proportion of civil servants at all levels, from primary-school teachers to government ministers. In spite of the socioeconomic differences among these areas, by the mid-1990s there were every-

where some individuals, mostly women, who sold salaula and tailored clothing from their homes.

Through Zambia's urban areas, the populations are very heterogeneous in
ethnic terms, and unlike in some West African cities, distinct ethnic residential clusters are rare. Marriages across ethnic lines are common. The vast majority of urban residents form an established population of whom many are
urban born-and-bred. The extent of interurban mobility is great (Republic of
Zambia 1995:39–42). Civil servants, in particular, have diverse experiences
from transfers across the country, and those in the upper ranks have often
lived abroad. In short, urban residents bring a wide range of comparative insights to bear on clothing consumption.

In my attempt to capture both the economic and cultural significance of
salaula consumption, I draw on several sources, including surveys of clothing-consumption practices, budget diaries, essays on clothing written by female and male adolescents, and participant observation in many different
situations and walks of life in Zambia. Most of the specific observations in
this chapter were made in 1995, and I discuss some points of methodology
along the way. Exploring what kinds of access and choice in the clothing market different individuals and groups have and why, the chapter first investi-
gates how Zambian urban residents construe the consumption of salaula as
compared to other clothing demands and consumption priorities in general.
But while purchasing power plays an important role in clothing consumption, so do cultural practices. I demonstrate this when describing the cultural
skills involved in the work of consumption and how consumers construe
proper dress. I expand these points in describing how one style of dress, the
chitenge suit, embeds normative practices about constructions of the
woman's dressed body. As in the previous chapters, the last section focuses
on shifts in meaning that accompany the transformation of the West's used
clothing into salaula, in this case, on its journey from the retail market, ready
to play untried parts in the lives of its new owners.

Sally's Boutique

Salaula markets are "our shops," as some of the householders I interviewed
about clothing consumption in 1995 put it. And Zambians will readily tell
you that three-fourths of the population shops "from salaula." "Because the
economy is biting in this part of the world and therefore the salary of my parents [a superintendent of an automotive department and a nurse] being that of
average Zambians, I buy most of my clothes from salaula," wrote Lukonde, a
twelfth-grade student in Kabulonga Secondary School for Girls in Lusaka,
one of several secondary schools where in 1995 twelfth graders ranging in

age from seventeen to twenty years wrote essays in their English composition class on clothing practices in their homes. Her description captures local attitudes to salaula better than any summary I could provide.[2]

> The bales of salaula come from the well developed countries and they usually contain very nice and modern fashions. Some of the clothes at salaula look like the ones one can find in boutiques. Many of my friends also buy their clothes from salaula and it is now popularly known as "Sally's Boutique." Salaula has really helped Zambians dress for without this kind of trade, many Zambians would be wearing rags . . . Even the foreigners and Indians also buy salaula since the nice clothes in the shops cost almost the salary of some people . . . When salaula was first introduced in Zambia, very few had the courage to go to a salaula shop and choose what he/she wanted. But now it is different. One can walk up to a salaula shop with his/her head high without feeling low or embarrassed.

My 1995 survey of clothing consumption practices substantiates Lukonde's description. When estimating clothing expenditures, the consumer price studies carried out by the Central Statistical Office and a variety of NGOs are of limited use for questions about salaula, since they do not distinguish between new and used clothing (Republic of Zambia 1997). Some studies do not include clothing at all when measuring the changing costs of consumption.[3] In my effort to understand who buys salaula and why, I deliberately oversampled the medium- to high-income population, which is the only socioeconomic segment with effective choice in the clothing market. In fact, I considered it inappropriate to impose a barrage of questions about clothing purchases and dress practices on the most disadvantaged population category, which has no clothing alternative but salaula and whose limited resources exclude them from much of the world of consumption.[4]

Below a certain income level, demand for clothing does not vary greatly but is rather uniform. By contrast the *apamwamba,* as the high-income group is referred to, a Nyanja term that literally means "those on the top," are trendsetters in many matters of lifestyle, including clothing consumption. Their dress practices display the styles that make heads turn either in admiration or disbelief, and as such they play a more important role in dress debate and dress practice than other groups. The issues I explored in the survey were deliberately broad and meant to stand in for very specific questions about household income and expenditure, which some people cannot answer, either because they do not know, because they will not reveal them, or because they are unable to specify them due to the very complicated borrowing, lending, and installment arrangements they are involved in. In my judgment the last factor is the most important, and I shall have more to say about it shortly.

Consumers in Zambia go to salaula markets for many reasons. White-col-

lar workers of both sexes in Lusaka's center often spend their lunch hour going through the stalls as a pastime, sometimes making purchases at whim.
Others go to find just that right item to go with a particular garment. Some
women who tailor in their homes search the salaula markets for interesting
buttons, belts, and trim to accent garments. And some go to purchase garments with the intention to resell. But the vast majority go to salaula markets
to buy clothing for themselves and their families. They come into town from
residential areas such as the ones in which I explored clothing-consumption
questions, where roughly two-thirds of all households supplied most of their
members' clothing from salaula. In addition to purchasing salaula, more than
half of the adult members of these households also regularly used a tailor, but
less so in the low-income households. And indeed the apamwamba, as I suggested above, is the only group that has an effective choice in the clothing
market.

These general observations can be further detailed in terms of specific socioeconomic background, gender, and age. An interesting observation that
emerged from the survey was that proportionately fewer married women
earn incomes in their own right in the low-income areas than in the higher-in-
come areas. It is possible that some of these women who do not earn incomes
on a regular basis engage in trade or marketing from time to time. Their lower
level of education helps to account for their absence from wage labor. Their
intermittent participation in trade is likely to be affected by a cultural reluc-
tance of men to allow wives to work away from home, an attitude that seems
to be less marked among people who are better situated. In Kamanga, for example, where most husbands did manual or unskilled jobs, only one-fifth of
the wives earned money in any way. In Kaunda Square, where husbands
tended to have more skills than in Kamanga, working in clerical positions,
technology, and communications, one-third of the wives worked to earn
money. This contrasts to the high-income areas, where many husbands held
civil service jobs while a few worked in private firms or had their own business, and two-thirds of the wives earned incomes, the majority as teachers,
clerks, businesswomen, and traders.

There are other differences among these neighborhoods. More than half of
the households in Kamanga lived in rooms or houses rented from private
landlords, compared to one-third in Kaunda Square. Much housing in the
high-income areas is government owned and tied to the job.[5] That is to say,
the level of disposable income depends not only on employment and whether
both spouses work but also on housing costs, which make up a higher proportion of available income in the low-income areas. When estimating the proportion of income spent on basic requirements, food ranked highest in all
these areas. Rent ranked second in the low-income areas, while education

Figure 56 Customers walking through the Gabon section of Kamwala market, Lusaka, 1995. Author's photograph.

Figure 57 Window-shopping at the outside section of Soweto market, Lusaka, 1995. Author's photograph.

Figure 58 Customers looking at salaula at DAPP store, Monze, 1993. Author's photograph.

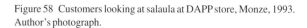

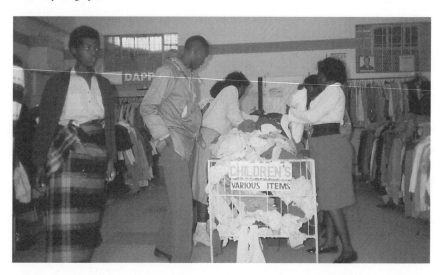

held that place in the high-income areas. Transportation in the low-income areas and water and electricity charges in the high-income areas took third place, with clothing tending to rank fourth among the items on which house-holders spent money on a monthly basis in all of these neighborhoods. While the irregularity of clothing purchases compared to rent and food, for example, and complicated credit arrangements make these rankings impressionistic, they nevertheless convey the self-reported expenditure priorities of consumers.

With this backdrop it comes as no surprise that in the least well-off of these households, most clothing needs are met from salaula, save for children's school uniforms and shoes. Even then, parts of school uniforms such as stockings, shirts, jerseys, and shoes are often bought from salaula. So are garments that are pieced together into nurses' uniforms, for example. "There is no clothing allowance," one nurse who worked in a township clinic told me; "a new uniform costs more than my monthly salary." Because of strained household budgets at this level, less clothing is obtained from the tailor than at the medium- and high-income levels. Yet while economic factors restrain consumption, there is room for cultural factors to enter decisions of what to buy. This was noted in a survey from the late 1980s and confirmed in my own observations from the 1990s: "Most people with little money prefer second-hand clothes to hand-made [tailor-made] items, not because of lower costs but because of better quality and higher fashion" (Hartman [1988?]:4).

Among medium-income households, adult women obtain some of their clothes from salaula, some from tailors, and some from shops; they also source clothing from "outside" from friends or acquaintances who are suit-case traders. Many women at this level own church uniforms, which they commission from small-scale tailors. Men at this income level obtain some clothing from shops and some from salaula even if they do not go into the markets themselves. And with the exception of school uniforms, most of the clothes of children and young adults like Lukonde are purchased at salaula markets. Money is tight at this income level, where the purchase of new clothing has become a rarity, an event for special occasions like birthdays or Christmas, if then. My question of when they last bought any new clothing was often met with a sad smile, for instance by men who recalled how several years ago they bought their first formal suit from the local firm Serioes, when assuming white-collar jobs after completing their education. School uniforms and underwear are the chief garments purchased new at this level. Even these garments are also sourced from salaula markets, though some householders had a hard time admitting that they bought underwear from salaula, if not their own, then their children's.

Body size is an important factor influencing which garments are bought where. Many salaula dresses are too tight and men's trousers and jackets too large for adult female and male Zambian bodies, which perhaps is why the salaula markets are particularly popular with young adults. Women's skirts and blouses are fairly easy to adjust to size, as are men's shirts, which make them among the most popular items in this market. It is also for size and fit reasons that there is scope for tailoring of women's dresses and men's trousers. Indeed, some women at this income level frequently call on one or two tailors.

"Only housewives have the time to go to the salaula market," a male secondary-school teacher told me. And some adult men informed me that they would not be caught dead in the salaula markets. Still, many men do go into these markets, as I have seen when spending time there, but I have also observed men hiding in the stalls when trying on garments. Some men send their wives to select the right-sized shirts and trousers for them. Yet some men who claim that they won't be caught dead in the salaula markets will nevertheless admit to buying secondhand clothes. They do so from the extensive workplace trade in which salaula traders circulate in office buildings, selling their goods on credit.

Consumers with connections and discretionary income, regardless of its source, may or may not purchase clothing from the salaula market. Some adult female heads of households in upper-level jobs told me plainly that they could afford to buy new clothing, that they did shop in Lusaka's exclusive boutiques but sourced most of their clothing from "outside." Other women at this level might not go into the salaula markets but nevertheless purchased garments from home-based salaula sellers in their neighborhoods. Such traders look out for specific types of garments their special customers are interested in. Yet many people with better means do frequent the salaula markets, for example, purchasing clothing for their servant staff, dependent kin, or up-country relatives. They buy garments on a whim for themselves, too.

The apamwamba shop for clothing everywhere, visiting salaula markets as a pastime, buying in the boutiques, frequenting their own tailors, but sourcing most of their clothing from "outside." For them, going into salaula markets is akin to a sport, something to do for entertainment. In the local terms I have identified, *apamwamba* is a lifestyle designation, referring to people of ample economic means who work in private business or government office. They are well educated, often abroad; own homes and farms; and have several vehicles, including four-wheel-drive cars; and their children attend exclusive local or foreign boarding schools. Their residences have satellite dishes and top-of-the-line electronic home-entertainment equipment. They are members of social clubs and often engage in sports like tennis and golf. Some go to gyms. The apamwamba might have had overseas posts, their present work frequently takes them outside the country, and they go on vaca-

Figure 59 Customer scrutinizing curtains at Kamwala market, Lusaka, 1995.
Author's photograph.

Figure 60 Bargaining over the price of a pair of trousers at Kamwala market, Lusaka, 1993.
Author's photograph.

tions both in the game parks in the region and abroad. They often pursue business activities at the same time as they hold top-level government jobs or positions in private firms. By a conservative estimate, eleven of the fifty-five households in the high-income areas where I inquired into clothing consumption fit this description.

Clothing in apamwamba households is expensive and exquisite in both quality and style, some of it was brand names, and some men's suits are bought from London's Savile Row tailors. Accessories in particular, jewelry, and high-quality shoes are among the diacritica by which the discerning observer is able to distinguish between dress styles at this level and salaula ensembles put together with flair for style. When it comes to style, some apamwamba women flaunt dress conventions by wearing short and tight garments in public if they have the body to carry it off and, if they are of ample size, by wearing elaborately constructed and ornamented flamboyant dresses and hats. Heavy makeup, complicated hairdos, and lots of jewelry often accentuate the apamwamba look.

Consumption Credit

One reason that household incomes are difficult to estimate is that many people engage in sideline economic activities while holding formal jobs. Much like the salaula traders I quoted in the previous chapter, these people "don't see" their earnings because they "go into the pot," that is, disappear into daily consumption budgets. Another factor affecting budget practice is credit. Large segments of Zambia's urban populations live on informal credit, and some use moneylenders as well (Hansen 1985; Roeber 1994). In fact, clothing consumption is greatly helped by credit practices. Anderson, a twelfth-grade student at St. Clement Secondary School at Mansa, the headquarters of Luapula Province, explained in 1995 how the household of his guardian, his older brother, a road inspector married to a bank employee in Lusaka, made out.

> It is almost impossible for working couples to clothe their family on the peanut salaries they earn. As a result, they have improvised a system. A businesswoman who buys goods from Zimbabwe, Botswana, and South Africa gives these goods on credit. She goes door-to-door to her estimed [*sic*] customers to advertise that she has goods from those countries . . . So most of the clothes if not all that we put on is bought from these women on credit; my guardian finds it easy and more advantageous to buy from these businesswomen because you can get more goods even if you are still paying for the previous ones.

"We live on credit," said one of four secondary-school teachers in Lusaka who kept account of their earnings and expenditures for me during a four-to-five-month period in 1995. Three of them were accommodated rent-free in tiny flats in a converted dormitory on the school campus. They used many kinds of credit when purchasing household appliances and furniture, food, and most certainly clothing. The advantage of the home-based salaula vendor, the tailor, and the suitcase trader is the availability of credit on individually negotiable terms. Not only that, individuals who owe money because of such arrangements often in turn lend money themselves. This is why default is not common in these arrangements. When I asked one of these teachers how people who extend credit can be sure of being repaid, she answered matter-of-factly, "We all depend on one another."

My specific aim with this budget exercise was to learn more about how people on tight money manage to purchase clothes for themselves and their families, as well as what types of clothes they bought: salaula, tailor-made, new from the shops, or from suitcase traders. Scrutinizing such accounts makes it possible to explain how a teacher who in 1995 had a monthly take-home pay of K93,000 was able to spend an average of K46,000 per month on clothes for herself and her two children. During this period she paid monthly installments on three dresses she had custom-ordered from one of two tailors who provided more than 90 percent of her personal wardrobe as well as on one dress from the tailor for her little girl; she bought brand new school shoes and socks for her children, and several children's garments from salaula. She also paid her daughter's nursery school fees of K50,000 for the term, installments on a couch with two matching chairs and a coffee table, and her housemaid a monthly wage of K10,000 that increased to K15,000 by the end of the period. While she was involved in credit arrangements with her tailors, she lent a friend K50,000 and some smaller amounts to neighbors for food purchases. She kept her budget viable by earning extra income from private tutorials and occasionally did some contract work in language teaching for a private firm. And she regularly prepared snacks for sale in the school cafeteria. She received additional formal pay by marking examinations toward the end of the term and from a long-overdue salary increment. In effect, she received more money from her sideline activities taken together than she did from her regular salary.

None of the three other teachers who kept track of their budgets were quite as entrepreneurial, although they, like many other teachers, gave private tutorials and occasionally engaged in trade, for example, buying and reselling farm produce or chickens, or suitcase trade. Two of the other teachers were married and had children, thus with larger combined household incomes but also more claims on earnings. Their clothing expenditures were neither at the level of the first teacher nor as regular. Both these households purchased clothing from salaula as well as tailors. The fourth teacher, who was not married and did not have children, spent an average of about half of her take-home pay of K60,000 on clothing, purchased on monthly installments. She borrowed regularly from a cousin and gave money frequently to her mother and sister. To be sure, as Anderson put it, credit allows persons on peanut salaries to go on buying while continuing to pay off what they owe.

Consumption as Work

Consumption is hard work that has complicated implications in the realm of production. For an illustration of some of the many detailed considerations that are brought to bear on salaula consumption, I describe a shopping trip at Lusaka's Kamwala market with Betty Miyanda, a thirty-five-year-old primary-school teacher. The sketch synthesizes many individual observations from this particular market. Because Mrs. Miyanda teaches morning sessions and does not have any private tutorials in her home on the afternoon of this trip, she has planned to go shopping from salaula. As the mother of four children in school, she keeps track of their clothing needs. With her own earnings she pays for most of their ordinary clothes, except for school uniforms that are paid from the salary of her husband, a road surveyor in a government job. In fact, she does most of the clothes shopping; only the oldest, a youth aged fifteen, who receives a bit of pocket money for performing chores at home, does some of his own clothes shopping. Mrs. Miyanda tells us that she hardly ever buys clothing "from the shops," and that although her husband will not readily admit it, she buys for him from salaula, especially shirts and cold-weather clothes.

Big markets like Kamwala are salaula's shop window. They create an atmosphere much like the West's shopping mall where consumers can pursue almost unlimited desires with an abandon not possible in the capital's formal shops, where they often are dealt with offhandedly or are pressured to purchase. Salaula markets thrive on the importance most Zambians attach to personal interaction and the attention they pay to keeping up pleasant interpersonal terms. In fact, these markets are important sites for both economic and social pursuits.

Our walk up and down the salaula aisles might appear to be casual window shopping, yet it is in fact very strategic. Mrs. Miyanda is looking for particular garments for her children and a top to fit a charcoal gray skirt she likes to wear to school to make up a two-piece outfit like the kind of "office wear" so popular with urban women in white-collar jobs. When working the salaula market, she always looks for shirts of the kind her husband likes to wear. What is more, one never knows what might be available, and she is on the lookout for "the latest." On this occasion she had heard that someone had just opened a bale of shoes.

We make many stops. Mrs. Miyanda turns garments inside out, carefully scrutinizing the neatness of the sewing and the quality of the fabric. Will the print run when washed? She pays attention to color, pattern, and style. Buying salaula is not a matter of "anything goes" but of getting the best value for money, combined with attractiveness and style. Above all, she gathers information, both from traders and other customers: where did you purchase that jacket, who has good shoes, she asks, and occasionally she stops passers-by not only to admire their clothes but also to inquire about sourcing: which tailor can make this outfit, where did you find gold buttons, and who sells black lace trim?

On this occasion Mrs. Miyanda purchased a pair of trousers and two T-shirts for her twelve-year-old son and dresses for her two daughters, aged ten and seven, to wear to church. She bargained over the price of the dresses, which the trader reduced because Mrs. Miyanda purchased two. She scanned the men's shirts at several stalls but considered the shirts not to be quite to her husband's taste; they were too colorful; some were checked and others had loud colors; he likes them plain, she explained. In fact, most adult men show the same preference. She spent a long time looking for a top for herself.

In the end Mrs. Miyanda bought a hip-length shocking pink top to go with her charcoal gray skirt. She was satisfied with the reduced price she had paid for the dresses for her daughters but felt that she had paid too much for the shirt in spite of arguing with the trader, who was not prepared to yield. Still, Mrs. Miyanda wanted that particular shirt, and so she paid. We took the shirt, and the pair of shoes she bought on a whim, to the shops on the periphery of the market. A shoe-repair man was asked to build up the heels and soles to give the shoes a platform look, and the top was taken to a tailor for alteration. Mrs. Miyanda did not care for the effect of the shoulder pads, and wanted them removed. The top was slightly longer than she liked; she wanted it shortened, and in addition, she asked for two rows of gold buttons to be sewed onto the front, which she considered too plain. While at the tailor's, we admired the latest styles of chitenge dresses. Mrs. Miyanda would like a new chitenge outfit, as she had to attend a kitchen party (Hansen 1995:140–42) at the end of the month; we inquired about the tailor's fees and the necessary yardage, and received advice about shops that sell good-quality and attractive imported chitenges.

Salaula consumption is hard work. In this brief sketch we glimpse the household power relations and norms that inform clothing-consumption practices and their allocation by gender and age. Having monitored the clothing needs of the members of her household, when setting about the task of purchasing salaula, Mrs. Miyanda gathers information and screens and sorts products. She is careful in negotiating price, if not always successful. Her final decisions not only are need-based but also reflect clothing desires as she combines garments from salaula into the style that is considered "the latest" in Lusaka. What is perhaps the most striking is the extent of clothing competence in matters of quality and style that Mrs. Miyanda displays as she skillfully works her way through the market, scrutinizing salaula. Her clothing competence is only to some extent a product of media exposure to local print and television advertisement, both of which are limited in scope, and to foreign television channels, music and film videos, and magazines presenting a range of visual impressions. Above all, her clothing competence is performance-based, drawn from the display of dressed bodies in streets, homes, and work in everyday interaction and at special events. It is informed as well by normative ideas about dress and body comportment, which women are taught from when they are very young.

Involving both needs and desires, the work of salaula consumption has implications for the entire system of provision that embeds this commodity. The effects of Mrs. Miyanda's decisions when shopping from salaula flow into many ancillary activities around and beyond the market, in this case most obviously the shoe-repair man and the tailor. Beyond the salaula market the popularity of chitenge dresses in recent years, made of colorfully printed cloth imported from India and the Far East, has turned consumers off buying local prints. The local textile factories in turn have stopped weaving chitenge in favor of gray cloth for the export market. Yet small-scale tailors are busier than ever making chitenge dresses of imported fabrics. Above all, the consumption of salaula is influenced by and has complex effects on household activities and welfare. These effects flow into the domains of distribution and production, which is why consumption does not constitute the end point of the economic process but helps fuel its beginnings.

Clothing Competence

Shopping from salaula does not mean that anything goes. A point made by Appadurai (1986:29) is pertinent here when he observes that demand "emerges as a function of a wide variety of social practices and classifications rather than a mysterious emanation of human needs, a mechanical response to social manipulations." Consumers in Zambia neither put together their clothing ensembles at random nor in passive imitation of the West. Negotiating both clothing needs and desires, consumers are influenced by a variety of sources when they purchase garments. Above all, clothing consumption implicates cultural norms about gender and authority. Local notions of what to wear, when to wear it, and how to present the dressed body construe dress practice on Zambian terms that influence how people dress in clothing from salaula. Clothing consumers speak of these terms in the language of tradition. Because this is a made-up tradition, it is subject to change. That is why the normative terms for how to dress delineate rather than determine how people dress, leaving room for idiosyncratic and provocative dress practices as well. Yet as I demonstrate in chapter 9, they are the culturally dominant terms that approximate a dress code, and they affect women's and men's scope to dress very differently.

The cultural terms that construe "traditional" dress practice were captured well by Benard, a twelfth-grade student in Mansa, in a 1995 essay on clothing consumption in his family. When school was not in session, he lived with his guardian, an older brother employed on a commercial farm on the outskirts of Kitwe on the Copperbelt. Benard explained:

> I'm of a family of five boys and four girls. Boys are supposed to wear trousers starting from their adolescence; this is due to our traditional dressing. For girls, they are not allowed to wear trousers because it's against our culture and it is part of family rules. Because if they start wearing trousers, they will show no respect to our parents who bought our clothes. Therefore girls in our family are only allowed to wear dresses with vitenge material [Bemba for printed cloth] covering the bottom part of their dress.

The normative notions about gender and clothing that Benard identifies are products of socialization and everyday social interaction. They hinge on social constructions of gendered and sexed bodies, comportment, and presentation. How much these constructions matter has to do with context, for example, home versus work. It also has to do with the structure of the interaction in terms of gender and authority, for example, a situation involving people of the same sex and age category or one where young people interact with people of the opposite sex in a senior generation. Religion also influences clothing norms, predominantly Christianity, as Islam claims such a small following in Zambia that its prescribed dress style hardly is evident in public settings.[6] Religious explanations of proper dress make reference to the Bible, which is claimed to forbid women to wear trousers, short and tight clothing, and makeup. These claims have much in common with the general normative aspects of Zambian dress practice that I describe below. Like all other dress conventions, this one is highly context dependent and largely confined to church attendance. Outside of that setting, according to a male journalist, "even Christian women are dressing 'to kill'" (*Weekly Post,* 16–22 April 1993).

To flesh out the normative aspects of Zambian dress practice, I asked the people I interviewed about clothing consumption to describe both a well-dressed woman and a well-dressed man and to explain what made someone look not well dressed. These questions followed discussions of their favorite types of clothes and what they did not like to wear and why. In fact, the two sets of questions complemented one another. The descriptions of well-dressed people were remarkably uniform across the different residential areas in which I interviewed, constituting what amounts to a culturally dominant notion of how to dress. Questions about hairstyles, makeup, and accessories supported these notions as well. Only in apamwamba households and women-headed households with good economic means were these notions occasionally challenged in everyday interaction. Some of the young adolescents who wrote clothing essays for me also challenged, or wanted to challenge, these norms that circumscribed their clothing desires.

The composite clothing profiles of a well-dressed woman and a well-dressed man that arise from these interviews have much in common. The adult dress profile of both sexes is tidy with smooth lines and careful color coordination. It is loosely fitting rather than tight. "Too many" different garments, colors, and fabrics distort the smooth profile, making the person look dishevelled and drawing undue attention to the dressed body. Women's moderate use of jewelry and makeup, and hairstyles for both sexes enhance the total look to make it appear natural rather than artificial. In short, dress should complement the body structure rather than putting it on conspicuous display.

For both sexes these formal dress profiles convey notions about respectability, maturity, and being in charge. Regardless of urban or rural residence, the accepted notion of how to dress makes adult men insist on suits, ties, long-sleeved shirts, and, when men are a certain age, hats for their public ensemble. Leather shoes, not boots, sneakers, or sandals, mark the man as properly put together. And irrespective of occupation and location, adult women insist on skirts below the knee, short-sleeved loose blouses, or dresses, on top of which a chitenge can be worn if necessary and, when women are a certain age, head scarves; shoes with heels, not sandals, and certainly not sneakers, are part of their ensemble in public. But on the matter of how to present the dressed body, the clothing profiles of women and men differ significantly. Women must cover their "private parts," which in this region of Africa includes their thighs. This means that dress length, tightness, and fabric transparency become issues in interactions with men and elders both at home and in public. I return to these observations in chapter 8.

The active concern with cutting a good figure on Zambian terms is evident in the hard work of salaula consumption in Mrs. Miyanda's market tour. That work extends beyond the market. A well-dressed person is well kempt herself and her clothing is well kept. Producing the smooth, tidy clothing profile involves processes that easily escape the gaze of the casual observer or traveler who sees salaula only as the West's used clothes. The desire to be well turned out, even if the garments are secondhand, makes clothes-conscious Zambians insist on immaculate ensembles whose elements are carefully laundered and ironed. For this reason the faded and torn jeans that are part of salaula bales imported from the United States are particularly unpopular. The desire to look spick and span prompts the kind of scrutiny of fabric quality we saw in Mrs. Miyanda, who sought to ascertain that colors of printed fabrics would not run in washing. Fading in sunlight is an issue as well. Most households do their laundry in cold water using strong detergents containing bleach, and clothes are usually hung up in the sunlight to dry. So color fastness and fabric quality are important issues in identifying clothes that are durable and will keep their good looks. And everyone pays great attention to shoes, commonly carrying a piece of cloth under the waist of chitenge wrappers, in handbags, or in pockets to remove Lusaka's dust when entering public buildings and private homes.

The attraction of salaula to clothing-conscious Zambian consumers goes far beyond the price factor and the good quality for money that many of these garments offer. Above all, salaula makes available an abundance and variety of clothes that allow consumers to add their individual mark on the culturally accepted clothing profile. The fact that we can identify Zambian terms for acceptable dress does not mean that everyone dresses alike. Nor does the desire to dress in "the latest" produce passive imitation and homogeneity. It is precisely the opposite effect that consumers seek to achieve from salaula and that they find missing from much store-bought clothing: uniqueness. What they want are clothes that are fashionable rather than common. One of the women I interviewed in a high-income area put it this way when explaining why she shopped from salaula: "I don't want to wear what everyone else is wearing." "Clothes from salaula are not what other people wear," said another woman, explaining why they are viewed as "exclusive."

The desire for uniqueness, to stand out, while dressing the body on Zambian terms, produces considerable variations in dress in public workplaces and offices. Women never wear the same dress to work every day, according to their own reports, but rotate their garments and make new combinations of dresses and skirts. Their rotation occasionally includes dresses in a cut and style that in the West might be considered cocktail or evening wear. They may wear a chitenge dress to work as well, something rarely seen in the 1980s. In some banks and private firms, women wear suited uniforms but have a "free dress" day once a week when they dress with their own sense of style.

Men work hard to achieve uniqueness in clothing presentation, too. Suits are worn in Zambia across a much wider range of white-collar and civil service ranks than in the midwestern United States, for example. Civil servants rotate their immaculately kept suits, including older suits that wear the marks of time but always are crisply pressed. Young male bank tellers and clerical workers vary their suited look by wearing different types of shirt, tie, and handkerchief combinations. Some men also wear jewelry such as necklaces, tie-pins, bracelets, and rings, which they rotate. In fact, men's suits are worn so commonly in Lusaka's downtown that, unlike in Harare in neighboring Zimbabwe, you hardly ever encounter an adult Zambian man wearing shorts in public.

Because notions of proper dress are context dependent, their constraining effects may be temporarily put aside. This is the case on the urban disco and evening entertainment scene, which in the 1990s often displayed miniskirts and women's tight and transparent garments. Men who attend such events dress in well-styled jeans and trousers. And some could very occasionally be seen wearing the very high waisted trousers inspired by Zairean rhumba musicians. Specially styled jackets go with them, adorned with a variety of inserted contrastive fabric or special collar, button, and pocket details. The majority of those who can afford to attend such events are of apamwamba background, the only group with an effective choice in the clothing market.

Last but not least, both idiosyncracy and pragmatics enter into how some people dress. I met many young male traders in the salaula markets who enjoyed dressing in a striking manner in garments they took a liking to. Examples include one young man who wore what looked like a hospital orderly's white uniform topped by a pink peignoir. Another young man dressed proudly in a church elder's purple gown. Dress practices such as these are not so much deliberate attempts to develop personal style distinctions as they are examples of the playfulness of young men who relish dressing up and showing off. What is more, the Zambian clothing scene is full of what to the Western eye may appear unorthodox or incongruous styles, such as men wearing combinations of women's clothing, including coats, sweaters, and shorts, and women wearing men's dust coats and jackets. Such dress practices do not represent deliberate cross-dressing but reflect the differential availability of women's and men's seasonal garments in salaula consignments. Such clothing efforts are pragmatic aims at combining cold-weather garments or work clothes from what is available from salaula.

What Zambians describe as their dress "tradition" is not a static mold but an evolving set of practices in which different influences with various backgrounds are affecting one another, making it subject to variation over time as well as to resistence among some segments of consumers. Recent scholarship provides rich examples of the making and changing of "traditional" dress practices and their shifting cultural and political valuations (Ong 1990; MacLeod 1992). I noted earlier the change from the safari suit to the double-breasted suit in the wake of the third republic in 1991 and the "new culture" of opening up both in dress and politics. Whether or not it has to do with politics, the profile of Zambian men's suited look has begun to loosen up in the period during which I have paid close attention to dress practices.

"Old people's styles are coming back," said one of the men I interviewed in 1997, no doubt thinking of the big trousers that were popular in the 1950s. The looser cut of men's suits may in fact be influenced from the Zambian grassroots, by young male street vendors who since the early 1990s have been wearing looser and bigger clothes inspired by the American hip-hop and rap scene. Zairean styles have an impact too, although they are far less widespread. Men used to insist on wearing shirts tucked in, well settled under their belts. Now not only street vendors wear their shirts loose but also some white-collar workers. The loose-shirt vogue has been legitimized by President Mandela, who after taking office in South Africa began wearing colorfully printed shirts, untucked, without jackets and ties, in public. "Mandela shirts" often feature paisley-inspired prints, and they are among the garments the suitcase traders are bringing back from South Africa. Less has changed in the realm of women's clothing except perhaps for the sleeveless blouse and dress, which have become fairly widespread among younger consumers. But issues about women's wearing short skirts and dresses, tight clothing, and trousers continue to agitate some segments of society.

Chitenge Wear

The cultural constraints on women's dress practices are far more pronounced than on men, who can create a smooth, continuous line, enveloping their bodies to perfection with the combination of suit, shirt, and tie. Although Anne Hollander's work is inspired by clothing in Western art, some of her arguments resonate with the history of clothing consumption in Zambia. Her recent book emphasizes the enduring appeal of the suit in creating the "perfect man" (Hollander 1994:92). She suggests that women's dress always makes a strong, almost theatrical visual claim, while men's tailored suit sets the real standard (8). Zambian women's commentaries on male and female clothing practice acknowledge such a difference almost in the same terms. Indeed they complain that men have a much easier time dressing. In addition to being concerned with quality issues, color coordination, fit, and the right accessories, women have to worry about decency and respectability in dress. Yet there is one clothing platform where women take safe clothing conventions in their own hands and develop them to the fullest. This is the two-piece chitenge outfit, the postcolonial creation of a women's national dress "tradition" that continues to take on new shapes, influenced in particular by Zairean and West African clothing trends. By contrast, West African–inspired loose gowns and print shirts have not appealed to Zambian men.

In the 1960s and 1970s the chitenge suit consisted of a wrapper or plain skirt with a minimally tailored, short-sleeved, matching top and at times a head scarf. When the local textile factories still produced chitenge, their lines included not only colorful patterns but also commemorative designs, prints to promote wildlife conservation or immunization, and announcements that made them into wearable political slogans (*New York Times,* 26 November 1989). Women commonly then, as they still do, wrapped lengths of chitenge cloth on top of a skirt or dress when working around the house or in the fields; traveling by public transportation; shopping in the public markets; waiting for a long time, for example, on hospital grounds; and attending overnight wakes and funerals. The most widespread use of chitenge is for carrying infants on the back. The chitenge holds bundles, serves as blanket when people sit on the ground, and has many usages. As a constructed garment, the chitenge suit gradually became more elaborate during the 1980s. It has now evolved into a fashion that holds the ample breasts and hips that fit so uneasily into ready-made clothing and many of the dresses in salaula markets.

During the mid- to late 1980s chitenge outfits were simple skirts or wraps and tops of printed cloth at times with contrasting ribbons sewn around necks and sleeves; tie-dye became common then, often locally produced by West African women who taught Zambian women the technique; tie-dye was sewn up into loose garments, including trouser and top combinations, often with Nigerian-style embroidery around necks, sleeves, and edges. This may have been influenced by the feminization of the men's two-piece outfit of trousers and oversized tops that was popular in Nigeria in the late 1980s (Bastian 1996). The trouser and top profile changed during the first half of the 1990s to skirts and tops of printed cloth or tie-dye with marked waistlines, peplums, increasingly elaborate built-up sleeves supported by interfacing, and collars, necklines, and fronts embellished by contrasting material, buttons, ruffles, or smocking. There were several types of skirts to choose from: plain wrappers, double wrappers, and Tshala Muanas, tight skirts reaching below the knee with a long slit in front, named after a popular Zairean singer. In 1997 the latest style was inspired by West African dress that locally was referred to as "Nigerian boubou."[7] This style consisted of huge flowing gowns of single-colored fabrics, damask or damask-weave imitations with elaborate embroideries in contrasting colors and with built-up headgear. Chitenge fashions will no doubt continue to change, as their popularity rises or declines in interactions with pan-African and global clothing trends. Perhaps in Zambia, as has been suggested for Kenya, this "global African dress signifies not

Figure 61   Woman displaying part of her chitenge wardrobe, Mtendere township, Lusaka, 1997. Author's photograph.

Figure 62   Dressing in chitenge for office work in a township bar, Mtendere township, Lusaka, 1997. Author's photograph.

Figure 63   Tailor making chitenge wear, Kamwala shopping center, Lusaka, 1995. Author's photograph.

tradition but modernity . . . [that constructs] an elusive and ambiguous . . . national identity" (Rabine 1997:63).

"You can do so many things with chitenge," explained one of the teachers who kept a budget book for me. Her wardrobe consisted largely of chitenge outfits in some of the different styles I just described and only a couple of "European-style" two-piece outfits. Chitenge outfits are much more comfortable to wear, she argued, than dresses and skirts "where you have to worry about belts and matching blouses." Wearing chitenge is closely related to income in that the price of fabric and the tailor's charges might be too high for many low-income consumers. A chitenge suit in 1995 easily cost K35,000 when the price of fabric, trimmings, and labor were added up, and more if the suit was highly embellished. This is why the self-reported ratio of "European-style" to chitenge wear by householders in Kamanga and Kaunda Square was heavily skewed toward the European end, which in this case means predominantly salaula. No one there claimed to wear only chitenge, although some women had one or two outfits that they wore for special occasions. In the high-income areas, by contrast, a small proportion of residents, one-eighth of the total, reported wearing only chitenge. Others wore chitenge with some regularity and reported owning many suits. But "European-style" clothing, which includes a high proportion of salaula, was the most widespread dress style there also.

Some women will tell you that they do not like chitenge styles at all. If pushed, they will explain that their dislike has to do with size, or "body structures" in the local dress language, meaning that they are "too" thin. Because of the body-size factor, age plays into this preference as well, and young adult women do not in fact agree on whether or not they like chitenge fashions. "They do make big women look nice," said one young woman, while another complained that chitenge dresses are only for "old" women.

A good deal of clothing competence is entailed in purchasing attractive chitenge fabrics and identifying tailors who are able to deliver a finished product to the satisfaction of customers. Discriminating customers considered the chitenge fabric produced by Kafue Textiles and Mulungushi Textiles until the early 1990s to be of poor quality and unattractive design. Those who had money paid a lot for Dutch wax prints available on the black market and chitenges brought across the border from Zaire and Burundi. The evaluation of chitenge depends not only on the attractiveness of the design but also on how well the fabric stands up to washing. Some chitenges contain a lot of starch, and some have colors that run. In fact, chitenge dresses may not be very durable, which is one reason they have less appeal at the low-income level. Their short life is a product of mediocre fabric, frequent washing with strong detergents, and constant ironing,[8] often with a heavy charcoal iron as many Zambian homes in the low-income areas are not electrified.

The increased availability in recent years of imported chitenge fabrics from India and Pakistan with attractive designs at more affordable prices and superior quality to those that used to be manufactured locally has helped to make chitenge fashions part of more women's wardrobes than in the 1970s and 1980s. Office workers and teachers wear them to work as do bank clerks on their "free dress" day. Above all, chitenge outfits are worn on formal visits and special occasions such as weddings and kitchen parties, where they are displayed proudly by mature women who have the body to carry them.

Our Shops

In the early 1990s salaula markets were sometimes described as Patelo's Boutique, perhaps with the acknowledgment that many people of Indian background (Patel is a common Indian name in Zambia) were involved in wholesaling imported secondhand clothing. In the mid-1990s salaula markets were popularly referred to as Sally's Boutique. These terms put a fresh gloss on secondhand clothing, erasing its origin and hiding its history. Some of the people with whom I discussed clothing consumption in 1995 described salaula markets as "our shops," using terms that provide additional evidence of localization: almost everyone shops "from salaula" and you can buy nearly everything there.

To be sure, shopping from salaula provides lots of excitement because of the profusion and variety of clothing that allows people to dress rather than wearing rags, as young Lukonde put it. But while many consumers have no qualms telling you that they buy their clothes from salaula, there are still some, particularly men in civil service positions, who are reluctant to admit that they wear salaula even if their wives bought it for them. Their reaction, I suggest, is not so much embarrassment as disappointment over the country's postcolonial economic and political developments, which have not increased the number of options and improved the livelihoods of the many, but rather reduced them. If everything else were equal, such men would no doubt prefer to purchase brand-new suits. But few are able to do so now. Instead such men participate, directly or indirectly, in the recommodification of secondhand clothing.

There is no doubt that consumption is serious work "if by work we mean the disciplined (skilled and unskilled) production of the means of consumer subsistence . . . this labor is not principally targeted to the production of commodities but is directed at producing the conditions of consciousness in which *buying* can occur" (Appadurai 1997:42, emphasis in original). As I have argued throughout this book, Zambian consumers work hard at making the West's used clothing their own, incorporating this imported commodity on terms that are locally conditioned. The local mark on salaula is a product of many activities, including wholesale and retail practices that shift the register of meaning of this commodity from used to new; physical changes achieved by alteration, mending, and recycling; extensive concerns with the care of clothing and its presentation; and putting salaula garments together into new local ensembles. The local mark has also to do with what consumers consider to be good taste, proper dress, and acceptable demeanor for women and men of different ages.

This transformation of meanings does not stop at the point when people put on their carefully selected and cared-for garments. The process continues, and perhaps more compellingly, as I discuss in the next chapter, in everyday interaction and at special events that support and challenge the delineations of what most consumers in Zambia consider to be the local terms for acceptable dress.

9 Clothing, Gender, and Power

Who defines what is acceptable dress in Zambia and why? The previous chapter about the work of consumption implied questions about clothing practices and their meanings to which I now turn. The meanings of clothes do not inhere in the garments themselves but are attributed to them in ongoing interaction. How clothing, both new and used, is constructed and how it matters has a lot to do with the context in which it is worn. Even then, because individual dress practice does not always conform to widespread norms, the body surface becomes a battleground where questions about dress and its acceptability are tested. That is, the dressed body both conceals and reveals deeply entangled issues about gender, sexuality, and power.

Focusing on context, this chapter is about what people wear and how they wear it in different social settings and the reactions the presentation of their dressed bodies provokes. I explore how meanings of clothing are constructed in a number of specific events, situations, and settings that range from everyday interaction in homes and public places to more explicit performance acts such as celebrations. These and other contexts serve as structuring backdrops for the presentational form or "look" of particular combinations of clothing, both new and used.

The chapter begins with the all-female context of the kitchen party, an event for which women dress with particular care. As a created tradition that celebrates women's submission to men through dance, song, and dress, the kitchen party is a particularly interesting context with which to begin a discussion of what amounts to a dress code. The second section turns to young adult women whose scope for dressing as they wish is severely circumscribed. Their self-conscious preoccupations with miniskirts hide adolescent worries over growing up in a male authoritarian society that is becoming increasingly sexually violent. Many young men also feel powerless but not for the same reason as young women, as I discuss in the third section. Here I explore the relative freedom of young men to dress as they want. Ultimately, questions about dress and salaula, about who dresses how and where, and from what source the garments are obtained, are about power, not only or always about purchasing power and household authority but also about the power of institutions and the state to privilege one sex over the other.

The specific insights in this chapter draw on extensive participant observation, essays written by young adult women and men about clothing, and interviews with young men who dress in order to draw attention to themselves. The essays on clothing consumption were written in 1995 by twelfth-grade students of both sexes in English composition classes in Lusaka and two provincial towns, Mansa and Kawambwa, in Luapula Province. I constructed this exercise to invite young adults to describe clothing practices in their homes; how they liked to dress, what they disliked wearing, and why; and where their clothes were bought. The resulting "clothing autobiographies" are rich in descriptions of clothing practices in the terms of the young people.

Kitchen Parties and Dress

During my years of comings and goings in Lusaka, kitchen parties have become increasingly popular. They are a product of the postcolonial urban situation, crossing ethnic, occupational, and class backgrounds, involving women from across residential areas. Although only some women can afford to stage such events, many attend such parties. I never came across kitchen parties in the early 1970s, but by the mid-1980s even women in the low-income areas spoke of organizing them, if not in their own residential settings then in the homes of friends or acquaintances in more affluent neighborhoods.[1]

Kitchen parties are all-female events at which relatives and friends, including expatriates, come together with presents to help the bride-to-be with kitchen utensils for her new home. Some of these parties are quite large, with more than a hundred women; they tend to take place outdoors, in a spacious garden on Saturday afternoons toward the end of the month, when wage earners have received their paychecks. They are modeled on a loose version of initiation ceremonies and feature a senior marriage instructor who, before the party, has taught the bride-to-be how to behave toward her husband, both sexually and interpersonally.

A kitchen party gets going in the afternoon after a night-long private instruction session and the bride-to-be's demonstration of her dancing skills, especially how "to dance in bed." The marriage instructor and senior relatives then bring out the bride-to-be covered in a chitenge cloth, followed by women drummers. The matron and the young woman seat themselves on the ground in front of the visitors. After an opening prayer, and in Christian homes sometimes a brief Bible lesson, the young woman is unveiled. She remains seated with downcast eyes for the duration of the party. Subsequent events include individual performances, as each guest who cares to, or can be coaxed by the mistress of ceremonies into dancing, steps into the center, com-

Figure 64 The bride-to-be, covered in chitenge cloth, leaving the house accompanied by marriage instructor *(right)* and mother *(left)* to the kitchen party, Lusaka, 1995.
Author's photograph.

Figure 65 Bride-to-be seated next to her mother, receiving a gift from a guest who is telling her about its usage. Matron on the right, and gift-wrapped present in front, Lusaka, 1995.
Author's photograph.

menting on the present she has brought "for the kitchen" in terms of its importance to the marital relationship.

Regardless of the ethnic background of the bride-to-be, the senior marriage instructor and the female drummers tend in Lusaka to have Eastern Province origins. "They know about these things," I was told. The drummers are usually recruited from the low-income areas. While some of the dances and songs may be regionally specific and derive from another era, kitchen parties are characterized by their ethnic and socioeconomic heterogeneity, and above all by their preoccupation with male-female relations and heterosexual norms. Guests at such events are served individually wrapped portions of food, in apamwamba households sometimes catered by hotels. Except in some Christian homes, such events feature a good deal of drinking, especially of beer but also, in wealthier homes, of wine and alcohol-spiced punches. One of the Zambian friends with whom I attended several kitchen parties in 1995 used to inquire not only about what present I was bringing but also if I had remembered to put my "baby" (a tiny bottle of rum or brandy to mix with soft drinks) in my handbag.

Kitchen parties offer entertainment and merrymaking, as mature women who can dance shake their hips and bottoms and are sometimes joined by other women who enjoy displaying their skills. Women who are less amply endowed produce some of this effect with the help of a prop, a chitenge cloth wound around their hips; the cloth has been thrown at them by the mistress of ceremonies, who opens and comments on the presents and cajoles the givers into dancing. She is herself a very skilled dancer and improviser. For instance, at one party when showing a present to the audience, a broom, she demonstrated how not to use it: strapping her loose black skirt with a long back slit around her hips, she danced, bending over with the broom in a posture revealing both her thighs and "masecrets," the local term for women's underwear. The guests screamed. As the afternoon progresses, the sexual gestures of dancing often become more explicit. Any literal interpretation of the sexual enactment in dance and gestures must be tempered with acknowledgment of the subversive atmosphere this entire performance event generates.

Kitchen parties are one of the few events that bring adult women together in Zambia to share experiences about their joys, successes, troubles, and tribulations as well as information with which they assist one another. Given the male authoritarian atmosphere that characterizes sociability across all class levels in Zambia, it comes as no surprise that some men view kitchen parties as events where married women get drunk and indulge in social evils, such as exposing unmarried women to "offensive" songs about sex and gossip about extramarital relationships (*Zambia Daily Mail,* 27 November

Figure 66 Guests kneeling to present gifts to the bride-to-be; drummers in the background, Lusaka, 1997.
Author's photograph.

1984; *Times of Zambia,* 5 December 1985). But aside from the alcohol, sex talk, and gossip, what also irks some men about women's attendance at such parties is their own lack of control. While some men may help sponsor kitchen parties by providing money to cover expenses, they have no input to their organization and staging. In effect, through participating in kitchen parties women act as independent consumers, spending money both on presents and clothing.

Many young women are ambivalent about kitchen parties but do attend them when the bride-to-be is a special friend or colleague. If you do not dance or drink, they say, these afternoons can be very long. And some young women are rather reluctant to enter the dance ground. They know that in the cultural terms that inform these events unmarried women ought not to be exposed to the presentation of special dance skills that are considered to be the exclusive domain of married women.

Fewer younger women than mature married women follow the overwhelming dress practice at such parties, the wearing of chitenge outfits. At parties where either the bride- or groom-to-be's relatives, or both, are Lozi, some women wear *misisi* dresses, the missionary-inspired dress of the Lozi home region. In its contemporary version the *misisi* is sewn of floral print fabric and consists of a top with gathered sleeves, a yoke around the neck, and a tiered skirt with a marked bustle and a shawl worn on top. The kitchen-party dress scene includes a very large proportion of chitenge wear, in wealthy homes a veritable chitenge fashion show, as well as some "European-style" dresses and two-piece suits, both from salaula and the tailor. I have seen several young women in stylish jeans with decorative tops receive critical remarks by women of the senior generation, insisting that trousers have no place at a kitchen party. One young woman who turned up at a kitchen party in 1995 in a chitenge outfit consisting of a short-sleeved top and loose bermuda shorts got so much flak that she wore a chitenge cloth as a wrapper for the rest of the afternoon. And one of the worst commentaries I have heard was directed toward a heavy-set woman who turned up at a "Christian" kitchen party in black tights and a T-shirt hugging her waist. That is to say, short and tight garments, displaying "private parts" and "body structures" for all to see, are not comme il faut at this event. In effect, the cultural terms informing the kitchen party celebrate women's subordinate roles to husbands, who are the only ones these terms allow to gaze at the "private parts" of a wife's body.

Figure 67 Guests at kitchen party, dressed (from left to right) in two-piece office wear, "Nigerian-inspired boubou" fashion, and chitenge dresses, Lusaka, 1997.
Author's photograph.

As a competitive presentation a kitchen party may be viewed as a social situation set apart from everyday life in terms of place, setting, and props. The most important prop is women's dressed bodies. At kitchen parties, the participants' evaluation of and commentary on heterosexual behavior extends into preoccupations with stylish appearance and dress. The focus on competitive display in sexually inflected dances, songs, presents, and clothes and the status politics that take place between women turn kitchen parties into what Appadurai (1986:21) has defined as tournaments of value,

> complex periodic events that are removed in some culturally well-defined way from the routine of economic life. Participation in them is . . . both a privilege . . . and an instrument of status contests. . . . The currency of such tournaments is also set apart through well understood cultural diacritics . . . What is at issue . . . is not just status, rank, fame, or reputation of actors, but the disposition of the central tokens of value in the society in question. Finally, though such tournaments of value occur in special times and places, their forms and outcomes are always consequential for the more mundane realities of power and value in ordinary life.

The currency of the kitchen party's tournament of value is the female body, clothed in dress. At such parties participants evaluate and judge both behavior and dress, collect information, trade, and share insights into the sources of clothing design and style. In effect, the participants constitute a specialized knowledge group that on such occasions work out, in conflict and accommodation, the meanings that distinct clothing styles convey. As Appadurai advises, such tournaments of value should not be isolated analytically from everyday life. Their articulations with other domains of life are rather complicated.

Taken together, the marriage counseling and the consumption aspect of the kitchen party make this new pan-ethnic tradition into a contemporary, uniquely Zambian ceremony, and as such, it is shaped by some of society's general problems in both the economic and the cultural domain. As an occasion for giving presents "for the kitchen" to help a bride-to-be look after husband and home, the kitchen party articulates with the domain of consumption. In effect, careful calculations go into the planning of such parties, since the expenses involved can easily exceed the value of gifts. Calculation takes place among those who are invited as well. Women with medium-income earnings such as the teachers who tracked their expenses for me limited the number of kitchen-party invitations they accepted. One of them said that teachers did not receive many invitations since "everybody knows" that they have little money to spend. While the party unfolds, guests scrutinize both performance and dress as well as the quality of the presents. They comment not only on the dancers' skills but also on the food and drink they are served.

From the participant's point of view, the success of a kitchen party often hinges on those aspects. In short, while kitchen parties offer marriage counsel to brides-to-be, they are a performance production of entertainment and consumption for both organizers and invited guests.

Perhaps the kitchen party's most marked contradiction lies in the celebration of the subordinate wifely role as enacted in the performance and dressed bodies of mature married women, many of whom in fact work in their own right. While young unmarried women who are contemplating proactive agendas for themselves may enjoy some of the merrymaking and socializing that kitchen parties offer, they may not fully agree with their message. One woman journalist recently pointed out how the traditional marriage counseling provided in connection with these events "reduces a woman to a house servant." The problem, she argued, "is exaggerated respect. Women are taught to regard their husbands as bosses . . . respect should certainly be there but not to the exent where a wife becomes a slave" (*Zambia Daily Mail,* 11 January 1998).

Miniskirts and Dangerous Dress

Clothing practices assume different meanings depending on where garments are worn and in whose presence. Normative ideas about gender and authority are among the dominant cultural representations through which Zambians interpret clothing practices. These representations strongly privilege men over women, as the discussion of the kitchen-party performance demonstrates. For another context I turn to young women, whom I have already described as ambivalent about how to dress. Their dress universe is potentially much wider than that of their mothers, yet they feel hemmed in. To illustrate how, I turn to my survey of clothing-consumption practices for an interview I conducted in 1995 with an air-traffic controller in one of Lusaka's medium-to high-income areas. It was late morning, and he had just completed a night shift and was relaxing at home, wearing shorts, a T-shirt, and sandals. At one point I asked him what he thought of the clothes of the young male street vendors who in 1995 dressed in oversized jeans and unlaced hightop sneakers. "It is all right," he said. "Even though our parents didn't like it at all, my generation loved jeans and we insisted on wearing them." When I asked how he viewed miniskirts for young women, his tune shifted markedly. "I can't allow that," he said vehemently, "not even for my own daughters. Young women are not supposed to show their legs in the presence of their father." This remark, with its unequal scope for male and female dress practice, echoes my discussion in the previous chapter.[2]

The remarks of the air-traffic controller turn on the miniskirt and pertain to

Figure 68   Women going shopping, dressed in chitenge wrappers: everyday dress practice, Mansa, Luapula Province, 1995.
Author's photograph.

Figure 69   Women dressed for a public event: the Annual Agricultural and Commercial Show, Lusaka, 1992.
Author's photograph.

tight and revealing clothing in general. As we learned from Benard's commentary, women's clothing competence is a product of early socialization. It hinges on what young women describe as "private parts," which include thighs, and "body structures," which refer to size and weight, and it also has to do with comportment and presentation. As Benard explained, young girls are taught to wrap a chitenge cloth around their waist when working around the home, and to wear loose and unrevealing dresses and skirts below the knee when in public. When sitting, their legs should neither be apart nor exposed. And their clothes must, of course, be clean and well ironed.

These presuppositions make many young women apprehensive about exposing their body in public. While this concern arises from the need to show respect for elders, it also pertains to the issue of decency and the implications raised by miniskirts about loose morals. Above all, this concern expresses young women's fear of sexual violence. As Abigal, a twelfth-grade student in Lusaka, explained in her essay on clothing: "The clothes I like least are short (mini) and tight clothes; and I like them least because here in Zambia when you dress in such kinds of clothes, people may start having ideas about you, because some people think that if you dress in mini skirts or dresses, you are a prostitute because they think prostitutes dress like that. I can give you one example," she went on. "Here in Zambia, if you put on mini and tight clothes, men can easily rip your clothes and you might be raped at the same time. And some people think you are of an unrespectable family if you dress in such kinds of clothes."[3]

But if young women's clothing competence is in part a product of early socialization, their clothing practice is also a result of their experiences in social and institutional settings of home, school, street, and work. Abigal's remarks touch on a highly charged issue that preoccupied at least one-third of her forty-nine Lusaka classmates, who made direct associations between miniskirts and rape. The specific backdrop for this close association was the public stripping of a woman wearing a miniskirt by street vendors at Lusaka's Kulima Tower (a major bus stop) on 18 March 1994 (*Zambia Daily Mail*, 23 March 1994). This particular event was not the only one of its kind. Five women had been raped in the melee that broke out when a concert by a popular Zairean rhumba group was called off in 1993, allegedly because men were provoked after watching the dance routines of the scantily dressed "dancing queens" that are part of such performances (*Times of Zambia*, 6 December 1993). Attempts at and incidents of stripping women who wear short skirts in public continue to occur, and they, sadly, help to account for Jessie's apprehensions: "Here in Zambia when you go to town the street vendors tear your dress or whatever you are wearing because it is very short. And they call you all sorts of names, for instance hule [prostitute] and they can rape you."

Cleopatra was more explicit: "In Zambia there is no freedom of dressing. If you wore mini skirts, bicycle shorts or leggings and decided to go shopping in town, you would be stripped naked . . . ; this kind of dressing arouses men's emotions."

Young men, as I discuss shortly, enjoy considerably more freedom in their dress than do young women, whom society blames for provoking men's uncontrollable desires when they wear short or tight clothes. Perhaps this understanding of dress is involved in many young women's liking for jeans; the preferred style in 1995 was a loose cut, giving a slightly baggy silhouette. "The reason why I like jeans," explained Habenzu, "is that when I wear jeans, I feel comfortable when I am sitting with boys because I can sit the way I want." And according to Sameta, "if I am on a journey or taking a stroll with friends I wear jeans. I walk without being worried. Secondly, when I am in a minibus or where most of those grown up people are, I don't have to worry about how I am supposed to sit." Hlupekile brought home the point about jeans: "The clothes I like best is office wear, that is, skirt and blouse, or suit, skirt and jacket . . . I like these clothes because in our country Zambia there are lots of rape cases. When you put on a mini skirt, you cannot go around town without being attacked by street boys or even raped. I prefer jeans because when you are surrounded by these kinds of people, it will take time for them to undress you. You can scream and at least people might be able to hear your screaming and come over."

The miniskirt is not the only item of clothing that gives rise to conformity in some areas of life and dissent in others. Trousers for women do so too, depending on context. In general, the association between miniskirts and rape was less explicit in rural female twelfth-grade students' dress practices. The young women at St. Mary's Secondary School at Kawambwa expressed less concern about the body-exposing issue in relationship to notions of decency, respectability, and sexual violence than their urban peers. Many liked dress and suit combinations, and quite a few liked to wear jeans. Yet jeans were not acceptable everywhere. Astridah dramatically related the following incident: "When I visited my aunt last month I wore jeans. Immediately she saw me, she started shouting. Is this the way you dress as a daughter of Lupupa? Our clan or family does not allow a woman to put on male clothes. I am telling you Astridah, in our family with your father, we don't allow such a way of dressing." Astridah added: "I was so shocked. She even complained that we learned this type of dressing from my mother which is not true."

When criticizing Astridah's mother for not teaching her daughter proper dress manners, the aunt might have implied that Astridah's mother was from a different ethnic group than her father, in which case the blame pointed to the mother's not knowing how to keep home and children properly. The blame might also imply that Astridah's mother worked away from home and thus ignored instructing her daughter. But her mother, according to Astridah's description of her family, was a "full time housewife." Still, from then on, Astridah made sure not to wear trousers when visiting her aunt.

Women's dressed bodies receive considerable critical scrutiny, and cases involving miniskirts worn in public provoked additional debate when in May 1997 popular television announcer Dora Siliya was suspended from the government-controlled Zambia National Broadcasting Corporation for "insubordination arising from her wearing miniskirts" (*Post,* 22 May 1997). The discussion took a new twist when in April 1998 one of Zambia's very few women members of parliament, Minister of Health Nkandu Luo, stormed out of the National Assembly after a male colleague raised a point of order about dress code. Ms. Luo was wearing a knee-length skirt. A male MP asked the deputy speaker if MP Luo's dress was in order, claiming that it would "provoke the feelings of the male members of the House" (*Zambia Daily Mail,* 4 April 1998). And in September 1998 parliamentarians watched in silence when the deputy speaker ordered Minister of Finance Edith Nawakwi to leave the National Assembly because of "inappropriate dressing," in this case a short skirt (*Zambia Daily Mail,* 17 September 1998).

The intensity of public reactions to events involving miniskirts is a telling indicator of the widespread social acceptance of what constitutes acceptable dress for women (*Zambia Daily Mail,* "Speaker" and "Gender Focus," 24 September 1998). I shall not enter into the tortuous discussions that took place in the print media in the wake of these events except to highlight a couple of issues that pertain directly to the substance of this chapter. These reoccurring events show that women's dress options in public settings where men are present are very circumscribed, that challenge of what amounts to a dress code easily provokes men to verbal harassment and more. But above all, such events demonstrate that some women who work in full public view dare to insist on their freedom to dress.

Adolescents like Astridah and Jessie are more self-conscious and less daring than Ms. Siliya, Ms. Luo, and Ms. Nawakwi. With so much public attention on women's dressed bodies, it is not at all surprising that the young women who wrote essays for me were preoccupied with managing their bodies through dress. But while these cultural norms inform young women's dress practices, they do not contain their desires. When away from the controlling sphere of the home, where they are supposed to wear chitenge wraps when working around the house, and outside the regulatory space of the school, where they wear uniforms, young women balance their pursuit of "the latest" with caution. Some young urban women who want to "move with fashion" dress in miniskirts when their parents are out, whereas others dare to wear miniskirts in public. For young adults attending school, weekends are times to dress up. In medium- and high-income areas, you will find young people "taking a stroll," often in heterosexual groups on weekend afternoons. This is the time for display of women's dress-up jeans and tops, skirts, dresses, and shoes, and for young men to show off their casual wear. It is a time for assignations as well and a part of the local culture of dating. Even in this situation miniskirts are rarely seen, and young women remain apprehensive about exposing their body.

There were three reactions to approaching adulthood and sexual maturity among the young female writers. A small group said that they were called tomboys and that they preferred to wear jeans and casual clothes. Several young women looked forward to wearing suits and dresses. They included Sameta, whose mother had given her a tailor-made long skirt with a slit at the back and a matching top for Christmas. Sameta explained: "I was very happy . . . I liked myself that day and I looked like I was working class even though I am still schooling. Sometimes when I wear office wear I feel comfortable and it makes me feel that one day I will become a grown-up woman." Finally, quite a few young women were approaching sexual maturity with unease and saw dresses as icons of female adulthood. Describing how she hated wearing dresses, eighteen-year-old Tanera explained: "Clothes like dresses really make me feel uncomfortable . . . I feel as if I look married or like a mother." Carolyn did not like wearing dresses either, because they made her look "old fashioned"; what is worse, "when you wear such clothes people will not even talk to you because they will think that you are running a home or you are somebody's grandmother." In short, the social and sexual identity of those young women is very much lodged in the way in which the body is worn through clothes. They have little room within which to maneuver because of the cultural meanings that society at large attaches to their clothing.

Although the government schools they attend are far from being Zambia's elite secondary educational institutions, these young women and the young men I turn to shortly are a relatively privileged group. This is so because of the mere fact that they made it to the final grade in school and expected to graduate within the year. Approximately equal numbers of girls and boys enroll in grade one, but the attrition rate of girls is higher than that of boys at all levels. Close to half of Zambia's school-age girls do not attend school (GRZ and UN 1996:47). These gender disparities have become more marked since the mid-1970s. They reflect societal norms, discriminatory school place-allocation ratios, and the fact that girls drop out of schools because of pregnancies. According to a recent assessment two-thirds of Zambian women have either had children or are pregnant by the age of nineteen. From fifteen years on, a large and growing proportion of teenage girls become pregnant, usually by men who are much older (GRZ and UN 1996:58–59). Taking advantage of girls and young women, men not only make them pregnant but also infect them with HIV/AIDS. In fact, rates of infection among adolescents are reported to be seven times higher for women between the age of fifteen and nineteen than for men of the same age (Webb 1996:2). Added to that are marked increases in the reported incidence of child sexual abuse, incest, domestic violence, and rape (Rude 1996; Shinkanga 1996; YMCA 1994).

Against this backdrop it is not surprising that the young female essay writers felt under pressure to construct their physical bodies into a particular model of femininity through dress, expressing their anxieties over sexuality in their preoccupation with the miniskirt. The dress practices they described drew on their understanding of their own gender as very much constructed through sexuality and on their knowledge that their place in society is shaped by that construction. Unlike their age-mates who never went to school or dropped out because they were pregnant, these young women had "kept themselves." The world is potentially within their reach, and it is a much broader world than their mothers encountered at their age. When writing brief introductions of themselves for a pen-pal project I facilitated with American peers,[4] these young women indicated that they wanted to be, for example, computer programmers, doctors, veterinarians, and airline pilots, and one even expressed her desire to become president. Among them some are likely to succeed. Dora Siliya did, and so did Nkando Luo and Edith Nawakwi.

Suit Aesthetics and Provocative Wear

Unlike young women who carefully monitor the way they dress in public, young men like to draw attention to themselves, in different ways to be sure, depending on their socioeconomic circumstances and regional location in Zambia's declining economy. Similar observations are available from Malindi on the Kenya coast, where Johanna Schoss (1996:167–75) noted young male tour guides in the late 1980s dressing in two versions of distinctive Western-style clothing, "professional" and "beachboy," that both were marked by the clothing's quality, newness, and foreign manufacture. In Zambia "newness" is an attribute not only of brand-new clothing but also of novel ownership of imported secondhand clothing. It includes such meanings as "fresh" from the source, and "new" from an unopened bale, among others. When understood in this way, newness captures young Zambian men's active preoccupation with a smart appearance that is both fashionable and neat. Young men's self-conscious concern with suits and jeans illustrates different constructions of these attributes of dress.

If miniskirts, jeans, and dresses indexed young adult women's anxieties about their future possibilities and position in Zambia during the last half of the 1990s, so did suits and jeans for their young male age-mates, yet with different ramifications. Few of the young men who wrote essays for me were preoccupied with their sexuality in any explicit way; their concerns focused more sharply on their future as adult men, holding jobs, and being in charge of households. Formal suits index that desire. I indicated in chapter 8 that suits are worn very widely across the civil service ranks and other white-collar work in Zambia. In today's popular discourse, because formal employment is declining, wage labor is coming close to meaning white-collar work. In fact, such employment is popularly referred to as "work," in contrast to "business" or "trade," and its job holders as "officers," "workers," or simply "working class." Sameta's commentary about looking as if she were "working class" when wearing a two-piece outfit of the kind that locally is called "office wear" means precisely that she looked like someone in a clerical position. The implication of this social categorization is clear. White-collar work is one of the few wage-labor opportunities to which young adults can aspire in Zambia's declining formal economy. Dressing in office wear conveys something important about educational background, respectability, and responsibility, and this association was particularly strong in the young men's essays. In short, cutting a fine figure in a smart suit implies that the wearer is a man in charge.

Many young adult urban men aspire to this dress ideal and the responsibility and social respectability that follows from holding a steady, monthly paid job and thus being a man in charge. "I want to be wearing clothes like those that people who work wear, because I want to be looking like a man rather than a boy," wrote Arnold, a twelfth-grade student in Lusaka. "Suits are the clothes I like most," explained Simon, "because they make me look decent and soon I will be joining the society of workers." Morgan, one of their classmates, described a pair of trousers and a jacket he recently had received: "I was full of joy . . . I like these clothes because a lot of people say that I look like a general manager and not only that, they also say that I look like a rich man." Other classmates liked jeans, particularly because they are durable, but also because "they are in style now." Lubasi put it this way: "I try by all means to be in line with style because when I am watching video music tapes like those recorded on MTV, I have noticed that most of the singers wear jeans."

But wearing jeans has a flip side. In the view of many of these young urban men, jeans too readily call forth the image of scruffy youths and street vendors. Simon, who preferred suits, said that he did not like jeans "because they make me look like a 'call boy.'" Call boys are young men at the minibus ranks who call out the destination of the bus, round up passengers, and collect fares. According to Moses, "I hate jeans because people may fail to distinguish between cigarette sellers and myself." Martin also hated wearing jeans "because they make me look like one of the naughty boys and thieves who hang around the corridors in town." Lusaka's downtown streets are full of young male traders in all kinds of goods. They put much effort into being seen, and many of them dress in a striking manner. The preferred style of the street vendors in 1995 when the students wrote their essays included oversized jeans, high-top unlaced sneakers, and flashy T-shirts; a baseball cap was almost de rigeur; and the most daring wore bandannas as headgear. Since domestically manufactured garments of this type were not readily available, most of these clothes were imported, either new or secondhand. Regardless of their source, such garments look costly.

There are at least two issues at stake in the young men's commentaries on the street vendors' get-up. First, because they are close to completing secondary school, they have higher economic aspirations for themselves. To be sure, young male secondary students do not want to be mistaken for the school dropouts turned street vendors who are viewed in some circles as a threat to society's stability and security. And second, the apparent expense of the street vendors' outfit readily implies that the clothes have been acquired by illicit means, thus the association with thieves. Conspicuous display of wealth raises suspicion in any case, and, in fact, *gangster* is a term residents of high-income areas use frequently to describe the street-vendor clothing style, including the air-traffic controller I quoted previously. The term *gangster* also refers to the rap-music scene that is inspiring local appropriations in some young men's dress.

Thus suits and jeans frame young urban adult men's desires for a better life. Young adult men in rural areas have similar desires, but they are more circumscribed by the conditions in which they live. Some twelfth-graders in a secondary school in Mansa expressed this clearly. Joshua explained: "Of all the clothes, I like strong ones which can serve me longer such as jeans. I like them because it is not easy for me to buy soap, and most of the time I do manual work in order to earn my living." The suit figures in the desires of these young rural men mostly by its absence. According to Cepas, "I dislike these types of clothes because they are very expensive and only meant for working class people. Since we do not work or get paid and only lead our lives by subsistence farming, I cannot go for this type of clothes." Nicholas used fairly similar language to describe why the suit combination did not fit his situation: "Such clothes can easily be torn and I think they are for office working people, so they don't suit me." Yet he added as an afterthought, "If I had a choice, I would really like to wear suits."

Figure 70 Young men in crisply ironed shirts and trousers with ties, tiepins and hats, imported from South Africa; inside Kamawala market, Lusaka, 1995. Author's photograph.

Figure 71 Young man assuming new accountant job in his first store-bought suit from Serioes, visiting friends in Kabwe's salaula market, 1993. Author's photograph.

Figure 72 Two young men overseeing a friend's salaula stand in main market while temporarily laid off from Mulungushi Textiles, Kabwe, 1993. Author's photograph.

Young men said far less in their essays than their female age-mates about clothing in reference to the opposite sex and their own physical bodies. There were exceptions, of course. The main reason Justin gave for liking jeans was to "please the cute girls so that I can be of attraction to them . . . cute girls never bother to say hi to you when you are putting on clothes that are rather old fashioned." Moses was very body conscious. Describing his delight over a double-breasted jacket that his father, a civil servant who tailored from home, recently had made for him, he elaborated: "After wearing it I surveyed myself in the mirror. I looked like a film actor . . . it was really a nice jacket. I like jackets because they suit me like a second skin. I have plenty of beef and muscles around my shoulders which forms a good round shape if I wear one [a jacket]." The reverse applied to Norman, who felt physically awkward. He complained: "Whenever I am wearing a suit, I am always thinking that everybody is looking at me . . . My physical structure does not earn me the prestige of wearing suits. I am slightly short and very thin. So whenever I put on a suit, it does not accord me the beauty of appearing best in clothes."

The flip side of jeans comes with new spins, as do all dress styles and their evaluation. A loose profile for men's suits is replacing the more formal suit silhouette of the late 1980s. Because I was curious about the evolving street-vendor style and its influence on mainstream men's dress in Zambia, I explored it in more detail in 1997. A young male assistant did purposeful sampling, interviewing twelve young men whose dress stood out from the crowd.[5] Aside from exploring the source of these young men's clothing, he engaged them in conversation about why they dressed in this manner. He asked questions about their personal circumstances as well. For an impressionistic comparison of young men's dress styles, he also interviewed four entry-level civil servants who wore formal suits to work every day.

The young men were interviewed in public places where they work and relax, such as markets, streets, bus stops, and bars, while the young civil servants were interviewed in a basketball club. The twelve young men included three barbers and a variety of street vendors. Some of the street vendors sold goods on commission for established shopkeepers, some hawked on their own behalf, and some had set up their own stands. They ranged in age from nineteen to twenty-two; a few of them had completed grade twelve, while the rest had dropped out of school earlier. The most striking observation that complements my findings from interviewing salaula traders of this age range in the markets is that no one was married; most of them lived with their parents or guardians, intermittently helping out with household expenses; some of them lived in rented rooms they shared with friends who all were "in business," in one case the salaula trade in exchange for rural produce, and in another the suitcase trade in the south. They all preferred to dress in jeans styles.

In addition to the style explanations I describe below, their preference for denim fabric has a clear practical reason. Jeans, one of them explained, "are durable; they are nice and easy to keep especially by bachelors like me who have no one to look after our clothes."

What these young men did for their own pleasure was to dress up in public in variations on the baggy-jeans look, several sizes larger than in 1995, and sometimes wearing more than one set of clothes. The interviews did take place during the Southern Hemisphere's coldest months, when people often wear garments on top of one another, yet the layered look was definitely in. A couple of young men wore oversized shorts, the kind that hang down below the knee and locally were referred to as "hot pants." Unlike American rappers whose brand-name underwear often is visible underneath the layer of pants, these young men's underwear did not show. They all wore oversized tops, often with hoods. The preferred headgear had changed since 1995 from the baseball cap to knitted wool caps locally referred to as "headsocks," often with a pattern in multicolored stripes, and occasionally a name or a logo. There were fewer hightop sneakers around than in 1995; the preferred footwear of the 1997 season was shoes with thick-treaded rubber soles, leaving tractor-like imprints called "galagata" (in Bemba, *ukukalakata* refers to walking with footwear making noise). The shoes were often worn without socks. Several of the young men had an earring in their left ear, one sported a nose ring, and several wore bracelets.

These young men purchased their clothing from the Zambia-Zaire sections on the periphery of the city markets where garments from "outside" were for sale, some used the tailor for special wear, and most of them scoured the salaula markets for just the right items. As one of them explained, "In salaula you will find things you can't believe how good they are." They readily pinpointed the inspiration of their style: friends from around town, local people that are admired, and foreigners. Foreign influences enter through magazines, posters, music videos, television, and the cinema. Although a television set is far from being a common fixture in all households in Zambia's low- and medium-income residential areas, viewing it is often a shared experience that may include neighbors and friends. Many bars have televisions and VCRs. What is more, informal video parlors are appearing in these areas, where music videos draw a particularly enthusiastic audience of young men. Clearly, young men such as these are exposed to multiple dress influences.

"I wear the big look because it is fashion," one of these young men said, while another explained that he like to "move with time." "I don't like common clothes and imitations," said yet another. When shopping for clothes, these young men look for garments that will contribute to the overall creation of a particular style, in this case "the big look," rather than for brand-name items. Their dress style is far less glamorous than that of the *sapeurs* in Congo-Brazzaville who, at least according to accounts prior to the recent civil war, celebrated appearance by parading expensive, upscale clothing they had obtained in Paris, proudly displaying *la griffe,* the label (Gandou-lou 1989:12–13). Like the women I described in the last chapter who wanted fashion and pieced their dress ensembles together from salaula to achieve what they considered to be uniqueness and exclusivity, these young street vendors strive for a particular look, and they also want fashion. And fashion does not mean homogeneity; while dressing almost alike, these young men in fact were striving to achieve "distinction," which is why they do not like "common clothes and imitations" but something that is "outstanding" and makes people look. "The big look," one of them said, "gives me confidence in myself."

The big look has been incorporated into the casual wear that young civil servants put on during weekends, and it has affected the general suit profile. How young civil servants dress depends on the situation, and they have more choices than the street vendors. These young men who ranged in age from twenty-two to twenty-six wore formal suits to work, and they liked them. They were all married with children, except for one who lived with his fiancée in housing that came with her job. Shopping from the same sources as the street vendors, they strove for the executive-designer look, which they explained in terms fairly similar to those used by the street vendors. Clothes like these, one said, "make me look good and elegant and different from my age group. I don't like common clothes. Besides," he added, "ladies like nice clothes and I like to attract ladies." Two of these young civil servants spoke specifically about disliking "West African attire" with loose big tops in bright colors and prints and simply pajamalike trousers underneath. The few young male essay writers who commented on the West African style of men's wear used much the same language of dislike. Zairean-inspired high-waisted trousers were not popular at all with any of these young men.

The big look the young street vendors work so hard to achieve through what they consider to be the right combinations of clothes sometimes comes with an attitude that is inflected in language use and intonation, which has given them the name "yoo boys." "They are performing," said an elderly man who was commenting on the big look, "they want to identify differently from ordinary people. They can take these clothes off again." But even if these young men take their clothes off again, their life chances are not likely to improve considerably. Their dress style is not part of a subculture, in the sense described by Dick Hebdige (1988), that sneers at mainstream dress conventions. Instead they dress to escape their own economic powerlessness, momentarily and vicariously, and so they put on clothes they equate with the power and success achieved by popular music performers. The young male secondary-school students who in their essays wrote disparagingly about the street vendors' getup fear ending up like them. Will they themselves after completing secondary school face unemployment and perhaps dead-end jobs like street vendors who earn too little to set up households of their own? It is not in the least surprising that many of them liked suits, which on their horizon, given the economic situation in Zambia, index formal employment, wages, household comforts, and the power that comes from being men in charge.

Dressing and Dressing Up: *Chokako Weka*

Because young people, both women and men, are fairly powerless in Zambian society, dress practices give them some space. *Chokako weka* means "move yourself" in Nyanja. Written on the sign of the salaula Caroussel Botique in Soweto market in 1992, these words capture some of the popular attractions of salaula in Zambia. Putting themselves together with clothing, the major part of which is from salaula, young people are dressing to explore who they are and whom they would like to become. But the meanings that clothes convey do not inhere in the garments themselves; as I have demonstrated in this chapter, meanings are attributed to clothes by acting social beings in particular situations and relationships.

Making associations between specific articles of clothing and behavior, young people construct an understanding of their world and of how they inhabit it. For reasons that I have explained here, young women work much harder than young men on the social management of their bodies and sexuality through clothing. Because revealing "private parts" is considered as leaving women's bodies open to invasion, women need to manage and contain their sexed bodies through clothing, whereas men's bodies follow second nature, dressed in that social skin that envelops their sexed bodies to perfection: the suit.

Clothing consumption constitutes a rich site from which to examine how young women and men are experiencing the possibilities and constraints of growing into adulthood in a poor country like Zambia. The local clothing-consumption politics is marked with structures of difference based on class, age, and gender, among others. These structures of difference comprise the local cultural norms that influence what is acceptable dress. These norms are both contested and redefined, and so they leave space for the social actor; and they vary both contextually and biographically as we have seen through the examples I have given involving young adults and their elders, and home, street, and public settings. We also saw this in the young adult, fairly well educated men's interpretation of the street vendors' clothes and the suit.

Adult women's concerns with their dressed bodies at kitchen parties and young people's preoccupations with dressed-body management and display offer dramatic evidence both of the power of dress and its gender limitations in Zambia. The cultural terms that shape women's and men's dress practice are emphatically unequal. Some carry much more social leverage and reward than others, and some are negatively sanctioned. If this habitus of gender relations is to change in Zambia, it will involve destabilizing its most powerful icons—the suit and the dress reaching below the knee—and the behaviors associated with them in the organization of everyday life and in the wider setting. And this depends not only on individuals but also on institutional practices and the importance that changes in schooling, employment, and family life may have on shaping people's opportunities, providing them with new terms with which to construct a differently gendered landscape than that in which they now find themselves.

The availability of salaula is threatening the holding power of this clothing habitus in a variety of ways. Fewer men than previously earn enough to perform the ideal male-gender role: as breadwinners in control of households and decision making. Women's informal-sector work is contributing critically to the viability of many households in the face of the declining real value of earnings and men's loss of formal-sector jobs. And few women today expect husbands to fulfill the cultural expectation of a bygone era of buying new dresses for them. Instead they purchase their own, sourcing from all available outlets, depending on the level of their spending money, their body size, and their personal desire for specific types of garments.

"You won't believe it, but it is from salaula" is a common explanation of the source of attractive clothes. Some husbands' suspicion linger that particularly good-looking garments are the presents of lovers or boyfriends. Anything that looks extravagant and expensive, for example, some of the young street vendors' garments, lends itself to the suspicion that it has been acquired by illicit means. The ready availability and affordability of salaula confound the gendered allocation of consumption tasks that for a long time has placed men as heads of household in charge of such decisions. While that structure of household authority is upheld ideologically in some domains of life, for example, in the kitchen party's celebration of a woman's wifely subordination, it is increasingly challenged by what goes on on the ground. To be sure, there is an agentive power entailed in the work of secondhand clothing consumption that affects relations within households, consumption priorities, and therefore the wider world of production. Last but not least, the dream of moving oneself, *chokako weka,* by putting oneself together with salaula empowers its wearer to imagine a world where freedom to dress stands for new opportunities.

10 The Politics of Salaula

Because the meanings people from different walks of life in Zambia attribute to the import and consumption of secondhand clothing are always in process, salaula provokes debate and dispute at many levels of society. Highly charged political, economic, social, and cultural issues have arisen from the international export of secondhand clothing, its local import, and retail connections as well as from the consumption practices it is giving rise to. The ramifications of these issues reach far into everyday life, affecting hierarchical relations between the sexes and generations, and across Zambia's urban and rural areas. The value contests embedded in these issues can be explored at many levels as I do briefly now, among them through popular reactions, import and tariff regimes, developments in the garment and textile industry, and the regulation of informal-sector markets.

Salaula is at the center of a local battle that takes place in the context of the liberalization of Zambia's economy and polity. In the newly democratic third republic, groups and individuals from across the socioeconomic spectrum are making claims for space and opportunity to make a living. When it comes to salaula, the Zambian government is caught in a balancing act of mediating between its different constituencies: the overseers of the IMF/World Bank–sponsored structural adjustment program, who insist on obtaining conditions to encourage a "free" market; local garment and textile manufacturers, who argue for import regulation to protect their ailing industry; and three-fourths of the population, who have seen both their formal job prospects and purchasing power erode over the years of the third republic. It is hardly surprising that the government's stance has been equivocal. The policy twists and turns that I discuss here capture the ambiguity that is at the very core of salaula consumption. For while it covers basic clothing needs, salaula also satisfies desires for attractive and stylish appearance through dress that today are more widespread than ever before. Because rags are a metaphor for lack of access, salaula stands for opportunity, choice, and new chances. In short, clothing needs and desires converge in a politics of salaula that the state can ill afford to ignore.

In the debates about salaula that I examine in this chapter, some groups speak about clothing needs, others of clothing desire, while the majority of the clothing-consuming public in fact conflate the two. Exploring popular reactions, I focus first on the local music scene that in songs and videos has celebrated salaula, often in the language of development. In such narratives salaula plays a creative role in shaping visions of personal and collective futures, which postcolonial developments so far have failed to deliver to the majority of Zambia's population. Then I turn to formal debates about regulation if not outright prohibition of the commercial import of salaula into Zambia. In a general sense the two-phased debate on this issue, in 1992–93 and again in 1998, revolves around questions of economic liberalization versus political restraint. The regulatory debate also reflects on the place and scope for domestic garment and textile manufacturing. The future prospects of this industry hinge not only on local politics but also, and perhaps more so, on whether the products it delivers can compete in the global commodity chain of garment production. Finally, I discuss how the twists and turns in the regulatory policy directed toward salaula parallel shifting policies toward the informal sector in general. Debates about the informal sector are value contests over manufacturing versus trade and wage-labor versus self-employment that are important for questions about consumer income and purchasing power.

Popular Reactions

In popular songs from the colonial era, clothing conveyed excitement about city life and the "civilization," wealth, and opportunity it stood for and, by contrast, the remoteness, poor access, and lack of sophistication implied by villagers' rags. Distinct clothing styles were commented on in songs, such as Alick Nkatha describing the new fashions brought back by migrants from the Congo, the "new look" of the 1950s available to people with money, and Kenneth Kaunda singing disparagingly about preoccupations with suits in the face of the pressing needs of nation building on the eve of independence. In postcolonial Zambia clothing has remained central to widespread sentiments about well-being. As urban and rural Zambians have come to rely increasingly on secondhand clothing, salaula has entered popular narrative, including songs. Working out widespread understandings of well-being, songs about salaula argue about the rights and wrongs of clothing consumption, in this way casting light on the power of clothing to mediate livelihoods and aspirations.

The growing availability and acceptability of secondhand clothing was the theme of a 1988 song in the Bemba language, "Salaula, Mayo" by popular singer Teddy Chilambe (*Zambia Daily Mail,* 21 April 1989). Composed in a mixture of Zairean rhumba and Zambian *kalindula* styles, this song's story of the growing popularity of salaula unfolds between a twice-repeated chorus.[1] I include a few excerpts.[2]

Chorus:

Salaula, salaula, salaula, mayo	Select, select, select, mother
Salaula, salaula, salaula, mayo	
Salaula, salaula, salaula, mayo	
Ishi nsapato balefwala ishawama	These nice shoes they are wearing
Namatoloshi balefwala ayawama	And the nice trousers they are wearing
Namashirti balefwala ayayemba	And the nice shirts they are wearing
Ni salaula, salaula, salaula, mayo	It is salaula, mother
Uno mwaka tuletasha kubena Zaire	This year we are praising the Zaireans
Pali uyo balo mwatupela tata	For this bale you have given us, father
Pantu emulesangwa salaula mayo, salamo	Because that is where salaula is found, mother, pick from there

The lyrics in this song tell of a time now past, when people were somewhat self-conscious about wearing salaula. Now even fashion-conscious office workers dress in suits from salaula. The song praises Zaireans for bringing salaula to Zambia and blames those who shunned it for wasting money they should use to feed their children. As salaula enters social relations in this song, it is implicated in personal projects of improving lives.

But in 1990 Teddy Chilambe changed his tune on salaula. In his "Mukonka Ifya Basungu," which in Bemba means "you follow the ways of white people," Chilambe blamed epidemics in Zambia on certain patterns of consumption, including salaula. According to a news write-up the song held secondhand clothes responsible for formerly uncommon ailments now afflicting Zambians such as herpes and AIDS (*Zambia Daily Mail,* 26 January 1990). While I have been unable to obtain the lyrics,[3] I do not doubt that this song's changing depiction of salaula tells a story with political and economic implications about problems affecting everyday life in Zambia during the waning years of the second republic. Its reference to AIDS is a matter to which I return later.

As the importance of salaula increased in the third republic, so did narratives testifying to its popularity. Among them was Daddy Zamus's snappy 1995 song entitled "Salaula," composed in reggae style with lyrics in "Caribbean"-inflected Zam-English. While Zemus's salaula song made many of the same observations as Chilambe's early piece, it was Zemus's music and performance that made the real difference between the two productions. Zemus's song does not lament the past, and it is more upbeat in its praise of salaula.

A music video was produced for Zemus's song. It shows Zemus in neatly tailored dark trousers and a colorful, loose, "silk" vest against the backdrop of one of Lusaka's main salaula markets, Kamwala. It then has shots of different parts of Lusaka, including office buildings and low-income townships, the kinds of settings the song's lyrics refer to. The chorus lines in Zemus's song have everybody buying salaula.

> *Chorus:*
> Everybody them buy it—salaula.
> Everybody them get it—salaula.
> Everybody looks good in it—salaula.
> Pretty girls look nice in it—salaula.
>
> Well enough in a country we've a lot of bankers
> in Livingstone, Ndola, and Lusaka
> And if we take it on the Mr. Big Spender
> they have got a lot more money than most of us malova [loafers]
> for any banker know that they must look right, yah.
> They ought to look like most of us so far, so far
> The . . . Bankers run to Kamwala
> the mighty shirts and the trousers and the mighty bamba [underwear]
>
> *Chorus*
>
> We know this little girl to have a big family
> Yah, we know yet a friend of me what kind of work she do
> that of a secretary and she don't ever earn a big salary
> and yet I know she ever look fancy
> I say no, the salaula are the only remedy
> Yes of course they go to Soweto and spend the money
> and next thing you know she look nice and ready.

Bankers, police, nurses, and "the masses in the ghetto" today all buy salaula, according to Zemus's song, which also points out that Indian traders were angry that they could not sell their poor-quality clothes. The MMD, the governing party, cannot stop this industry, the song continues, because everybody is buying salaula. In Lusaka's low-income townships, among them Kanyama and Chawama, everybody is happy, the song concludes, as they are in Garden, Mandevu, and Bauleni. Much like the popular outcry against formal prohibitions on salaula that I discuss below, Zemus's song highlights the political unacceptability of banning salaula.

Songs like this one reached to the core of widespread understandings of the importance of salaula. What these were was revealed particularly clearly during debates about prohibiting the importation of salaula. Finance Minister Ronald Penza's proposal in the 1998 annual budget address to increase the tariff on imported salaula provoked commentary not only from representatives of the manufacturers' associations, salaula importers, and retailers, but also from the general public.

The Salaula Tug of War

Clothing is an important wage good, accounting for a significant part of consumer expenditure. Because clothing consumption is a force to be reckoned with, the salaula phenomenon mobilizes public opinion at many levels both inside and outside Zambian society. Extrapolating from the not altogether uniform experience of the industrializing West, the social science literature on modernization and development has conventionally assigned a progressive role and many trickle-down effects to the textile and garment sector of the economy, pointing to the relative ease with which factories can be established and workers provided with the skills to quickly develop an industry with growth potential. Several countries in the Far East and Mauritius are given as examples of the role of textile industries as engines of growth, often without acknowledgment of the degree of political and economic intervention, including incentives to foreign firms, that has driven this growth (Elson 1994; Park and Anderson 1991). With this model as a backdrop, it is not surprising that the rapidly expanding trade and consumption of secondhand clothing in Zambia—as in some other countries in Africa, including Kenya, Zimbabwe, and South Africa—has tended to be portrayed negatively in accounts of the economy's performance problems by local and external observers, who draw a direct connection between the popularity of salaula, the closure of textile and garment factories, and the loss of jobs.[4]

A few caveats are in order before considering these debates. It is easy, but too facile, to blame salaula for the dismal performance of Zambia's clothing and textile manufacturing industries. At the launching of the third republic in 1991, that sector was saddled with a number of problems that dated back to the last half of the 1980s, if not earlier, during President Kaunda's leadership. I touched on some of them in chapter 4. In effect, unfavorable fiscal, monetary, and exchange-rate policies prompting skyrocketing inflation had helped to bring this sector into a precarious state by 1991 (Seshamani 1994:120). The sector's problems were accentuated by its high import dependence, high capital intensity, inappropriate technology, poor management, and lack of skilled labor, especially in textile-printing technology that resulted in gross underutilization of capacity.

As I demonstrate below, it is not surprising that the ad hoc and unsystematic import policies of the first years of the third republic were unfavorable to the local clothing and textile industry. On first sight this story is less about salaula than about a combination of policies that encouraged rapid increase in import penetration without providing incentives to promote local production and employment. Even then, unless the country experiences substantial economic growth combined with a more equitable income distribution, the local market is unlikely to support any considerable growth of the clothing and textile industry. And that is the reason why, after all, this debate revolves around salaula.

The Zambian debate about the relationship between imports of second-hand clothing and the clothing and textile sector of the economy began inter-mittently when the salaula trade started growing in the mid-1980s. It has since had two marked peaks, the first between 1992 and 1993, and the second in 1998. Such debates will no doubt continue unless the government pro-hibits commercial import of this particular commodity. Even then, African borders are highly permeable, and Zambia's border areas are not only vast but often unprotected. Unless consumer incomes and the purchasing power of the great majority of the population improve markedly, the effective market for salaula consumption will remain massive.

Tariff Issues

During the second republic when severe import restrictions applied to so-called nonessential commodities, licenses to import secondhand clothing were occasionally granted to people who, judging from popular commen-tary, were closely linked by kinship, marriage, and connections to the powers that be. In 1986 the chair of the Clothing and Allied Industries Association of Zambia, Michael Miti, complained that it "was not right to allow traders to use the scarce foreign exchange on secondhand clothing" (*Times of Zambia*, 1 July 1986). Most clothing factories then were reported to be "running at 50% capacity and some of them [were] on the point of closure." The indus-try's difficulties were attributed to the declining purchasing power of the pub-lic in the wake of the foreign-exchange auctioning system practiced at that time (*Times of Zambia*, "Salaula Defended," 21 June 1986).

Local critical discussion of the import of salaula intensified in 1992 and es-pecially 1993 when representatives of the manufacturers of textiles and gar-ments blamed salaula for "killing" their industries and called for an outright ban on imports. Textile firms in the Copperbelt began complaining in 1992 of a "serious slump in business due to a high influx of cheap imported goods such as that of second-hand clothing" (*Zambia Daily Mail*, 28 August 1992). The arguments were leveled at the new government, which was slow to im-prove the circumstances for local industrial production, retaining unfavor-able tariffs on necessary inputs while allowing the importation of finished goods, including salaula, at lower rates. High interest rates, lack of domestic credit, and high tariffs on imports of new machinery and raw materials like dyes, chemicals, and artificial fibers made it difficult for industry to rehabili-tate its outmoded machinery and manufacture goods at a price that consumers could afford, not to mention of a quality and style that they would purchase. Added to that was a severe drought in 1992 in the entire southern African region, which caused local cotton production to fall behind and water-based power generation to drop, causing most factories to lay off workers because of reduced production capacity.

The 1992–93 season was indeed a bad one for local production of textiles and garments. The clothing manufacturers complained of the "government's tolerance of the thriving 'salaula' business," expressing fear that "Zambia would be reduced to a mere dumping ground if nothing is done to restore decency to its trade." The assistant director of Ndola's Piper Clothing, Dickson Chitambala, who made these comments, was "sad to note that salaula traders had trading licenses for their businesses yet these clothes were donated for distribution to the poor" (*Times of Zambia,* 1 March 1993). In May 1993 eighteen textile and clothing factories in Southern and Copperbelt Provinces were reported to have closed, and thirteen more were earmarked for closure "because they have been priced out of business by secondhand (salaula) traders" (*Zambia Daily Mail,* 25 May 1993). The chief executive of the Zambia Confederation of Industries and Chambers of Commerce, Bernhard Chisanga, "blamed the collapse of the clothing industry on high import tariffs and the unfair competition from the sale of salaula which were brought into the country tax-free" (*Times of Zambia,* "18 Firms Fold Up," 7 June 1993). But rather than complaining, some manufacturers looked for ways out of this impasse. When a research team of which I was part in 1993 called on the manager of Deetex, formerly a major producer of clothing in Lusaka's light industrial area, the premises displayed a big sign that in bold type told the story of the industry's decline: "Salaula at sale here in bales at wholesale prices." Aside from taking up salaula, this firm had begun to diversify into the general wholesale business (*Profit,* January 1994, p. 13).

The response of government was ambiguous, alternating between statements about ruling out banning "because it was not the solution to the poor performance of the textile industry" (*Times of Zambia,* 1 June 1993) to advocating imminent prohibition of salaula imports (*Zambia Daily Mail,* 19 June 1992). Salaula traders, not surprisingly, "saw red" over the impending ban, arguing that the "best thing government could do was to help the textile owners improve their products, especially their quality, to encourage competition" (*Zambia Daily Mail,* 21 June 1993). The national chairman of the Zambia National Council of Commerce and Industry, Stabin Mutale, appealed to government to rescind the decision to ban salaula, arguing that "its existence is helping in alleviating the impact of the harsh Structural Adjustment Programme (SAP)." Banning the salaula trade, he went on, "was tantamount to government defeating its own policies of liberalising of the economy" (*Zambia Daily Mail,* 26 June 1993).

By September 1993 fifty-one clothing firms out of a total of seventy-two in the country had closed (*Times of Zambia,* 13 September 1993). Those that survived tried to rationalize production by aiming at niche markets such as industrial clothing and protective wear. Several production lines were closed, and workers were laid off at the two parastatal textile mills, Kafue Textiles of Zambia and Mulungushi Textiles. Kafue Textiles of Zambia was on the verge of financial collapse in 1992, and Mulungushi Textiles ceased operating temporarily in 1993. Both mills were slated for sale in the government's industrial privatization efforts. Mulungushi Textiles reopened only in 1997 after a takeover exercise by Chinese investors who also bought up some of the shares of Kafue Textiles of Zambia (*Times of Zambia,* 17 February 1997). In 1999 production at Kafue Textiles had ground to a halt. Accumulated debts made potential investors reluctant to purchase the firm, making its future uncertain (*Times of Zambia,* 16 August 1999).

The 1992–93 debate did not produce any immediate result. Importation of salaula kept increasing, and the tariff regulations remained unchanged. Meanwhile the major textile manufacturers began reorienting production toward a changed target: the nontraditional export market, which in Zambia means anything but copper and is encouraged as a way of shifting the economy's long-standing foreign-revenue dependence on the global metal market. In the liberalized spirit of an open economy, most of the second republic's import restrictions have been lifted, making available manufactured goods from all over the region and overseas, including textiles and clothing. With the ready availability of affordable, high-quality, good-looking, printed textiles imported from South and Southeast Asia, Kafue Textiles of Zambia in 1995 ceased printing chitenge cloth for the local market, concentrating instead on production of unfinished cloth (gray or loomstate cloth) for export mainly to the European market. The manufacturers now complained not only about salaula but about "cheap imports" in general, alleging subsidy and dumping by Southeast Asian producers aiming to get a foothold in the local market. At the regional level, the government has repeatedly called for changes in the tariff regime and in particular for South Africa to change its protective trade policy (EIU 1997:13).

Imports, Exports, and Dumping

Since the mid-1990s the most adverse import duties on industrial production inputs have been removed, yet textile and clothing manufacturing firms have continued to close. A major South African holding company, Pepkor, Ltd., has opened several stores in Zambia, beginning in 1995 in Lusaka with PEP, which sells inexpensive clothing, and Ackerman Stores, also in Lusaka, in 1996 catering for the upmarket in trendy and quality fashion clothing, and establishing outlets in Kitwe and Ndola in the Copperbelt in 1997 (*Times of Zambia*, 23 September 1996; *Post*, 25 April 1997). By 1999, additional South African garment manufacturing firms had opened stores on Lusaka's Cairo Road, as had a discount store selling clothing that was made in Zimbabwe (*Post*, 2 March 1999; *Financial Times*, 2–8 August 1999). At the end of the 1990s, hardly any garment manufacturers were left in Zambia, save for small-scale tailoring workshops and individual tailors. In fact, the number of small-scale workshops appears to be growing, confronting the salaula import by turning to niche production of garments in styles, including chitenge wear, and sizes not readily found in the secondhand clothing markets.

Of the thirty-one textile mills that were in operation in 1992, some twenty-one were still producing in 1995. The cotton spinners were doing well, according to an industry report on 1994, "because most have relatively newer machinery and can afford to export their yarn. Weavers and knitters on the other hand have relatively old machinery and were established mainly to service the domestic market which has somewhat collapsed" (Export Board of Zambia 1995:3). Between 1992 and 1994 employment figures in the subsector dropped from 8,093 to 5,335. An estimated labor force of 5,854 in 1995 indicates a slight growth, suggesting, according to a report, that the employment situation is stabilizing (Ministry of Trade, Commerce and Industry 1996:2).

For lack of a local market, the textile manufacturers still in operation have oriented production away from weaving, dyeing, and finishing (value added) toward the export market for loomstate cotton cloth and yarn. In fact, export from this reoriented production has increased steadily, becoming an important contributor to Zambia's nontraditional exports, second to engineering products in 1995 and to agricultural products in 1996 (Export Board of Zambia 1997:2), and assuming first position in 1997, when it was the leading foreign-exchange earner among the nontraditional exports (*Post*, 15 April 1998). The European Union is the largest market for Zambia's textile products that enjoy preferential access under the Lomé Convention (Ministry of Commerce, Trade, and Industry 1996:3).

Continued success in this export trade should not be taken for granted. The future development of nontraditional exports of textiles will depend on many factors, including renewal of the European Union's continued financing of Lomé IV's Export Development Program, improved export access to regional markets in the Southern African Customs Union (SACU), and shifts in the domestic market. For a recent example, realizing the potential use of cloth by the small-scale tailoring sector, one industry spokesperson told me in 1997 that some of the privately owned weaving firms had begun to produce value-added cloth again, specifically targeting the retail level rather than factory garment production, which has almost collapsed (Export Board, Lackson Kanyemba, 21 July 1997, Lusaka).

With their own tariff problem largely behind them, representatives of the textile and garment manufacturers have occasionally continued to blame salaula for the sector's problems. Their repeated demand was for assessments of realistic import tariffs on salaula, which industry representatives tended to characterize as entering the country illegally, either smuggled or as "donations" free of tariffs. While some of these processes do occur because of Zambia's vast borders, salaula did carry tariffs, even on charitably donated consignments. DAPP, for example, an NGO that for years held a special dispensation, paying lower tariffs because of its import of unsorted garments in bulk, has since the mid-1990s paid the same tariff as the commercial importers. During this period the ZRA embargoed consignments and assessed fines on some salaula importers who ignored or violated customs regulations, in an effort to enhance revenue collection. When industry spokespersons are making arguments about salaula imports escaping regulation, they appear to be no better informed about the international secondhand clothing trade than the thousands of small-scale traders who resell imported salaula from bales they have purchased from local wholesalers.

Public debate about salaula picked up momentum again in 1998 when the effects of economic liberalization had become clearer than they were in 1992 and 1993, shortly after the change in politico-economic regime at the end of 1991. Purchasing power continued to decline, and within the first year of its operation in Lusaka, the new PEP store "faced stiff competition from traders of secondhand goods." The manager of the PEP stores in Zambia explained that "people preferred to buy secondhand clothes, shoes, ties and leather handbags because of their low prices" (*Times of Zambia,* November 1995). The open importation of goods in general and extensive smuggling from neighboring countries of anything from soap and biscuits to coffee and margarine were beginning to have negative effects on other firms that manufactured locally. Reckitt and Coleman, Colgate-Palmolive, and Lever Brothers restructured from manufacturing into marketing and distribution, significantly reducing their local operations. In 1997 Johnson & Johnson and Dunlop Tyres moved their production to Zimbabwe. Dunlop, the only tire-manufacturing company in Zambia, ceased operating locally because it was unable to make a profit in the face of the growing import of retreaded tires (*Financial Mail*, 16–22 September 1997). While the growing import of salaula in the first half of the 1990s served as an easy scapegoat for long-standing problems of Zambia's textile and garment producers, the experiences of Dunlop and other manufacturers in recent years reveal problems facing the manufacturing industry in general in a political setup geared toward economic liberalization.

The 1998 annual budget proposal aimed to lessen some of the problems experienced by local manufacturers hardest hit by smuggling and "underevaluation by some importers," by proposing specific duty rates for "imported tyres, sugar, soft drinks, edible oil, beer, batteries, and flour." The budget proposal included concerns about "rescuing industry" by proposing a higher import tariff on salaula, increasing the duty from U.S.$1.50 to U.S.$5 per kilogram (*Zambia Daily Mail,* 30 January 1998). Both wholesalers and small-scale retailers of salaula reacted sharply. The tariff increase was too high in the view of the salaula wholesalers, who not only had to pay VAT since 1995 but also confronted ever-growing costs of their imported consignments because of the continued depreciation of the Zambian currency. With the likelihood of higher costs being passed on to the small-scale retail level, salaula traders complained. Who would be able to afford their goods? The consumer price index, which measures costs of new goods, for clothing and footwear for metropolitan low-income households had increased tenfold between 1992 and 1997, from 27.9 to 279.7 (and that of high-income households from 24.6 to 281.7; Republic of Zambia 1997, tables 1L and 1H).

During the first week after the proposal to increase tariffs was announced, many salaula wholesalers in Lusaka closed their outlets, and salaula traders marched to the office of the minister of Lusaka Province to express their disappointment (*Times of Zambia,* 5 February 1998). Neither group was averse to tariffs per se but considered the proposed ones to be too high. From their different positions both groups argued that improvement of the textile and garment manufacturing industry should not be achieved at the expense of salaula, but that there should be some symbiosis between the two (*Zambia Daily Mail,* 9 April 1998). Both groups claimed that the people who would be adversely affected by the increase were the very poor Zambians. According to the chairman of the Salaula Dealers' (wholesalers) Association, Layton Simbeye, "the key issue here is that salaula is for poor people and it has given them an opportunity to dress decently despite the hardships they have to go through and the increase is not fair, how can you justify a poor man going about in torn and tattered clothes?" (*Zambia Daily Mail,* 4 February 1998).

Wary about grassroots expressions, the president began to waver, making statements in public about the need to revisit the proposed $5 duty on salaula (*Sunday Times of Zambia,* 8 February 1998). The parliamentary debate about the amendment to the customs and excise bill highlighted much ambiguity about the issue when one MP, Bennie Mwiinga, made far-fetched and unsubstantiated statements about deaths from diseases people caught by wearing salaula, and accused traders of being criminals. He was countered by MP Vernon Mwaanga, who argued that the "politics of salaula are real and should not be trivialized." Mwaanga went on to explain that it was not only the "common man in the compounds who is heavily depending on salaula but also most of the members of parliament. If there was no salaula," he said, "most of the members of this House would not have come here properly dressed." Speaking matter-of-factly, MP Samuel Chipungu said that "these measures will not help anybody because the [clothing and textile] manufacturing industry is dead" (*Post,* 18 February 1998). The association that MP Mwiinga drew between skin diseases and salaula was disconfirmed in a statement by doctors at the University Teaching Hospital a few days later (*Sunday Times of Zambia,* 22 February 1998).

For a short while a program to phase out the new tariff over three years was discussed. Then on 7 March 1998 President Chiluba suspended the proposal for a duty tariff increase for the next year, directing traders to revert to the prices at which they had sold their goods before the announcement of the proposed tariff change. He did stress that the suspension was a temporary measure, asking rhetorically: "Are you ready to continue to salaula ourselves?" (*Times of Zambia,* 7 March 1998.[5] Commenting on the dilemma of whether to listen to the salaula traders and buyers or the wider national concern to increase revenue collection, one observer said: "On this one, however erm it's better to put your smart money on issues of political expediency. After all, it is better to please the majority salaula traders than the tiny minority Zambia Association of Manufacturers (ZAM) who may not even supply the demand of quality clothes [that] salaula so far has faithfully done" (*Zambia Daily Mail,* 10 February 1998).

Unlike in South Africa and Zimbabwe, where labor unions in the textile and clothing sector actively engaged in the secondhand clothing debate, organized labor in Zambia has kept a low profile on the saluala issue. There were occasional statements already in 1986, for example, when the National Union of Commercial and Industrial Workers demanded an immediate ban on the importation of secondhand clothes "to save local industry from total collapse" (*Times of Zambia,* "High Prices," 21 June 1986), and in 1993 when the union announced plans for campaigns against continued imports of salaula (e.g., *Times of Zambia,* 17 December 1993), yet I have seen little evidence of sustained public interventions into this debate by unions in Zambia. Even before the closures, textile and clothing workers constituted a small proportion of the wage-labor force. They earn low wages. Several workers are likely to be retrenched or pruned as the firms for which they work reorient production or close due to IMF/World Bank directives to reform or rationalize the economy.

While the outcome of the most recent efforts to regulate the commercial import of secondhand clothing remains inconclusive, the government has advanced a policy formulation that it has relied upon after all previous occasions when the battle over salaula was waged. At issue are licenses, levies, or taxes to be imposed on vendors in general (*Times of Zambia,* "Street Vendors," 7 June 1993; *Zambia Daily Mail,* 20 July 1993, 10 June 1998, 17 July 1998). Such pronouncements have never been implemented and are unlikely to be so at present, due to no small degree to the enormous logistical problems that arise from the mobility, irregularity, and informality of this trade.

To be sure, some commentators are less convinced than the majority of Zambian consumers about the "goodness" of salaula. The point of such critics is that salaula consumption glorifies the free market and sidesteps concerns with more "productive" forms of employment. As I have explained, there is no straightforward causal relationship between the growing import and consumption of salaula and the decline of the local textile and garment manufacturing sector. The problems of that sector stem rather from the contradictory forces that are operating on its various components. These forces have been prompted by government policies that have curtailed the development of a competitive textile and garment sector while they have reduced incomes and the purchasing power of the great majority of the population.

Revitalizing Zambia's Clothing Manufacturing Sector?

Might Zambia's ailing garment manufacturing sector obtain a new lease on life by producing for export? In that way, it would contribute to employment generation and foreign-exchange earnings, and perhaps eventually satisfy local demand for good-quality and stylish clothing at prices the country's poor consumers can afford. Many odds are against the export scenario. The contemporary global system of clothing manufacturing is penetrated by complex, competitive commodity chains in which countries like Zambia are caught in "a backwash, competing for markets which are far less buoyant than in the 1970s and 1980s" (Elson 1994:208). What is more, the global garment trade is structured by a range of restrictive rules and regulations. The most important of these regulations were established by the General Agreement on Tariffs and Trade (GATT) and its successor, since 1995, the World Trade Organization.

At its formation in 1947, GATT established guidelines for more open trade, reducing restrictive barriers that had evolved since the outset of the Great Depression. But GATT ideals were soon modified, and the United

States and many European countries have used a variety of measures to restrict import of textiles and garments, especially from the developing countries. To accommodate the problems of the textile and garment trade, GATT developed a series of special arrangements, including multifiber arrangements (MFAs), establishing bilateral export guidelines. That is, the Multi-Fibre Agreement permits quantitative restrictions and makes it possible to set quotas not only on a specific product but on imports from a specific country (Dickerson 1991:296–337). Developing countries have led the push for a gradual dismantling of the agreement in order to return the textile and garment trade to normal GATT rules. Changes in trade rules have been under way since the Uruguay Round concerning provisions on MFAs, which according to a 1995 agreement are to be eliminated entirely by year 2005 in a three-stage process.

The removal of all quotas on textiles and garment exports in 2005 will create, according to one analysis, "gainers and losers among the developing country suppliers" (Majmudar 1996). Cost concerns and product differentiation are important factors in this process. Given the policies that have shaped the performance of the textile and garment sector in Zambia, that sector is not very likely to become competitive in export markets. In effect, because it is a very minor international supplier, Zambia may not benefit from the phase-out of the Multi-Fibre Agreement.

Might Zambia's garment manufacturing sector benefit from establishing export processing zones (ETZs)? Several garment-producing countries in the developing world, including Bangladesh, Mauritius, and Namibia, have used such zones as a strategy to increase exports, create jobs, and attract foreign investments. Malawi recently established several ETZs, and the issue was being debated and encouraged in Zambia in 1997 (*Times of Zambia,* 5 August 1997, 9 September 1997). While ETZs might create more local jobs, the proposition is problematic. Establishing ETZs depends on attracting foreign investors by tax incentives, favorable import and export arrangements, developed infrastructure, and a trained but relatively low-cost labor force. Both infrastructure and labor are in need of extensive upgrading in Zambia, and the country's landlocked location is not ideal for market access. And while ETZs might generate employment, they offer few enduring benefits to the local economy because of the low pay. The results might be along the lines of what has been observed in Bangladesh, where ETZ workers cannot afford to purchase the garments they produce and rely instead on that country's large market of imported secondhand clothes (*Toronto Star,* 13 November 1993).

There are other scenarios. The U.S. Congress, for example, is contemplating a trade bill for Africa that would lower tariffs and increase the volumes of imported textiles and garments (*Journal of Commerce,* 19 October 1998).

External incentives for production of clothing for export might be envisioned under the Lomé Convention of the European Union. Under such an arrangement exports are temporarily granted tariff- and quota-free access to European Union markets. But how Zambia's clothing manufacturing sector would perform either in an ETZ or in a Lomé/European Union arrangement will depend on overhauling the sector's aging machinery and upgrading the skills of garment workers, to improve productivity and quality and thereby produce garments that meet standardized specifications at the importing end.

Garment manufacturers in Zambia seeking to enter the global clothing market without external support might try to identify niche markets, for example, in "safari-style" leisure wear or Afrocentric garments. Another option might be acting as an assembly base in CMT (cut, machine, trim) production. The long-term viability of all these efforts depends not only on cost and specific market identification, but also on design and quality and on a steady output of consistent quality. In short, there are several problems to overcome to develop a export-oriented garment industry, including matters of technical competence, business culture, and management as well as infrastructural developments, labor, finance and markets, and import and export regulations (Biggs et al. 1994).

The most striking ramification of the scenarios sketched above is that, in today's global system of clothing manufacturing, countries like Zambia have, in Gary Gereffi's words, to "run faster just to stay in place" (1994:226). In the U.S. congressional debate about the proposed Africa trade bill, concerns have been raised that large manufacturers of textile goods, including China and other major Asian textile/apparel suppliers, might use African countries for illegal transshipment of their own goods into the United States (*Journal of Commerce,* 29 March 1999). Indeed, Zambia's textile and garment manufacturing sector is vulnerable to more efficient competitors both internationally and regionally who outperform them in quality and price. In regional terms, regardless of how attractive Zambia's legal and policy regime is toward the textile and clothing sector, South African and Zimbabwean firms with access to much larger markets can apply economies of scale.

In an ironic twist of economic liberalization and its ideal goal of expanding local growth, large regional chains such as South Africa's Pepkor holding company now supply Zambia and the broader regional markets with goods produced in South Africa. Zambian manufacturers continue to have reduced access to South African markets. While concluding trade deals between Zambia and SACU may improve access for Zambian manufacturers to SACU markets, it is unlikely to boost their export role appreciably because of the cost and quality issues alluded to above. At the moment, given its uncertainty about how to plug into the global economy of textiles and garments, it is not surprising that the Zambian government remains ambiguous about its salaula policies and has, in the short run at least, allowed itself to be convinced by political arguments about the "goodness" of salaula.

The "Real Economy"

On the night of 27 April 1995 a section of Lusaka's largest market, Soweto, caught fire. Overnight several salaula traders lost their goods. Newspapers carried photographs of crying women who had found their source of income reduced to ashes (e.g., *Zambia Daily Mail,* 29 April 1995). On the day of the fire, PEP, a South African chain store selling inexpensive apparel and clothes, opened its first outlet in Zambia, on Lusaka's main thoroughfare, Cairo Road. Newspaper photographs depicted the long queues of people who had lined up overnight in the hope of buying stylish, affordable clothing (*Times of Zambia,* 1 May 1995, 6 May 1995).

These events, and others like them during subsequent years, bear directly on the politics of salaula through connections between clothing consumption, informal-sector marketing, and the decline of formal-sector employment in Zambia. In the 1990s' strained economic atmosphere the informal sector engaged long-term traders as well as recently retrenched workers, out-of-school youth, and rural migrants. It also included wage-employed people whose purchasing power was so reduced that they were compelled to pursue economic sidelines to tide their households over. Over this period the growth of the secondhand clothing trade outpaced that of other informal-sector activities.

Lusaka's huge informal sector in the mid-1990s comprised an astonishing variety of retail, service, and small-scale economic enterprises that spilled into the main streets. The variety of merchandise was so vast that some vendors no doubt were fronting for established businesses. Much like during the previous government, during the third republic various policy formulations were advanced to regulate this sector, including licenses, levies, taxes, and, most often, relocation, that is, pushing it out of sight. The most common intervention was police sweeps, ostensibly because of violations of by-laws concerning trade in public places.

Regulation of markets and street vending remains a sensitive issue in Zambia and elsewhere (Clark 1988). Many Zambians recall vividly what happened in 1990 after subsidies were removed from mealie meal, the staple food, when riots erupted and street vendors participated in the looting of state-owned stores in the Copperbelt towns and Lusaka. When in the early part of 1993 the Lusaka City Council undertook one of many sweeps—assisted by policy and military—it clashed with street vendors, and a riot ensued. President Chiluba intervened strongly on behalf of the street vendors, blaming council authorities for not finding alternative places before moving the vendors off the streets. His action was subsequently interpreted to mean that anyone was allowed to trade and erect a stand anywhere on the streets. Since then, such stands have been referred to as *tuntembas* (singular *intemba*), which is Bemba for "areas of operation." The term captures accurately what vendors are doing: making claims on economic space.

Reactions to the 1998 government effort at regulating salaula by increasing its cost and thus possibly forcing many wholesalers and small-scale traders out of this market support popular impressions about salaula. A group of former Standard and Chartered Bank employees, for example, who began selling salaula after losing their jobs, described "the latest development as their second retrenchment" (*Zambia Daily Mail,* 10 February 1998). The spokesperson for the salaula wholesalers, who noted that salaula trading is the major way of engaging people in income-generating work in Zambia, argued that the "increase of duty on secondhand clothes will create problems in the informal sector as some (salaula traders) might be forced out of employment" (*Zambia Daily Mail,* 4 February 1998). And one vendor predicted that crime among youth was likely to increase "if salaula traders will be forced out of business by increased duty" (*Zambia Daily Mail,* 10 February 1998).

Because nonregulated economic practices are pervasive throughout Zambian society, government intervention in salaula in particular and in street vending and informal markets in general is a highly charged issue. Such economic activities are in fact central to efforts at making a living and constitute what Janet MacGaffey (1991) called the "real economy" for the case of neighboring Zaire in the last half of the 1980s. The tug of war over salaula regulation and trading space in Zambia in the 1990s provides telling evidence of the difficulties that are accompanying the country's economic transformation. The result is a dramatic confrontation between "free market" policies and informal economic activities (Dilley 1992). Such informal operations reproduce livelihoods and, along with them, the social relations by gender and age on which household reproduction depends. In effect, the struggle for a living in a developing country like Zambia requires more radical reforms than regulating salaula and moving vendors off the streets.

The Politics of Need and Desire

The rapidly growing import of salaula since the mid- to late 1980s has been a stage for political debates over liberalized import and trade practices and their contradictory effects on local production and consumption. The different constituencies in these debates have not agreed on the significance, or damage, of salaula although they understand its basic role in covering the clothing needs of poor consumers. Arguments by garment and textile manufacturers for reduction of salaula imports through increased tariffs have been neither politically expedient to the powers that be nor culturally acceptable to the vast majority of Zambia's consumers, for whom salaula offers better choice of both price and style than locally manufactured garments.

The commercial import of secondhand clothing does not everywhere give rise to the kind of politics that it has in Zambia, most likely because of different cultural constructions of this commodity and the variable roles it assumes within local systems of provision and in relationship to other activities with which it becomes entwined. Those roles satisfy both clothing needs and desires in Zambia, which is why the cultural meanings associated with consumption and dress practice affect the political contests involving salaula.

Salaula's shop window, the big markets like Kamwala, Soweto, and Lusaka's street-vending scene, display not only cost-effective prices but also everyday fashions and more. To be sure, clothing needs abound. One market vendor commenting on the 1998 proposal to increase the import tariff on salaula argued, "A good leader must listen to the problems of the people." He explained: "I buy my family's clothes from salaula as well. I don't remember when I last bought clothes from the shops which, most of the time, are unrealistically expensive. Some people would never afford to buy any clothes if there was no salaula" (*Zambia Daily Mail*, 18 February 1998). It is equally certain that style issues matter. Another commentator was well aware of the appeal of salaula to a broad consuming public that engages actively with clothing uniqueness and style: "Some 'salaula' clothes are unparalleled on our local market . . . They are incomparable clothes which Zambian manufacturers cannot match" (*Zambia Daily Mail*, 10 February 1998).

Even in making need-based decisions when shopping from salaula, consumers' choice of garments is influenced by their desire to achieve a particular look. Noting this convergence, one observer pointed out that "in fact, even in terms of quality, salaula beats most of the shops in town which are expensive for nothing." Turning to matters of style, he explained that the "other good side of salaula is that the clothes are not as common as those bought from the shops . . . Sometimes people will even wonder where one bought their attire from when they are clad in very nice salaula which cannot be found in most of the shops." If salaula once was seen as clothing for the underprivileged or downtrodden, this man remarked, "now, almost everyone buys salaula. We see people even driving Mercedes Benz cars coming to buy salaula because they have discovered that it is good and goes at unbeatable prices for that matter. Some of them have standing arrangements with salaula traders [who] reserve good clothes for them and inform them when [they] open new bales" (*Zambia Daily Mail,* 18 February 1998).

Because of the power of clothing to mediate notions of self and society, consumer desire has an important place in debates about garment and textile production. For salaula the work of production does not end in consumption; it begins there. This is why policies affecting salaula reach far into everyday life. As a sociocultural phenomenon salaula has engaged the hearts and minds of many Zambians who consider wearing salaula rather than rags to be an improvement of lives. This widespread meaning of clothing helps to explain why first lady Vera Chiluba's donations from the Hope Foundation of salaula to poor villagers represent much more than political handouts. It is also why, in the view of large segments of the Zambian population, the dressed bodies of the president and first lady concretize both the limits and challenges of abstract phenomena like development, "the nature of society," and possible directions of its future. Yet it remains to be seen whether politico-economic processes within Zambia and in its relationship to the world at large will alter the cultural significance that secondhand clothing has had for local consumers since the late 1980s.

Conclusion: Other People's Clothes?

Imported secondhand clothing has many names. It was called *Vietnam* in Kivu in the eastern part of Zaire in the 1970s, *Kennedy* in Haiti in the 1980s, and *calamidades* in Mozambique in the 1990s. It is known by local terms that mean "dead white men's clothes" in Ghana, "died in Europe" in northwestern Tanzania (Weiss 1996:138), and "shake and sell" in Senegal (Heath 1992: 28).[1] In East Africa it is called *mitumba,* which is Swahili for "bale." In Malawi it is *kaunjika,* which in Nyanja means "to pick," while *salaula* means in Bemba "selecting from a pile in the manner of rummaging."

What these terms do is to bring a variety of local understandings to bear on imported secondhand clothing, naming at least two types of relationships or situations. Some of these names share a source reference: to the West in general, and more specifically to clothing that is cast off and no longer in use, in some instances provided for humanitarian aid. Among the sources these names point to are army surplus shipped to Zaire, locally understood to come from dead soldiers in Vietnam; used American clothing provided as support to Haiti during the Kennedy administration; and anything the West delivered as relief and aid during the civil war in Mozambique, where imported used clothing continues to be referred to as *calamidades.* The other names refer to market situations such as packing in a bale, shaking, sorting, and selecting from a wide range of garments.

What we make of these references to the West's clothing surplus depends on the case at hand and the economic and cultural politics of its time. In Zambia, I have argued, the point of origin is not the most important issue. What matters here is the way salaula names how people deal with clothing, selecting and choosing garments to suit both their clothing needs and desires. Rather than elaborating the obvious, that is, how the export trade of secondhand clothing provides yet another example of inequitable north/south relations, a major effort of this book has been to highlight the agency of the consumer, suggesting that a cultural economy of judgment and style is at work in local appropriations of the West's unwanted clothing. For secondhand clothing is not just any commodity but rather a very special one: as dress, it mediates both individual and collective identities and desires, and as an imported commodity, it opens a special exposure on interactions between the local and the West.

The "magic of clothing" of which Hans Christian Andersen wrote more than a century ago still works in this case. Combining garments from salaula to produce desired clothing looks and styles, consumers in Zambia erase previously drawn clothing distinctions, transforming the West's "old" clothes into "new" by their context. As a local phenomenon, salaula is part of a countrywide wholesale and retail scene with its own consumption politics and cultural economy of taste and style. And as a global phenomenon, the explosion of Zambia's salaula trade and its associated trading activities and consumption practices are the products of a little-known, almost entirely unregulated global commodity trade that is fueled by the West's clothing surplus and penchant for charitable giving. A transformation is at work here as well that turns charity into big business and that is making its own commercial offer and demand.

I have suggested in this book that an explanation of Zambian preoccupations with clothing, both new and used, puts the recent intellectual preoccupation in anthropology and other disciplines with consumption to the test of a broader analytical frame by examining the entire economic circuit, linking questions pertaining to historically specific processes centered on production and distribution with consumption issues shaped by local cultural practices. The interaction of local and global processes in the secondhand clothing system of provision raises crucial and perhaps unusual questions that I probe in this conclusion. The questions arise from the fact that, while salaula creates colorful market and consumption scenes that affect the state of Zambia's textile and garment sector, it is also part of an expanding global economy whose operation casts light on important development issues. Yet in spite of, or perhaps because of, the international forces that impinge on this trade, the essence of the salaula phenomenon is Zambian and local. This is why I have analyzed the popularity of salaula as a context for teasing out some of the striking contradictions of Zambia's ongoing political and economic liberalization.

What is the role of "the West" in this, and how can we speak of "local" practices involving garments that are not products of domestic manufacture? I begin my probing with the international connections as they are understood at the local end, pointing out some of the inequalities of power and knowledge that complicate the way the West and Zambia come together in engagements with clothing. Although secondhand clothing consumption on first sight appears so inextricably bound to "the West," the Western attribution of salaula is highly problematic, as I discuss below. Then I turn to the charitable connection and to questions about what we are to make of it, adding a Zambian perspective to the "win situation" described by a spokesperson for the commercial textile recyclers. Finally, I address Zambian preoccupations with salaula in the context of the country's development predicament, emphasizing the need not to lose sight of our own complicity in this process.

Salaula: An Assault?

"Aren't we all just a secondhand lot?" asked popular columnist Jowie Mwiinga in 1993 when the debate about banning or restricting the salaula import was heating up. "Who would ever have guessed that dress and fashion could have become a volatile political issue?" he asked. Tongue in cheek, he explained that "people are upset because the government is trying to force them to wear brand new clothes . . . some poorly cut things from, say, Deetex . . . when they are perfectably comfortable with the ones the DAPP sells in its secondhand section." These preferences made a lot of sense: "We resigned ourselves to leading our second rate lives on secondhand things a long time ago," he explained, listing as examples secondhand cars, often stolen, secondhand spare parts, secondhand airplanes, and secondhand maize donated by the United States during the drought of 1992. What is more, he continued, the president seems keen on secondhand things like secondhand religion from the United States as well as several previously used ministers from the Kaunda era. The only thing that is new about them is the "New Culture suits they wear so religiously." His point was obvious, namely that banning the secondhand trade would "contradict the second-hand free market ideology Chiluba has been preaching so ardently" (*Weekly Post*, 2–8 July 1993).

The rapid growth of the salaula trade in recent years in Zambia is indeed a product of political contradictions arising in the process of liberalizing an economy that is unable to employ a large proportion of its able-bodied population in conventional wage labor, including textile and garment production. But Mwiinga's points may be pushed even farther. We need to reckon with questions of culture and history, if we are to understand why clothing, in particular, becomes central in discussions about liberalization and democratization. In this situation Zambian preoccupations with salaula is one of many unexpected local results of their engagement with "the market."

Past and present, people in Zambia want to wear clothes that make them look good. Given the multiple dress and fashion inspirations they are exposed to in today's global market, it is not surprising that some of their local creative dress appropriations are beginning to destabilize long-held dress conventions. "Free dress" days in offices and challenging the parliamentary dress code are two examples. In recent controversies over miniskirts, women have interpreted freedom to dress as an important dimension of democracy.

The bulk of these clothes and of dress fabric in Zambia has always been imported, and secondhand clothing is merely one of those imports. Locally produced chitenge material is no longer the national fabric but has been replaced with better quality and more attractive imported prints produced in South and Southwest Asia. Today many Zambian women wear dresses they call traditional that are made from these imported print fabrics. Indeed, past and present converge in Zambia in imported goods. But clothing is among the most important of those imported goods in mediating widely shared notions of well-being. Intermittent antisalaula commentary, particularly from nonlocal observers, about the relationship of production to consumption in the developmental context treats this issue in a one-sided way. Such arguments differ from the approach of this book, which has sought to explain the shifting meanings of clothing in people's lives in terms of changing processes that have opened up for complex interactions between this part of Africa and the world beyond it.

There can be no doubt that the accelerated global commodity flow of secondhand clothing and the widespread consumption of salaula in Zambia in recent years are both products of globalization and its results. But it is misleading to think of the import of salaula as merely an assault on the local that turns everything over in its own image. The involvement of Zambians in the global market through consumption does not by itself result in increasing cultural uniformity. For globalization is not only, or mainly, about the effects of macrolevel economic processes; it also involves cultural and subjective matters. This is Roland Robertson's view (1992:164–81, 183) when he suggests that the essence of globalization lies in the consciousness of the global, in people's awareness of the global situation, specifically that we all inhabit this world. That is to say, Zambian preoccupations with salaula make up a politics of consumption that tells us something about "being-in-the-world" (Friedman 1994a:112–16) on local terms.

Western Commodities and Local Histories

"What is in a commodity? Is it the quality or the origin or perhaps the price that influences people's choices?" asked a Zambian journalist, wondering why imported goods are so popular in his country (*Zambia Daily Mail*, 1 September 1995). The answer to that question depends a good deal on the commodity in question. Save for the origin of salaula garments, there is nothing particularly "Western" about how people in Zambia deal with them. Salaula clothing practices and their incorporation of nonlocal cultural inspirations are not adequately explained as a result of hegemonic domination by the West. The process is interactive, as I have demonstrated in this book by way of specific events and contexts, and it draws importantly on local cultural notions of how to dress. In effect, the meanings people in Zambia attribute to the West's used clothes are informed in important ways by the structure of social relations and the norms that underpin them. When the social and cultural presuppositions that inform clothing practices come into focus, it becomes difficult to view the salaula phenomenon as wholly externally driven.

The work of clothing consumption provokes a set of arguments about the possibilities of leading different and better lives. Practices involved in dressing, and dressing well, are understood by their wearers as being among the prerequisites of modern society, including suits, dresses, and shoes, not to mention other paraphernalia, and going without them, like wearing rags, marks their wearers' premodern status. The implicit model behind this clothing engagement is a rather unspecified sense of "the West." To be sure, when it comes to clothing, Africa and the West cannot escape one another. Unequal integration into the regional and wider world economy took place a long time ago in this part of Africa. As I have argued throughout, people in Zambia have dealt with garments "from the West" for such a long time now that we must recognize the resulting clothing practices as their own.

What is striking about this clothing argument in Zambia is that people there rarely use the category "the West." Instead they talk generically about the "outside," which includes neighboring countries in the region as well as Hong Kong and the United States. Or they invoke the "well-developed countries" or "the donor countries." They also use terms that emerge in the context of specific encounters, for instance the United States or the United Kingdom. Their narratives are not static but employ idioms of time and place that are indicative of the different exposure to the world beyond home by the generations who grew up prior to and after independence. The connections they draw today among "the well-developed countries," "the donor countries," and clothing availability indicate the extent to which Zambians commonly associate consumption with the modernizing project of development agencies and NGOs. This association is not surprising because, after all, in the postcolonial era especially from the mid-1970s on, "development" has been the principal avenue through which "the West" has affected the lives of people "on the periphery."

The ready availability of secondhand clothing has redrawn the map of clothing into a global one in which nations do not matter very much (Gereffi 1996). Consumers in Zambia are not particularly concerned about the provenance of used garments as long as they are not Zambian. We saw this in the designation of clothes from graves as "third-hand," and in the care salaula traders take to demonstrate that their merchandise is fresh from the bale and not previously worn by Zambians. Hardly any of the hundreds of traders and consumers of salaula I have interviewed since the early 1990s asked questions or raised concerns about why or how the West's discarded clothes end up as a cherished commodity in Zambia. Their overwhelming answer when I asked if they knew the source of salaula was that these clothes were "donations" from the "well-developed" countries as is the case with so much else in

Zambia. Some ventured comments about affluence: "They have so many clothes there, you know." When I explained to them the commercial connection between charitable organizations and textile recyclers, most were surprised.

Some of the people I interviewed about their understanding of imported secondhand clothes did ask me if it were true that salaula is "dead people's clothes," and a few wondered if salaula really could transmit AIDS. Judging from Chilambe's 1992 song, "Mukonka Ifya Basungu" (you follow the ways of white people), some Zambians associate salaula with ailments "from the West." But the far-fetched connections MP Mwiinga drew between secondhand underwear and skin diseases during the parliamentary debate about increasing the salaula tariff in 1998 were not elaborated by any of his colleagues, and they were immediately dismissed by medical experts. Still, public disclaimers are one thing, and popular understandings another. "Sharing clothes of someone with AIDS" was mentioned as a mode of transmission by less than one-third of women interviewed in the demographic and health survey of Zambia conducted by USAID and the UN Population Fund in 1991 (UNZA et al. 1992:21). While clothing, and along with it salaula, is embedded in understandings that in specific instances may draw connections to AIDS and foreground the West, this argument is but one of several possible explanations of processes that might have "something" to do with disease transmission.

In everyday talk in Zambia the generic West carries little political salience. Few would think of blaming it for affecting clothing consumption whether new or old, and there is no suggestion of salaula being the flip side of Western fashion. What the West is, above all, is an imagined place, associated with power, wealth, and an abundance of consumer goods that surpass most local products in quality and style. From it comes, for example, via American youth subculture the hip-hop- and rap-inspired style of young male street vendors in Zambia. Yet women's two-piece outfits are not American derived, but influenced rather by British and South African fashions. Distinctions between Zambia and dress styles in the United States, Britain, South Africa, and elsewhere obscure dynamic relationships and influences that cross such boundaries. There is a multiplicity of heritages at work here with complex dialectics between local and foreign influences, and between what is considered to be "the latest" and what is current, in a reconfiguration process that generates distinct local clothing-consumption practices.

Winners and Losers

Recycling used clothing in order to help needy and poor people both at home and abroad is a good idea. But few individuals in the West who donate used clothing are aware of the vast surplus of salable garments they help to generate or that half, or more, of their donated clothing in fact never reaches a charity thrift store. For their part many small-scale salaula traders and textile and garment manufacturers in Zambia believe that salaula clothes are donations directly from charitable organizations. Commercial transactions between the major source of donated clothing in the West, the established charitable organizations, and the commercial textile recyclers and rag graders who purchase the bulk of our donations are not commonly known either in the West or in Zambia. In effect, the charitable guise of the secondhand clothing trade hides the profitable business that private clothing donations help to fuel.

When the international commercial trade in secondhand clothing is explained, it draws mixed responses. Some textile recyclers in the United Kingdom have won awards because of their export of a commodity that is in great demand in Third World countries. Yet major charitable organizations are subject to intermittent media criticism, especially around the charitable season, about their extensive dealings with commercial textile recyclers without full accounting to the public. And contracting with commercial recyclers to collect in the name of an official charity has seen widespread misuse, leading to bad press for the charities.

The relationship between business and charity in the developing world casts revealing light on the uneasy relationship between the international humanitarian-aid industry and local governments, specifically on questions about state autonomy when faced with international groups with their own agendas. These issues have been explored especially in the context of food emergency aid (de Waal 1997; Raikes 1988; Smith 1990). Clearly, the business of charity in the secondhand clothing export trade invites more scrutiny than the scope of this book offers. To be sure, charitable organizations and commercial recyclers alike want to make the most money possible from clothing donations, the former in order to relieve a variety of human needs largely at home and the latter in order to profit. But even if the different profit motives of the two groups are removed, the underlying social and economic factors that help recycle clothing and support export trade will not disappear. Given the way in which the world does business today, discussions about ways of eliminating the commercial middlemen from this process are not very realistic. The vast surplus of used clothing that consumers donate to the major charitable organizations in the West turns charity into business. Regardless of how we evaluate the role of the charitable organizations in this process, there is no doubt that a rhetoric of giving and helping hides a very profitable business both from public view and from scrutiny.

While the results of our own consumerism, used clothing, may not deliver freedom from general want when it is exported, it certainly helps to relieve the clothing needs and desires of those on the receiving end. From their perspective, as this book demonstrates for Zambia, being poor and being a consumer are not mutually exclusive conditions. Aside from its affordability, the immense crossover appeal of secondhand clothing to poor consumers stems from the very special power of clothing as a commodity in mediating notions about the self and society.

Have the charitable organizations of the West become the clothiers of Zambia? Yes and no. In Zambia today, secondhand clothing consumption extends across all social strata except the top. But in the act of appropriating the West's used clothes into locally desired styles, the new wearers are undercutting the history of salaula, which is Western only in its origin. The style tensions and creativity these appropriations entail arise because of global and transnational transformations of the world within which we all live, which in fact the secondhand clothing system of provision is instrumental in setting into motion.

Development Predicaments

The economic history of textile and garment production goes to the heart of classical political economy and the expansion of the West, with present-day production practices that link north and south in a hostile embrace (Bonacich et al. 1994; Gereffi and Korzeniewicz 1994; Morawetz 1981). While the international secondhand clothing trade brings the asymmetry of north/south relations into sharp focus, it also adds surprising twists to this story, as do the dress practices that are arising around the growing consumption of the West's discarded clothing both at home and abroad. Viewing the commodities that flow along the international secondhand clothing chain in terms of how people in Zambia deal with them casts unusual light on how they resolve, or accommodate, some of the contradictions between surplus and wants that fuel this international trade. Salaula consumption both draws and erases distinctions in clothing-consumption practices between classes and across urban and rural areas at the same time as it attaches new meanings to notions of us versus them, rich versus poor, or in the words of young Lukonde, average Zambians versus the well-developed countries.

When I completed this research, the salaula phenomenon appeared to have settled in Zambia, certainly not growing by leaps and bounds as in the first half of the 1990s. Imports from major sources such as the United States were no longer increasing from year to year but seemed to be stabilizing. The sudden removal of street vendors, among them salaula traders, in 1999 affected the volume neither of import nor of wholesale to urban and provincial retailers. While salaula trading temporarily lost its most visible operational space on city streets, it continues unabated in established city and township markets and in private homes, and it is appearing in new modes of mobile trade. As an important consumption good that engages a large sector of the informal economy, the salaula trade carries on in a variety of forms, persisting in the face of formal efforts to regulate it.

The salaula phenomenon will not disappear overnight, nor will large segments of the population stop wanting salaula. As long as the Zambian government maintains its liberalization policy on imports, including secondhand clothing, and does not empower the local clothing and textile industries, the distinction between rags and salaula will continue to be redefined in local terms that transform the West's used clothing into desirable garments. This result of today's development predicament saddens those consumers who know that it does not have to be that way, for example, middle-aged civil servants, who are reluctant to be seen buying salaula. They recall buying their first formal suits from the local clothier, Serioes, remembering that things were not always so. But in the time of structural adjustment programs, what governments can do is restrained by external policy formulations. Widespread frustration with unemployment and high prices provoked by the government's austerity policies and the economy's downward spiral are dashing many Zambians' hopes of leading better lives. We the donors are complicit in this as consumers in a global world where Third World products rarely earn a fair price.

Understanding how the West's used clothes have become redefined as "new" in Zambia and how differences have emerged between second- and thirdhand clothing invites attention to the drawing and erasing of distinctions in clothing-consumption practices. In effect, these very designations and their shifts constitute arguments over the meaning of salaula. I have suggested that these meanings are shaped, in conflict with or accommodation to, the cultural politics of gender, generation, and class of their time. Explaining secondhand clothing practices in this way turns them into much more than a passive imitation of the West. What is more, this view enables us to understand how and why the practices that surround secondhand clothing consumption in Zambia may differ from those elsewhere, for example, in Ghana, where the very same commodity, after its tangled journey from the West, is also in great demand.

The tug of war over values that salaula consumption has fueled in Zambia is also social and cultural. It gives rise to conformity in some areas of life and creativity and rebellion in others. Because the commodity salaula is also a social thing, people's dealings with it have ramifications on social and cultural relations in society at large. For example, buying their own clothes from salaula rather than being presented with them by men as customary conjugality once prescribed, women are shaking men's domestic imperialism. And while clothing used to mark social distinctions, the ready availability and affordability of salaula to youth and rural residents is mediating desires for social mobility and visions of different lives. Of course, dreams of better lives must not be mistaken for equality, and therefore the leveling influence of salaula beyond the domain of clothing consumption must not be overdrawn. Salaula may well mediate desires, but it also dresses bodies. Above all, because clothing constitutes a major dimension of well-being in Zambia, the widespread satisfaction of both clothing needs and desires from salaula offers concrete evidence of the country's development predicament and the uneasy coexistence of freedom and constraint from which it arises.

Notes

Introduction

1. Stallybrass (1996:307) refers to Andersen's story and reminded me of its contemporary relevance. William Kennedy drew my attention to this work.

2. Japan both imports and exports secondhand clothing, receiving a growing portion of top-range used garments from the United States with values nearly doubling from $20.4 million in 1994 to $35.5 million in 1998. The Japanese market for vintage clothing and specialty wear is especially large (*Newsday,* 22 February 1998).

3. Bermingham (1995:12) is suggesting that many arguments about emulation are developed on the basis of Thorstein Veblen's analysis ([1899] 1957) of conspicuous consumption of the nouveaux riches in the late nineteenth century.

4. I wish to thank Beverly Lemire for her constructive suggestions about historical sources on the export of secondhand clothes.

5. In a recent assessment of poverty, rural respondents were asked to describe a poor person. Wearing rags played a major role in characterizations of poverty, and more so for women than for men. These perceptions were drawn from a combination of household-survey data in the analysis of which gender profiles of poverty were constructed, attributing proportional weight to specific aspects of poverty. Both women and men referred to lack of food and clothing as the most important characteristic of a poor person, with women giving emphatically more weight to these basic items than men. In their composite poverty profile women weighted "wearing rags/no clothing" as 21 percent and "having no food/does not eat well" as 20 percent. Men assigned 14 percent to "wearing rags/no clothing" and 15 percent to "having no food/does not eat well." Although the overall poverty assessment was conducted in both urban and rural settings, the published report does not include any urban poverty profiles (World Bank 1994:30–31).

6. Geographers have been in the forefront of this work. For an overview see Jackson and Thrift 1995.

7. For criticism and debate, especially about Fine's analysis of food as a system of provision, see for example Glennie and Thrift (1993), and several contributors to the *Review of International Political Economy,* among them Friedmann (1994) and Watts (1994), as well as responses by Fine (1993, 1994).

8. In recent disasters, some relief organizations have urged the public to give money rather than foodstuffs and used clothing. According to the Red Cross such donations can impede relief efforts because of the time and cost involved in their collection, sorting, transportation, storage, and distribution (*Tampa Tribune,* 3 October 1998, p. 3).

Chapter 1: Clothing Encounters

1. This oral history project was conducted by the Department of History at the University of Zambia (UNZA) by second-year students Raban Chanda and Daniel Yambayamba in Mansa District of Luapula Province around 1974. The transcripts and tapes are deposited in the UNZA library special collection. I am grateful to Mwelwa Musambachime

for enabling me to read his edited and annotated manuscript version of the interviews. The numbers that appear in my references refer to the numbers assigned to the interviews in the Musambachime manuscript.

2. From about 1850 and for over 100 years, Lancashire printworks were the world's leading producers of specialty prints for West African markets. Their main output was two types: wax prints and fancy or roller prints. An African wax print is a printed cotton fabric of plain weave to which the design is applied with wax or resin on both sides of the cloth. It is often dyed indigo, leaving a blue pattern on a white background after the resin is washed out. Roller prints are printed fabrics with a design on one side of the cloth, applied through a continuous process by engraved metal rollers (Nielsen 1979:468). By 1995 there were only two wax-printing manufacturers left in Europe: Brunnschweiler and Company just outside of Manchester and Vlisco bv in the Netherlands.

I have not come across European manufactured prints made specifically with designs for central Africa during the colonial period. My preliminary research consisted of reading relevant literature, communications with textile scholars and art historians, and examination of print samples in museum/gallery collections in Manchester. In 1995 the textile collection at the Whitworth Art Gallery in Manchester, for instance, contained samples of printed cloth produced by Manchester manufacturers in the interwar period with distinct regional market references such as West Africa, East Africa, and South Africa, or specifications such as "Indian style," "Ceylon style," and "Malayan style."

The reasons that specifically designed prints never were produced for central Africa might have to do with the limited size of this region's market and the low purchasing power of its small population. The location might have been an additional factor, right in the middle of south-central Africa, and the end point perhaps of the flow of goods from either coast as well as from South Africa.

3. The medieval Arab trade had direct contacts with the coastal regions of East Africa and the hinterlands of Sofala and Zambezi. There is some archeological evidence of this trade in Zambia (Gray and Birmingham 1970:8).

4. *Ifya Bukaya* was used in many primary schools. Its first editions were printed at the White Fathers' printing press in Chilubula in Northern Province. Debra Spitulnik translated the title for me.

5. I thank Irene Manda for her translation of this text and for her clarifications of the meanings of specific Bemba words.

6. This proportion of wages spent on clothing seems large, as African mine workers at this time, and until the mid-1950s, received food rations in addition to their cash wage.

7. The African National Congress introduced a policy of moderation they termed "New Look" toward the end of 1956 (Rotberg 1965b:278–81). I am not sure whether the "New Look" in Nkata's song has any conventional political significance.

8. Wilk (1990:79) refers to V. S. Naipaul (1968) as a source for this formulation. I came across it as a title of a dissertation (Ichaporia 1980). Orlove and Bauer (1997) offer constructive insights into the significance of imports.

Chapter 2: Clothing Needs and Desires

1. Staff from the Rhodes-Livingstone Institute participated in these exercises under the guidance of director J. C. Mitchell, who provided advice on fieldwork methodology (NAZ/SEC 4/1863).

2. In Brelsford's budget study (1946:109) of a fishing village in the Bangweulu swamps in Luapula in 1944, households spent 58 percent of their incomes on store-

bought goods, out of which clothing accounted for 24 percent, and 50 percent when blankets were included. Very little food was purchased; most of it was obtained in exchange for fish. Allan et al. (1948:171) observed in a survey among the Plateau Tonga in Mazabuka District in 1945: "Given a cash income the Tonga's first item of expenditure will be on clothing for himself and then his wife, children and other dependents." Their budget survey shows that small- and medium-income farmers spent almost half of their income on clothes for the family. And Kay's study (1964:87) in an Ushi-speaking village in Luapula in 1959–60 showed that households spent 41 percent of their incomes on clothing and blankets, and 22 percent on food.

3. The table shows a very provisional listing of the not always very comparable findings about clothes and food consumption of the major urban household budget surveys.

	Percentage of Urban Household Consumption	
Year of Study	Clothing	Food
1945–46 (Deane 1953:293)	30	50
1947 (*Final Report of Commission of Inquiry* 1950:193)	36	32
1960 (*Urban African Budget Surveys* 1965:22)	16	51

4. See Burke 1996 (117, 217–28) for this in Southern Rhodesia, where household budget surveys were conducted with much more regularity than in Northern Rhodesia (Barber 1961:169–70).

5. In monetary terms in 1952, African wages and salaries made up about £12 million out of total national income of £62.4, according to the Overseas Economic Survey (1955:67).

6. See also Ranger 1975. Mitchell's analysis of the kalela dance continues to be a subject of discussion; see Argyle 1991 and Matongo 1992.

7. I am grateful to Roger Sanjek (personal communication, December 1998) for pointing this photograph out to me. He explains that Jimmie Rodgers was the father of American country music. First recorded in 1927, his records had sold in the millions by the early 1930s and his tunes had found their way to Fort Jameson (Chipata) in Northern Rhodesia well before John Barnes arrived in 1946.

Chapter 3: Secondhand Clothing and the Congo Connection

1. I have not been able to trace the origin or etymology of the term *kombo*. The specialists in the Bemba language whom I have consulted have not offered any suggestions. Swahili specialists suggest that *kombo* is a word in the version of the Swahili language spoken in Katanga/Shaba. Mwelwa Musambachime (personal communication, 28 April 1999) confirms that the term stems from Katanga. He remembers from his childhood in Mansa in the early 1950s that the term applied to "used clothes" from abroad. It was used "only for imported secondhand clothes which came in bales," not used clothing bought in shops.

2. I use the name Luapula throughout this chapter although this region has been referred to by different terms since the early colonial period. Administratively, the region known as Luapula Division was renamed Fort Rosebery in the late 1890s, and Mweru-

Luapula District in 1911. In 1929 Mweru-Luapula became a province, which in 1934 was incorporated into Northern Province. After a reorganization in 1947, Mweru-Luapula was linked to Western (now Copperbelt) Province. This proved cumbersome, and the area was linked to Northern Province again in 1953. Luapula province with Mansa (Fort Rosebery) as headquarters was established in 1958 (Gould 1989:16–17).

3. Moss (Morris) Dobkins, born in London in 1894, was the son of Jewish immigrant parents from Vilna in Russia. Like his grandfather before him, his father was a master tailor. At age seventeen young Dobkins sailed to South Africa and traveled north, working a variety of jobs in trade, prospecting, and shopkeeping, at times for relatives who had preceded him. On the journey described in this chapter, he walked from Northern Rhodesia all the way to the terminus of the Benguela railway at Lobito Bay in Angola; he seemed not to have returned to Northern Rhodesia until 1926. He eventually settled in Chingola, assuming a prominent role in commerce on the Copperbelt. I thank Wally (Walter) Dobkins for allowing me to read his father's autobiographical notes about his life and times in this region during the early 1900s.

4. Before 1908 the Congo (known then as the Congo Free State) belonged to Leopold II. Even after 1908, when the Belgian government took control of the entire region, the administration of Katanga was separate from that of the rest of the Congo (Fetter 1976:16).

5. These customs arrangements, which were established under terms of the Berlin Treaty of 1885 and the convention of St. Germain-en-Laye of 1919, stipulated complete freedom to the "trade of all nations," in this way precluding preferential trade arrangements. The Congo Basin embraced the entire Belgian Congo, Kenya, Uganda, Tanganyika, and Nyasaland, while the southern line cut through Angola, Northern Rhodesia, and Portuguese East Africa; the northern line cut through the French Congo and French Equatorial Africa, a small part of the Sudan and Abyssinia, and Italian Somaliland (NAZ/ SEC1/289, 1927–47).

6. Colonial officials in Northern Rhodesia intermittently discussed the matter of repealing the Congo Basin treaties. In 1956, when Northern Rhodesia was part of the Federation of Rhodesia and Nyasaland (1953–63), the Congo Basin treaty was abrogated and a common federal tariff imposed (Kanduza 1986:196). Barber gives 1957 as the date of the abrogation (1961:141). At that time several border posts were set up on the Northern Rhodesian side of the Congolese border.

7. I am indebted to the Reverend Léon Verbeek, who made transcriptions of these two interviews available to me. They were taped in Congolese kiBemba and translated into French by Jean Kibuye Mufwakalibu.

8. The appendix in Musambachime's unpublished dissertation (1981) contains English translations of interviews conducted in the Bemba language with twelve individuals and four groups of elders who had been involved in the early fishing industry in Luapula. One elder, Kauseni Mwewa, explained that he walked to Elisabethville in the Congo as a young boy around 1908 "because I needed some decent clothes" (Mwewa interview, p. 5). Secondhand clothing is a frequent topic in these interviews, with fishermen explaining that they bought kombo for the money they earned from fish sales and that some began selling it themselves. In the 1930s Fisto Mulenga bought kombo at Kasenga and Katabulwe, while others purchased it from itinerant traders (Mulenga interview, p. 10).

9. According to the interviews described in note 7, Luka Mumba was an important hawker of secondhand clothing in Mokambo in the early 1940s and one of the first three African traders to pass a formal test in Elisabethville in 1942 in order to obtain a hawker's license.

Chapter 4: Dressing the New Nation

1. This information, which I have been unable to verify, was provided by Irene Manda, then a research officer at the National Assembly (November 1997, Lusaka). Judging from photographs I have seen of Kaunda wearing wraps, I am not sure that in fact he was wearing a Ghanaian kente cloth. In a frequently reproduced photograph Kaunda's wrap is purple and black with a dotted pattern in white and blue running across it.

2. This comparison is not systematic but mainly indicative of an active level of production in the garment and textile sector. The listings provide little basis for differentiation, with no indication of ownership, size of firm, number of employees, or extent of dependence on domestic or imported inputs.

3. Although the term *salaula* may have been applied to used clothing earlier, it first drew my attention in a newspaper in 1986 in a photograph caption: "Typical Scene of Zambian Market: Ndola's Masala market, one source where salaula or second-hand clothes which contain polo-neck sweaters can be found" (*Sunday Times of Zambia*, 16 November 1986).

4. These commentaries contain allusions to the long-winded debate about whether President Chiluba was son of a Zambian or Zairean (Congolese) father. An amendment to the constitution prevents anyone not born of Zambian parents from pursuing the office of president.

Chapter 5: The Sourcing of Secondhand Clothing

1. These circumstances parallel those Janet Poppendieck (1998:36) notes in her work on the donation of emergency food aid in the United States. In none of the annual reports I collected from Chicago-area nonprofit organizations during the course of this research (Amvets, Goodwill Industries, Salvation Army) were used-clothing donations listed separately nor were commercial sales to textile recyclers referred to. In fact, these organizations do not mention such sales in either their fund-raising efforts or the annual reports they present to the public.

2. DAPP and Humana are associations connected with the Federation for the Pan-European Benevolent Organizations of UFF and Humana, an educational body and an aid organization that is headquartered in Denmark and operates in eleven countries in Europe. UFF is the acronym for the Danish Ulandshjælp fra Folk til Folk (Development Aid from People to People). It is commonly referred to as "The Federation" and described as an international membership organization, comprising associations in several countries in Africa and Europe. It also has projects in St. Lucia, Brazil, and Malaysia. Started in the early 1970s in Tvind, Denmark, by a group of teachers who pooled their wages and lived a collective lifestyle, it has expanded into what critics call an "empire," with boarding schools focusing on alternative education in Scandinavia, two schools until recently in the United Kingdom, and one in the United States (the Institute for International Cooperation and Development in Massachusetts). The federation is alleged to own a property company, a shipping line, plantations, houses and factories, and charitable trusts centered on a financial base in the Cayman Islands. In spite of frequent media exposure and numerous investigations in different European countries, the relationships among income generated through DAPP/Humana secondhand clothing collections throughout Europe, development projects largely in southern Africa, and the other activities of the federation remain unclear. The federation opened its new headquarters outside of Harare in Zimbabwe in October 1998.

3. The department store Hudson Belk in Chapel Hill, North Carolina, recently

announced such a trade-in: "$10 Jeans Trade-in . . . Bring in your old, tired jeans and get $10 off a new pair of brand name jeans like Levi, Lee, Union Bay, Squeeze, plus your favorite designers" (*Chapel Hill News,* 10 October 1997).

4. This group was launched by the International Association of Wiping Cloth Manufacturers with the goal of increasing textile recovery from waste.

5. In addition the United States did not follow the Standard International Trade Classification codes (SITC) until 1978, when it began disaggregating used clothing from rags.

6. I am drawing on statistics from the UN *International Trade Statistics Yearbook,* which lists exports by value in U.S. dollars and does not provide information about volume or weight.

7. The European Union proposal to introduce control procedures for export of certain kinds of waste was adopted in December 1994 and ratified in December 1997. Non-OECD members were invited to express whether or not they wished the control procedures applied to exports to their country of wastes in general or of specific categories of waste. Secondhand clothing is included on the list of so-called green waste (*Official Journal of the European Communities* 1997). Zambia signaled to the European Union that it would accept shipments of such waste from the European Union without recourse to any of the control procedures. In principle, secondhand clothing continues to be shipped from European Union countries to Zambia under the same conditions that apply to ordinary commercial transactions (personal communication, European Commission, Directorate E [industry and environment], waste management, Brussels, 12 October 1998). I thank Hans Minor Vedel for his assistance with these clarifications.

8. There are some commonalities between the lack of information concerning the disposal of used-clothing donations by charitable organizations and the promotion practices of overseas child-sponsorship organizations. In the wake of press reports about discrepancies between fund-raising appeals and the realities of lives of children featured in such campaigns, attorneys general in some states are investigating the accuracy of such funding appeals by several organizations that sponsor children abroad (*Chicago Tribune,* 15 March 1998, 22 March 1998).

9. In Denmark this particular discussion had been fueled by union representations from the clothing and textile sector in reaction to reports from unions in South Africa and Zimbabwe in 1992 about the adverse effects of used-clothing imports on the local industries. This issue was on the agenda of the world congress of clothing and textile workers in Portugal in 1992. During 1993 the Danish foreign ministry commissioned a study of the effects of used-clothing sales in Zambia and Zimbabwe, with particular focus on the activities of DAPP (Denconsult 1993).

Chapter 6: Import, Wholesale, and Distribution
1. The duty rate on imported finished goods was lowered from 40 percent to 25 percent in 1996. For more on duties, see chapter 10.

2. SGS, based in Geneva, is the world's largest organization in the field of inspection and verification, offering control services for the international shipment of goods. The Zambian government entered a contract with SGS some twenty years ago. Questions have been raised about reviewing the need to continue the costly contract with SGS in Zambia's liberalized economy (*Financial Mail,* 22–28 July 1997).

3. Unlike in 1995, when I called on the SGS Lusaka office in 1997, I was not able to obtain information about secondhand clothing imports, for which, I was told, SGS no longer provides records. For statistical data I was referred to the ZRA, which in turn referred me

to the Central Statistical Office, where I have been unable to obtain systematic data. ZRA officials allege that SGS "does not work."

4. Because the UN annual publication on world trade statistics lists only value of commodities, and not weight, I arrived at this informal estimate by extrapolating from the U.S. export figures that list both value and volume in the commodity trade statistics series for individual countries (to which Zambia has not reported since 1978). U.S. secondhand clothing exports to Zambia for 1994 weighing 4,008 tons were reported at a value (U.S.$3,598,000) that is slightly more than half of the estimate of Zambia's total imports (U.S.$6,393,000) from all sources that year. For a conservative estimate I suggest that the weight of Zambia's total import that year might be about twice that reported for the U.S. part of the import, some 7,000 tons. There are some discrepancies in the UN estimates. The 1994 *International Trade Statistics Yearbook* (UN 1995:60) estimates total exports to Zambia in 1994 at a value of U.S.$6,393,000 whereas the 1995 yearbook estimates $4,546,000 for 1994 (UN 1996:60).

5. My request for data from the UN International Trade Branch for exports of secondhand clothing to Zambia from the major reporting export partners, the United States, the United Kingdom, Canada, Belgium-Luxembourg, and the Netherlands, over the 1990–97 period did not produce consistent data. Only from the United States and the United Kingdom were data available for the entire period. In the data set I was provided with, reporting from Belgium-Luxembourg begins in 1992 and from Canada in 1996. There were no reported data for the Netherlands. The German record is spotty, and German export to Zambia is negligible, showing a value of U.S.$27,000 in 1991, declining to $5,000 in 1997.

6. I have not come across specifically identifiable bales from Japan, Hong Kong, or Pakistan, either in wholesalers' warehouses or in retail markets. Perhaps these listings reflect reexport of secondhand clothing from the West, which is imported into those countries in considerable volumes (see chapter 5).

7. I interviewed twelve wholesalers in person in 1992 and have data about eight whom a cooperating Danish colleague interviewed in 1993; I interviewed ten wholesalers in person in 1995, made informal calls on several, and did full interviews with two in 1997.

8. I am very grateful to Bradford Strickland, who conducted interviews with the Khatry Brothers on my behalf (30 August and 27 September 1995), introduced me, and facilitated my follow-up interview (12 August 1997).

9. The exchange rate of the kwacha has changed dramatically during the 1990s (EIU 1994:3, 1998:6). The average exchange rates of Zambian kwacha for U.S.$1 were 1990, 28.99; 1991, 61.73; 1992, 175.00; 1993, 452.76; 1995, 857.23; 1997, 1,325.00.

10. I am grateful to Phillemon Ndubani for assisting me with these interviews.

11. I thank Bradford Strickland for offering these observations from 1993 (April; August through October) and 1995 (August).

12. Chris Simuyemba tracked this journey for me in January 1993.

13. Personal communication, Jakkie Potgieter, Institute for Security Studies in South Africa, 25 February 1998.

Chapter 7: Clothing Retail Practices

1. My retail surveys of the secondhand clothing trade reckon with the range of garments and apparel that is sold, the range of persons involved in terms of age and gender, and the trader's status as an independent operator or a paid worker. I interviewed a total of 83 traders in Lusaka in 1992, of whom 23 worked in the periurban township Mtendere,

31 in Kamwala market, and 29 in Soweto market. In 1993 a Danish colleague and I did a rapid assessment of some 50 traders, at Kamwala, Soweto, and Mandevu township in Lusaka, at Ndola's main Masala market, and at Kabwe. In 1995 I extended my previous work through 172 interviews in Lusaka, 30 in Mtendere township, 60 in Kamwala market, and 82 at Soweto market, as well as 22 in Mansa and 12 in Kawambwa in Luapula Province. I have also monitored the tailor's trade, interviewing 12 tailors in 1993 and 49 in 1995, all in Lusaka, and 27 in Luapula Province in 1995. As always, Norah Rice worked with me as my chief assistant in Lusaka, while my research in Luapula in 1995 was facilitated by the Bemba translation skills of Damiano Chonganya. Monica Macmillan and Chris Simuyemba were helpful with a variety of activities in 1993. Several other individuals have assisted me with specific tasks, as is evident in notes to previous chapters.

2. For their funerals deceased persons in Zambia are dressed in their Sunday best. Mourners and participants at the night-long wakes and participants in funerals do not dress up or put on garments with particular cultural significance. Instead they wear very plain clothing, including, for women, chitenge wrappers and head scarves.

3. Long-term observers tell me that these grave robbings are not recent phenomena, but that they have been noted for some years.

4. A similar practice has been observed in the secondhand clothing markets in Gambia, where "traders do not iron or alter the clothes in any way but sell them in the condition in which they come from the bales. This is because Gambian consumers prefer to buy clothes they know have originated in the West, not those previously worn and donated by the Gambian elite" (Field et al. 1996:372).

5. The question of who purchases the very expensive garments at the high end of the clothing market is intriguing. Boutique owners and attendants offer anecdotal evidence: the president's wife and ministers' wives. In my clothing-consumption survey, which I discuss in chapter 8, I interviewed two wives of ministers who indeed did frequent such shops. There is no doubt that there is a good deal of money in circulation that does not filter across class, and that some of it is spent on conspicuous consumption. Zambia has the most liberal banking regulations in the region. An unintended effect of this, according to one report, has been the "growth of money laundering" in the country (EIU 1997:25), some of it probably drug money.

Chapter 8: The Work of Consumption

1. Squatter settlements are areas where people live without security of tenure. In common parlance they are illegal, yet they house more than half of Lusaka's population. The city council provides plot allocation and basic services in site-and-service schemes where residents build their own houses.

2. This and subsequent excerpts are direct quotes from the students' essays without any editing on my part except for occasional clarifications. I have discussed the essay as an ethnographic genre and the circumstances under which this essay was constructed and written elsewhere (Hansen n.d.). For more about the contents of these essays, see chapter 9, note 3.

3. The Social Research Project of the Jesuit Center for Theological Reflection, for example, which has investigated the changing costs of living in Lusaka since 1991, focuses on basic food, charcoal, and soap. For a family of six the price of those items more than tripled between 1991 and 1997, from K6,363 to K201,200 (*Times of Zambia,* 8 July 1998).

4. In deciding on the scope of my systematic investigation of clothing-consumption practices, I was influenced by Bourdieu's discussion of the class delimitations of his survey about art consumption in France (1984:505). I was also inspired by Rick Wilk's invi-

tation to explore not only what people like but also what they "hate to" consume, which he presented in a conference paper in 1994. I refer to the published version here (1997). In fact, my question about what clothes Zambian consumers hate to wear provoked rich answers pertaining to the construction of acceptable and proper dress. My survey comprised a total of 107 interviews in private households: 32 in Kamanga and 20 in Kaunda Square undertaken by Chris Simuyemba, as well as 55 in Rhodes Park, Woodlands, and Kabulonga, carried out by Norah Rice and me. As a pilot project, Violet Chuula interviewed 14 teachers. Aside from collecting brief information on home ownership, household composition, education, income sources, and rural, urban, and overseas experiences, the survey questions revolved around identifying dress preferences, dislikes, and clothing-consumption practices related to salaula, tailor-made garments, and ready-made clothing from the shops or "outside." We also explored who purchased which items of clothing from whom, and where and when clothing was last acquired; estimated the proportion of chitenge wear to "European-style" clothing in women's wardrobes (in several cases I actually saw the wardrobes); and examined consumption practices in general. And we took informal notes about home furnishings and interior decoration as well as of how the person with whom we spoke was dressed, including hairstyle, makeup, and jewelry.

5. As part of a general policy, many of the government-owned houses in these areas are now for sale.

6. Islam was not widespread during the precolonial era in this region; some influences came from Malawi, where Islam played a larger role. Islam developed more of a profile among immigrant Indian communities, and the first mosque was built in Chipata on the border with Malawi in the post–World War II era. Exposed to these influences, some Africans converted to Islam. In the postcolonial era Islamic proselytization efforts in Zambia have come from various parts of the Arabian peninsula.

7. The term *boubou* is used in the Francophone West African countries for women's tuniclike dress. The reference to "Nigerian boubou" in Zambia offers evidence of the crossover influences in pan-African dress styles.

8. Larvae from eggs laid by putsi flies on wet laundry easily enter human skin, producing a boillike swelling. To prevent this from happening, local and expatriate women alike insist that all clothing that has been dried in the open must be carefully ironed.

Chapter 9: Clothing, Gender, and Power

1. There is little substantive work on this topic. Preliminary observations are presented in Pegg 1996 and Rasing 1997, whereas Kamlongera 1986–87 provides a poorly informed interpretation drawing on secondary sources from Malawi. Magazine articles are sometimes sensationalist, like one in *Lovelines* (October 1994), a publication I had never seen before and have not seen since.

2. For reasons of space I am not here engaging with the rich scholarship on youth in the West, which has obvious relevance but also raises difficult issues in the empirical context of my work.

3. I received permission to undertake this exercise in 1995 from the provincial education officer in Lusaka and the district education officer in Luapula Province. Secondary-school principals or department heads allowed me to contact English teachers, who in turn administered the essay after I had explained to them my interest in the subject and my particular aims. The teachers subsequently described my interests to the students. A total of 173 students wrote essays, 49 young women at Kabulonga Secondary School for Girls and 57 young men at Kabulonga Secondary School for Boys in Lusaka, and 38 young women

at St. Mary's Secondary School at Kawambwa and 29 young men at St. Clement's Secondary School at Mansa in Luapula Province. The question was worded as follows: "How do you dress in your family? Describe who buys the clothes for your family and where most of your clothes are bought (from the shop, tailor, salaula, or any other source). When was the last time you were bought or received clothes and what kind of clothes were they? What kind of clothes do you like best and why? And what kind of clothes do you like least and why? Please indicate where you live, the size of your family, and what your parents or guardians are doing (farming, fishing, office work, business, trade, etc.)."

4. The young women in grade twelve at Kabulonga Secondary School for Girls in Lusaka were keen to make contacts with peers in the United States. They asked for pen pals. I coordinated an exchange of letters with their English teacher and a friend of mine who is a public-school teacher in Chicago. The project, including the personal introductions I refer to in this chapter, was set up by the young women themselves and handed on to me in the form of an exercise book, which I sent to Chicago.

5. Oscar Hamangaba assisted me in this exercise, and I learned a lot from his keen interest in the topic.

Chapter 10: The Politics of Salaula

1. The orchestration of kalindula consists of acoustic guitar, a two-string bass, drum(s), and percussion. The characteristic sound of kalindula, according to Wolfgang Bender, "arises from the bass . . . Kalindula has a continuous rhythm over which the voice sings. The drum has to adjust to the voice" (1991:147).

2. I wish to thank Chris Simuyemba for his translations and transcriptions of the songs discussed in this chapter.

3. Chris Simuyemba in Lusaka and I have in vain attempted to locate a copy of this song, Chris by calling on friends and acquaintances and the music archive at the Zambia National Broadcasting Corporation, and I by asking subscribers to the Zambia list on the Internet about its lyrics.

4. These questions have been discussed in several evaluation/consultative reports, commissioned by development organizations and NGOs. Their results depend very much on the specific terms of reference under which the work was conducted. I am best informed about the nature of the reports that have been commissioned in Scandinavia as indicated in the list below. Only in rare instances are such reports attributed to the individual consultants who undertook the research. The most detailed of these reports is Haggblade's on Rwanda before the civil war (US Agency for International Development 1989), a rather special case, as Rwanda had neither local textile nor clothing factories. The full publication details about these reports are available in the reference section of this book. I list them here by the organizations in charge of the studies. They include Area Forecasting Institute, Sweden (Abrahamsson 1988); US/AID, Washington, DC (Haggblade 1989); Interconsult, Sweden (1990); Swedish Red Cross (1992a, 1992b); Denconsult, Denmark (1993); Südwind Institut für Ökonomie und Ökumene, Germany (1994); SIDA, Sweden (Wicks and Bigsten 1996).

5. The announcement of the 1999 budget did not contain any reference to tariffs on secondhand clothing.

Conclusion: Other People's Clothes?

1. I am grateful to Lisa Cliggett, Jacques Depelchin, Roger Sanjek, Kathie Sheldon, and Teodosio Uate for these insights.

References

Articles, Books, and Reports

AAFRC Trust for Philanthropy. 1998. *Giving USA: The Annual Report on Philanthropy for the Year 1997*. Ed. Ann E. Kaplan. New York: American Association of Fund-Raising Council.

Abrahamsson, Hans. 1988. *Den nakna sanningen: De Svenska enskilda organisationernas klädstöd till Moçambique och dess inverkan på lokal textilproduction* (The naked truth: the clothing aid of Swedish private organizations to Mozambique and its effects on local textile production). Göteborg: Area Forecasting Institute.

Advisory Committee on Industrial Development. 1949. First, Second, and Third Reports. Lusaka: Government Printer.

Alessandro, Bonanno, Lawrence Busch, William F. Friedland, Lourdes Gouveia, and Enzo Mingione. 1994. *From Columbus to ConAgra: The Globalization of Agriculture and Food*. Lawrence: University of Kansas Press.

Allan, William, Max Gluckman, D. U. Peters, and C. C. Trapnell. 1948. *Land Holding and Land Usage among the Plateau Tonga of Mazabuka District: A Reconnaissance Survey*. Rhodes-Livingstone Papers, no. 14.

Alpern, Stanley B. 1995. What Africans Got for Their Slaves: A Master List of European Trade Goods. *History in Africa* 22:5–43.

Andersen, Hans Christian. [1835] 1976. *80 Fairy Tales*. Translated by R. P. Keigwin. Reprint, Odense: Skandinavisk Bogforlag, Flensteds Forlag.

Anderson, W. O. 1919. *On the Trail of Livingstone*. Mountain View, CA: Pacific Press Publishing Association.

Annuaire de l'État Indépendent du Congo et Annuaire Colonial Belge réunis. 1948. *Annuaire du Congo Belge*. Livre d'addresses et recueil. Brussels.

Annual Report on African (Native) Affairs. 1958. *Luapula Province*. Lusaka: Government Printer.

———. 1959. *Western Province*. Lusaka: Government Printer.

———. 1960. *Luapula Province*. Lusaka: Government Printer.

Appadurai, Arjun, ed. 1986. *The Social Life of Things: Commodities in Cultural Perspective*. Cambridge: Cambridge University Press.

———. 1997. Consumption, Duration, and History. In David Palumbo-Liu and Hans Ulrich Gumbrecht, eds., *Streams of Cultural Capital: Transnational Cultural Studies*. Stanford: Stanford University Press, pp. 23–46.

Argyle, John. 1991. *Kalela, Beni, Asafo, Ingoma,* and the Rural-Urban Dichotomy. In Andrew D. Spiegel and Pat A. McAllister, eds., *Tradition and Transition in Southern Africa: Festschrift for Philip and Iona Mayer*. Johannesburg: Witwatersrand University Press, pp. 65–86.

Ash, Juliet. 1996. Memory and Object. In Pat Kirkham, ed., *The Gendered Object*. Manchester: Manchester University Press, pp. 219–24.

Baldwin, Robert E. 1966. *Economic Development and Export Growth: A Study of Northern Rhodesia, 1920–1960.* Berkeley: University of California Press.

Barber, William J. 1961. *The Economy of British Central Africa: A Case Study of Economic Development in a Dualistic Society.* London: Oxford University Press.

Barnes, John A. [1951] 1959. The Fort Jameson Ngoni. 1951. In Elizabeth Colson and Max Gluckman, eds., *Seven Tribes of British Central Africa.* Manchester: Manchester University Press, pp. 194–252.

Bastian, Misty. 1996. Female "Alhajis" and Entrepreneurial Fashions: Flexible Identities in Southeastern Nigerian Clothing Practice. In Hildi Hendrickson, ed., *Clothing and Difference: Embodied Identities in Colonial and Post-Colonial Africa.* Durham: Duke University Press, pp. 97–132.

Batchelor, Peter. [1997?]. Intra-State Conflict, Political Violence, and Small Arms Proliferation in Africa. In Virginia Gamba, ed., *Society under Siege: Crime, Violence, and Illegal Weapons.* Towards Collaborative Peace Series, vol. 1. Halfway House, South Africa: Institute for Security Studies, pp. 103–28.

Bates, Robert H. 1976. *Rural Responses to Industrialization: A Study of Village Zambia.* New Haven: Yale University Press.

Bates, Robert H., and Paul Collier. 1993. The Politics and Economics of Policy Reform in Zambia. In Robert H. Bates and Anne O. Krueger, eds., *Political and Economic Interactions in Economic Policy Reform: Evidence from Eight Countries.* London: Blackwell, pp. 387–443.

Bean, Susan. 1989. Gandhi and Khadi: The Fabric of Independence. In Annette Weiner and Jane Schneider, eds., *Cloth and Human Experience.* Washington, DC: Smithsonian Institution Press, pp. 355–76.

Bender, Wolfgang. 1991. *Sweet Mother: Modern African Music.* Chicago: University of Chicago Press.

Bermingham, Ann. 1995. Introduction: The Consumption of Culture: Image, Object, Text. In Ann Bermingham and John Brewer, eds., *The Consumption of Culture, 1600–1800: Image, Object, Text.* New York: Routledge, pp. 1–20.

Bettison, David G. 1959. Numerical Data on African Dwellers in Lusaka, Northern Rhodesia. *Rhodes-Livingstone Communication,* no. 16.

Biggs, Tyler, Gail R. Moody, Jan-Henrik von Leeuwen, and E. Diane White. 1994. *Africa Can Compete: Export Opportunities and Challenges for Garments and Home Products in the U.S. Market.* World Bank Discussion Papers no. 242. Africa Technical Department Series. Washington DC: World Bank.

Bigland, Eileen. 1939. *The Lake of the Royal Crocodiles.* New York: Macmillan.

Board of Trade. 1954. The African Native Market in the Federation of Rhodesia and Nyasaland. London: Her Majesty's Stationery Office.

Bonacich, Edna, Lucie Cheng, Norma Chincilla, Nora Hamilton, and Paul Ong, eds. 1994. *Global Production: The Apparel Industry in the Pacific Rim.* Philadelphia: Temple University Press.

Bourdieu, Pierre. 1984. *Distinction: A Social Critique of the Judgement of Taste.* Translated by Richard Nice. Cambridge: Harvard University Press.

Braudel, Fernand. 1973a. *Capitalism and Material Life, 1400–1800.* London: Weidenfeld and Nicolson.

———. 1973b. *The Mediterranean and the Mediterranean World in the Age of Philip II.* Vol. 2. New York: Harper and Row.

Brelsford, Vernon W. 1946. Fishermen of the Bangweulu Swamps: A Study of the Fishing Activities of the Unga Tribe. *Rhodes-Livingstone Papers,* no. 12.

———. 1965. *The Tribes of Northern Rhodesia.* Lusaka: Government Printer.

Burawoy, Michael. 1972. The Colour of Class on the Copper Mines: From African Advancement to Zambianization. *Zambian Papers,* no. 7.

Burke, Timothy. 1996. *Lifebuoy Men, Lux Women: Commodification, Consumption, and Cleanliness in Modern Zimbabwe.* Durham: Duke University Press.

Busschau, W. J. 1945. *Report on the Development of Secondary Industry in Northern Rhodesia.* Lusaka: Government Printer.

Campbell, Colin. 1987. *The Romantic Ethic and the Spirit of Modern Consumerism.* Oxford: Blackwell.

———. 1998. Consumption and the Rhetorics of Need and Want. *Journal of Design History* 11(3):235–46.

Carrier, James G., and Josiah McC. Heyman. 1997. Consumption and Political Economy. *Journal of the Royal Anthropological Institute* 3(2):355–73.

Chapman, Stanley. 1993. The Innovating Entrepreneurs in the British Ready-Made Clothing Industry. *Textile History* 24(1):5–25.

Clark, Gracia, ed. 1988. *Traders versus the State: Anthropological Approaches to Unofficial Economies.* Boulder, CO: Westview Press.

Colonial Annual Report of Northern Rhodesia. 1947. London: His Majesty's Stationery Office.

Colson, Elizabeth. 1958. *Marriage and the Family among the Plateau Tonga of Northern Rhodesia.* Manchester: Manchester University Press.

———. 1962. Trade and Wealth among the Tonga. In Paul Bohannan and George Dalton, eds., *Markets in Africa.* Evanston: Northwestern University Press, pp. 601–16.

Comaroff, John L., and Jean Comaroff. 1987. The Madman and the Migrant: Work and Labor in the Historical Consciousness of a South African People. *American Ethnologist* 14:191–209.

———. 1997. Fashioning the Colonial Subject: The Empire's Old Clothes. In John L. Comaroff and Jean Comaroff, *Of Revelation and Revolution,* vol. 2, *The Dialectics of Modernity on a South African Frontier.* Chicago: University of Chicago Press, pp. 218–73.

Cosgrove, Stuart. 1989. The Zoot Suit and Style Warfare. In Angela McRobbie, ed., *Zoot Suits and Second-Hand Dresses: An Anthology of Fashion and Music.* Boston: Unwin Hyman, pp. 3–22.

Council for Textile Recycling. [1997?]. Textile Recycling Fact Sheet.

Cunnison, Ian. 1959. *The Luapula Peoples of Northern Rhodesia: Custom and History in Tribal Politics.* Manchester: Manchester University Press.

———. 1961. Kazembe and the Portuguese, 1798–1832. *Journal of African History* 2(1):61–76.

Customs Department. 1950. *Annual Report 1949.* Lusaka: Government Printer.

Danmarks Statistik. 1988–97. *Udenrigshandel Fordelt på Varer og Lande* (Foreign trade by commodity and country). Copenhagen: Danmarks Statistik.

Davies, Kenneth G. 1975. *The Royal Africa Company.* New York: Octagon Books.

Davis, J. Merle. [1933] 1968. *Modern Industry and the African: An Enquiry into the Effect of the Copper Mines of Central Africa upon Native Society and the Work of the Christian Missions.* 2d edition. New York: Augustus M. Kelley.

Davison, Patricia, and Patrick Harries. 1980. Cotton-Weaving in South-East Africa: Its History and Technology. In Dale Idiens and K. G. Ponting, eds., *Textiles of Africa*. Bath, United Kingdom: Pasold Research Fund, pp. 175–202.

Deane, Phyllis. 1953. *Colonial Social Accounting*. Cambridge: Cambridge University Press.

de Certeau, Michel. 1988. *The Practice of Everyday Life*. Translated by Steven Kendall. Berkeley: University of California Press.

de Grazia, Margreta, Maureen Quilligan, and Peter Stallybrass, eds. 1996. *Subject and Object in Renaissance Culture*. Cambridge: Cambridge University Press.

de Grazia, Victoria, ed., with Ellen Furlough. 1996. *The Sex of Things: Gender and Consumption in Historical Perspective*. Berkeley: University of California Press.

Denconsult. 1993. *Virkninger af brugttøjsalg i udviklingslande* (The effects of used-clothing sales in developing countries). Report commissioned by the Danish Foreign Ministry on DAPP in Zambia and Zimbabwe. Copenhagen.

Denzer, LaRay. 1997. The Garment Industry under SAP with a Special Case Study on Ibadan. Paper presented in workshop, SAP and the Popular Economy, August, at Development Policy Centre, Ibadan, Nigeria.

Department of Overseas Trade. 1939. *Report on Economic and Commercial Conditions in Southern Rhodesia, Northern Rhodesia, and Nyasaland*. London: His Majesty's Stationery Office.

de Waal, Alex. 1997. *Famine Crimes: Politics and the Disaster Relief Industry in Africa*. Bloomington, IN: James Currey.

Dickerson, Kitty G. 1991. *Textiles and Apparel in the International Economy*. New York: Macmillan.

Dilley, Roy, ed. 1992. *Contesting Markets: Analyses of Ideology, Discourse, and Practice*. Edinburgh: Edinburgh University Press.

Dixon-Fyle, Mac. 1983. Reflections on Economic and Social Change among the Plateau Tonga of Northern Rhodesia, 1890–1935. *International Journal of African Historical Studies* 16(3):423–39.

Dobkins, Morris. N.d. Unpublished autobiographical notes.

du Mortier, Bianca M. 1991. Introduction into the Used-Clothing Market in the Netherlands. In Centro italiano per lo studio della storia del Tessuto, ed., *Per una storia della moda pronta: Problemi e ricerche: Atti del V Convegno Internazionale del CISST*, Milano, 26–28 February 1990, pp. 117–25.

DuPont, Ann. 1995. Captives of Colored Cloth: The Role of Cotton Trade Goods in the North Atlantic Slave Trade, 1600–1808. *Ars Textrina* 24:177–83.

Durham, Deborah. 1995. The Lady in the Logo: Tribal Dress and Western Culture in a Southern African Community. In Joanne B. Eicher, ed., *Dress and Ethnicity*. Oxford: Berg Publishers, pp. 183–94.

Economist Intelligence Unit (EIU). 1994. *Country Report: 4th Quarter: Zambia*. London: Economist Intelligence Unit.

———. 1997. *Country Profile, 1997–98: Zambia*. London: Economist Intelligence Unit.

———. 1998. *Country Report: 2nd Quarter: Zambia*. London: Economist Intelligence Unit.

Ehlers, Tracy Bachrach. 1993. Belts, Business, and Bloomingdale's: An Alternative Model for Guatemalan Artisan Development. In June Nash, ed., *Crafts in the World Market: The Impact of Global Exchange on Middle American Artisans*. New York: State University of New York Press, pp. 181–98.

Eicher, Joanne B. 1969. *African Dress: A Select and Annotated Bibliography of Sub-Saharan Countries.* East Lansing: Michigan State University.

Elias, Norbert. 1978. *The Civilizing Process: The History of Manners.* New York: Urizen Books.

Elson, Diane. 1994. Uneven Development and the Textiles and Clothing Industry. In Leslie Sklair, ed., *Capitalism and Development.* London: Routledge, pp. 189–210.

Epstein, Arnold L. 1981. *Urbanization and Kinship: The Domestic Domain on the Copperbelt of Zambia, 1950–1956.* New York: Academic Press.

———. 1992a. Response to Social Crisis: Aspects of Oral Aggression in Central Africa. In Arnold L. Epstein, *Scenes from African Urban Life: Collected Copperbelt Papers.* Edinburgh: Edinburgh University Press, pp. 158–207.

———. 1992b. The Role of the Urban Courts. In Arnold L. Epstein, *Scenes from African Urban Life: Collected Copperbelt Papers.* Edinburgh: Edinburgh University Press, pp. 22–41.

Export Board of Zambia. 1995. *Report on the Audit of Textile Producers 1994.* Lusaka: Export Board of Zambia.

———. 1997. *Report on the Export Performance of Textiles in 1996.* Lusaka: Export Board of Zambia.

Fabian, Johannes. 1986. *Language and Colonial Power: The Appropriation of Swahili in the Former Belgian Congo, 1880–1938.* Cambridge: Cambridge University Press.

———. 1990. *History from Below: The "Vocabulary of Elisabethville" by Andre Yav: Text, Translations, and Interpretive Essays.* Philadelphia: John Benjamins Publishing.

Fallers, Lloyd. 1961. Are African Cultivators to Be Called Peasants? *Current Anthropology* 2:108–10.

Feldman, Egal. 1960. Jews in the Early Growth of New York City's Men's Clothing Trade. *American Jewish Archives* 12(1):3–14.

Fetter, Bruce. 1976. *The Creation of Elisabethville, 1910–1940.* Stanford, CA: Hoover Institution Press.

Field, Simone, Hazell Barrett, Angela Browns, and Roy May. 1996. The Second-Hand Clothes Trade in the Gambia. *Geography* 81(4):371–74.

Final Report of the Commission of Inquiry into the Cost of Living. 1950. Lusaka: Government Printer.

Fine, Ben. 1993. Modernity, Urbanism, and Modern Consumption: A Comment. *Environment and Planning D. Society and Space* 11:599–601.

———. 1994. A Response to My Critics. *Review of International Political Economy* 1(3):579–86.

Fine, Ben, and Ellen Leopold. 1993. *The World of Consumption.* London: Routledge.

Fraenkel, Peter. 1959. *Wayaleshi.* London: Weidenfeld and Nicolson.

Francis, Sally K., Sara L. Butler, and Kelly S. Gallett. 1995. Disposition of Donated Clothing: An Ecological Concern. *Journal of Family and Consumer Sciences* 87(3): 25–30.

Friedman, Jonathan. 1991. Consuming Desires: Strategies of Selfhood and Appropriation. *Cultural Anthropology* 6(2):154–63.

———. 1994a. *Cultural Identity and Global Process.* Thousand Oaks, CA: Sage Publications.

———. 1994b. Introduction to Jonathan Friedman, ed., *Consumption and Identity.* London: Harwood Academic Press, pp. 1–22.

Friedmann, Harriet. 1994. Premature Rigour; or, Can Ben Fine Have His Contingency and Eat It, Too? *Review of International Political Economy* 1(3):553–61.

Gallo, Marzia Cataldi. 1991. Il commercio degli abiti usata a Genova nel XVII secolo. In Centro italiano per lo studio della storia del tessuto, ed., *Per una storia della moda pronta: Problemi e ricerche: Atti del V Convegno internazionale del CISST,* Milano, 26–28 February 1990, pp. 95–106.

Gandoulou, Justin-Daniel. 1984. *Entre Paris et Bacongo.* Paris: Centre George Pompidou.

———. 1989. *Dandies à Bacongo: Le culte de l'élégance dans la société congolaise contemporaine.* Paris: L'Harmattan.

Gann, Lewis H. 1969. *A History of Northern Rhodesia: Early Days to 1953.* New York: Humanities Press.

Geisler, Gisela, and Karen Tranberg Hansen. 1994. Structural Adjustment, the Rural-Urban Interface, and Gender Relations in Zambia. In Nahid Aslanbegui, Steven Pressman, and Gale Summerfield, eds., *Women in the Age of Economic Transformation: Gender Impacts of Reform in Post-Socialist and Developing Countries.* London: Routledge, pp. 95–112.

Gereffi, Gary. 1994. Capitalism, Development, and Global Commodity Chains. In Leslie Sklair, ed., *Capitalism and Development.* London: Routledge, pp. 211–31.

———. 1996. Global Commodity Chains: New Forms of Coordination and Control among Nations and Firms in International Industries. *Competition and Change* 4:427–39.

Gereffi, Gary, and Miguel Korzeniewicz, eds. 1994. *Commodity Chains and Global Capitalism.* New York: Praeger.

Gertzel, Cherry, with Carolyn Baylies and Morris Szeftel. 1984. *The Dynamics of the One-Party State in Zambia.* Manchester: Manchester University Press.

Ginsburg, Madeleine. 1980. Rags to Riches: The Second-Hand Clothes Trade, 1700–1978. *Costume* 14:121–35.

Glennie, Paul D., and Nigel J. Thrift. 1993. Modern Consumption: Theorising Commodities and Consumers. *Environment and Planning D. Society and Space* 11:603–6.

Goldthwaite, Richard A. 1992. Identity and Consumerism in Renaissance Florence. Transcript of twelfth annual Phi Alpha Theta Distinguished Lecture on History, 16 March, State University of New York, Albany.

Gould, Jeremy. 1989. *Luapula: Dependence or Development?* Zambia Geographical Association Regional Handbook 6, Finnish Society for Development Studies Monograph 3 in Cooperation with Scandinavian Institute of African Studies.

Gouldsbury, Cullen, and Hubert Sheane. 1911. *The Great Plateau of Northern Rhodesia.* London: Edward Arnold.

Government of the Republic of Zambia and the United Nations System in Zambia (GRZ and UN). 1996. *Prospects for Sustainable Human Development in Zambia: More Choices for Our People.* Lusaka: Pilcher Graphics.

Gray, Richard, and David Birmingham. 1970. Some Economic and Political Consequences of Trade in Central and East Africa in the Pre-colonial Period. In Richard Gray and David Birmingham, eds., *Pre-colonial African Trade: Essays on Trade in Central and Eastern Africa before 1900.* London: Oxford University Press, pp. 1–23.

Green, Nancy. 1997. *Ready-to-Wear, Ready to Work: A Century of Industry and Immigration in Paris and New York.* Durham: Duke University Press.

Guille, Jackie. 1995. Southern African Textiles Today: Design, Industry, and Collective

Enterprise. In John Pickton, ed., *The Art of African Textiles: Technology, Tradition, and Lurex*. Catalogue produced for the Barbican Art Gallery. London: Lund Humphries, pp. 51–54.

Gussman, Boris W. 1952. *African Life in an Urban Area: A Study of the African Population of Bulawayo*. Part 1. Bulawayo: Federation of African Welfare Societies in Southern Rhodesia.

Haggblade, Steven. 1989. A Review of Rwanda's Textile Clothing Subsector. *Employment and Enterprise Policy Analysis Discussion Paper*, no. 24.

———. 1990. The Flip Side of Fashion: Used Clothing Exports to the Third World. *Journal of Development Studies* 26(3):505–21.

Hansen, Karen Tranberg. 1985. Budgeting against Uncertainty: Cross-Class and Transethnic Redistribution Mechanisms in Urban Zambia. *African Urban Studies* 21:65–74.

———. 1989. *Distant Companions: Servants and Employers in Zambia, 1900–1985*. Ithaca: Cornell University Press.

———. 1994. Dealing with Used Clothing: *Salaula* and the Construction of Identity in Zambia's Third Republic. *Public Culture* 6(3):503–23.

———. 1995. Transnational Biographies and Local Meanings: Used Clothing Practices in Lusaka. *Journal of Southern African Studies* 21(1):131–45.

———. 1997. *Keeping House in Lusaka*. New York: Columbia University Press.

———. 1999. Second-Hand Clothing Encounters in Zambia: Global Discourses, Western Commodities, and Local Histories. *Africa* 69(3):343–65.

———. N.d. Gender and Difference: Youth, Bodies, and Clothing in Zambia. In Victoria Goddard, ed., *Gender, Agency, and Change: An Anthropological Perspective*. London: Routledge. Forthcoming.

Hartman, Michael. [1988?]. Social Relations and Access to Informal Sector Services: Some Examples from Tailors in Lusaka. Unpublished paper, Institute for African Studies, University of Zambia.

Heath, Deborah. 1992. Fashion, Anti-fashion, and Heteroglossia in Urban Senegal. *American Ethnologist* 19(2):19–33.

Hebdige, Dick. 1988. *Subculture: The Meaning of Style*. London: Routledge.

Helmreich, J. E. 1983. The Uranium Negotiations of 1944. In Académie Royale des Sciences d'Outre-Mer, ed., *Le Congo durant la Seconde Guerre Mondiale: Recueil d' études*. Brussels: Académie Royale des Sciences d'Outre-Mer, pp. 253–84.

Hendrickson, Carol. 1996. Selling Guatemala: Maya Import Products in U.S. Mail-Order Catalogues. In David Howes, ed., *Cross-Cultural Consumption: Global Markets, Local Realities*. New York: Routledge, pp. 106–21.

Hendrickson, Hildi. 1996. Introduction to Hildi Hendrickson, ed., *Clothing and Difference: Embodied Identities in Colonial and Post-colonial Africa*. Durham: Duke University Press, pp. 1–16.

Higginson, John. 1989. *A Working Class in the Making: Belgian Colonial Labor Policy and the African Mineworker, 1907–1951*. Madison: University of Wisconsin Press.

Hobson, Dick. 1996. *Tales of Zambia*. London: Zambia Society Trust.

Hollander, Anne. 1978. *Seeing through Clothes*. New York: Viking Penguin.

———. 1994. *Sex and Suits: The Evolution of Modern Dress*. New York: Alfred A. Knopf.

Holleman, J. F., and S. Biesheuvel. 1973. *White Mine Workers in Northern Rhodesia, 1959–1960*. Leiden: Afrika-Studiecentrum.

Hopfinger, Hans. 1985. Geographische Aspekte des internationalen Handels mit gebrauchter Bekleidung: Perfektes Recycling oder Verlängerung asymmetrischer Handelsbeziehungen mit der Dritten Welt am Fallbeispiel Syrien. *Erdkunde* 39:206–17.

Ichaporia, Niloufer. 1980. Crazy for Foreign: The Exchange of Goods and Values on the International Ethnic Arts Market. Ph.D. dissertation, University of California, Berkeley.

Industrial Corporation, Ltd. (Indeco). 1970. *A Survey of Zambian Industry.* Lusaka: Indeco.

Interconsult. 1990. *Klädfrakt för projektbistand: Studie av SIDAs fraktbidrag till foreningen U-landshjaelp Från Folk till Folk i Sverige (UFF)* (Clothing freight as project aid: A study of SIDA's freight aid to the Swedish organization Development Aid from People to People). Stockholm.

Jackson, Peter, and Nigel Thrift. 1995. Geographies of Consumption. In Daniel Miller, ed., *Acknowledging Consumption.* London: Routledge, pp. 204–37.

James, Deborah. 1996. "I Dress in This Fashion": Transformations in Sotho Dress and Women's lives in a Sekhukhuneland Village, South Africa. In Hildi Hendrickson, ed., *Clothing and Difference: Embodied Identities in Colonial and Post-colonial Africa.* Durham: Duke University Press, pp. 34–65.

James, Jeffrey. 1992. *Consumption and Development.* New York: St. Martin's Press.

Johnson, Marion. 1974. Cotton Imperialism in West Africa. *African Affairs* 73(291): 178–87.

Jubb, Samuel. 1860. *The History of the Shoddy-Trade: Its Rise, Progress, and Present Position.* London: Houlston and Wright.

Kallmann, Deborah. 1998. Projected Moralities, Engaged Anxieties: Northern Rhodesian News, Women's Pages Advertisements, and Advice Columns in Three Newspapers. M.A. thesis, University of Arizona.

Kamlongera, Christopher F. 1986–87. Denigration of a Culture or Cultural Change in Malawi: The Kitchen Party. *Bulletin of the International Committee on Urgent Anthropological and Ethnological Research* 28–29:53–65.

Kanduza, Ackson M. 1986. *The Political Economy of Underdevelopment in Northern Rhodesia, 1918–1960: A Case Study of Customs Tariff and Railway Freight Policies.* Lanham, MD: University Press of America.

Karmiloff, Igor. 1990. Zambia. In Roger Riddell, ed., *Manufacturing Africa: Performance and Prospects of Seven Countries in Sub-Saharan Africa.* London: James Currey, pp. 297–335.

Kasengele, Mwango. 1998. Differentiation among Small-Scale Enterprises: The Zambian Clothing Industry in Lusaka. In Anita Spring and Barbara E. McDade, eds., *African Entrepreneurship: Theory and Reality.* Gainesville: University Press of Florida, pp. 93–106.

Kasoma, Francis P. 1986. *The Press in Zambia: The Development, Role, and Control of National Newspapers in Zambia, 1906–1983.* Lusaka: Multimedia Publications.

Katzenellenbogen, Simon I. 1973. *Railways and the Copper Mines of Katanga.* Oxford: Clarendon Press.

Kaunda, Kenneth. 1962. *Zambia Shall Be Free: An Autobiography.* London: Heinemann.

Kay, George. 1964. Chief Kalaba's Village: A Preliminary Survey of Economic Life in an Ushi Village, Northern Rhodesia. *Rhodes-Livingstone Papers,* no. 35.

———. 1967. *A Social Geography of Zambia.* London: University of London Press.

Kopytoff, Igor. 1986. The Cultural Biography of Things: Commoditization as Process. In Arjun Appadurai, ed., *The Social Life of Things: Commodities in Cultural Perspective.* Cambridge: Cambridge University Press, pp. 64–91.

Legros, Hugues. 1996. Chasseurs d'ivoire: Une histoire du royaume Yéké du Shaba (Zaire). Brussels: Editions de l'Université de Bruxelles.

Lemire, Beverly. 1988. Consumerism in Preindustrial and Early Industrial England: The Trade in Secondhand Clothes. *Journal of British Studies* 27:1–24.

———. 1990. The Theft of Clothes and Popular Consumerism in Early Modern England. *Journal of Social History* 24(2):255–76.

———. 1991a. *Fashion's Favourite: The Cotton Trade and the Consumer in Britain, 1660–1800.* Oxford: Oxford University Press.

———. 1991b. The Nature of the Second-Hand Clothes Trade: The Role of Popular Fashion and Demand in England, c. 1700–1850. In Centro italiano per lo studio della storia del tessuto, ed., *Per una storia della moda pronta: Problemi e ricerche: Atti del V Convegno internazionale del CISST,* Milano, 26–28 February 1990, pp. 107–16.

———. 1997. *Dress, Culture, and Commerce: The English Clothing Trade before the Factory, 1660–1800.* New York: St. Martin's Press.

Levitt, Sarah. 1991. Bristol Clothing Trades and Exports in the Georgian Period. In Centro italiano per lo studio della storia del tessuto, ed., *Per una storia della moda pronta: Problemi e ricerche: Atti del V Convegno internazionale del CISST,* Milano, 26–28 February 1990, pp. 29–41.

Long, Norman. 1968. *Social Change and the Individual: A Study of the Social and Religious Responses to Innovation in a Zambian Rural Community.* Manchester: Manchester University Press.

Luig, Ulrich. 1997. *Conversion as a Social Process: A History of Missionary Christianity among the Valley Tonga, Zambia.* Hamburg: LIT.

MacGaffey, Janet, with Vwakyanakzi Mukohya, Rukarangira wa Nkera, Brooke Grundfest Schoepf, Makwala ma Mavumbu ye Beda, and Walu Engundu. 1991. *The Real Economy of Zaire: The Contribution of Smuggling and Other Unofficial Activities to National Wealth.* Philadelphia: University of Pennsylvania Press.

MacLeod, Arlene E. 1992. Hegemonic Relations and Gender Resistance: The New Veiling as Accommodating Protest in Cairo. *Signs* 17(3):533–57.

Magubane, Bernhard. 1971. A Critical Look at Indices Used in the Study of Social Change in Colonial Africa. *Current Anthropology* 12:419–31.

Majmudar, Madhavi. 1996. Trade Liberalisation in Clothing: The MFA Phase-Out and the Developing Countries. *Development Policy Review* 14:5–36.

Makgetla, Neva Seidman. 1986. Theoretical and Practical Implications of IMF Conditionality in Zambia. *Journal of Modern African Studies* 24(3):395–422.

Maren, Michael. 1997. *The Road to Hell: The Ravaging Effects of Foreign Aid and International Charity.* New York: Free Press.

Marsden, Terry, and Jo Little, eds. 1990. *Political, Social, and Economic Perspectives on the International Food System.* Aldershot, United Kingdom: Avebury.

Martin, Phyllis M. 1994. Contesting Clothes in Colonial Brazzaville. *Journal of African History* 35(3):401–26.

———. 1995. *Leisure and Society in Colonial Brazzaville.* Cambridge: Cambridge University Press.

Marwick, Max G. 1974. Some Labour Histories. Appendix B in Helmuth Heisler, *Urbanisation and the Government of Migration: The Interrelation of Urban and Rural Life in Zambia.* New York: St. Martin's Press, pp. 144–50.

Matongo, Albert B. K. 1992. Popular Culture in a Colonial Society: Another Look at Mbeni and Kalela Dances on the Copperbelt, 1930–1964. In Samuel N. Chipungu, ed.,

Guardians of Their Time: Experiences of Zambians under Colonial Rule, 1890–1964. London: Macmillan, pp. 180–217.

Matthews, T. I. 1981. Portuguese, Chikunda, and Peoples of the Gwembe Valley: The Impact of the "Lower Zambezi Complex" on Southern Zambia. *Journal of African History* 22:23–41.

McGrath, J., and A. Whiteside. 1989. Industry, Investment Incentives, and the Foreign Exchange Crisis: Zambia: A Case Study. In Alan W. Whiteside, ed., *Industrialization and Investment Incentives in Southern Africa.* Pietermaritzburg, South Africa: University of Natal Press, pp. 167–83.

McKinley, Edward H. 1986. *Somebody's Brother: A History of the Salvation Army's Men's Social Service Department, 1891–1985.* Lewiston, NY: Edwin Mellen Press.

McRobbie, Angela. 1989. Second-Hand Dresses and the Role of the Ragmarket. In Angela McRobbie, ed., *Zoot Suits and Second-Hand Dresses: An Anthology of Fashion and Music.* Boston: Unwin Hyman, pp. 23–49.

Miller, Daniel. 1987. *Material Culture and Mass Consumption.* Oxford: Blackwell.

———. 1994. *Modernity: An Ethnographic Approach.* New York: Berg.

———. 1995a. Consumption as the Vanguard of History: A Polemic by Way of an Introduction. In Daniel Miller, ed., *Acknowledging Consumption.* New York: Routledge, pp. 1–57.

———. 1995b. Consumption Studies as the Transformation of Anthropology. In Daniel Miller, ed., *Acknowledging Consumption.* New York: Routledge, pp. 264–95.

———. 1997. *Capitalism: An Ethnographic Approach.* New York: Berg.

Miller, Joseph C. 1988. *Way of Death: Merchant Capitalism and the Angolan Slave Trade, 1730–1830.* Madison: University of Wisconsin Press.

Ministry of Commerce, Trade, and Industry. 1996. Report on the Textile Sub-sector. Lusaka.

Mintz, Sidney. 1985. *Sweetness and Power: The Place of Sugar in Modern History.* New York: Viking Penguin.

Miracle, Marvin P. 1969. Trade and Economic Change in Katanga, 1850–1959. In Daniel F. McCall, Norman R. Bennett, and Jeffrey Butler, eds., *Western African History.* New York: Praeger, pp. 214–58.

Mitchell, J. Clyde. 1956. The Kalela Dance. *Rhodes-Livingstone Papers,* no. 27.

———. 1987. *Cities, Society, and Social Perception: A Central African Perspective.* Oxford: Clarendon Press.

Mitchell, J. Clyde, and Arnold L. Epstein. 1959. Occupational Prestige and Social Status among Urban Africans in Northern Rhodesia. *Africa* 29:22–39.

Moore, R. J. B. 1937. Industry and Trade on the Shores of Lake Mweru. *Africa* 10(2): 137–58.

———. 1948. *These African Copper Miners.* Revised, with appendices by A. Sandilans. London: Livingstone Press.

Morawetz, David. 1981. *Why the Emperor's New Clothes Are Not Made in Colombia: A Case Study of Latin American and East Asian Manufactured Exports.* New York: Oxford University Press.

Morrow, Sean F. 1985. "To Build the City of God in Their Midst": Motives and Methods of the London Missionary Society in Northern Rhodesia, 1887–1941. Ph.D. dissertation, University of Sussex.

Musambachime, Mwelwa C. 1981. Development and Growth of the Fishing Industry in Mweru-Luapula, 1920–1964. Ph.D. dissertation, University of Wisconsin.

———. 1995. The Role of Kasenga (Eastern Shaba) in the Development of Mweru-Luapula Fishery. *African Studies Review* 38(1):51–68.

———. N.d. The Oral History of Mansa, Zambia. Edited and annotated version of oral-history research conducted by second-year students Raban Chanda and Daniel Yambayamba. Department of History, University of Zambia.

Musiari, Antonio. 1991. Commercio di abiti usata o gia confezionati a Parma nei secoli XVII e XVIII. In Centro italiano per lo studio della storia del tessuto, ed., *Per una storia della moda pronta: Problemi e ricerche*. Atti del V Convegno Internazionale del CISST Milano, 26–28 February 1990, pp. 69–84.

Mwaanga, Vernon J. 1982. *An Extraordinary Life*. Lusaka: Multimedia Publications.

Mwangilwa, Goodwin B. 1982. *Harry Mwaanga Nkumbula: A Biography of the Old Lion of Zambia*. Lusaka: Goodwin B. Mwangilwa.

Mwansa, Maximus. 1992. The Emergence of African Entrepreneurs in Fort Rosebery (Mansa)–Samfya Area, 1930–1964. M.A. thesis, University of Zambia.

Naggar, Betty. 1990. Old-Clothes Men: 18th and 19th Centuries. *Transactions: The Jewish Historical Society of England* 31:171–91.

Naipaul, V. S. 1968. *An Area of Darkness*. Harmondsworth: Penguin.

Narotzky, Susana. 1997. *New Directions in Economic Anthropology*. London: Pluto Press.

Nielsen, Ruth. 1979. The History and Development of Wax-Printed Textiles Intended for West Africa and Zaire. In Justine Cordwell and Ronald A. Swarz, eds., *The Fabrics of Culture: The Anthropology of Clothing and Adornment*. The Hague: Mouton, pp. 467–98.

Nonprofit Almanac. 1996–97. *Dimensions of the Independent Sector*. San Francisco: Jossey-Bass Publishers.

Official Journal of the European Communities. 1998. Written Question E-0016/98 by Jean-Pierre Bebear. Subject: Controls on the Movement of Waste. Answer by Mrs. Bjerregaard on Behalf of the Commission. 17 July, C223/84-86.

Ong, Aihwa. 1990. State versus Islam: Malay Families, Women's Bodies, and the Body Politic in Malaysia. *American Ethnologist* 17(2):258–76.

Orlove, Benjamin, and Arnold J. Bauer. 1997. Giving Importance to Imports. In Benjamin Orlove, ed., *The Allure of the Foreign: Imported Goods in Postcolonial Latin America*. Ann Arbor: University of Michigan Press, pp. 1–29.

Overseas Economic Surveys. 1950. *Southern and Northern Rhodesia and Nyasaland, 1950*. London: His Majesty's Stationery Office.

———. 1955. *The Federation of Rhodesia and Nyasaland, 1954*. London: His Majesty's Stationery Office.

Park, Young-Il, and Kym Anderson. 1991. The Rise and Demise of Textiles and Clothing in Economic Development: The Case of Japan. *Economic Development and Cultural Change* 39(3):531–48.

Parpart, Jane L. 1994. "Where Is Your Mother?" Gender, Urban Marriage, and Colonial Discourse on the Zambian Copperbelt, 1924–1945. *International Journal of African Historical Studies* 27(2):241–71.

Pegg, Jacquelyn. 1996. The Proper Woman: The Kitchen Party as Contested Site of Gender Construction in Urban Zambia. M.A. thesis, Northwestern University.

Perrings, Charles. 1979. *Black Mineworkers in Central Africa: Industrial Strategies and the Evolution of an African Proletariat in the Copperbelt, 1911–1941*. New York: Africana Publishing Company.

Perrot, Philippe. 1994. *Fashioning the Bourgeoisie: A History of Clothing in the Nine-teenth Century.* Translated by Richard Bienvenu. Princeton: Princeton University Press.

Pickton, John, with Rayda Becker, Pauline Duponchel, Jackie Guille, Elizabeth Harney, David Heathcote, Julia Hilger, Atta Kwami, Pat Oyelola, and Simon Peers. 1995. *The Art of African Textiles: Technology, Tradition, and Lurex.* London: Barbican Art Gallery; Lund Humphries.

Pickton, John, and John Mack. 1989. *African Textiles.* 2d edition. London: British Museum Publications.

Piore, Michael J., and Charles F. Sabel. 1984. *The Second Industrial Divide: Possibilities for Prosperity.* New York: Basic Books.

Poewe, Karla O. 1976. Religion, Kinship, and Labor in Luapula: Prosperity and Economic Stagnation of Lake and River Fishing Communities. Ph.D. dissertation, University of New Mexico.

———. 1981. *Matrilineal Ideology: Male-Female Dynamics in Luapula, Zambia.* New York: Academic Press.

Poppendieck, Janet. 1998. *Sweet Charity? Emergency Food and the End of Entitlement.* New York: Viking.

Potgieter, Jakkie. [1997?]. The Price of War and Peace: A Critical Assessment of the Disarmament Component of United Nations Operations in Southern Africa. In Virginia Gamba, ed., *Society under Siege: Crime, Violence, and Illegal Weapons.* Towards Collaborative Peace Series, vol. 1. Halfway House, South Africa: Institute for Security Studies, pp. 129–68.

Powdermaker, Hortense. 1962. *Copper Town: Changing Africa: The Human Condition on the Rhodesian Copperbelt.* New York: Harper and Row.

Prins, Gwyn. 1990. The Battle for Control of the Camera in Late Nineteenth Century Western Zambia. *African Affairs* 86(354):97–105.

Quinn, K. 1965. A Consideration of the Economics of Central Africa. In George J. Snowball, ed., *Science and Medicine in Central Africa.* Oxford: Pergamon Press, pp. 673–80.

Rabine, Leslie W. 1997. Not a Mere Ornament: Tradition, Modernity, and Colonialism in Kenyan and Western Clothing. *Fashion Theory* 1(2):145–68.

Raikes, Philip L. 1988. *Modernising Hunger: Famine, Food Surpluses, and Farm Policy in the EEC and Africa.* Portsmouth, NH: Heinemann.

Ranger, Terence. 1975. *Dance and Society in Eastern Africa, 1890–1970.* Los Angeles: University of California Press.

———. 1980. Making Northern Rhodesia Imperial: Variations on a Royal Theme, 1924–1938. *African Affairs* 79(316):349–74.

Rasing, Thera. 1997. Globalisation and the Making of Consumers: Zambian Kitchen Parties. Paper presented at conference organized by EIDOS/WOTRO, Globalization, Development, and the Making of Consumers: What Are Collective Identities For? 13–16 March, at the Hague.

Record of the Second Meeting of the Western Province African Provincial Council. 1951. Luanshya, 23–25 April.

Reikat, Andrea. 1997. *Handelsstoffe: Grundzüge des Europäisch-Westafrikanischen Handels vor der industriellen Revolution am Beispiel der Textilien.* Studien zur Kulturkunde, 105 Band. Köln: Rudiger Koppe Verlag.

Reynolds, Barrie. 1968. *The Material Culture of the Peoples of the Gwembe Valley.* Manchester: Manchester University Press.

Ribeiro, Aileen. 1991. Provision of Ready-Made and Second-Hand Clothing in the Eighteenth Century in England. In Centro italiano per lo studio della storia del tessuto, ed., *Per una storia della moda pronta: Problemi e ricerche: Atti del V Convegno internazionale del CISST,* Milano, 26–28 February 1990, pp. 85–94.

Richards, Audery I. [1939] 1969. *Land, Labour, and Diet in Northern Rhodesia.* Oxford: Oxford University Press.

Roberts, Andrew D. 1970. Pre-colonial Trade in Zambia. *African Social Research* 10:715–46.

———. 1976. *A History of Zambia.* London: Heinemann.

Robertson, Roland. 1992. *Globalization: Social Theory and Global Culture.* Newbery Park, CA: Sage Publications.

Roche, Daniel. 1996. *The Culture of Clothing: Dress and Fashion in the Ancien Régime.* Translated by Jean Birrell. Cambridge: Cambridge University Press.

Roeber, Carter A. 1994. Moneylending, Trust, and the Culture of Commerce in Kabwe, Zambia. *Research in Economic Anthropology* 15:39–61.

Roseberry, William. 1996. The Rise of Yuppie Coffees and the Reimagination of Class in the United States. *American Anthropologist* 98(4):762–75.

Rotberg, Robert I. 1962. Rural Rhodesian Markets. In Paul Bohannan and George Dalton, eds., *Markets in Africa.* Evanston: Northwestern University Press, pp. 581–600.

———. 1965a. *Christian Missionaries and the Creation of Northern Rhodesia, 1880–1924.* Princeton: Princeton University Press.

———. 1965b. *The Rise of Nationalism in Central Africa: The Making of Malawi and Zambia, 1873–1964.* Cambridge: Harvard University Press.

Rude, Darlene. 1996. Nagging Wife–Killer Freed after Custody: A Gender Analysis of Domestic Homicide in Zambia. M.A. thesis, University of East Anglia.

Schoss, Johanna. 1996. Dressed to "Shine": Work, Leisure, and Style in Malindi, Kenya. In Hildi Hendrickson, ed., *Clothing and Difference: Embodied Identities in Colonial and Post-colonial Africa.* Durham: Duke University Press, pp. 157–88.

Schuster, Ilsa M. G. 1979. *New Women of Lusaka.* Palo Alto, CA: Mayfield Publishing.

Seidel, Jutta Zander. 1991. Ready-to-Wear Clothing in Germany in the Sixteenth and Seventeenth Centuries: New Ready-Made Garments and Second-Hand Clothes Trade. In Centro italiano per lo studio della storia del tessuto, ed., *Per una storia della moda pronta: Problemi e ricerche: Atti del V Convegno internazionale del CISST,* Milan, 26–28 February 1990, pp. 9–16.

Sendwe, Floribert Kabongo. 1994. La production et l'importation des produits textiles au Congo-Belge, 1928–1960. Travail présenté en vue de l'obtention du grade de gradué en histoire. Université de Lubumbashi.

Sennett, Richard. 1992. *The Fall of Public Man.* New York: Knopf, 1977. New York: W. W. Norton and Company.

Seshamani, Venkatesh. 1994. Inflation, Policy Reforms, and the Manufacturing Sector in Zambia. In Moses Banda, Caleb Fundanga, and Chiselekwe Ng'andwe, eds., *Economic Development and Democracy: Critical Issues in the Third Republic.* Lusaka: Economics Association of Zambia, pp. 119–27.

Shammas, Carole. 1990. *The Pre-industrial Consumer in England and America.* Oxford: Clarendon Press.

Sharpe, Pamela. 1995. "Cheapness and Economy": Manufacturing and Retailing Ready-Made Clothing in London and Essex, 1830–1850. *Textile History* 26(2):203–13.

Shinkanga, Monica G. 1996. *Child Sexual Abuse in Zambia: Results from a Rapid Assess-*

ment of Child Sexual Exploitation in Chainda, Kamanga, and Luangwa Bridge. Lusaka: YWCA.

Siyolwe, Yolishwa W. 1994. Makwebo Women: A Study of the Socio-economic Activities of a Select Group of Women Traders in Lusaka, Zambia, 1980–1990. Master of Letters thesis, University of Oxford.

Smith, Brian H. 1990. *More Than Altruism: The Politics of Private Foreign Aid.* Princeton: Princeton University Press.

Sogge, D., ed. 1996. *Compassion and Calculation: The Business of Private Foreign Aid.* London: Pluto Press.

Spufford, Margaret. 1984. *The Great Reclothing of Rural England: Petty Chapmen and Their Wares in the Seventeenth Century.* London: Hambledon Press.

Stallybrass, Peter. 1996. Worn Worlds: Clothes and Identity on the Renaissance Stage. In Margreta de Grazia, Maureen Quilligan, and Peter Stallybrass, eds., *Subject and Object in Renaissance Culture.* Cambridge: Cambridge University Press, pp. 289–320.

Steiner, Christopher B. 1985. Another Image of Africa: Toward an Ethnohistory of European Cloth Marketed in West Africa, 1873–1960. *Ethnohistory* 32(2):91–110.

———. 1994. *African Art in Transit.* Cambridge: Cambridge University Press.

St. John, Christopher. 1970. Kazembe and the Tanganyika-Nyasa Corridor, 1800–1890. In Richard Gray and David Birmingham, eds., *Pre-colonial African Trade: Essays on Trade in Central and Eastern Africa before 1900.* London: Oxford University Press, pp. 202–30.

Südwind Institut für Ökonomie und Ökumene. 1994. Der deutschen alte Kleider: Schaden Kleider Spenden der Zweidrittelwelt? (German old clothes: do clothes donations hurt the Second and Third Worlds?). Siegburg: Südwind.

Sutherland-Harris, Nicola. 1970. Zambian Trade with Zumbo in the Eighteenth Century. In Richard Gray and David Birmingham, eds., *Pre-colonial African Trade: Essays on Trade in Central and Eastern Africa before 1900.* London: Oxford University Press, pp. 231–41.

Swedish Red Cross. 1992a. In Need of Clothes: Second-Hand Clothing for Poland. Stockholm.

———. 1992b. In Need of Clothes: Second-Hand Clothes for Uganda, Zimbabwe, Mozambique, Sierra Leone, and Vietnam. Stockholm.

Tapson, Winifred. 1957. *Old Timer.* Cape Town: Howard Timmins.

Tarlo, Emma. 1996. *Clothing Matters: Dress and Identity in India.* Chicago: University of Chicago Press.

Thirsk, Joan. 1978. *Economic Policy and Projects: The Development of a Consumer Society in Early Modern England.* Oxford: Clarendon.

Turner, Terence S. 1993. The Social Skin. In Jeremy Cherfas and Roger Lewin, eds., *Not Work Alone: A Cross-Cultural View of Activities Superfluous to Survival.* London: Temple Smith, 1980. Reprinted in Catherine B. Burroughs and Jeffrey Ehrenreich, eds., *Reading the Social Body.* Iowa City: University of Iowa Press, pp. 15–39.

United Nations. 1994. *Commodity Trade Statistics 1994: United States.* Statistical Papers, series D, vol. 44, nos. 1–13.

———. 1995. *International Trade Statistics Yearbook 1994.* Vol. 2, *Trade by Commodity.* New York: United Nations.

———. 1996. *International Trade Statistics Yearbook 1995.* Vol. 2, *Trade by Commodity.* New York: United Nations.

United Nations and Economic Commission for Africa (UN/ECA). 1964. *Report of the UN/ECA/FAO Economic Survey Mission on the Economic Development of Zambia (Seers Report)*. Ndola: Falcon press.

United Nations Development Programme (UNDP). 1995. *Human Development Report 1995*. New York: Oxford University Press.

United Nations. International Trade Branch. 1998. Unpublished data on SITC 269 (worn clothing): imports into Zambia reported by major trade partners, 1990–97.

University of Zambia (UNZA), Central Statistical Office, and Demographic and Health Surveys. 1992. *Zambia Demographic and Health Survey 1992: Preliminary Report*. IRD/Macro International.

Urban African Budget Surveys held in Northern Rhodesia May to August, 1960. 1965. Reprint, Lusaka: Central Statistical Office.

U.S. and Foreign Commercial Service and U.S. Department of State. 1997. *Used Clothing Market Overview*. Washington, DC: Department of Commerce.

U.S. Department of Commerce. 1993. Used Apparel Markets in Sub-Saharan Africa: Market Notes and Contacts. Washington, DC: International Trade Administration, Office of Africa.

Vail, Leroi, and Landeg White. 1991. *Power and the Praise Poem: Southern African Voices in History*. London: James Currey.

van Groen, Barth, and Piet Lozer. 1976. La structure et l'organisation de la friperie à Tunis. *Groupe d'Études Tunis* (Université Libre Amsterdam).

Veblen, Thorstein. [1899] 1957. *The Theory of the Leisure Class*. New York: Mentor.

Verbeek, Leon. 1987. *Ombres et clarières: Histoire de l'implantation de l'église catholique dans le diocèse de Sakania, Zaire, 1910–1970*. Rome: Libreria Ateneo Salesiano, Instituto Storico Salesiano.

Watts, Michael. 1994. What Difference Does Difference Make? *Review of International Political Economy* 1(3):563–70.

Weatherill, Lorna. 1988. *Consumer Behavior and Material Culture in Britain, 1660–1760*. London: Routledge.

Webb, Douglas. 1996. The Socio-economic Impact of HIV/AIDS in Zambia. *SafAIDS News* 4(4):2–10.

Weiner, Annette B. 1992. *Inalienable Possessions: The Paradox of Keeping-while-Giving*. Berkeley: University of California Press.

Weiss, Brad. 1996. Dressing at Death: Clothing, Time, and Memory in Buhaya, Tanzania. In Hildi Hendrickson, ed., *Clothing and Difference: Embodied Identities in Colonial and Post-colonial Africa*. Durham: Duke University Press, pp. 133–54.

White Fathers. 1931. *Ifya Bukaya: Second Bemba Reader*. Chilubula, Zambia: White Fathers.

Wicks, Rick, and Arne Bigsten. 1996. Used Clothes as Development Aid: The Political Economy of Rags. Report of a study about the effects of freight aid conducted for Swedish International Development Cooperation Agency (SIDA). Department of Economics, Göteborg University.

Wilk, Richard. 1990. Consumer Goods as Dialogue about Development. *Culture and History* 7:79–100.

———. 1997. A Critique of Desire: Distaste and Dislike in Consumer Behavior. *Consumption, Markets, and Culture* 1(2):175–96.

Williame, J.-C. 1983. Le Congo dans la guerre: La coopération economique Belgo-Alliée de 1940 à 1944. In Académie Royale des Sciences d'Outre-Mer, ed., *Le Congo durant la Seconde Guerre Mondiale: Recueil d'études.* Brussels: Académie Royale des Sciences d'Outre-Mer, pp. 213–52.

Wilmsen, Edwin. 1989. *Land Filled with Flies.* Chicago: University of Chicago Press.

Wilson, Elizabeth. 1985. *Adorned in Dreams: Fashion and Modernity.* Berkeley: University of California Press.

Wilson, Godfrey. 1941–42. An Essay on the Economics of Detribalization. Vols. 1 and 2. *Rhodes-Livingstone Papers,* nos. 5 and 6.

Winchester, Sarah Hart. 1995. Textile Recycling 101. *Scrap Processing and Recycling,* 24 May.

Woldring, Klaas, ed. 1984. *Beyond Political Independence: Zambia's Development Predicament in the 1980s.* The Hague: Mouton.

World Bank. 1994. Zambia Poverty Assessment. Vol. 1, Main Report (no. 12985-ZA). Human Resources Division, Southern Africa Development, Africa Regional Office.

Wright, Marcia. 1993. Cloth Weaving in the Rukwa Valley: 1915 as a Moment within a History of Production and Marketless Exchange. Paper presented at conference, Artisans, Cloth, and the World Economy: Textile Manufacturing and Distribution in Africa and Southern Asia, April, Dartmouth College, Hanover, NH.

Yelengi, Nasa T. 1997. The PFB Railroad, Society, and Culture in Rural Katanga (Colonial Zaire). *Africa* (Rome) 52(2):182–211.

Young Women's Christian Association (YWCA). 1994. Violence against Women: Zambian Perspectives. An Evaluation Report of the Initiatives of the YWCA of Zambia. Lusaka: YWCA.

Zambia. 1971. *House of Chiefs Debates.* Tuesday, 28 September–Wednesday, 29 September 1971. Lusaka: Government Printer.

———. 1995. *Internal Migration and Urbanization: Aspects of 1990 Census of Population, Housing, and Agriculture.* Lusaka: Central Statistical Office, Population and Demography Division.

———. 1997. *New Consumer Price Index, December 1997 Release.* Lusaka: Central Statistical Office, Prices and Consumption Studies Branch.

Zambia Industrial and Mining Corporation (Zimco). 1976. *Directory of Zambian Industry.* Lusaka: Zimco Information and Publicity Unit.

Newspapers

United States

Big Red News. 1990. Clash at Domsey: Pro Union Workers vs. Scabs. 21 July, p. 3.

Business America. 1988. Now Is the Time for U.S. Firms to Look Again at Sub-Saharan Africa. 25 April, p. 18.

———. 1991. Reputation Is Growing as Good Place to Do Business: Togo World Trade Outlook 1991. 22 April, p. 17.

Business First–Columbus. 1989. Labels Don't Matter When You Buy Clothes by the Pound. 6 November, section 1, p. 1.

Chapel Hill News. 1997. Advertisement for jeans trade-in at Hudson Belk Department Store. 10 October, p. A5.

Chicago Tribune. 1992. Firms Told to Look to Africa. 26 March, business section, p. 1.

———. 1992. French Firm Helping Jobless Move from Rags to Enrichment. 13 October, section 3, pp. 1, 6.

———. 1998. The Miracle Merchants: Myths of Child Sponsorship. 15 March, section 2; 22 March, section 2.

———. 1998. Looking for Job, Outfit to Fit. 5 October, section 2, pp. 1, 4.

Courier-Journal (Louisville, KY). 1996. Old Clothes? Your Donation's Destination Could Be a Thrift Shop or a Ship Overseas: If You Care, It Pays to Ask. 30 December, p. F1.

Houston Chronicle. 1998. Out of Houston: Port Trade with Africa on the Rise: U.S. Initiatives May lead to a Boost. 2 April, business section, p. 1.

Journal of Commerce. 1978. Ships and Shipping. 23 May, p. 1.

———. 1996. Ships and Shipping. 1 March, 12 June, 7 November.

———. 1997. Tradeleads. 9 April, 19 November.

———. 1998. Caribbean, African Bills Fail in Congress. 19 October, p. 3A.

———. 1999. Chinese Web Site Hints at Textile Strategy. 29 March, pp. 1A, 3A.

———. 1999. Tradeleads. 20 April.

Los Angeles Times. 1987. Charity Thrifts: Donated Goods Form Heart of Billion-Dollar Family Empire. 27 September, part V.

———. 1992. Garb Go-Round: Recycling of Clothing in Thrift Shops and Elsewhere Keeps Tons and Tons from Taking Up Vital Landfill Space. 29 October, p. J16.

———. 1997. Turning Donated Rags into Riches. 28 July, pp. A1, A13.

Milwaukee Journal Sentinel. 1999. Goodwill Collection Proposal Upsets Other Charities. 11 February, p. 1.

The News and Observer (Raleigh). 1997. Old-Sneaker Prices Go Air-Borne. 22 November, pp. A1, A18.

Newsday (New York). 1998. Making Money off U.S. Charity: Sales of Donated Clothes Abroad Fueling Bin Thefts. 22 February, p. A30.

New York Daily News. 1991. Not So Sweet Charity: Domsey Strikers Rip Clothing Connection. 23 April, pp. 20, 22.

The New York Times. 1985. Used-Clothes Dealers Tied to Salvation Army Payoffs. 25 May, section 1, p. 6.

———. 1987. Used U.S. Clothes a Best Seller in Africa. 16 February, section 1, p. 48.

———. 1987. West African Women: Political Inroads. 10 August, p. A8.

———. 1989. Zambia's Social Fabric. 26 November, section XX, pp. 6, 26.

———. 1992. Clothing Bins Being Removed as Eyesores. 9 February, p. L1.

———. 1994. Used American Jeans Power a Thriving Industry Abroad. 22 August, pp. A1, C3.

———. 1995. In the High Season for Giving, Competition for Castoffs Begins. 14 November, p. B7.

———. 1996. Glad Rags to Riches in the Resale Market. 4 June, p. B11.

———. 1997. U.S. Victory Is Empty to Brooklyn Workers. 9 June, p. A15.

———. 1997. Secondhand Souvenirs. 28 September, travel section, p. 27.

———. 1997. Clothes Sold by Pound Attract Mexican Buyers. 12 November, p. A14.

———. 1997. Big-Men's Wear, from a Stranger's Closet. 14 December, p. B14.

The Plain Dealer. 1998. America's Old Clothes Finding Homes Abroad. 25 January, p. 6H.

Scramento Bee. 1990. Cash from Castoffs: "Ragman 1" Helps Clothe the Poor Worldwide. 26 March, p. C1.

The Sun (Baltimore). 1997. Ugandans Hunt for Fashion Castoffs: Fashion: Third World

People Dress like New in Secondhand Clothes and Shoes from the US. 28 September, p. 1K.

———. 1997. Whitehouse: One of the Giants of Used Clothing. 28 September, p. 27A.

The Tampa Tribune. 1998. Red Cross Needs Cash to help after Georges. 3 October, p. 3.

Wall Street Journal. 1997. Second-Hand Rows: These Thrift Shops are Classy—and Doing a Booming Business. 20 January, pp. 1, 6.

Women's Wear Daily. 1991. ILGWU Protests at Salvation Army. 8 May, p. 25.

Zambia

Financial Mail. 1997. Do We Still Need SGS? 22–28 July, p. 5.

———. 1997. Dunlop Forcibly Abandons Manufacturing. 16–22 September, p. 8.

———. 1998. Stalls Still Go Begging at New Market. 3–9 November, p. 2.

Financial Times. 1999. Guys and Girls . . . Fashion for Zambia. 2–8 August, p. 14.

Lovelines. 1994. Kitchen Parties an Outlet for Lesbianism? (by a correspondent). October, pp. 4–5.

The Post. 1994. Soweto Marketeers Plan to Riot if Their Stalls Are Razed. 30 September, p. 4.

———. 1994. Soweto Market Traders Sue Government. 7 October, p. 4.

———. 1994. Soweto Marketeers Agree to Vacate the Site after 45 Days Grace Period. 28 October, p. 3.

———. 1995. Announcement by the Ministry of Finance: Pre-shipment Inspection Program. 11 July, p. 3.

———. 1995. Price in Eastern Province. 11 July, p. 12.

———. 1997. FTJ Threatens Customs Clerk over His Imported Neckties. 9 April, p. 1.

———. 1997. Ackermans Opens Shops on C/belt. 25 April.

———. 1997. Dora Siliya's Minis Annoy ZNBC Bosses. 22 May, pp. 1, 6.

———. 1997. Vera's Mannerisms (letter to the editor). 29 May, p. 9.

———. 1997. Vera Chiluba Defended (letter to the editor). 4 June, p. 11.

———. 1997. Poverty Datum Line (editorial). 18 July, p. 12.

———. 1997. Caution Kabila (editorial). 22 July, p. 10.

———. 1997. Lusaka Council Sets Tuntemba Ablaze. 11 August, pp. 1, 3.

———. 1997. Vera's Mannerisms Were Disgusting (letter to the editor). 26 November, p. 7.

———. 1998. Salaula Traders Are Criminals, says Mwiinga. 18 February, p. 5.

———. 1998. Non-traditional Exports Increase. 15 April.

———. 1998. NGOs Gang Up against Vera. 20 May, p. 1.

———. 1999. Clothes at Queenspark. 2 March, p. 8.

Profit. 1994. Smaller Manufacturers Also Hit by SAP: Len Aked Looks at the Effect of Liberalisation on Smaller Companies. January, pp. 12–13.

Sunday Mail. 1995. Don't Be Deceived by My Wearing Suits: Between the Lines by Geoff Zulu. 12 February, p. 5.

———. 1997. Lusaka Riots Have Lessons for All Sides. 17 August, p. 5.

———. 1998. Why Are Marketeers Ditching New Soweto? 15 February, p. 7.

Sunday Times of Zambia. 1986. Photograph caption: "Typical Scene of Zambian Market." 16 November.

———. 1993. "Salaula" Levy Quashed. 19 September.

———. 1995. Priests' Tax Evasion Tricks Exposed. 7 May, p. 1.

———. 1997. Chiluba Opens New Market. 10 August, p. 1.

———. 1998. Revisit Salaula Tax. 8 February.

———. 1998. Salaula Medically Safe. 22 February.

———. 1999. Stalls Razing Leaves Lusaka Vendors in Shock. 2 May, p. 9.

Times of Zambia. 1981. Made in Zambia? Kapwelwa Musonda on Tuesday. 11 August, p. 4.

———. 1985. Dress Decently (letter to the editor). 4 February.

———. 1985. Kitchen Parties Turned into Beer Dens. 5 December.

———. 1986. High Prices Killing Clothing Industry. 21 June.

———. 1986. Salaula Defended. 21 June.

———. 1986. Stop Salaula Imports, Urges Trader. 1 July.

———. 1986. How Can Police in "Pata-Pata" Nab Thieves? 26 October.

———. 1987. Erring Soldiers Punished. 28 January.

———. 1987. Poorly Dressed Teachers (letter to the editor). 28 April.

———. 1987. Dress Up Newspaper Sellers (letter to the editor). 6 June.

———. 1988. Garment Sector Has Stagnated. 30 June, pp. 12, 14.

———. 1989. Garment Industry Demise Blamed on Imported Clothes. 25th Zambia International Trade Fair Supplement, 29 June, pp. 5, 11.

———. 1990. Refugees' Clothes Racket Exposed. 10 January, p. 1.

———. 1990. "Salaula" Sales Okay—Sata. 10 January, p. 2.

———. 1991. Shops Shift to Salaula. 13 June.

———. 1991. Salaula Trade Faces Doom. 19 November.

———. 1992. Customs Change Import Rules. 28 June, p. 7.

———. 1992. Salaula Sale: Advertisement by the Rotary Club of Kabwe. 28 August.

———. 1993. Ban "Salaula" Traders. 1 March.

———. 1993. State Won't Ban "Salaula." 1 June.

———. 1993. 18 Firms Fold Up. 7 June.

———. 1993. Street Vendors to Pay Levy. 7 June.

———. 1993. Announcement from the PTC about cash-on-delivery service by Sonny Boys mail-order specialists from Cape Town. 19 June, p. 5.

———. 1993. YMCA Donates "Salaula." 5 August, p. 3.

———. 1993. "Salaula" Loophole Sealed. 9 September, p. 1.

———. 1993. Clothing Firms Shut Down. 13 September.

———. 1993. Erring Customs Officials to Be Axed. 7 October, p. 3.

———. 1993. Kitwe Shocker! Thieves Strip Body at Cemetery. 22 October, p. 1.

———. 1993. Cash Lust Leads Cemetery Looters to Strip Bodies of Clothes. Feature article by Ben Phiri. 3 November, p. 9.

———. 1993. Five Raped after Koffi Rhumba Show. 6 December.

———. 1993. NUCIW to Launch Anti-salaula Campaign. 17 December.

———. 1994. "Salaula" Splits Church. 27 May, p. 1.

———. 1995. Photo of shoppers lined up in front of recently opened PEP shop in Lusaka. 1 May, p. 5.

———. 1995. New SA Shop Causes Stir in Lusaka. 6 May, p. 7.

———. 1995. Dar Port Records Low Cargo. 25 July, p. 7.

———. 1995. Wanted: Quality Clothing in Zambia. By Samuel Ngoma. 26 August, p. 4.

———. 1995. SA Shop Moans. November, n.d.

———. 1996. Suspects Admit Stealing from the Dead. 7 August, pp. 1, 3.

———. 1996. When Grave Clothes Reappear. 8 August, pp. 1–2.

———. 1996. Ndola in Reburial Fracas. 9 August, p. 3.

———. 1996. High Class Fashion Shop Eyes Lusaka. 23 September, p. 7.

———. 1996. Villagers Barter Crops for "Salaula." Provincial round-up by Lawrence Liandisha. 13 October.

———. 1997. Mulungushi Textiles Stirs Back to Life. 17 February.

———. 1997. Graves Ransacked. 25 April, p. 1.

———. 1997. The Graveyard Prowler Confesses . . . "I Stole from the Dead." 30 April, p. 1.

———. 1997. Export Zone Concept on Course, Says Nkole. 5 August, p. 7.

———. 1997. Export Zones Good for Zambia. 9 September.

———. 1998. Lusaka Salaula Traders Protest. 5 February.

———. 1998. Grave Thieves Admit Trespassing Charge. 5 February.

———. 1998. Salaula Duty Suspended. 7 March, p. 1.

———. 1998. Lusaka City Market: From a Showpiece to a White Elephant. 13 June.

———. 1998. Food Basket Tops K200,000: How Do People Survive? 8 July, p. 5.

———. 1999. Kafue Textiles Audit Begins. 16 August, p. 7.

The Weekly Post. 1993. Even Christian Women Are Dressing to "Kill." By Anthony Kunda. 16–22 April.

———. 1993. Aren't We All Just a Secondhand Lot? By Jowie Mwiinga. 2–8 July, p. 7.

———. 1993. PTC Suspends Mail Order System. 11–19 August, p. 11.

———. 1993. First Lady's Dressing Too Flashy (letter to the editor). 20–26 August, p. 2.

Zambia Daily Mail. 1982. Why Zambian Women Prefer Foreign Dresses? Local Fashions Not Inferior. 7 January, p. 7.

———. 1984. Adolescents Should Not Attend Kitchen Parties (letter to the editor). 27 November.

———. 1989. Between the Lines. By Geoff Zulu. 21 April.

———. 1990. Chilambe Goes Anti-salaula. By B. Katongo. 26 January.

———. 1992. Salaula Wreaks Havoc. 28 August.

———. 1993. 18 Firms Shut. 25 May, p. 1.

———. 1993. State to Check "Salaula" Imports. 19 June, p. 1.

———. 1993. Salaula Traders See Red over Pending Ban. 21 June, p. 7.

———. 1993. Do Not Ban Salaula—ZNCCI. 26 June, p. 3.

———. 1993. Vendors to Pay K5,000 Levy. 20 July, p. 7.

———. 1994. Vendors Blasted for Undressing Woman. 23 March.

———. 1994. Check Those Cross-Border Women "Salaula" Dealers. 16 October, p. 4.

———. 1995. Announcement by the Zambia Revenue Authority: Scheme for the Pre-clearance of Imported Goods. 4 March, p. 2.

———. 1995. "Striptease" at Border Irks Zambian Women. 26 April, p. 6.

———. 1995. Soweto on Fire: Inferno Shocks Marketeers as 800 Stalls Are Burned to Ashes. 29 April, p. 1.

———. 1995. Zimbabwe Locks up 700 Zambians. 17 August, p. 1.

———. 1995. Why Prefer Imported Goods? 1 September, p. 5.

———. 1996. Salaula: People Walking Dead? 24 August, pp. 1, 5.

———. 1996. Chiluba Bends Backwards for Church, Vendors. 10 December, p. 4.

———. 1997. Lusaka City Market Doomed? 2 September, p. 7.

———. 1998. Let Not Bad Rituals Hijack Noble Meaning of Kitchen Parties. Story by Isabel Chimangeni and interviews by Alinedi Ngoma. 11 January, p. 5.

———. 1998. Budget Address by the Honourable Ronald D. S. Penza, MP, Minister of Finance and Economic Development, Delivered to the National Assembly on Friday. 30 January, pp. 3–7.

————. 1998. Salaula Dealers Call for Tax Relief. 4 February.

————. 1998. Salaula Dirge Persists. Feature article by Sylvia Mweetwa. 10 February.

————. 1998. Best Attire in Town Is from Salaula. By Newton Sibanda. 18 February, p. 7.

————. 1998. Parley Bars Luo over Short Dress. 4 April, p. 1.

————. 1998. Thanks So Much for Rejecting Salaula Tax (letter to the editor). 9 April.

————. 1998. Vendors Ready to Pay Tax. 10 June.

————. 1998. Living from a Wheelbarrow. 15 July, p. 7.

————. 1998. Vendors' Taxation Explained. 17 July.

————. 1998. Edith Nawakwi Event. 17 September.

————. 1998. Gender Focus: Is Parliament Dress Code Exclusively for Female MPs? 24 September.

————. 1998. The Speaker Must Apologise to Nawakwi (letter to the editor). 24 September.

————. 1998. Gender Sensitive Eroding Our Culture. 5 October.

————. 1999. LCC Clears Vendors. 29 April, p. 1.

Other Newspapers and News Services

Africa News Service. 1988. Bits and Pieces. 25 January.

————. 1997. Zambia: Development Aid from People to People Cries for Tax Relief. 4 November.

————. 1997. Ghana Bans Imports of Second-Hand Goods from EU Countries. 31 December.

The African Listener. 1957. The Well-Dressed Woman. Part 1: March, p. 12. Part 2: April, p. 9.

BBC World Broadcasts. 1980. Middle East and Africa: Zambia: Restrictions on Import of Non-essential Goods. 17 June.

————. 1998. GBC Radio, Accra, Ghana: End of EU Export of "Green Waste" Worries Second-Hand Dealers. 6 January.

Central African Post. 1949. Some illusions of the Bantu. 27 October, p. 5.

The Daily Telegraph (United Kingdom). 1997. Queens Awards: Rags to Third World Riches. 21 April, p. 29.

Financial Times (United Kingdom). 1998. The Textiles Sector: From Rags to Riches. 21 April, p. 6.

The Herald (Zimbabwe). 1994. Second-Hand Clothes Imports Curtailed. 10 February.

The Independent (London). 1999. Gucchi? No, Darling, It's Oxfam. 10 February, features section, p. 8.

The Indian Ocean Newsletter (Indigo Publications). 1998. US Doing Well in the Rag Trade. 10 January, economics section, N. 794.

Inter Press Service. 1994. Cameroon-Economy: Secondhand Clothes Market Booms, But . . . 10 October.

IPS Service Francophone. 1998. La Friperie refait les garde-robes dégarnis. 4 July.

Knack (Belgium). 1996. Hoedt u voor zakkenrollers (Beware of pickpockets). 29 May, pp. 20–23.

MNet (South Africa). 1997. *Carte Blanche* program on secondhand clothing imports and charitable organizations. 9 November.

NBC Nightly News. 1997. Old Clothes Donated to Charity Sometimes Are Sold for Huge Profits Overseas. Transcript of news feature. 7 December.

Politiken (Denmark). 1996. Hjælpeorganisationer strides om brugt tøj (Charitable organizations fight over used clothing). 28 August, section 1, p. 13; section 4, p. 3.

Southern Africa Chronicle (South Africa). 1996. Zimbabwe: An Yves Saint Laurent Jacket for a Few Cents. 7 October, p. 15.

TASS (Telegraph Agency of the Soviet Union). 1993. South African and Namibian Police Detain Arms Smugglers. 9 November.

The Toronto Star. 1993. The Vicious Cycle of Textile Trade. 13 November, p. B5.

United Press International. 1991. Clothing Company Ordered to Rehire 200 Strikers. 1 August.

Archives

Archives Africaines, Ministère des affaires étrangères et du commerce extérieur, Brussels.

OC 393/201.385.01. 1935. Renseignements economique sur different pays. No. 25 Japon.

National Archives of Zambia, Lusaka

NAZ/KDF 6/1/11. 1923–24. Annual Report: Mweru-Luapula, Kawambwa Subdistrict.

NAZ/KDF 6/1/11. 1926. Annual Report Mweru-Luapula. Native Trade and Industries.

NAZ/MH 1/5/2. 1931–62. Public Health/Infectious Disease Regulation.

NAZ/SEC 1/289. 1927–47. Customs Treaties and Agreements. Congo Basin Treaty. Vol. 1. J. C. Maxwell, Governor's Office, Livingstone, to L. S. Amery, Colonial Office. 14 September 1927.

NAZ/SEC 1/1363. 1943–49. Report by Mr. A. L. Saffrey on Cost of Living.

NAZ/SEC 1/1970. 1943. Public Opinion Reports (Central Province).

NAZ/SEC 2/294. 1939–47. Box System.

NAZ/SEC 2/875. 1948. Kawambwa Tour Reports. No. 3 of 1948. Appendix 8: Trade.

NAZ/SEC 2/876. 1949. Kawambwa Tour Reports. No. 4 of 1949. Annexure 5: Trade.

NAZ/SEC 2/877. 1950–51. Kawambwa Tour Reports. No. 2 of 1950. Annexure 3: Visit to Kasenga Boma; D.C.'s comments. No. 9 of 1950. Annexure 2: Trade.

NAZ/SEC 2/878. 1951. Kawambwa Tour Reports. Comment on tour report 6/1951. No. 6 of 1951. Annexure 5: African Trading. No. 10 of 1951. Annexure 6: Trade and Communication.

NAZ/SEC 2/879. 1952. Kawambwa Tour Reports. No. 5 of 1952. Annexure 2: Trade and Industry.

NAZ/SEC 2/882. 1955–56. Kawambwa Tour Reports. No. 8 of 1955. Annexure 4: Special Annexure on Kasenga Riots.

NAZ/SEC 2/894. 1949. Fort Rosebery Tour Reports. No. 13 of 1949. Chief Chimese's area.

NAZ/SEC 2/896. 1951–52. Mansa Tour Reports. Comment on tour report 3/1951.

NAZ/SEC 2/902. 1954–55. Mansa Tour Reports. Fort Rosebery. No. 25 of 1954. Annexure 7: Village Shops and Trade.

NAZ/SEC 2/1234. 1940–49. Uniforms for Chiefs (Robes).

NAZ/SEC 4/1863. 1953. Cost of Living Index: Africans. Vol. 2. Letter from J. C. Mitchell to Director of Cost of Living Commission, 28 January.

NAZ/ZA 7/4/26. 1931. Mweru-Luapula Province Tour Reports. Letters appended to tour report of Kawambwa District.

Pretoria Archives, South Africa
SAA/SAB/DEA 204 A10/16/IX. 1928–42. Prohibited and Restricted Imports. Second-Hand Clothing.

Zambia Consolidated Copper Mines Archives, Ndola
NCCM/KMA 20. 1943. Comments on the Saffrey Report. H. H. Field, Compound Manager, Mufulira, to General Manager, Mufulira, 13 July.
NCCM/KMA 131. 1945. Minutes of the sixth meeting of the Supplies Board (Government Committee), 20 March.

Index

advertising: of clothing and textiles in colonial newspapers, 47–48; in visual and print media today, 196, 225

AIDS, and secondhand clothes, 231, 253

Amvets (American Veterans of Foreign Wars), 105, 123

Andersen, Hans Christian, 1, 249

Angola, transborder trade, 25, 121, 154

apamwamba, Zambian high-income group, 186, 190–91; and clothing, 196, 205, 213

Appadurai, Arjun, 13, 184, 196, 205, 213

barter, of secondhand clothing, 142, 148, 150, 154. *See also* weapons

Belgian Congo, 29–31, 35, 36, 45, 47, 61–68; in regional secondhand clothing trade, 64–70, 71–76, 77, 89; role of Mokambo, 70–72

Belgium: export from Belgium-Luxembourg today, 130; historical role in international secondhand clothing trade, 66, 105, 108, 112–14, 119

Bemba, ethnic group in Zambia: colonial interest in clothing, 27; *Ifya Bukaya* language reader, 23, 29, 39, 260n. 4

Benin, role in transshipment of secondhand clothing, 15, 125

Bermingham, Ann, 5–6, 13, 259n. 3

Bettison, David, 44

blue jeans. *See* jeans

botiques (sic), upscale secondhand clothing stands in Zambia, 156, 170, 181, 183, 185

Bourdieu, Pierre, 266n. 4

"box system," for storing clothing, 35; and legal regulations, 35. *See also* clothing, as wealth

brand names, 182, 192, 225

Broken Hill (now Kabwe), mineworkers and clothing, 27, 34, 36, 40, 48, 52

Carrousel Shopping Centre, Lusaka, 170, 183

charitable organizations, and secondhand clothing, 11, 100–102, 103, 104, 105, 254; clothes scandal in Britain, 123; Abbé Pierre, 100; Goodwill Industries, 23, 100–103, 124; Hu-

mana, 100–102; Oxfam, 100, 104, 130; Salvation Army, 11, 103–4, 112–13, 124–25; St. Vincent de Paul, 100–102, 105, 124. *See also* DAPP

Chiluba, Frederick, Zambia's president since 1991, 92, 232; controversies over dress, 93; "new culture" dress style, 91, 94, 95, 250. *See also* MMD; third republic

Chiluba, Vera, first lady of Zambia, 92, 247; dress style, 94–95; and Hope foundation (NGO), 94–95, 130, 247

Chipungu, Samuel, Zambian MP, 240

Chisco Asaar, Ltd., Zambian general wholesaler, 135

chitenge, printed cloth, 37, 82, 201–5, 212, 215; growth of import, 196, 236, 259; local production, 202; "national dress," 82–83; popularity as dress fabric, 92, 177, 181, 195; versatility of use, 204; young women's attitude toward chitenge fashions, 204

chokako weka (Nyanja expression), "move yourself," 227, 228

clothing: clothing as status marker, 4, 8, 55–57; colonial attitude toward African clothing, 33, 40, 45, 48; and gender relations, 40, 57–59, 196–97, 228; historical importance in Africa, 10; mission influence, 26, 31–32; and religion, 197, 267n. 6; as wealth, 35, 36, 40

clothing, care for, 28, 198–99, 204

clothing, meaning of: display, 38–39, 52, 200, 227; in performance, 52, 196, 207, 225

clothing, special commodity, 3, 4–6

clothing competence, 196–201, 204

clothing consumption survey, 186–92

clothing producers. *See* garment manufacturing

Colson, Elizabeth, 28, 42, 58

Comaroff, John, and Jean Comaroff, 23, 27

commodity chains/circuits in global apparel market, 2, 19, 241, 255

commodity fetishism, 5

consumer demand, 167; buying practices, 186, 189, 190, 194–98; gender differences, 190; pay cycles, 167; seasonal fluctuations, 167

consumption: anthropological research, 12,

methodology (*continued*)
  of representatives of charitable organiza-
    tions, 18; statistical sources, 101, 114–17,
    265nn. 4, 5; student essays, 185–86, 207–8,
    267n. 3; survey of clothing consumption,
    184, 186–92, 266n. 4; survey of traders and
    wholesalers, 131–34, 265–66n. 1
Mexico: prohibiting secondhand clothing imports, 112, 116; transborder smuggling from
  the U.S., 115
migration, 31, 35; and clothing consumption
  knowledge, 27–28, 29–32, 57; *icibalo* (contract labor), 69; returning migrants and clothing, 35, 69–70; rural-urban, 40, 57, 84; to the
  Belgian Congo, 33, 67, 69–70; from Eastern
  Province to Southern Rhodesia, 34; from
  Gwembe Valley to Southern Rhodesia, 27–
  28, 32
Miller, Daniel, 3, 4, 6, 14, 39
miniskirts, 214; controversies about, 81–82;
  and high-profile women, 218; and sexual
  violence, 216–17
missions: education and clothing, 31–32; influence on clothing, 26, 31–32; Christian Mission to many lands, 27; London Missionary
  Society, 26, 33–34; Salesian Mission and
  secondhand clothing, 66–67; Seventh Day
  Adventists, 32
Mitchell, Clyde, 40, 50–51
MMD (Movement for Multi Party Democracy),
  ruling party in current Zambian government,
  232. *See also* Chiluba; third republic
Mobutu Sese Seko, former president of Zaire,
  and *authenticité* in dress, 122
modernity, 15, 23, 24
Moore, R. J. B., 34, 37, 50, 59, 60
Mozambique: port of entry, 127–28; smug-
  gling, 118
Mukampalili, secondhand clothing outlet in
  Lusaka, 135; change to restaurant, 136
Multi-Fibre Agreements. *See* GATT
Mulungushi Textiles, 84, 88, 148, 204, 236
Musambachime, Mwelwa, 23–24, 36, 61, 69,
  70, 73, 259–60n. 1, 261n. 1, 262n. 8; and
  University of Zambia, oral history project in
  Luapula Province, 23, 259
mutomboko, Lunda ceremony, 79, 80 fig. 8
Mwaanga, Vernon, Zambian politician, 81, 240
Mwinga, Bennie, Zambian MP, 240, 253

names, popular: for secondhand clothing, 1, 89,
  182, 248; for secondhand clothing markets,
  185, 205

national dress, question of, 78–81
Nawakwi, Edith, MP, minister of finance, 218
Netherlands, historical role in international secondhand clothing trade, 101, 108, 112–14,
  119
"new culture," 92, 201, 250
newspapers, Zambia: colonial, 47; postcolonial, 19
Nigeria, 115, 117; import restrictions on secondhand clothing, 122
Nkumbula, Harry, Zambian political leader, 72,
  80; and dress, 80; participation in secondhand clothing trade, 71
north/south relations, 21, 255

office wear. *See* fashion
one party state. *See* second republic

Penza, Ronald, Zambian finance minister, 232
Pepkor, Ltd. (South African apparel retail firm),
  236–38, 243, 244
Perrot, Philippe, 7, 8, 9, 10
Plateau Tonga, ethnic group in Zambia, 28, 32;
  desertion case in native court, 57
popular songs, and clothing: politics and
  dress, 77; women and paramours, 59;
  Teddy Chilambe, 230–31, 253; Alick
  Nkatha, 37, 38, 52, 230; Daddy Zemus,
  230–32
Powdermaker, Hortense, 48, 50, 52, 59
"private parts," 91, 198, 212, 216, 227. *See also*
  sexuality

rag trade. *See* secondhand clothing industry
ready-made clothing manufacture: early development of, 8–9, 10; slop shops, 8–9; Zambia, 179–82
recycling, of textile and clothing. *See* secondhand clothing industry
regulatory policy. *See* tariff issues
Richards, Audrey I., 27
Roche, Daniel, 7, 8
Rotary Club of Kabwe, 130
Rwanda, former involvement in secondhand
  clothing trade, 115, 117, 118–19

safari suit, 81, 93. *See also* Kaunda; national
  dress
Saffrey, A. L., report on African consumption,
  36, 40, 43–45
salaula: criticism of import, 90–91; defined, 1–
  2, 15; "genuine," 171–73; global nature of
  trade, 2; name first appearing, 89; popularity,